CURSED HORR

Mark Iveson

First published in 2015 by Telos Publishing Ltd,
5A Church Road, Shortlands, Bromley, Kent BR2 0HP, UK

www.telos.co.uk

Telos Publishing Ltd values feedback. Please e-mail us with any comments
you may have about this book to: feedback@telos.co.uk

ISBN: 978-1-84583-113-4

Cursed Horror Stars © 2015 Mark Iveson
Cover design: David J Howe
Image colourisation: Stuart Humphryes
Index: Ian Pritchard

Dedication

Dedicated to the memory of Robert Quarry

Acknowledgements

With so much wonderful support from friends, I would love to claim a long list of thank yous, but in the interests of space I will limit the acknowledgments to those whose have gone beyond the call of duty.

First to my mother Inga, who believed in me from day one, to my close friends Reece Williams and Carolyn Eastgate for providing solid back-up, and to writer Daniela Norris, whom I can't thank enough for her kind words of wisdom.

My thanks to American writers Andrea Griffith, Deborah Del Vecchio, David del Valle and Mark Redfield, and to British writer R J Ellory, all of whom have been an inspritation for different reasons. I reserve my greatest thanks to American writer Sally Franz, whose help with completing the book I will always be indebted for.

My special thanks to Telos Publishing for giving me this extraordinary opportunity.

Finally a big thank you to the Writers' Retreat at Swanwick in Derbyshire. The first time I went there I didn't have a clue, and without the support and friendship of my fellow residents, I would not have come even this close.

Contents

Introduction

'If I played Hamlet, they'd call it a horror film.' – Peter Cushing

The popularity of the horror film is equalled only by its notoriety, controversy and critical disdain. It can also be unforgiving to the actors associated with it. Typecasting in a specific genre is difficult enough for any film star, but to those linked to horror, the effects can be disastrous.

Because many long-dead horror stars suffered at the unmerciful hands of the genre, I often asked myself the question, 'What went wrong? Were they in some way cursed by horror typecasting?' It was this, along with my admiration for these actors, that prompted me to research and write this book.

Cursed Horror Stars charts the rise and fall of five actors associated with the genre. There was certainly more to their career declines than just horror typecasting. Personal demons, serious health issues and professional missteps were also important factors in their seemingly inevitable downhill slope.

As the cinema's definitive werewolf, Lon Chaney Jnr became haunted by the spectre of his legendary father. Blighted by alcoholism throughout his life, he hid his personal demons behind an affable if abrasive everyman persona, until the booze got the better him.

Basil Rathbone could do no wrong in Hollywood until he earned cinema immortality as the definitive Sherlock Holmes. Unable to shake off the Great Detective's mantle, he returned to the stage but never equalled his early success, as the spectre of his fictional *alter ego* continued to dominate him.

Once the toast of the German stage, Peter Lorre found fame with his mesmerising performance as the child killer in *M* (1932), yet Hollywood had no idea how to make use of his talents. Dogged by poor health, morphine addiction and financial problems, he never achieved his full star potential.

Fellow morphine addict Bela Lugosi became an overnight screen success as Dracula. However, his sinister presence, limited acting range and peculiar accent all handicapped his career. Unable to escape the Count's clutches, he ended up starring in some of the worst movies ever made.

Robert Quarry was set to replace Vincent Price as America's horror king following his excellent performance in the title role of *Count Yorga, Vampire* (1970). But despite his versatility and star quality, bad luck and near death experiences hampered his promising career.

INTRODUCTION

Thanks to the various horror and fantasy conventions held all over the world, the popularity of these wonderful actors will remain for many years to come. I hope this book stands as a valuable record and tribute to the memory of these great men.

Mark Iveson
June 2015

The Curse Of The Phantom: Lon Chaney Jnr

'They had to starve me to make me take his name.' – Lon Chaney Jnr

Lon Chaney Jnr lived and died in the self-imposed shadow of his fabulously famous father, Leonadas Frank Chaney, aka Lon Chaney, one of the greatest stars of early cinema, renowned for his portrayal of grisly and macabre roles – most notably the title characters of *The Hunchback of Notre Dame* (1923) and *The Phantom of the Opera* (1925). And like many actor children of the rich and famous to follow (Carrie Fisher, Tatum O'Neil, Christopher Lawford,

Margaux Hemingway), Lon Jnr gained Hollywood notoriety that others would kill for, but it was never enough. Surely the younger Chaney died as much from an inability to enjoy his accomplishments, as from the horrors of the self-punishment he chose?

Chaney was born in the dusty state of Oklahoma on 10 February 1905, and christened Creighton Tull Chaney. He kept the name Creighton during the early part of his acting career; until the curse of his father's distinguished name pursued and eventually overtook him, with devastating results. Forced by lack of work to assume the identity Lon Chaney Jnr in a final attempt to best his old man, he became more miserable than ever.

The name change initially brought about little improvement in his situation, until he followed his father's footsteps into the type of movies for which he was best known. Horror films of the '20s had carried less notoriety, so Chaney Snr had been able to work successfully in other types of role as well. By the '40s, however, the genre had become nasty and unforgiving to its leading actors, and as a consequence, Creighton, like many other of its noted performers, was unable to escape the real horror of typecasting.

By the time he achieved a similar level of success to his dad, the horror genre represented all things wrong in Hollywood. Being pigeonholed as the monster for most of his career, he had trouble finding decent roles in other films.

But who was the father who loomed bigger than life itself for poor Creighton? What were the skeletons that rattled in the Chaney family closet that drove the tormented young man into his own private madness?

Lon Chaney Snr died young, and with most of his movie output now considered 'lost' (only his horror films have survived), there is an aura of mystery surrounding the actor. The son of deaf mutes, who were strict Roman Catholics, he was born in Colorado Springs on 1 April 1886. His love for theatrical drama stemmed from childhood. As a boy, he honed his future acting skills by communicating with his parents through pantomime.

According to some sources, Chaney refused to utter a word until he was 8 years old out of sympathy for his parents. This was in all probability just a Hollywood publicity story, but it did give him an understanding about people born with disabilities, an important factor that influenced his future film career. In any case, the boy still had to go to school like many other children.

Chaney's father, Frank H Chaney, wasn't born deaf, as many stories seem to indicate. A childhood illness rendered him unable to hear when he was two years old, although he said he could still pick up certain sounds. His handicap didn't stop him from becoming a reasonably successful barber. The family, which had Irish and French origins, descended from John Chaney, an American congressman and representative of Ohio. The family also has a distant relative in present-day Republican politician Dick Cheney.

Chaney's mother Emma Alice Kennedy was born deaf, as was her own mother, who founded the Columbia State Institute for the Deaf and Dumb. She worked as a teacher at a school for the deaf until inflammatory rheumatism left her a bedridden invalid for the rest of her life. The second of four children – the others being named John, George and Caroline – Chaney was taken out of school when he was in fourth grade to care for his mother and younger siblings.

To supplement the family's meagre finances, Chaney worked as a prop boy at a local theatre. With the pantomime skills he developed as a child, and an attraction to the smell of greasepaint, he discovered the joy of performing in front of an audience. His brother John had his own travelling theatre company, and this further influenced the desire to act.

Chaney's disapproving father had other ideas and sent him on an apprenticeship as a carpet-layer and paperhanger. He spent three years as a sales assistant in a drapery store but continued working in the theatre and later joined the stagehands' union. He finally succumbed to the acting bug by joining John on the road.

When John's company folded, Chaney continued touring, now with the Columbia Comedy Repertory Company. Arriving in Oklahoma City in 1904, he met the Company's newest member, a 16-year-old singer called Cleva Creighton; they married that very same year.

'I was born black and dead.' Dramatic words from Creighton Chaney, but this later statement added to the mystery surrounding his birth in 1905. He was rumoured to have been a premature stillborn at 2½ pounds. According to Hollywood legend, his father revived him after submerging him in the freezing waters of the Belle Isle Lake, not far from the family's log cabin home. He was then placed in an incubator made from a shoebox. It's a great story, but complete fiction, according to Chaney's son Ron and Cleva Creighton's daughter (from her second marriage) Stella George. No doubt it was created by the tabloid press of the day, just like Chaney's early silent relationship with his parents.

But if there *was* some truth to the story, could the trauma of his birth have had some kind of impact on Creighton's young life? Could it have affected his decision to become an actor? Did the health problems and demons that plagued him later in his life come about as a result of his dramatic 'jump-start' in the world?

Creighton's tiny years were spent touring America with his parents. 'My father would improvise a hammock slung over the dressing-room table for me, or else I slept in a cotton-lined shoebox,' he later recalled. 'One or other of my parents would race backstage whenever they could to check on me.'

Arriving in Chicago in 1909, his father met an old actor friend, Lee Moran, who got him a job on a show called *The Red Kimono*. However, as for many performers of the day, times were extremely hard. Creighton remembered an incident one Christmas Eve that summed up his father's early struggles:

'Dad put most of the money in the gas meter. When he came to the first saloon, he placed me up on the bar close to the free lunch. Then he did his dance and picked up the small change. Meanwhile I filled my overcoat pockets with pretzels and sandwiches.

'When we got home, he went out, broke a limb off a park tree, fixed it in a box in our room, and spent the night making tree decorations out of a roll of red crepe paper he had bought with a few pennies.'

Despite the hardship, the family made enough money that in 1912 they were able to move from the windy city, with its harsh, snowy winters, to the relatively serene warm, sunny climes of Los Angeles, fulfilling Chaney's lifelong dream to live on the West Coast. His brother John got him a job at a local theatre where he was working as a stage manager.

Chaney worked seven days a week as a singer and comedian in various musical revues produced at the Olympic Theatre in Los Angles. A naturally gifted dancer, he performed in comic opera and vaudeville, and also toured San Francisco with a German comedy duo. 'As a comedian he was irresistible,' according to his biographer Michael F Blake. Although there are no audio recordings in existence, many of Chaney's friend and associates have spoken about his rich baritone voice.

Meanwhile Cleva Chaney was making a name for herself as a singer, and her newfound success quickly overtook her husband's modest stage achievements. Because of his puritan upbringing, Chaney considered himself essentially the breadwinner of the family, so not surprisingly he was deeply unhappy with Cleva's fast rising career.

It was only a matter of time before the cracks showed in their marriage – a result of Chaney's dented professional and masculine pride getting the better of him. The pressures of maintaining a career and bringing up her son on top of her husband's deep-seated resentment and insecurity got too much for Cleva. Her only solace for alleviating the constant stress was booze.

The marital tension eventually exploded into a trauma that would curse Creighton into adulthood. As the arguments between the couple increased, so did Cleva's alcohol dependence. The situation had got so bad that Chaney accused her both of neglecting their son in favour of her career and of being unfaithful. Whether or not this was true, the booze had already affected Cleva's fragile state of mind. Following a heated argument with her husband, she attempted suicide by drinking poison in the very theatre he was working in. She survived, but the poison ruined her voice. With her singing career over, Cleva was despondent, a situation made more unpleasant when Chaney had her committed to an asylum as an alcoholic.

Chaney clearly had a ruthless streak, and his attitude toward his poor wife was nothing short of vicious. Now with sole custody of Creighton,

Chaney cut off all communication with Cleva and ignored her letters. Nor did he want her to have anything to do with the boy. The couple divorced in 1914.

Chaney did not remain single for long. He met chorus dancer Hazel Hastings at a San Francisco theatre and they married in 1915, following Hazel's own previous divorce. Hazel gave up showbusiness to bring up Creighton, a decision that the staunchly old-fashioned Chaney happily approved of. Hazel's former husband was said to have been a legless man who ran the cigar counter at the theatre she worked in – somewhat ironic, given that she then married a man would later specialise in playing movie cripples. Once again, though, this appears to have been just a story generated by the Hollywood publicity machine.

By the time of the marriage, Creighton was 10 years old, and well aware of his birth mother's absence. At first Chaney told his son his mother had died. Creighton's life was a jumble of grief and adjusting to his new stepmother. Then, a few years down the line, he found out that Cleva was still alive. How does a child negotiate the feeling of being betrayed by his father? Even with the truth known, Chaney forbade the boy from contacting his mother. With the father/son relationship already extremely tense following the break-up of the first marriage, learning the truth about Cleva caused further estrangement between Creighton and his workaholic dad; a sad case of life being stranger and more horrifying than fiction.

In between meeting Hazel and divorcing Cleva, Chaney had already relocated to the hubbub of Hollywood, where he began looking for better-paid film work. With the help of Lee Moran, he started out as a $5-a-day dispatch rider at Universal Studios.

Meanwhile, Creighton, a gawky adolescent, had to deal with new surroundings once more, making new friends and starting at a new school, all while seeing more of his stepmother and less and less of a father constantly looking for film work.

Making his film debut in *Poor Jake's Demise* (1913), Chaney found his comedy skills quickly got him noticed by Universal. After appearing in several comic shorts, he wanted to take performing a stage further by using his self-taught make-up skills to create new and distinctive characters. According to Creighton, 'He used to sit in the bullpen at Universal, which was a room about the size of a TV studio. He'd sit there, and an assistant director would come out and say, "Anybody here that can play a college boy?" Dad would say, "Yeah, I can play a college boy." Then he'd come back and they'd come out and say, "Anybody here that can play a Chinaman?" Well, this went on a few times and there wasn't anybody who could. So my dad, being a natural artist from the word go, got his make-up kit and his own stuff together and took it to Universal. And when they asked, "Anybody play a Chinaman?" he'd say, "Yeah I can play a Chinaman."

He'd make himself up as a Chinaman, go and work for ten minutes, come back, then go out and play a Greek. And this way, make three or four pictures a day.'

Chaney took a break from acting to direct a series of films starring silent star J Warren Kerrigan – with some success too. According to writer John Brosnan, '[Chaney was] a competent director, but he decided that he enjoyed acting most of all and returned to it. He [had] already formed the opinion that his best chance of success lay in character acting, lacking, as he did, the good looks necessary for a leading man.' Chaney knew there was something extra-special about creating a vivid character by using make-up and mime.

Chaney was still earning only $5 a day at Universal and, considering his increasing prominence as an actor, approached studio manager William Sistrom and demanded $125 per week and a five-year contract. 'It was a reasonable request,' noted Brosnan. 'Chaney had become a relatively valuable member of the studio's stock company. But Sistrom turned him down. According to Chaney, Sistrom told him he knew a good actor when he saw one, but looking directly at Chaney he saw only a wash-out. So Chaney walked off the lot.'

Chaney went freelance at this point in the early part of his movie career; a stressful endeavour that only added to his distance from young Creighton. He had saved enough of his Universal income to enable him to look for film work elsewhere, but away from the studio he was virtually unknown. As the weeks turned to months, it was only a matter of time before the money ran out. Chaney began to wonder if Sistrom had been right all along.

Salvation came courtesy of cowboy actor William S Hart who, after seeing Chaney in several Universal shorts, cast him as a villain in the Western *Riddle Gwane* (1919). Unlike most leading men, who needed to be the star of a picture and resented being upstaged by their fellow actors, Hart wanted his supporting cast to hold their own. Chaney also enjoyed working with Hart and remained grateful for the opportunity to prove himself a good actor. More parts quickly followed.

Making his horror debut in *The Glory of Love* (1919), Chaney took it a step further with his next effort, *The Miracle Man* (1919), a film that arguably defined his career. Director George Leone Tucker offered him the role of Frog, a criminal who dons several disguises, including that of a fake cripple. 'Tucker didn't really want me for the role of the cripple,' said Chaney. 'He wanted a professional contortionist, but the five he tried out couldn't act. Tucker explained to me that the first scene he would shoot would be the one where the fake cripple unwound himself in front of his pals. If I [managed] that, I got the job.'

But Chaney was not a contortionist. 'It would have been a lot easier in my subsequent work if I had been.' Pondering over the part, he thought about a trick he hadn't tried since childhood. 'I crossed my legs, then double-crossed them, wrapping my left foot across my right ankle. When I came to the studio on the test day, Tucker was already behind the camera. He gave me one glance and called, "Camera!" I flopped down, dragging myself forward along the floor, my eyes rolling, me face twitching and my legs wrapped tighter and tighter around each other. Tucker didn't speak, and the sweat rolled off me. Finally I heard a single whispered word from him. "God," Tucker said. I wanted to say that too, but not for the same reason.'

The Miracle Man was a box-office hit that secured Chaney's future. Now close friends, he and Tucker would have made several more films together, had it not been for the director's sudden death at the age of 30. Although deeply upset by the loss of his friend, Chaney continued his good work with the gangster thriller *The Penalty* (1920). Playing a legless crime boss, he achieved the effect by designing a leather harness that bound the calves of his legs against his thighs so he could walk only on his knees.

Thanks to these amazing efforts, Chaney emerged as one of Hollywood's most enduring silent stars – and, as previously noted, not one affected by horror typecasting, despite creating truly grotesque characters such as Fagin in *Oliver Twist* (1922) and Quasimodo in *The Hunchback of Notre Dame*. His remarkable and gruesome disguises, coupled with his unique use of theatrical mime, earned him his legendary nickname 'The Man of a Thousand Faces'.

'Don't step on that spider, it might be Lon Chaney!' or so the classic Hollywood saying went. Chaney was 100% dedicated to his profession. Future star Joan Crawford, who as a newcomer worked with the actor in *The Unknown* (1927), was completely impressed by his total absorption into his character – an armless man called Alonso. 'Lon Chaney was my introduction to acting,' she said. 'The concentration, the complete absorption, he gave to his characterisation filled me with such awe, I could scarcely speak to him. He never slipped out of character. Watching him gave me real desire to be a real actress.' Chaney's close friend and frequent collaborator director Tod Browning also noted, 'The more grotesque his characters, the better Lon likes them. You probably read how much he suffers in some of his make-ups. That isn't publicity. He will do anything for the sake of his pictures.'

And he certainly suffered for his art! Chaney often went to extreme and very painful lengths to perfect his creations. In *The Hunchback of Notre Dame* he wore a 70lb hump, a leather harness to prevent him from staying upright and rubber skin to cover the hump. Watching the movie, one can all but smell and feel the acrid sweat of working with that hump under huge spotlights. He also inserted a painful device into his mouth to prevent him from closing it. It was excruciating but well-rewarded work; Universal was paying him $2,500 per week to play Quasimodo, and the film's success led to a lucrative contract with MGM.

'The parts I play point out a moral,' he said of his work. 'They show individuals who might have been different, if they had been given the chance.' And Chaney's characters were definitely individuals, thanks to his painful make-up effects. But it was always for art, not for exploitation. 'I hope,' he added, 'I shall never be accused of striving merely for horrible effect.' Writer and film historian Denis Gifford had his own theory about the extraordinary lengths that Chaney took to create his cripples: 'His world appeal [came] at a time when genuine grotesques, the victims of war, begged at every corner.' Whether Gifford's analysis is correct or not, there is little doubt that these deformed characters were an unintentional reflection of the horrors of World War I.

But it was *The Phantom of the Opera* (1925) that featured Chaney's finest creation. To achieve Erik the Phantom's distinctive but hideous skull face, Chaney inserted a device up his nostrils to flare them out and raise the tip of his nose. He then used metal prongs to distort his face. The end result was an outstanding piece of make-up that complemented a truly remarkable performance – and one that was certainly not without its problems. After years of struggle, Chaney Snr was now determined to maximise his stardom to the full. The film's cinematographer Charles Van Eager once commented, 'It was a terrific strain, because Chaney and [Rupert] Julian [the director] wouldn't talk to each other. I had to be the messenger boy. Rupert would ask me to tell Lon to do this and that, and Lon would tell him to go to hell! So Lon did whatever he wanted.'

'When a make-up is as painful as that,' Chaney said, 'it takes a good deal of imagination to forget your physical sufferings. Yet, at that, the subconscious mind has a marvellous way of making you keep the right attitudes and make the right gestures when you're actually acting.'

But why should Chaney have put himself through such an ordeal to achieve his performances when he really didn't have to? Not exactly healthy to go through so much pain for days on end! As someone who felt more at home with the technicians than with the other actors, Chaney despised all forms of weakness – a by-product of his strict puritan upbringing, which might also explain his nasty attitude toward his first wife. He often felt acting was a bit of a soppy occupation for a grown man, so to achieve any kind of perfection on screen, he had to go through a lot of pain to justify the living he was earning.

But there was more to Chaney's acting than this. His odd childhood, failed first marriage and early struggles contributed to an introverted and dour persona, a situation that was then made more complex by his father's death. While Chaney was making *The Phantom of the Opera*, his father Frank started losing his sight – which, for a deaf mute, was nothing short of a nightmare. This added further stress to the pain his son was already experiencing under his make-up. 'It was a time of great strain for Chaney, until his father died a few days after the picture was completed,' said writer John Brosnan. 'But it's more likely that the pain he inflicted upon himself was merely a combination of professional pride and the results of his puritan upbringing.' For a man who could not show any weak emotions, such a situation can't have made things at home with his wife and son very happy.

The Phantom of the Opera cost $630,000 to make, the lion's share of the budget being spent on the superb Parisian sets that included the interior of the Paris Opera House and the maze-like underground sewer system. But although no expense was spared, the film still turned a healthy profit of $540,000. Despite being creaky in spots, due to primitive film techniques, it still stands up reasonably well today, and Chaney's unmasking can still pack a punch to those unfamiliar with Erik's famous appearance. The Phantom will always be the actor's definitive grotesque character – and it was one that followed Creighton's future career like an unwanted albatross around his neck.

Chaney himself insisted he never went out of his way to play grotesques. 'People seem to think I study scripts all the time,' he said. 'I don't even try to find stories for myself like some stars. I wouldn't know where to look for them. I trust my producers to look out for my own good. All I want to know is what the character is and what rules him. It takes me two to four weeks to work out a make-up for a new picture. That said, I don't worry.'

But whatever his reasons for enduring them, these lengthy, gruelling and painful make-up designs affected Chaney's health. He had to wear glasses off camera when the primitive contact lenses he used on set impaired his vision. The heavy rig he wore on *The Hunchback of Notre Dame* ended up damaging his spine, and by 1927, he admitted, 'I can't play these cripple roles anymore. That trouble with my spine is worse every time I do one, and it's beginning to worry me.'

Against all odds, Chaney's personal life at this time was reported to be a happy one. A private man by nature, he lived with Hazel and Creighton in quiet, wealthy obscurity at their log cabin in the Sierra Nevada, as far from the Hollywood glamour and beeping horns of the city as possible. 'Between pictures there is no Lon Chaney!' he said, further summing up his desire for anonymity by adding, 'My whole career has been devoted to keeping people from knowing me.' Shying away from Hollywood's social scene, he hardly spoke in public and rarely gave interviews; he had little time for the press, following the bad publicity surrounding Cleva's attempted suicide.

Chaney also seemed relaxed and settled with his career. 'The chief thing for an actor to remember is that it wasn't his brains that got him to stardom. It was only his acting. He isn't paid to think about production plans, and when he starts, he usually sinks his career.' Although he was labelled unfriendly by the press, his friends and colleagues knew different.

According to writer Clarence Locan, 'On his days off he would be around the studios talking to the workers. He knew all their troubles and the first name of every worker in the studio. At Christmas there was a present for every worker from Lon. Every girl in the offices got a glove order, the office boys, the electricians and the rest all had presents. It was genuine.'

Creighton once said of his father, 'After witnessing the torture my father endured in his various make-ups, I was more than ready to heed his advice about not doing that type of work. And yet, I suppose the fact that I followed in his footsteps proves that some people just can't escape their destiny.' There was something prophetic in Creighton's words; but if it was destiny, his dad, realising his own years of struggle, was determined not to put his boy on the same path.

Chaney also extended his kindness to his fellow actors. One up-and-coming actress named Loretta Young recalled, '[He was] very co-operative and helpful, especially to those performers without much experience.' He was instrumental in giving noted African-American actor Noble Johnson his break in films, and once gave Boris Karloff a piece of advice that changed the course of his career. 'One day,' Karloff said, 'as I was leaving the studio, pretty discouraged at the way my career was going, I heard a car honk behind me – and Lon Chaney gave me a lift home. We talked for over an hour about the picture business and my own chances of getting somewhere. He said to me, "The secret of success in Hollywood lies in being different from everyone else." He cited his own career, his own unusual parts, as an example. He then said, "Find something no-one else can or will do – and they'll begin to take notice of you. Hollywood is full of competent actors. What the screen needs is individuality." Heeding every word Chaney uttered, the ever-grateful Karloff eventually achieved movie success, and later passed this advice on to another up-and-coming young actor named Christopher Lee.

According to John Brosnan's book *The Horror People*, Creighton Chaney had a happy childhood, and while many friends and colleagues confirm this as true, it wasn't a view shared by novelist and friend Curt Siodmak. 'I believe that Lon [was] badly treated as a child by his famous father, was never able to shed the hurts of his childhood.' Siodmak further added that Creighton's strict father beat him regularly, and got him jobs as a newsboy, a butcher's boy and a poultry dresser to avoid spoiling him and enable him to stand on his own feet in adulthood. This sums up a complex man who lived a different life at home from the one at work.

According to Siodmak, '[Creighton] always lived under his father's shadow, although I believe his acting had deeper roots and that he had more talent than his paternal tormentor.' Siodmak's assessment of Creighton's acting skills may be debatable to some critics, but it's clear that the desire to prove his worth over his father was extremely strong, perhaps too strong for him to handle on his own.

Brosnan's book also claims Chaney actively discouraged his son from acting, and that the boy himself showed little interest in performing. While the former is certainly true, Creighton was impressed by his dad's work in mime and make-up. 'Dad never wanted me to be an actor, so he made it unattractive.'

Creighton rarely saw his father working in the studios. 'I watched Dad work out his disguises at home, so it was pretty much a business with me. In the early days of motion pictures it was not considered a good thing to be married, much less to have a son of my age! Therefore I saw very few of his performances.'

Watching the way his father worked, the younger Chaney himself developed into a highly accomplished make-up artist, but he was prevented from using his self-taught skills later on because of the strict union rules the studios prevailed on him to abide by when he became an actor.

Creighton attended Hollywood High School – his classmates included other future movie stars Fay Wray and Joel McCrea. Already tall and well-built, he wanted to play for the school football team, but was turned down because he weighed 125 pounds. When he asked his father about being an actor, the ultra-strict Chaney removed him from school and enrolled him at the Commercial Experts Training Institute in Los Angeles, where he trained as a plumber. Hardly an occupation befitting the son of a Hollywood legend.

As an adult, the 6 foot 3 inch Creighton was nothing like his diminutive father ('He's too tall.' Chaney once said. 'They would have to build parts around him.'). Broad shouldered and powerfully built, with heavy facial features, he looked more like a construction worker than an actor. As someone whose appearance suggested he would be more at home on an oil rig wearing a tin hat and mucky blue overalls than treading the boards in a theatrical costume, Creighton would at the very least have made a decent Western outlaw or gangster's heavy.

In the late '20s, Hollywood underwent a major movie revolution with the coming of sound. Like many great silent movie stars, Chaney Snr feared the 'talkies'. Not only did it finish the careers of many big name actors whose voices disappointed the public, it meant a more naturalistic acting style came to the cinema. Chaney's skills at pantomime became redundant in the face of this new medium. Worse still, he started having trouble with his throat after swallowing a piece of artificial snow during the making of *Thunder* (1929). His tonsils were removed but the throat problems persisted.

Whether he liked it or not, the 'talkies' were here to stay (despite movie pioneer D W Griffith's stubborn insistence, 'We do not want sound and we shall never want the human voice with our films!'). Chaney's long-awaited sound debut came in *The Unholy Three* (1930), a remake of his 1925 film. Any fears he might have had about not surviving the transition were dispelled as critics and audiences alike were equally impressed by his distinctive voice; he actually spoke to great effect with four different accents – his own, plus the voices of an old lady, a ventriloquist's dummy and a parrot. 'The Man of a Thousand Faces' could easily have become 'The Man of a Thousand Voices' had fate not taken an ironic but tragic turn.

With his newfound success, Chaney Snr signed another lucrative MGM contract, to remake more of his silent films. There were also rumours that he was scheduled to play Count Dracula in director Tod Browning's forthcoming film version of Hamilton Deane's stage play about the Transylvanian vampire. Oddly enough, Bela Lugosi, who had achieved major stage success as the Count when the play first opened on Broadway in 1927, and who would become forever associated with the role when he was eventually cast by Browning, was not even considered for the film version at this point!

Chaney was set to star next in *The Big House* (1930), but the throat problems continued. He travelled to New York to consult a specialist, who diagnosed the actor as having bronchial cancer brought about by his heavy smoking. Cancelling his participation in the film (Wallace Beery replaced him), he returned to his mountain cabin to convalesce, only to be struck down later with a bout of pneumonia. He was rushed to a Los Angeles hospital, where he suffered a serious throat haemorrhage that, ironically, rendered him mute and left him resorting to sign language to communicate with others.

Lon Chaney, 'The Man of a Thousand Faces', died on 26 August 1930 at the age of 47. It was obvious his time as an actor remained rooted in the silent era. Because only his horror films have survived the years, his typecasting in that type of role has actually happened after his death, and this is how his legend has lived on. His son, however, would be very much alive and well when his horror star status took hold of him – with devastating results. And no matter what success Creighton achieved – and he did – the myth of his father grew bigger with time. Creighton simply could not outrun that ferocious beast.

By the time of his father's death, Creighton Chaney was married with two sons, Ron and Lon Jnr. After leaving school, he worked as a boilermaker. Following a stint as a secretary, he ran a moderately successful plumbing business. In his father's words at the time, 'He's happy in business and has a great wife.' Creighton Chaney had been married to Dorothy Hinckley since 1926.

As a final cruel blow, Chaney Snr's determination to have his son stand on his own two feet in adulthood continued after his death. The bulk of the late actor's fortune was left to his wife Hazel, with Creighton receiving only a small part of the estate. Even his father's surviving siblings were generously provided for. Considering his family commitments at the time, one can only wonder how Creighton viewed this final act of puritan defiance from his father.

Creighton Chaney had worked as a tradesman to keep his father happy. Once Chaney Snr was dead, the acting bug from high school resurfaced once more. 'The ham was there,' he said, knowing where his true destiny lay. But there were other factors that influenced the career-change. America was going through the most tumultuous decade of the early 20th Century, with banks and businesses folding in rapid succession following the infamous Wall Street crash of 1929. By 1932, the Great Depression hit Chaney hard. When his plumbing business folded, he was among the United States' 16 million unemployed.

The film industry however seemed immune to the slump – the introduction of sound turned out to be a temporary saviour in these bad times. Taking this factor into account, Creighton decided – against his late father's better judgement, and perhaps his own – to find film work.

Chaney Jnr had previously acted as a small boy in the silent film *Heart of a Wolf* (1922). His first official film appearance was in *The Galloping Ghost* (1931) as an uncredited henchman. His entry into a full time acting career came in a roundabout way. He had been invited to a party where he met some of his father's friends. After he sang a song he had written, one of the friends suggested he should take it to MGM's music department.

'When I went to the studio, I had to pass the casting office. The casting director looked at me, and said, "You're Lon Chaney's son. You ought to be in pictures!" "How about it?" I asked. He told me he'd have a job for me in a couple of days.'

Chaney waited for the phone to ring, and waited, and waited – nothing! Eventually the friend who had liked the song paid a visit to the casting director at RKO Studios and put in a good word. This led to a stock contract and a bit part as a chorus dancer in *Girl Crazy* (1932).

RKO had wanted to sign him under the name Lon Chaney Jnr, but at that stage Creighton refused. 'As I see it now,' he later said, 'I was foolish. I'd have gotten ahead much faster if I had. But I didn't feel I was entitled to take my father's name. I didn't feel I was an actor yet.' Chaney felt he had a lot more to offer than just being the son of a movie legend; it was only a question of convincing the powers-that-be in Hollywood.

For once, fortune smiled on Creighton, even though he was playing just bit parts. Not only was he kept constantly in work (even if it didn't amount to anything creatively rewarding), he was able to learn the technical side of film acting. His massive frame also served him well as a stuntman, his years as a tradesman having probably made him resistant to physical damage. More importantly, he was making a go of it in Hollywood under his own name.

'My father would be horrified if he knew I was making pictures and that

I'm not billed as "Creighton Chaney",' he once said, as his dad's great name began to haunt him. But work he did, and it wasn't just acting; anything went. 'I worked under five names. I did extras under one name, stunts under another name, bits under another name and leads under my own. I'd get a call to do a fight, so I'd get on the set and I'd go quickly to the assistant director and I'd say, "How long is the fight going to take? And how long am I going to be here?" And he'd say "About 20 minutes." "And when are you going to do it?" He'd say, "About an hour from now." "Okay, I'll see you." I'd run to the next set and work under a different name. And between the three or four sets I'd come off smelling like a rose.'

Because he acted under so many different names early on in his career, the exact number of films he appeared in may never be known. However, they included *Bird of Paradise* (1932), *The Last Frontier* (1932) *Lucky Devils* (1933), *Scarlet River* (1933), *The Three Musketeers* (1933), *Son of the Border* (1934), *Sixteen Fathoms Deep* (1934), *The Life of Vergie Winters* (1934), *Girl of My Dreams* (1934) and *Woman of Destiny* (1935). If anything, his time with RKO was beneficial, as he played reasonably decent supporting roles, achieving second billing in *Woman of Destiny*. More importantly, he was billed as 'Creighton Chaney' in all of them.

The RKO contract expired in 1935, and before long Chaney struggled to find work. But despite the fears of unemployment, he steadfastly he refused to change his name. 'I once told my father, "I wouldn't go into pictures on your name. If I could use another name – and top you – I'd give it a fling, but nobody's ever going to top you." Strong words; but sadly *that* name slowly but surely took over his life.

'I am most proud of the name "Lon Chaney" because it was my father's name,' he said. 'I am *not* proud of "Lon Chaney Jnr", because they had to starve me to make me take his name.' With a family to support in these desperate times, there was little else he could do but reluctantly jump on the bandwagon of his famous legacy. After an uncredited appearance in *Uniform Lovers* (1935), he officially became 'Lon Chaney Jnr' for *Accent of Youth* (1935). Soon after this momentous decision, the tides of fortune began to change in a way that he could not have foreseen.

Initially the gambit worked. He got the starring part of reformed gangster Silk Lennox in *The Shadow of Silk Lennox* (1935), and was top billed again in *A Scream in the Night* (1935), in the dual role of hero and villain. However, his inexperience as a leading man clearly showed in both these performances. In truth, the producers had merely taken the chance to exploit *that* name. The films were both made by tiny independents, and did not guarantee any kind of springboard to a long-term career – although Chaney fared well enough when gaining a supporting role opposite Gene Autry in Republic's *The Singing Cowboy* (1936).

Chaney remained with Republic for his first fantasy feature. *Undersea*

Kingdom (1936) is a 12-part serial set in Atlantis. And it is truly dreadful, with a bland cast and an extremely annoying kid whose character should have been brutally killed off in the first episode! Although Chaney stands out among the faceless leads, his part as a henchman called Captain Haker hardly stretched his acting abilities to any great lengths. But at least it was paid work.

Another 12-part serial followed, this time for Universal. *Ace Drummond* (1936) had Chaney cast as a henchman called Ivan. He followed that up with unbilled appearances in *Killer at Large* (1936), *O'Riley's Luck* (1936) and *Love is News* (1936). He worked with Gene Autry once more in *Texas Serenade* (1936), and then stayed with the Western genre, to which he looked ideally suited, for *Cheyenne Rides Again* (1937). Small supporting roles came in *Midnight Taxi* (1937), *Secret Agent X-9* (1937), *Angel's Holiday* (1937), *Wild and Woolly* (1937), *Wife, Doctor and Nurse* (1937) and *Joy Parade* (1937). There were also uncredited appearances in *That I May Live* (1937), *His Affair* (1937), *Slave Ship* (1937), *Born Reckless* (1937), *The Lady Escapes* (1937), *One Mile From Heaven* (1937), *Lovely to Look At* (1937), *Charlie Chan on Broadway* (1937) and *Second Honeymoon* (1937). However, despite this long list of jobs, the work was sporadic, and Chaney's services were required for only a few days on each production, leaving him with long spells of unemployment in between. That, coupled with the small and undemanding nature of his roles he did win, suggested that Chaney's decision to change his name had in the end made not a blind bit of difference.

It was a decision he was to regret throughout the rest of his career, because he never considered himself as good as his father. The motivation might have been all about money, but even Hollywood was unable fight off the grip of Great Depression any longer. With studios running into financial problems and star contracts getting suspended, the name change meant nothing now, and Chaney's modest acting abilities paled considerably in comparison with those of Tinsel Town's more established stars. So work was still hard to come by, and all he could get were bit parts.

The spiral down was much faster than the ride up had been. And the one solace for such a situation was booze. Like many tradesmen, Chaney liked to down a few beers at his local bar, but with the stress of unemployment eating away at him, he had inherited his mother's penchant for alcohol, which then led to serious weight gain problems. As the boozing increased, his marriage and family life began to suffer, finally buckling under the weight of drink and financial hardships, which led to the couple divorcing in July 1937. Dorothy was awarded alimony, property and custody of their sons.

But Lon Chaney Jnr was a survivor and a fighter. He was determined to make a living in Hollywood. He figured he could handle the booze as long as the work kept coming his way. In his personal life, things started to look up again when he married model Patsy Beck in October 1937. Professionally, however, his career continued to mark time, showing no real signs of advancement. There were a string of uncredited bit parts in *City Girl* (1938), *Happy Landing* (1938), *Sally, Irene and Mary* (1938), *Walking Down Broadway* (1938), *Alexander's Ragtime Band* (1938), *They're Off* (1938) and *Submarine Patrol* (1938). Other than being credited, he fared no better in *Mr Moto's Gamble* (1938), *Josette* (1938), *Speed to Burn* (1938), *Passport Husband* (1938), and *Road Demon* (1938).

It is probably stating the obvious to say that Chaney was difficult to cast. Because of his massive frame and brutish yet sympathetic features, he never went beyond playing simpleminded men unable to cope with life's misfortunes – a subtle reflection of his own life. It was this kind of dimwitted character that would later give him the best acting role of his otherwise disappointing career. But for now he still had to work and make the best of a bad situation. There were a trio of Westerns – *Jesse James* (1939), *Union Pacific* (1939) and *Frontier Marshal* (1939) – and a return to the Charlie Chan series with *City of Darkness* (1939). But the financial situation worsened. Chaney was now so broke that his car and all his furniture had been repossessed. He was a desperate man forced into an almost impossible situation.

Then, however, his fortunes suddenly changed for the better. This turning point came when he got cast as the tragic simpleminded giant Lennie Small in a stage production of John Steinbeck's acclaimed novel *Of Mice and Men*. The play had originally been a big hit on Broadway, with Broderick Crawford in the role. When it transferred to Los Angeles, Crawford left the production to repeat his stage success in a forthcoming film version co-produced by Hal Roach Studios and RK and directed by Lewis Milestone. Chaney stepped into the breach as Crawford's replacement, in the process making his theatre debut. The play was equally successful in Los Angeles, receiving excellent critical notices, with Chaney's performance being singled out for the highest praise.

One person who loved the play was Milestone, but despite Chaney asking for a screen test for the film version, the director already had his mind firmly fixed on Crawford for the role. He did however give Chaney the job of feeding lines from off-camera to the actresses auditioning for the part of the boss's wife (which eventually went to Betty Field). Seeing Chaney's performance during those auditions, Milestone changed his mind and gave the actor the job after all, without even requiring him to do the screen test he originally asked for.

The film version faithfully follows Steinbeck's novel. Set during the Great Depression, it tells the story of intelligent but cynical George and his strongly-built but mentally-challenged friend Lennie, both of whom find work at a ranch where they pursue an impossible dream of buying their own land and living the perfect utopian existence. The story ends in tragedy, with Lennie accidentally killing the boss's flirtatious wife and George having to kill his friend before the lynch mob arrives to administer their own brutal brand of justice. There was no room for glitzy artificial happy endings here; with the hardships of the Depression still ringing true to many people, the film struck a chord with the cinema-going public.

With the diminutive Burgess Meredith well cast as George, the film racked up four Oscar nominations, including the one for Best Picture; quite an achievement considering that two unknown actors played the leads. Although the production is now dated in parts, there is no denying Chaney's outstanding performance as Lennie. He perfectly captures the pathos and tragedy of the retarded strongman unable to control his innocent yet destructive emotions – his own past struggles, coupled with his heavy his drinking, no doubt providing inspiration for the actor. The distinctive childlike characteristics of this role – the one for which he is now most well known away from the horror genre – would serve as a useful grounding for playing his future monsters, and one cannot help but wonder if his tense childhood prepared him for it.

But to his friend Curt Siodmak, there was something to Chaney's performance that ran deeper than acting. 'He needed a father figure to guide him, which drove him to drink. His most telling performance is in *Of Mice and Men* by John Steinbeck. He played the giant halfwit Lennie, who is dominated by his friend, his substitute father.'

But brilliant though he was in the film, Chaney, like many actors of his day, quickly found himself being sent up in Warner Brothers' classic cartoons, and sadly this considerably diminished in his eyes his finest screen performance. Lennie would often turn up in the shape of a giant cat or a grizzly bear, harassing Bugs Bunny or Sylvester the cat with 'Which way did they go George?', 'I want a wittle mouse George!' or 'I've got a wittle bunny wabbit, and I'm going to squeeze him and hug him and I'm gonna call him George!' Thanks to Warner Brothers, Chaney's Lennie became a caricature.

Chaney too had his reservations about being identified with the role. 'When I got my break in pictures, in *Of Mice and Men*, I was Lennie, the imbecile. It haunts me,' he once complained. 'I get a call to play a dumb guy and the director tells me not to be Lennie, but he's never happy until I play the part like Lennie, and then he doesn't know why he likes it!' This pigeonholing as the simpleminded lug would indeed recur from time to time, but a new form of typecasting was just around the corner.

Chaney was set to star in *Cup of Gold*, a film adaptation of another Steinbeck novel. When the project fell through, he tested for the role of Quasimodo in RKO's big-budget remake of *The Hunchback of Notre Dame* (1939). What an opportunity to recreate a role made famous by his late father, and with the name 'Lon Chaney Jnr'! And having a hit movie behind him, how could he fail? Sadly, it wasn't to be, and the role went to Charles

Laughton instead. Chaney was still relatively unknown, and the name didn't seem to make much difference. His father had been dead ten years and motion pictures had moved on. Had his son been able to take on the role, he could have topped his father. Quasimodo, like Lennie, is a simpleminded misfit, a part Chaney could play now with his eyes shut.

'Nothing is more natural to me than horror,' Chaney said, and his feelings about the genre must have indicated where his future would lie – especially when Hal Roach assigned him a prominent supporting part opposite Victor Mature (in his first starring role) and Carol Landis in *One Million BC* (1940). This hilariously cheesy prehistoric fantasy suffers badly in comparison with Hammer's ultra-camp 1966 remake – its enlarged lizards are especially poor forerunners of Ray Harryhausen's classics stop-frame animated dinosaur figures. And having Mature as a clean-shaven, square-jawed pretty-boy caveman destroys what little realism the film could have had (given that dinosaurs actually disappeared long before man arrived) – although Landis looks more convincing than Raquel Welch's heavily mascaraed Hammer heroine.

What really gives the film credibility is Chaney's sympathetic turn as Akhoba, the scarred and crippled leader of the primitive and violent rock tribe. Unrecognisable under a thick beard and sweltering hot long matted wig, he uses his heavy frame to great advantage to give a reasonably effective performance. The fact that his dialogue consisted of grunts and groans meant that he could take a leaf out of his father's book by using pantomime. In that respect he comes closest to inheriting his father's skills. At least he makes a more convincing caveman than Mature!

Taking another leaf from his father's book, Chaney originally designed his own make-up for Akhoba. Celebrated film fan Forrest J Ackerman related an incident from the production that he learned about when he once visited the actor: 'He did tell me that he had assisted his father in many ways with his make-up and took pride in the fact that he could make himself up very well too. I would say, judging from the one or two stills that survive, he'd done a very original job for *One Million BC*. But he wasn't allowed to use it for the film, because by then the unions had come into Hollywood and they required a make-up man to do all the make-up rather than the actor himself. Actually I thought Chaney had done a better job on himself than the make-up man subsequently did on *One Million BC*, but he wasn't permitted to use that talent. It was a handicap that his father didn't have to face.' In light of this, it is somewhat ironic that *Variety* noted in its contemporary review: '[Chaney] has carved a fine characterisation from the role of a tribal chieftain and, in view of the make-up used, may be following in his father's footsteps as an interpreter of gruesome parts.'

As daft as it was, *One Million BC* did very well at the box office; enough for Chaney to catch the attention of Universal Studios, although this had more to do with his father's name and reputation than any real talent on his part, and also perhaps to the fact that his famous role of Lennie bore some resemblance to Boris Karloff's Monster in their hit production *Frankenstein* (1931). It seems the studio executives put two and two together and concluded that they had found themselves a new genre headliner. Chaney, now 34, was clearly aware of the reasons why Universal had offered him a long-term contract – an offer he had gratefully accepted. But after years of struggle in B-movies, he was now on good money and working for a decent studio; and it might even open a few doors for more rewarding roles – or so he thought!

Sadly, it was not to be. 'Now I'm typed as the horror man,' he admitted. 'I scare women and children and give men the shudders!' So began the curse of the Phantom.

It was a horror film that marked Chaney's Universal debut. Originally titled *The Mysterious Dr R, Man-Made Monster* (1940), it had been devised five years earlier as a vehicle for Boris Karloff and Bela Lugosi. Director George Waggner reworked the original treatment into a solid screenplay, with Universal putting up the $86,000 budget. With Karloff now off conquering Broadway in *Arsenic and Old Lace* and Lugosi reduced to making low-budget programmers, Universal, keen to promote their new horror discovery, cast Chaney in Karloff's role as the monster in question, while Lionel Atwill skilfully deputised for Lugosi as the slimy Dr Rigas.

Chaney's character, Big Dan McCormick, is essentially a superior version of Lennie, a simple, affable, easygoing man who is turned into an electromagnetic monster by the loopy Rigas. The role is within his range, but he invests it with a great deal of sympathy, especially when McCormick descends into uncontrollable madness. Shot in three weeks, the end result is a decent chiller with Chaney – billed as 'Lon Chaney Jnr' – giving a thoroughly agreeable and likeable performance that generates the kind of pathos that marked his upcoming signature role.

During the making of the film, an event took place that must surely have brought home to Chaney the strong spectre of his father and the realisation of the career path he would take. On 11 December 1940, he attended a ceremony that took place on the Paris set of *The Phantom of the Opera*. Five surviving members of the film's original crew unveiled a plaque. It read, 'Dedicated to the memory of Lon Chaney, for whose picture *The Phantom of the Opera* this stage was erected in 1924.' Denis Gifford summed it up best: 'Chaney was dead, yet Chaney lived. From his very next picture, Universal dropped Jnr's "Jr". Only in movies could the dead truly come back to life.'

Although *Man-Made Monster* had the trappings of an efficient, conveyor-belt film typical of Universal's '40s horror output, it did well at the box office following its release in March 1941. It was obvious the film's success owed less to Chaney's star turn than to the massive free publicity it gained from a headline-making sex scandal that engulfed Lionel Atwill at that time and effectively derailed his career. Nevertheless, it certainly helped Chaney's profile, and Universal knew they had a new horror star to promote. Little did they care that they were literally creating a monster. And so began Chaney's association with the studio, which could be best described as extremely turbulent.

With the success of *Man-Made Monster*, Universal needed to find the perfect horror vehicle for their new discovery. In the meantime, the studio kept Chaney busy with a string of supporting roles. He was third billed behind Rudy Vallee and Helen Parrish in *Too Many Blondes* (1941), and appeared in a quartet of Westerns – *Billy the Kid* (1941), *San Antonio Rose* (1941), *Riders of Death Valley* (1941) and *Badlands of Dakota* (1941). Although he was invariably cast in supporting roles, these were a step up from his countless bit parts of the '30s, and being under a well-paid contract, he had regular money coming in whether he worked on a film or not.

Finally Universal came up with a brand new monster; well, not quite new, since the studio had previously produced *Werewolf of London* (1935). Chaney sealed his horror immortality with the role he will always be remembered for, Lawrence Talbot aka *The Wolf Man* (1941). It was a role he was most proud of. 'He was my baby!' he exclaimed with great affection. 'Of course I believe that the Wolf Man is the best of my horror roles, because he is *mine!*' Producer Paul Malvern agreed. 'Lon Chaney Jnr was under contract, and as far as the public was concerned there were no other actors who could play the Wolf Man.'

The screenplay originated during a conversation between Curt Siodmak and George Waggner. 'The idea for *The Wolf Man* started when George Waggner gave me the title and the list of Universal's contract players: Claude Rains, Maria Ouspenskaya, Warren William, Evelyn Ankers – all seasoned actors. Since Karloff was busy working on another motion picture, Lon Chaney got the part that changed his life and made him an actor of standing.'

Siodmak further said, 'When Universal entrusted their major new horror project to George Waggner, he realised that the studio needed someone dependable to write the script. The picture, I was told, should be in the range of $180,000. My salary was $400 a week, no percentages of course, and I only had 24-hour cut-off employment.'

The film's make-up designer Jack Pierce had also been responsible for the unique make-up for *Werewolf of London* (1935), but he wanted to try a different tack for the creature this time. 'I combed numerous histories of England without finding a practical description of a werewolf. About all I learned was that the legend began, and still persists, among the people of Wales who live around the ancient castles. Sometimes the wind produces sounds like the howling of wolves. Apparently the werewolf legend started with these noises. Since no-one had ever seen one, I just sat down and tried to figure out what a werewolf ought to look like.'

With the Wolf Man make-up successfully devised by Pierce, Chaney would now experience the same kind of pain his father had previously endured in order to create his beloved monster. According to Pierce at the time, 'The Wolf Man make-up, though it takes four hours to apply, is not as complicated as for Frankenstein's Monster. It consists principally of an artificial nosepiece and bristles on the head, face and neck, which is literally applied yak hair by yak hair. The hair is then singed to give it that wild, unkempt look. I also make up Chaney's feet and give him claws.'

The make-up took three hours to remove. 'What gets me is when it's after work,' said Chaney, 'I'm all hot and itchy and tired, and I've got to sit in the chair for 45 minutes while Jack just about kills me ripping off the stuff he puts on in the morning! Sometimes we take an hour and leave some of the skin on my face!'

The transformation scenes were equally difficult to achieve, as the actor relates: 'The day we did the transformations I came in at 2.00 am. When I got in the position, they would take little nails and drive them through the skin at the edge of my fingers of both hands, so that I wouldn't move them anymore. While I was in this position they would build a plaster cast of the back of my head. Then they would take the drapes from behind me and starch them, and while they were drying them, they would take the camera and weigh it down with one ton, so it wouldn't quiver when people walked. They had targets for my eyes up there. Then, while I was still in this position, they would shoot five or ten minutes of film in the camera. They'd take that film out and send it to the lab. While it was there, the make-up man would come and take the whole thing off my face, and put on a new one, only less. I was still immobile. When the film came back from the lab, they'd put it back in the camera and then they'd check me. They'd say "Your eyes have moved a little bit, move them to the right ... Now your shoulder is up ..." Then they'd roll it again and shoot another ten frames. Well we did 22 changes of make-up and it took 22 hours. I won't discuss about the bathroom!' And for all that, Chaney loved his Wolf Man.

One thing was certain: Curt Siodmak kept his distance. 'Of course, I had access to the set,' he said, 'but I didn't like to go there. Lon wanted to kill me! He was angry, because it took five to six hours to get into the make-up and an hour to take it off; he couldn't talk in the make-up, and he had to eat through a straw. Chaney said, "If I find the s-o-b who made up this monster, I'm gonna hit him over the head!"'

Despite being a handsomely-mounted chiller with a good cast that includes Claude Rains, Evelyn Ankers, Bela Lugosi, Patric Knowles, Ralph Bellamy and the diminutive Russian actress Maria Ouspenskaya (in her career-defining turn as the old gypsy woman Maleva), *The Wolf Man* falls short of the standard of Universal's early horror classics. The famous werewolf folklore that also featured in future films never came from any ancient legends; Curt Siodmak made it all up! The death silver bullet and the pentagram were his ideas, as was the famous rhyme, 'Even a man who is pure in heart and says his prayers by night, becomes a wolf when the wolf bane blooms and the autumn moon is bright.' It was all Siodmak's doing!

Siodmak admitted, 'Lon Chaney Jnr became the accepted Wolf Man in history, since he had a sharply-defined character, which has often been repeated but has never been changed. It also might be that he identified himself with that character – a decent human being, murderer against his will. Like in a Greek tragedy, where the gods decide on man's fate, the actor as in life could not escape his destiny.'

Siodmak saw *The Wolf Man* as a metaphor for the Nazis; an otherwise good man transformed into a murderer. Like many Jews, Siodmak had lived a normal life in Germany before fleeing to America when Hitler rose to power. The pentagram idea was taken from the Star of David. However, Siodmak had little time for symbolism in film theory. He simply wrote what was expected of him. 'The producers would think, "Give it to Siodmak, so we can get the script fast, then we can shoot it in a few weeks." That was my reputation. It wasn't the value of my script; it was more that they just didn't want to lose their money. Every night I say "Heil Hitler!", because without the son of a bitch I wouldn't be in Three Rivers, California. I'd still be living in Berlin!'

As convincing as he is in his wolf guise, Chaney is miscast when he plays his human side. Looking more like an American farmhand than the son of a Welsh aristocrat (albeit one who has lived in the States for 18 years – Universal surpassed themselves here!), he can't get beyond playing the likeable lug – although at least Talbot is more intelligent than Lennie Small or Dan McCormack.

'In my first version,' said Siodmak, 'Larry Talbot was an American mechanic who is sent to England to install a telescope in a Scottish castle. The studio made him the son of the lord who owned that building. I could never imagine that Lon, with his American accent, could ever have been a British nobleman! Also, I thought the idea of a simple mechanic who finds himself changing into a wolf would be doubly frightening to an American who had not been brought up in Wales, which is still full of ghosts. Maybe my producer George Waggner was right. My ideas were too sophisticated for a B horror picture!'

If Chaney's improbable casting as a Welsh heir is too hard for some people to swallow, the casting of Claude Rains as his father Sir John Talbot is equally unconvincing. Although there was actually a 16-year age gap, Rains and Chaney look about the same age!

Even if the success of *The Wolf Man* owes more to Pierce's memorable creation, Chaney's affable performance generates a tragic sympathy that typifies a Universal monster. 'All the best monsters were played for sympathy,' he said. 'That goes for my father, Boris Karloff, myself and all the others. They won the audience's sympathy. The Wolf Man didn't want to do all those things. He was forced into them by circumstance.' Chaney honed that characterisation in four Wolf Man movies in all, and even though his performances became increasingly sloppy with each film, he still managed to get the audience behind him. The years of playing Talbot's hairy persona also left his face permanently scarred from the make-up.

'The one thing I remember [about making *The Wolf Man*] is that Lon Chaney was usually drunk,' said cameraman Philip Lathrop. It pretty much summed up the actor's stormy time at Universal. In many ways, his behaviour mirrored that of the title character of *Dr Jekyll and Mr Hyde* rather than that of the Wolf Man. When he was sober (which was very rare), he was always a friendly man. 'There was never a nicer guy,' recalled Universal producer Paul Malvern. 'He got along with everybody. He and Broderick Crawford and Andy Devine were all pals, and they used to get together and do a lot of drinking.' Evelyn Ankers, who was Chaney's frequent co-star, also said of the actor, 'He seemed to have the need to be liked by everybody. When he wasn't drinking, he was the sweetest. Sometimes he hid the drinking so well, we could never be sure.' But drinking was very much part of Chaney's life, and this caused endless problems at Universal. According to Ankers, 'If a dress was destroyed or a hair-do by the Pierce crew, then [Chaney] heard from the front office; for they were afraid production would be held up, and that meant money lost.'

In addition to his wild drinking sessions, both on and off the set, Chaney had a reputation for being a boisterous and aggressive practical joker. All too often his mischievous pranks – which included water buckets on top of half-open doors and jumping out of dark corners to frighten people – quickly annoyed his fellow actors. Chaney would frequently sneak up behind Ankers in full wolf regalia and scare her senseless, and this soured their working relationship, despite their natural on-screen chemistry.

But Chaney found a boozy kindred spirit in Broderick Crawford. They enjoyed many wild drinking sessions together and used to throw punches at one another in the dressing room they shared, until they were either covered in blood or one of them had been knocked out by the other! 'Monsters!' exclaimed actor Robert Stack of Chaney and Crawford. 'They were known as monsters around the Universal lot, because their drunken behaviour often ended in bloodshed.'

Unsurprisingly, Chaney was difficult to work with, and the more he drank, the worse he became. 'He had that drinking problem,' said director Charles Barton. 'By late afternoon he didn't know where he was. He had that problem all his life, even when he was very young. I don't know why. I guess *he* knew all along.'

Barton's comments point to a complex and emotionally troubled man hiding behind the boozing and schoolboy antics. His father's ghost continued to overshadow Chaney in some way; and although he was happily married, unsubstantiated rumours persisted that he was homosexual and that he repressed that side of himself behind the heavy-drinking, hard-talking macho-man image – so much so that he tried to join the Marines when America declared war on Japan, although he failed the physical.

Universal Studios *were* willing to overlook these over-the-top antics, because they had a new horror star to promote. Unfortunately Chaney's limited acting ability, coupled with his increased alcohol consumption, would turn out to be his major downfall when playing other roles, which would include three more classic screen monsters. None of these interpretations would generate the pathos, sympathy or tragedy he brought so well to the Wolf Man.

Production on *The Wolf Man* wrapped in November 1941 for release the following month. With America going into the war following the Japanese attack on Pearl Harbor, Universal weren't too sure if this would have a negative effect on audience figures. They need not have worried. *The Wolf Man* did excellent business and finally established Chaney as a major star. 'When the picture made its first million,' said Siodmak, 'the producer got a $10,000 bonus, the director a diamond ring for his wife, and I got fired, since I wanted $25 more for my next job!'

Following another supporting role for Chaney in *North of the Klondike* (1942) with Broderick Crawford and Evelyn Ankers, Universal planned a new horror vehicle for their genre headliner, now dubbed the 'Master Character Creator' by the studio. It was an ambitious title for an actor whose dramatic range was limited at best. Keen to keep its *Frankenstein* franchise going, Universal decided that Chaney would be a perfect replacement for Boris Karloff, who had decided long ago never to return to his most famous role again.

Playing Frankenstein's Monster in *The Ghost of Frankenstein* (1942), Chaney once more had to undergo the discomforts of Jack Pierce's make-up. 'It took four hours to make me up,' he recalled. 'Then they led me to the set. They dug a hole in the cliff and put me in. They stuck a straw in my mouth and covered me in cement. It took till 12 o'clock to get me sealed in. Then everybody went to lunch!' Chaney found the rubber headpiece extremely uncomfortable. He constantly complained about it during filming, and got so angry that no-one in the cast or crew listened to his protests that eventually he ripped it off, tearing open a gash in his forehead. Production was shut down for a few days. An allergic reaction to the greasepaint also kept the actor out of action for a week.

Unlike Boris Karloff, who was an easygoing man and extremely patient despite the difficulties he underwent when Pierce transformed him into the Monster, Chaney became increasingly short-tempered. The newfound stardom had started to make him a very difficult man to deal with. Not surprisingly, relations between Chaney and Pierce began to strain under the actor's aggressive behaviour.

Chaney felt that the best way to deal with the discomfort he was suffering was booze. Keeping a hip flask at the ready at all times, he drank throughout the shoot. One day he was so inebriated he got lost, in full costume, within the intricate mazes that formed the laboratory set. It took several minutes for him to find his way out.

But there was a gentle side to Chaney that went against his boisterous tough-guy image and difficult behaviour. William Smith, now famous for villainous roles, was a child actor who also appeared in the film. 'During breaks on the set of *The Ghost of Frankenstein*,' he recalled, 'Chaney treated all the children on the set to an ice-cream.'

Chaney's massive frame may have been ideal for the Monster but he lacked the facial mobility that had made Karloff so memorable. Following Karloff would have been a daunting task for any actor, and despite the similarities between the Monster and Lennie, Chaney simply wasn't up to it. 'When I had to take over the part of the Frankenstein Monster from Boris Karloff, the pressure was on,' he admitted. Too much pressure for the actor to handle. As he wanders around the set with his eyes apparently closed, his miserable facial expression fails to register any emotion at all; the pathos of the Wolf Man is seriously lacking, and alongside typically scene-stealing turns from Bela Lugosi and Lionel Atwill, Chaney is completely out of his depth.

The Ghost of Frankenstein is regarded as the first production-line *Frankenstein*. The law of diminishing returns had already affected the quality of the series in terms of script and direction. The film is flatly presented and not very inspiring. Chaney's one-dimensional performance shows he had insufficient talent, presence or ability to successfully challenge Karloff.

Like *The Wolf Man*, however, the film did extremely good business at the box office, proving there was still life in the series. Other than a supporting role in the Western *Frontier Badmen* (1943), and a gag appearance as himself in *Crazy House* (1943), Chaney's output remained entrenched in horror. But as his performance in *The Ghost of Frankenstein* showed, he could not escape the clutches of his father's shadow. Worse still, with his next role, starring in *Son of Dracula* (1943), he fell victim to another actor's nightmare – miscasting.

Son of Dracula is much better than *The Ghost of Frankenstein*, chiefly because of the dreamlike atmosphere effectively created by director Robert Siodmak. His brother Curt was briefly involved after writing the original story but was thrown off the production. 'They only wanted one Siodmak,'

Curt later said. 'This lasted 71 years, until he died. He started on *Son of Dracula* and they gave him $150 a week. Two years later he was making $2,000 a day at Universal.'

There was always a tremendous rivalry between the Siodmak brothers, and Robert wasn't too impressed with his sibling's original screenplay. 'Universal sent me the script of *Son of Dracula*,' he said. 'It was terrible. It had been knocked together in a few days. But we did a lot of rewriting and the result wasn't bad. It wasn't good, but some scenes had a certain quality.'

The mist-shrouded swamp of America's Deep South couldn't be more ideally suited as the Count's new home. Amongst the film's memorable moments are Dracula's coffin emerging from the marshes and vapour rising from the coffin to form the all-too-real vampire king. Siodmak keeps things going at a reasonable pace, making it one of Universal's better horror efforts.

But there is one massive flaw – Lon Chaney Jnr. Not looking remotely European, the actor is way too big and all-American to pass himself off convincingly as the Count. (Bela Lugosi was reported to be furious he wasn't even considered for the role.) Looking out of place in the starched scratchy collars of the formal evening attire and cape, Chaney was a bad choice to play Dracula. To his credit, he battled extremely hard against his miscasting and managed to give a half-decent performance. If anything his interpretation can be classed as something of a forerunner to Christopher Lee's. Chaney may lack Lugosi's aristocratic bearing, but he puts his massive physique to good use by creating a terrifying and formidable vampire presence, and one not afraid to get into a fight. He also cuts a more sympathetic figure on a par with the Wolf Man, especially when the Count's new bride (played by Louise Albritton) is using him to selfishly attain immortality for herself and her former fiancé. It's a winning turn played with complete conviction. Chaney's acting is unlikely to satisfy Dracula fans, but he deserves ten out of ten for doing his best in what could have been a total disaster for all concerned.

Even though he was required to wear only a moustache by way of special make-up this time, Chaney's difficult attitude and violent outbursts continued. During the making of *Son of Dracula*, he ended up smashing a vase over Robert Siodmak's head.

His performances as Dracula and the Monster may not have been horror classics, but they are ten times better than the three terrible films he then made as Kharis the Mummy. Universal had previously produced *The Mummy* (1932) and *The Mummy's Hand* (1940), the latter having no relation to the previous film. *The Mummy's Hand* is a well made and entertaining horror that features a memorable performance from Tom Tyler, normally known for playing cowboys, as the 3,000-year-old Kharis. The film having done very well at the box office, a sequel was inevitable. With Tyler unable to repeat the role because of crippling arthritis, Universal decided to promote their 'Master Character Creator' in another unsuitable monster role.

The first of the three films Chaney made in this series was *The Mummy's Tomb* (1942). Like *The Ghost of Frankenstein*, it has all the hallmarks of a third-rate assembly-line horror production. As it is a direct sequel to *The Mummy's Hand*, this sloppy effort is padded out with flashback footage from that previous film. Contrasting with the lean-looking Tyler, Chaney with his hefty presence gives the impression that Kharis has put on quite a bit of weight during his long slumber – a situation made all the more obvious because Tyler features quite a lot in the flashback footage. The only possible explanation for the change of appearance comes from sinister High Priest Andoheb, played as in *The Mummy's Hand* by George Zucco, when he says that the fire seen at the climax of the previous film did not kill Kharis but 'maimed and distorted him'. However, Chaney's Kharis doesn't look remotely singed or burnt; he must have needed an emergency change of bandages after he piled on the weight!

But then logic was never a great strong point of *The Mummy's Tomb*. If Kharis's new look stretches the viewer's credulity, then the fact that supporting players Dick Foran and Wallace Ford, repeating their roles from the previous film, have been given make-up that causes them to appear some thirty years older, gives the impression that the sequel is set around 1970!

Chaney's own make-up as the Mummy is also less effective than Tyler's in the previous film, time and budget constraints having worked against Jack Pierce's perfectionism. Whereas he had given careful attention to detail to Tyler's Kharis, Pierce devised a basic mask for Chaney to wear. Unfortunately this registers no facial expression bar showing just one eye; not that Chaney was an expert at showing emotion, judging by his performance as Frankenstein's Monster! Really it could have been anyone under the bandages. The role itself is limited to the actor shuffling about (drunk) and killing the odd victim. Chaney himself complained bitterly about its meagre size.

As bad as it was, *The Mummy's Tomb* turned out to be one of Universal's biggest money-makers, and this meant a further sequel was inevitable. *The Mummy's Ghost* (1944) is actually a slight improvement, with no flashback footage this time and the welcome presence of John Carradine as high priest Yuseuf Bey. But Chaney sleepwalks through his role. Still angry about the limited screen time he was being afforded, he had a several run-ins with fellow actor Frank Reicher. According to director Reginald Le Borg, 'Chaney as Kharis went overboard in a scene when he strangles Frank Reicher's character, although Chaney blocked the camera from picking up Reicher's reaction. Reicher later exclaimed, "He nearly killed me!"' Being a more professional actor than Chaney was, Reicher didn't complain, but Le Borg added, 'The next day, I noticed [Reicher's] neck visibly bore the effects.'

If the tantrums were bad, the boozing was worse. By midday Chaney was usually drunk as a lord. It came to the point that actress Ramsey Ames became terrified every time the intoxicated actor had to carry her across the steep boardwalk set. Logic got strained once again here, given that Kharis has only one good arm and should therefore be unable to carry anybody!

The next film, *The Mummy's Curse* (1944), followed the same pattern and contains nothing worth noting in any detail other than further lapses in logic. For starters, the Louisiana swamp where Kharis met his doom in the previous film has been mysteriously transferred to Massachusetts. Furthermore, the sequel takes place 25 years after the last film, meaning it would have to be set in the late 1990s!

Unable to generate any expression or sympathy, Chaney's one-note acting in all three films was in tune with their appalling nature. The drinking didn't help much either; writer Gregory Mank described Chaney as someone who 'had a thirst on the set for more than just [his character's] tana leaves.'

But for all his heavy drinking and violent outbursts, Chaney often befriended young actors and stood up for older ones that he felt were being given a hard time by the studio. One person he stood by was William Farnum. A one-time silent movie star, Farnum had been reduced to small roles with the coming of sound, and these included a bit part in *The Mummy's Curse*. According to co-star Peter Coe, 'Chaney demanded that Farnum be given his own chair and be treated with respect, or else he would walk off the picture.'

Although the least distinguished of Universal's monster cycle, the mummy mask worn by Chaney is the only surviving example of Jack Pierce's incredible work. At the time of writing, it is on exhibition at the Experience Music Project Museum in Seattle, Washington.

Chaney may have been Universal's top horror star, but his height proved something of a handicap when it came to him being considered for other roles. In a nutshell the studio had no idea what to do with him outside the horror genre, and his appearing in this kind of rubbish only served to illustrate his limited value as their contract player.

Thanks to his booze-fuelled antics and childish pranks, Chaney's relationship with Universal remained stormy, the situation not being helped by the studio casting him in inappropriate roles. Being under contract did at least enable him to do a certain amount of work in other genres, but the restrictions imposed on him by typecasting, his limited range and his erratic behaviour meant his non-horror output consisted of supporting roles that were merely extensions of his Lennie character. This all added to Chaney's increasing frustration that he could not escape his father's hold.

But his films were successful at the box office, and Universal, to their credit, tried their best to accommodate him – and wring out a few dollars on the strength of his name – even if the attempts to vary his image proved disastrous. In attempting to alter the status quo, the studio cast Chaney as college professors, teachers, intellectuals and academics for a series of low budget second features known as *The Inner Sanctum*. Based on a popular radio series, these films were effectively introduced by a misshapen head in a crystal ball! Unfortunately they did not live up to their offbeat premise.

The first of these productions was *Calling Dr Death* (1943). Directed by competent journeyman Reginald Le Borg and co-starring the excellent J Carrol Naish, it has Chaney playing Dr Mark Steele, a neurologist whose unfaithful wife has been brutally murdered. Suffering from memory loss, Steele, with the help of his attractive nurse, undergoes hypnosis to see if he is actually responsible for the murder. It's a decent enough premise to start the series, but the end result is little more than another misfire cashing in on the famous name. Looking sweaty and uncomfortable in double-breasted suits, ties, slicked back hair and Clark Gable moustache, a miscast Chaney, who was not especially handsome, just bulldozes his large physique through the film. Lacking the conviction he brought to *Son of Dracula*, he proves conclusively that the only tortured individuals he excelled at were ordinary or simpleminded guys, not professors, academics or other intellectual types.

Calling Dr Death did sufficiently well at the box office for Universal to continue the series. Each film, six in total, had a modest $150,000 budget and a 12-day shoot with Reginald Le Borg directing. The next, *Weird Woman* (1944), has Chaney, reunited with Evelyn Ankers, as Professor Norman Reed, a scientist who marries an exotic woman raised by natives who believe her to be a voodoo high priestess. In *Dead Man's Eyes* (1944), for a change of profession, Chaney plays artist David Stuart, a blind man given new eyes that have previously witnessed a murder. In *The Frozen Ghost* (1945), working once more with Ankers, he portrays mentalist Gregor the Great. Lower down the intellectual scale, *Strange Confession* (1945) has Chaney as downtrodden chemist and family man Jeff Carter, who takes revenge on those responsible for his son's death. The final film of the series went more or less back to the first effort. *Pillow of Death* (1945) has Chaney playing Wayne Fletcher, an attorney whose wife has been smothered. Because he is having an affair, he's the chief suspect.

Someone on the lines of Boris Karloff, Basil Rathbone or Bela Lugosi could have given *The Inner Sanctum* series the kind of acting class that Chaney simply lacked. Playing well-dressed, intellectual men dealing with unfaithful wives, jealous colleagues, voodoo priests and deranged hypnotists, simply wasn't his forte, because he had insufficient glamour to carry it off. Chaney's dramatic performances overall were at best unconvincing, at worst amateurish.

At least one of the actor's demons could have been exorcised if wasn't for a last minute attack of cold feet by Universal. The studio promised Chaney his father's role of Erik in the 1943 remake of *The Phantom of the Opera*. With the film due to be shot in Technicolor and budgeted at $1.75 million, this incredible offer was too good to pass up. Chaney relished the prospect of playing the role, because he saw it as an opportunity to bury his father's ghost once and for all. And starring in a high-profile film production meant Universal might take him more seriously as an actor – no typecasting, no monsters, no second-rate movies, none of that stuff. That paternal spectre that had haunted him all his life could now be eradicated for good.

But, once again, Chaney got short shrift. Fearing possible miscasting if he was hired, Universal replaced him, much to his lasting bitterness, with the more versatile Claude Rains, who ironically had played his screen dad in *The Wolf Man*.

Although lavishly shot, with excellent costumes and sets, the lacklustre remake is ultimately undermined by an equally miscast Rains. A fine actor who rarely gave a bad performance on screen, Rains is adequate enough, but he lacks the presence and that special magic that made the great Lon Chaney Snr's performance immortal.

On paper it's unlikely Chaney could have pulled it off; he simply did not have the talent or versatility of his father, or even of Claude Rains for that matter. As in *Son of Dracula*, he would have looked too uncomfortable wearing formal evening dress; and, as an actor more suited to working-class everyman roles, playing a brilliant but demented composer would have left him as miscast as with his *The Inner Sanctum* intellectuals. But such was Chaney's determination, it is just possible he could have overcome those obstacles and defied everybody's fears by delivering an excellent performance as Erik, leading Universal seriously to reconsider his position as a horror star. More importantly, Chaney could have achieved the major stardom that was always one step away from him.

But, as it was, he was back to the usual grind of B-movie chillers – including reprising the role of Talbot in *Frankenstein Meets the Wolf Man* (1943). This is a daft but reasonably enjoyable effort that pre-dates *Freddy vs Jason* (2003), the *Alien vs Predator* movies and *Godzilla vs Whatever Monster Toho Studios Decided to Throw at Him While he Destroyed Japan for the Umpteenth Time*! Aware of the declining standards of the *Frankenstein* series, Universal needed a fresh approach, so why not bring back the Wolf Man? 'When the monster died,' said Curt Siodmak, 'it didn't. Universal writers always found a way to bring it back to life, which proves that a financial return supersedes death.'

It was Siodmak who accidentally brought up the idea of bringing two of Universal's most popular monsters together in one film. 'Never make a joke in the studio,' he added. 'I was sitting down at the Universal commissary having lunch with George Waggner, and I said, "George, why don't we make a picture called *Frankenstein Wolfs the Meat Man* – er, *Meets the Wolf*

Man." He didn't laugh.'

It was inevitable that Chaney would return as Talbot, and the opening sequence where the long dead Welshman (!) is revived is very effective. Chaney's performance in the part is also vastly improved. Now settled into the role, he plays his human alter ego with great skill, care and commitment. His transformation from man to wolf is brilliantly done. The only drawback of the first half is the brief appearance of Dennis Hoey as Inspector Owen. Best known as the bumbling Inspector Lestrade in Universal's *Sherlock Holmes* series, he's dressed in Lestrade's bowler hat and top coat and is Lestrade in all but name. It's as if he has wandered in from the other series – perhaps not surprisingly, since Roy William Neill, who directed the *Holmes* films, is also director on this production.

As a sequel to *The Wolf Man*, the first half of the film hits the mark beautifully. Talbot then heads off to Mittel Europe to consult Dr Frankenstein about his affliction. This too is a welcome bonus, as it brings back the wonderful Maria Ouspenskaya, in excellent scene-stealing form as Maleva. Once again she acts everyone off the screen with her wise but sinister presence.

Hiding in the ruins of Frankenstein's castle after his werewolf persona attacks a girl, Talbot finds the Monster in a block of ice – hence the film's title. (Note that the name 'Frankenstein' has now been passed to his creation.) The Monster is now blind and extremely weak after what happened to him in the previous film.

The Monster has also changed his appearance. It was the intention for Chaney to reprise his role from *The Ghost of Frankenstein*, but budget restrictions and make-up demands made it impossible for Chaney's Wolf Man to meet Chaney's Monster. So Universal offered the Monster role instead to the 60-year-old Bela Lugosi. Lugosi had turned it down in 1931, but was now in such desperate financial straits that he had no choice but to accept it this time. On paper the casting switch was sound enough: in *The Ghost of Frankenstein*, Lugosi's hunchback Ygor had his brain transferred into the Monster, making the Monster able to speak in Ygor's voice. However, the studio ultimately decided to edit out all of Lugosi's dialogue and all references to his blindness, reducing the actor to just a few minutes' screen time. Lugosi also looked far too old and frail to pass himself off as scary. Even in the brilliantly orchestrated final confrontation between the monsters, both actors were replaced by stuntmen.

A heavy drinker on top of having a morphine addiction, Lugosi would find some emotional solace by drinking Chaney (whom he disliked intensely) under the table whenever possible. The sickly smell of booze and tobacco smoke that regularly wafted from the dressing room was a sad reminder of two men coping with their own separate demons through alcohol – Chaney with his whiskey and Lugosi with his Burgundy.

As his alcohol abuse and personal ghosts were eating him alive, Chaney was beginning to unravel. On top of his constant drinking and highly-charged emotional state, his mindset was further dogged by fears of unemployment that stemmed from his early struggles. An avid fisherman, hunter and marksman, he got so worried about the film work drying up that he spent a lot of time at his large farmhouse in the country, where he caught fish, shot game and proceeded to can everything for such a day as he might need to call on it to eat.

The stress of possible unemployment also prompted him to take on more work than he could handle, rather than hold out for better roles. Eventually overwork and personal problems began to take their toll on his marriage. Following a heated row with Patsy, an alcohol-fuelled Chaney overdosed on 40 sleeping pills. After spending 46 hours in hospital, close to death, he recovered and reconciled with his wife.

Chaney was struggling to hold on, to fight back his decline. It was at this time that he reached out to his birth mother. The reunion was a happy one, and at least it helped Chaney bury one of his childhood demons. Cleva Creighton, who had since remarried, eventually died in a Los Angeles nursing home in November 1967. From all accounts, Chaney was devoted to her until the very end.

Even if the rot was setting in, *Frankenstein Meets the Wolf Man* is an enjoyable movie, despite being undermined by studio interference. But once again Chaney found himself associated mainly with inappropriate horror roles, the appeal of which was falling due to a combination of the films' declining market, restricted budgets and downturn in actual quality. In between looking uncomfortable playing suits in *The Inner Sanctum* series and shuffling around drunk in the *Mummy* films, he was handed lesser material elsewhere. Billed behind Jon Hall, Sabu and the darkly exotic Maria Montez, he was reunited with director Robert Siodmak in *Cobra Woman* (1944), but this fell a long way short of the artistic highs of *Son of Dracula*. Playing Hava, a blind/mute beggar, the actor looks overweight and even more uncomfortable half-naked than he did in a suit. But it is actually camp fun if watched with a sense of humour. At least it is better than his brief appearance dressed as a bear in the Ole Olsen/Chic Johnson comedy *Ghost Catchers* (1944) and an uncredited turn as himself in *Follow the Boys* (1944).

If combining two monsters had worked successfully in *Frankenstein Meets the Wolf Man*, why not try out another monster fest? Universal clearly felt this would be a good idea to draw in the crowds, even if it reflected their desperation to get more money out of a dying genre. *House of Frankenstein* (1944) and *House of Dracula* (1945) more or less ended all things horrific for Universal. With a generous budget of $354,000, the first film, originally titled *The Devil's Brood*, is definitely the better of the two, with a stellar horror cast that includes, alongside Chaney (Talbot/Wolf Man), genre favourites Boris

Karloff (mad scientist), John Carradine (Dracula), J Carrol Naish (hunchback assistant), Lionel Atwill (police inspector) and George Zucco (travelling showman). Kharis the Mummy was also considered for inclusion, but budget restrictions prevented this. Giant cowboy actor Glenn Strange won a small measure of horror fame as Frankenstein's Monster, now billed twenty-second in the cast. Although the Monster is reduced to a little more than a prop, Strange manages to invest some feeling into the role – not surprisingly, since he was coached by Karloff. 'I'd never have been the Monster I was if it hadn't been for Boris Karloff,' recalled Strange. 'He had finished his scenes and could have gone home, but he stayed on and worked with me. He showed me how to make the Monster's moves properly and how to do the walk that makes the Monster so frightening.' Thanks to Karloff's coaching, Strange achieved more in his brief scenes in *House of Frankenstein* than Chaney had managed when he took centre-stage in *The Ghost of Frankenstein*.

Once again Curt Siodmak provided the initial concept for the film. 'The idea was to put all the horror characters into one picture. I only wrote the story. I didn't write the script.' Rather than provide a central story for the ghouls to appear in, *House of Frankenstein* opts for individual tales linked together by Karloff's Dr Nieman and his journey to Frankenstein's ruined castle. Carradine's Dracula makes a good impression at the start of the film but is killed off pretty quickly, allowing for Nieman to enter the next tale, where he meets the Monster and the Wolf Man.

Repeating his signature role, Chaney still invests a great deal of sympathy as the tormented Talbot, and at least has only one transformation scene toward the end. However, as the film progresses, he becomes more pathetic than sad, and therefore tiresome to an audience that is supposed to root for him. He is nevertheless as effective as ever in his werewolf persona. Actress Elena Verdugo, who played Talbot's love interest, recalls, 'They used to have professional screamers on the [Universal] set. Well, when the Wolf Man jumped out at me, I was so scared and screamed so wildly that they cancelled the professional screamer!'

It is all wonderful ghoulish fun, but *House of Frankenstein* suffers from an overkill of monsters, making it less effective than it might have been. The performances from all concerned are solid, but apart from Karloff, everyone suffers from limited screen time. And while it's entertaining in some parts, it is clear that Universal's production line horror would grind to a halt sooner rather than later.

Sadly the fun of the first film is lacking in *House of Dracula*. Chaney, Carradine and Strange all reprise their roles, although there is no explanation as to how Dracula and Talbot have been revived. Lionel Atwill, who was terminally ill with cancer, also returns, playing yet another policeman. Onslow Stevens takes over the mad scientist duties and, like Karloff in the previous film, provides the linking framework to several unrelated tales. In fact it is Stevens who steals the acting honours from the better known cast, all of whom are reduced to minor roles. Strangely, considering the film's title, Carradine's Count has even less to do than before.

While Chaney still evokes audience sympathy, his sloppy performance reduces Talbot to a caricature. Sporting a moustache for the first time in the series, he gives the impression of having rushed straight from a *The Inner Sanctum* movie. Now seemingly on autopilot, he reiterates the character's feelings of death and despair to the point of annoyance. There is one nice touch involving a hunchback woman, played with some distinction by Jane Adams, who later recalled that working with these horror luminaries had been quite an experience: 'At the Pasadena Playhouse, I had become familiar with the Stanislavski "method" of acting in serious drama. A horror film allowed you to become totally engrossed in what you were playing. On *House of Dracula*, my memory is that they were all very serious actors, and they were sitting around studying their scripts.'

For Glenn Strange, working on *House of Dracula* proved a difficult experience, and Chaney came to the rescue with a remedy he knew all too well. 'After sitting for three hours in the make-up chair in the morning,' Strange recalled, 'I spent the rest of the day buried in cold liquid mud, which doubled up for quicksand. Then everybody went out for lunch. By the time they came back, I was so cold I could barely feel my legs. Lon suggested I use alcohol to keep warm.' Taking Chaney's advice, Strange forgot about the other effects of booze. 'Throughout the day, Lon passed a bottle of whiskey, which I drank in between takes. By the end of the day, I was so drunk I could barely dress myself after removing the costume.'

House of Dracula isn't without interest, but it is a clear indication that Universal's classic monster cycle had been well and truly exhausted. There could be only so many monster rallies before the public grew fed up with it all. In terms of quality, the series was also at the end of its tether, and the fact that the Wolf Man was given a happy ending only served notice that Universal had taken the horror genre as far as it could. With *The Inner Sanctum* series also coming to a quiet end, and his only other film assignment at this time being the Western *The Daltons Ride Again* (1944), Chaney faced an uncertain future.

Although the horror films were still doing well at the box office, the rot had set in. John Carradine summed it up best shortly after completing his stint on *House of Dracula*: 'By the time they finished the script, millions of GIs were being shipped home. World War II had ended. Many of the GIs did not come home whole in mind and body. Thousands of families had their own horrors to contend with, and the studios were running scared from any type of horror films.'

Although Carradine makes a solid argument, some studios hadn't quite got wind of the situation and continued to churn out increasingly inferior production-line chillers to wring a final few dollars from the box office tills. But by 1946 the situation had taken a sharp change. The atomic bombs over Hiroshima and Nagasaki and the uncovering of the well-documented work of Dr Josef Mengele meant that the horror genre slowly became redundant as an entertainment medium. Also, studios were now dealing with major changes in film production, as television began to make inroads. Eventually cost-cutting meant that many of the contract players had to go.

Chaney was no exception. An actor of his modest talents was now expendable in the face of these changes, and by this time Universal had grown fed up with his boozing. The studio had been happy to overlook his drinking and practical jokes while he was a horror star, but with the genre played out, there was no need for him. Unsurprisingly his contract was not renewed. Chaney's star career was now at an end; and typecasting being what it was, he, like Bela Lugosi, was unceremoniously cast out to the wolves as a freelance actor. It was a brave new world out there, but not necessarily a good one.

He was perhaps a little luckier than most (certainly luckier than Lugosi). There was still a demand for supporting actors, and Chaney had already provided back-up in several Westerns produced at Universal. Unfortunately the return of another form of typecasting started to hang over his head; that of his other famous character, Lennie. So it looked like a career awaited playing dim-witted B-movie heavies.

And that was indeed the case when he was cast as the intellectually challenged Willie in the excellent Bob Hope comedy *My Favorite Brunette* (1947). Basically spoofing Lennie (Hope's character offers to buy his a rabbit), Chaney holds his own more than adequately, even if it isn't a great part. Still it was well-paid work in a high-profile movie. *My Favorite Brunette* is also notable for having cast Chaney alongside Peter Lorre as the sadistic knife thrower Kismet. Like Chaney, Lorre had just severed his links with Warner Brothers and was facing an uncertain future.

For Paramount studios, Chaney returned to the Western genre to star opposite Randolph Scott in *Silver City* (1948). His role of Steve Murkill is little more than the villain's henchman, required to be a totally loathsome low-life who terrorises everyone before Scott's hero knocks him out! He also gets a good fight scene with Scott where he memorably keeps his cigarette in place. It's a typical Randolph Scott effort, but being a Paramount picture, it kept Chaney's profile fairly high.

The Counterfeiters (1948) is a reasonable crime thriller, with Chaney playing gangster Louie Struber. Not quite as big as his previous films, but it gave him a chance to play an intelligent ringleader instead of a dim-witted heavy.

For director Irwin Allen, Chaney appeared alongside Lloyd Bridges in *16*

Fathoms Deep (1948), a seafaring yarn that sees the actor playing Dimitri, a crooked businessman at odds with Bridges' small entrepreneur. He makes the most of his role despite the lack of screen time.

Chaney's best screen work of the late '40s, however, came courtesy of an unlikely studio – Universal – and in an unlikely role – the Wolf Man. Despite his happy ending in *House of Dracula*, Talbot would succumb to his lycanthrope alter-ego one last time in *Abbott and Costello Meets Frankenstein* (1948). Previously one of Hollywood's most popular comedy double acts, Abbott and Costello were experiencing a career decline caused by failing box office and personal problems. In an attempt to revive the studio's flagging fortunes and resurrect their now defunct horror cycle – and make a bit more money from the paying public – Universal decided to team the struggling duo with their redundant monsters.

Lou Costello was reluctant take part in the film. 'No way I'll do this crap!' he exclaimed. 'My little girl could write something better than this.' However, all things were smoothed over with a $50,000 salary advance and an acquiescence to the duo's insistence that their old friend Charles Barton be taken on as director.

Originally called *The Brain of Frankenstein*, the film had a decent budget of $792,000. It went into production in February 1948, with Chaney and Glenn Strange both on board as the Wolf Man and the Monster respectively, and Bela Lugosi – although he wasn't initially considered for the role – making his second screen appearance as Dracula. For good measure, even Vincent Price's unmistakable voice briefly turns up uncredited as the Invisible Man!

As well as returning to past glories, Chaney could also take some comfort that his wolf make-up this time took only an hour to apply. Jack Pierce's time-consuming methods were considered obsolete by Universal, so he was dropped (to his lasting bitterness) in favour of Bud Westmore, who had a more economical approach. Not only did Westmore reduce the discomfort Chaney had to endure, he also created a rubber mask that allowed the actor to register facial expressions. As a result, Chaney is much more convincing than he ever was in the previous films.

Chaney rushed to the aide of Glenn Strange once more when the latter broke his foot during production. For the thrilling climax where the Monster throws Lenore Aubert's mad doctor (a nice touch, since the female of the species is deadlier than the male!) off the cliff-top castle to a watery grave, it was Chaney doing the honours instead of Strange.

Unfortunately the demon drink continued to follow Chaney throughout production. 'By late afternoon,' recalled Barton, 'he didn't know where he was.'

Abbott and Costello Meet Frankenstein is both funny and scary. As well as being one of the comedy duo's best-remembered vehicles, it boasts spirited scenes and excellent performances from the other cast members – especially

Lugosi, who is better this time as Dracula than he was 18 years earlier, and Chaney, who brings back some of the enthusiasm that was lacking in *House of Dracula*.

With such a great success behind them, Universal would go on to team the comedy duo up with their remaining monsters – with diminishing results. Only *Abbott and Costello Meet Dr Jekyll and Mr Hyde* (1953) would come close to the quality of the first effort. *Abbott and Costello Meet the Killer, Boris Karloff* (1949), *Abbott and Costello Meet The Invisible Man* (1951) and *Abbott and Costello Meet The Mummy* (1955) are shining examples of how a good but simple formula cannot sustain a series of films.

Despite it being his best screen vehicle in a long while, Chaney was not happy with *Abbott and Costello Meet Frankenstein*; he felt Universal had ruined the horror genre by allowing Abbott and Costello to spoof it. 'Gone now are the scares!' he lamented. 'The monsters are now figures of fun, for the kids.' Not that it mattered to Universal. The film grossed over $3 million at the box office and put Abbott and Costello, and everyone else involved, back on top, albeit very briefly.

Abbott and Costello Meet Frankenstein did not have any long-term effect on Chaney's career; and it did nothing whatsoever for Bela Lugosi. As the decade came to a close, Chaney landed a supporting role as John Colton in *There's a Girl in My Heart* (1949), a pleasant enough little musical for Allied Artists. The next decade would bring many highs and lows in his rollercoaster career, including extensive television work.

There might have been an occasional chiller to make it to the screen, but as far as the public was concerned, the horror genre was officially dead and buried. The '50s saw the rise of science fiction. The drive-ins were now packed with teenagers eager to watch giant spiders, sea monsters and a fire-spouting lizard from Japan causing havoc in a variety of trashy but endearing low-budget flicks. Chaney however wasn't too impressed with this new monster rally. 'The trouble with most monster pictures today is that they go after horror for horror's sake. There's no motivation for how monsters behave. There's too much of that science fiction baloney.'

Despite those persistent fears of unemployment, the '50s turned out to be a very busy period for Chaney as he made a reasonably successful transition from leading man to supporting player. He was burly sailor Red Lynch in *Captain China* (1950), Gus the sympathetic gangster in *Once a Thief* (1950) and a heavy called Shocker in the drama *Inside Straight* (1951). He returned to the Western genre opposite Gregory Peck in *Only the Valiant* (1951) and John Ireland in *The Rebel* (1951), the latter giving him a chance to excel in a spot of villainy as crippled landowner Artimus Taylor. There was also a brief turn in a rather silly comedy about a dog, called *Behave Yourself* (1951), and a touch of ham-slicing theatrics as red-bearded pirate Borka Barbossa in the Arabian nights flick *Flame of Araby* (1951).

Horror roles still followed Chaney, and despite his feelings about *Abbott and Costello Meet Frankenstein*, he worked with the duo again on TV in *The Colgate Comedy Hour*, playing Frankenstein's Monster in a sketch. This was his first known television work; and it was followed by his first in a drama anthology, with a guest appearance in the series *Cosmopolitan Theatre*.

While his films weren't cinematic classics, they provided respectable, decently paid work for Chaney. But in between his prolific but undistinguished output was a film that became a foretaste of the chillers he would make a decade later. *Bride of the Gorilla* (1951) marked Curt Siodmak's debut as director, and while his quick-fire scripts were reasonably decent, his direction lacked punch. Still, he rounded up a dependable cast of Raymond Burr (who took an immediate dislike to Chaney), Barbara Payton and Tom Conway, with Chaney unbelievably cast as South America policeman Commissioner Tora.

The plot is daft beyond words. Burr's character marries a plantation owner's widow (Payton) and gets cursed by a witch doctor so that every night he turns into a gorilla and goes on a rampage! It is cheap, cheesy and cheerful, with a good cast all at sea and Chaney looking rough, and only the glamorous Barbara Payton holding any kind of interest. One can only imagine that Chaney did the film out of loyalty to Siodmak – although a bit of fast drinking money must have helped!

At the beginning of 1952 Chaney returned to television with a serious interpretation of Frankenstein's Monster. Predating *The Twilight Zone* and *The Outer Limits*, ABC's *Tales of Tomorrow* was the first American TV anthology series to deal with science fiction. The series mixed classic tales with contemporary fantasy, and Chaney starred in the first television adaptation of Mary Shelley's classic tale. Thanks to the excellent make-up, Chaney's bald-headed, scar-faced Monster is far more convincing than the one in *The Ghost of Frankenstein*. Unfortunately his heavy drinking beforehand ruined an otherwise effective performance. Drunk during the rehearsals, he damaged some of the props, which had to be replaced at the last minute. In an ironic twist of fate, when the show got its live broadcast in January 1952, the booze-soaked Chaney thought he was going through another rehearsal, and instead of smashing up all the furniture as he was supposed to, he just waved it around before putting it neatly back in its place! He can be heard whispering to himself, 'Save for the show.' Unsurprisingly, his unreliable behaviour more or less ended his career on live television.

Despite the increasing alcoholism, and apparent misery, the film work continued, with a return to Arabian nights adventures as Sinbad in *Thief of Damascus* (1952) and to the reliable Western genre in *Springfield Rifle* (1952). One of his more interesting films of the time was *The Battle for Chief Pontiac* (1952). Playing the title role of the Indian chief in question, Chaney doesn't look remotely Native-American, but he gives a nicely restrained performance predating his major television success a few years later.

But the real high spot was his well received performance as Martin Howe in the highly acclaimed Western classic *High Noon* (1952). Starring Gary Cooper as a town marshal who must face a deadly enemy alone because the people he has protected for years refuse to help him, this is an unusually intelligent and perceptive Western, far removed from the standard shoot-em-ups. Unrecognisable behind a grey wig and thick moustache, Chaney gives a brief but unforgettable turn as the retired sheriff who wants to help but is prevented from doing so by his age, making him the only person Cooper forgives. Although not quite Oscar-worthy, his excellent performance should have helped pave the way for better acting assignments.

Unfortunately *The Black Castle* (1952) is the antithesis to *High Noon*. Starring Boris Karloff and Richard Greene, this was Universal's dismal attempt to revive the old gothic format. By this time, Karloff's horror career had slowly started the downward turn, even though he remained extremely busy with his stage and television commitments on both sides of the Atlantic. However, he hasn't much to do in the film. Chaney fares even worse as Gargon the mute servant, who spends much of his limited screen time hulking in the background – although he is allowed a great death scene when he falls into an alligator pit.

The movie work continued to come in, but by this time Chaney's famous name was simply marquee value for low-budget filmmakers. Peg-Leg the pirate in *Raiders of the Seven Seas* (1953), Spurge McNamee opposite James Cagney in *Lions in the Street* (1953), Pedro Martines in *Lost Treasure of the Amazon* (1953), and another burly henchman role as Castro alongside Raymond Burr in *Passion* (1954): these roles didn't amount to much and required Chaney to do little except look menacing – something he could do with his eyes shut.

Among the brief cinematic high spots were a small but nicely-played cameo as Bible-spouting drunk Crazy Charlie in *The Boy from Oklahoma* (1954) and a slightly larger appearance, against his usual standard villainy, as the sympathetic Padre Feilips in *The Black Pirates* (1954). Big-budget comedy was also on the menu when he worked once more with Bob Hope in *Casanova's Big Night* (1954). This was the last of Hope's major movies, and probably his worst, complete with mistimed laughs and a cast that included Joan Fontaine, Basil Rathbone, John Carradine and Vincent Price (uncredited as Casanova) looking all at sea. Chaney has one good scene as the sly Emo the Murderer, although he briefly lapses into his Lennie routine once more – he has a pet mouse!

No-one could say Chaney's output was greatly varied. In between the Westerns *The Silver Star* (1955), *I Died a Thousand Times* (1955) and *The Indian*

Fighter (1955), he was well cast as hardboiled prisoner Alamo Smith in the gritty drama *Big House USA* (1955). But his best performance, and one to equal his memorable turn in *High Noon*, was in the role of Robert Mitchum's alcoholic father Job Marsh in Stanley Kramer's glossy *Not as a Stranger* (1955). There is something of an eerie reminder of Chaney's own relationship with his father during his scenes with Mitchum. Mitchum plays ambitious medical student Lucas, who learns that his father has drunk away the tuition fees, leading to a vicious confrontation that results in Job hitting the bottle. 'You'll never make it,' Job says to his son. 'It's not that you don't have a brain. You have to have a heart.' Chaney's role lasts one scene, but it's a pivotal moment, and he gives a heart-wrenching performance full of pain and anguish – much like the actor's own life at that time.

Another intriguing film for Chaney was *Manfish* (1956), an adaptation of Edgar Allan Poe's *The Gold Bug*. Playing Swede, one of three unsavoury adventurers in search of treasure, he goes through his Lennie routine once more, but ends up being the only character with any redeeming features. The film's premise is promising enough, but it's a laboured effort torpedoed by variable acting, only Chaney emerging from the murky waters with any credit.

A couple more Westerns – *Pardners* (1956) and *Daniel Boone, Trail Blazer* (1956) – followed, but Chaney's horror career would be revived thanks to television. Universal's old monster movies were being screened on TV with increasing frequency, which meant that Chaney's old horror fame was rekindled with a new generation of fans. This also more or less coincided with Hammer Films successfully spearheading a revival of the genre following the success of their *The Curse of Frankenstein* (1957). Had Chaney been more astute, he could have maximised his newfound fame in quality film roles. But, due to financial and alcoholic necessity, he was now accepting any he was offered.

The first of these came in *The Indestructible Man* (1956), a sort of inferior version of *Man-Made Monster* and Boris Karloff's *The Walking Dead* (1935). Receiving top billing for the first time in years, Chaney plays Charles 'The Butcher' Benton, a recently-executed gangster who is brought back to life when a scientist puts several thousand volts through his system. Now indestructible following the experiment, all he has to do is eliminate the other gangsters who double-crossed him. The film itself is a workmanlike effort that is actually an improvement of several of Chaney's '40s features, and the actor is in fine menacing form as the wronged man out for revenge, even though he is mute for most of the time – perhaps the boozing had started to affect his ability to remember his lines.

The horror revival continued with *The Black Sleep* (1956), a mediocre chiller that has Chaney playing alongside a wonderful (but wasted) cast of Basil Rathbone, Bela Lugosi and John Carradine. Only Rathbone has a decent role, with Chaney and Lugosi playing mutes – in Chaney's case a lumbering giant called Mongo. But the film seems to have had some kind of pleasant effect on everyone involved. 'It's good to be working with old friends,' said Lugosi, obviously mellowed with age since the time when he resented Rathbone and actively disliked Chaney. He and Chaney even travelled to Washington with John Carradine and Tor Johnson – who also plays a lumbering mute – to promote the film.

Rounding off this trio of entertaining but undistinguished chillers, *The Cyclops* (1957) has Chaney as Martin Melville, one of four people on a plane that crash-lands in an isolated valley, which is actually radioactive, so that they have to deal with giants spiders, lizards and the title character. Directed by Bert I Gordon, this is the sort of so-bad-it's-good slice of science fiction hokum he was famous for. As the standard bad guy, Chaney, clearly drunk from the start, stumbles and sweats profusely with a performance that's a pale shadow of his earlier work. However, one poignant aspect of the making of the film was that Cleva Creighton regularly brought her middle-aged son his lunch. For all his demons, alcoholism and the ghost of his father refusing to go away, Chaney found great emotional solace spending time with his biological mother.

Chaney finally won a small measure of TV fame in the popular series *The Last of the Mohicans*, the first ever American-Canadian production. Based on James Fenimore Cooper's celebrated *Leatherstocking* novels, this starred John Hart as mountain man Nathan 'Hawkeye' Cutler, with Chaney as his Mohican blood brother with the amazingly tongue-twisting name of Chingachgook.

Effectively shot on location in Ontario, the series is a welcome departure from the studio-bound Westerns of the day. Although nothing like a Native-American, Chaney gives a dignified performance tinged with sadness at his character's situation – no place in the Indian world because he's the last of his kind, and not welcome in the white man's world because he's considered a savage.

The series was very popular and ran for 39 episodes. For Chaney, it brought a whole new generation of American fans, who became enthralled with this character, and few of whom had ever seen him as the Wolf Man. As each episode was a more like a television movie, they were released theatrically in several countries.

Despite his alcohol dependency, the success of *The Last of the Mohicans* revived Chaney's dormant television career. Now he was making guest appearances in just about every Western show going, including *Tombstone Territory, The Texan, Johnny Ringo, Bat Masterson, Wagon Train, Wanted Dead or Alive, The Rifleman* and *Rawhide*. He even squeezed in a Western feature, *Money, Women and Guns* (1958). If there was ever a movie genre Chaney was ideally suited to, it was the Western, where his increasingly weary looks made him a natural cowboy. The horror films he starred in merely capitalised on his name and reputation. If only he had been able to overcome the hardships of the '30s and retain his real name, perhaps celebrated Western director John Ford could have used him as a regular in much the same way as he used Ward Bond or John Carradine.

In 1957 Chaney sold the film rights to his father's life to Universal. The resulting film biopic was *The Man of a Thousand Faces* (1957), starring James Cagney as Lon Chaney Snr. As with most movie biopics at the time, the studio played around with the facts of the actor's life, a situation not helped by the fact they employed five writers to rework the whole thing. For example, in the film telling, Cleva Creighton abandons both husband and son, which was not the case in reality. Nor did she, as the film suggests, attempt suicide while performing on stage. Not surprisingly, Chaney wasn't pleased with the end result. However, he praised Cagney's excellent portrayal. Cagney looked nothing like Chaney's father – he was too old and too short – but he turned in a nice performance. Unfortunately the actor who on Cagney's recommendation played the young Creighton Chaney was Roger Smith, a slim, handsome, clean cut and debonair man and therefore completely miscast in the role.

With the money he made from selling the rights to his father's life story and from his extensive film and television work, Chaney bought a house overlooking the San Fernando Valley. It was as an act of revenge over the studio that had cast him aside a decade earlier. 'All my life I wanted to look down on Universal Studios,' he said. 'And now at last I can!'

One of the high spots of Chaney's film career was *The Defiant Ones* (1958), starry Tony Curtis and Sidney Poitier as convicts on the run from a chain-gang (and chained together). Reunited once more with director Stanley Kramer, Chaney gives an excellent performance as Big Sam, a former inmate who helps free the feuding pair from their chains. *The Defiant Ones* is a superb film that tackles racism in an intelligent way, making it an important forerunner of the civil rights movement of the '60s. Although it is basically a two-hander between Curtis and Poitier, Chaney makes the most of his brief screen time, showing that with the right role he could overcome the drinking and the demons to give a remarkable performance.

The horror revival continued with *The Alligator People* (1959), an interesting and quite original addition to the low-budget monster cycle. Playing the hook-handed alligator hunter Manon, a drunken Cajun, Chaney is good value, even if he constantly adjusts his hook in front of the camera. (Like Captain Hook, Manon lost his hand to one of those critters!) The character spends much of his time getting drunk (real booze no doubt), and Chaney chews the scenery with some gusto. There is also an unpleasant scene where Manon attempts to rape the lead female character, played by Beverly Garland, which was quite shocking for 1959.

Unfortunately, there was a serious problem that affected Chaney's performance in this film. His voice sounds extremely rough throughout, and this wasn't because of his drinking – in fact it was an early indication of the same throat cancer that had claimed his father. Chaney was clearly an ill man.

On the small screen, Chaney acted as host for the 1959 horror series *13 Demon Street*. This American-Swedish anthology series was filmed in Sweden with a Swedish cast. Chaney, who didn't appear in any of the episodes, was added to the cast along with the American voice artists who dubbed the Swedish on-screen actors. *13 Demon Street* has some curiosity value, but the series was aborted after four episodes and was never broadcast. It was later re-edited by Curt Siodmak and released in the cinemas as *The Devil's Messenger* (1961), with Chaney's host recast as Satan.

Chaney's horror career reached its nadir with a truly atrocious effort from Mexico. *La Casa del Terror* (1960) was originally a comedy-horror-musical starring the country's resident comedy star Tin Tan, aka German Valdes, as a bumbling night watchman who stumbles upon a mad scientist trying to bring the dead back to life. One of the subjects is a bloated-looking Egyptian mummy, played by Chaney. Once the bandages are opened, the actor, wearing a denim outfit similar to the one he had in *The Wolf Man*, then turns into a werewolf! Yes, it's as daft as that, with an overweight Chaney, playing the part mute since he didn't know any Spanish, going through the usual rampaging routine with no conviction whatsoever.

But it gets better, or worse, depending on one's sense of humour. Infamous zero-budget filmmaker Jerry Warren then got hold of the film and had it completely redubbed and reedited. He cut Valdes out the action altogether and added scenes from another Mexican horror film, *Attack of the Mummy*. He also added footage of Chaney kidnapping a woman and climbing up a skyscraper – although there are rumours that this material was actually shot by Edward D Wood Jnr. According to film editor Ewing Brown, 'It was 1957, we were shooting at Kenmore stage on Santa Monica – it was owned by Larry and Harry Smith. Ed [Wood] was directing this wolf man thing with Lon Chaney Jnr. We had this great set – the outside of a building, the corner, where the stones are notched together. And Chaney climbed this goddamn thing! We were shooting – he got a finger- and a toe-hold with this mask and furry hands, and we were breaking up – we were shooting silent. Chaney says, "If you think this goddamn thing's easy – you try it! Goddamn it!" We were cracking up as he was trying to climb this wall. Ed was trying to promote money on this. We did the scenes for promo material.'

The original Mexican movie came out to paying audiences in 1960, while Warren's edited version, renamed *Face of the Screaming Werewolf*, was released in 1964. The end result is an incomprehensible mess that must rank as one of the worst films Chaney ever appeared in. If Wood did have any involvement in it, he probably sold both footage and film rights to Warren in exchange for quick cash to buy booze. In any event, Chaney looks totally ashamed to be taking part in this piece of tenth-rate rubbish. But even worse was to follow

Apart from the obscure feature *Rebellion in Cuba* (1961), Chaney's career remained entrenched in TV Western shows, which included a recurring role as Chief Eagle Shadow in the comedy Western series *Pistols and Petticoats* and a guest spot as Lennie in *The Monkees* episode entitled 'The Monkees in Ghost Town'.

The final phase of Chaney's horror career then got off to a decent start with *The Haunted Palace* (1963). Having previously made a number of Edgar Allan Poe adaptations, director Roger Corman decided to bring H P Lovecraft's *The Case of Charles Dexter Ward* to the big screen, although he borrowed the title of a Poe poem for his version. Since American International Pictures were producing, their contract star Vincent Price played the dual roles of Satanist Joseph Curwen and his descendant Charles Dexter Ward, with Chaney assuming the role of Curwen's follower Simon Orme. *The Haunted Palace* isn't one of Corman's better cinematic efforts, but it's a typically lavish, atmospheric production that did well at the box office. Replacing Boris Karloff, who had fallen ill, Chaney, despite looking much older that his 57 years, gives a brief but excellent performance full of eerie menace.

As AIP were regularly hiring the old horror stars as solid support for Vincent Price in their Poe chillers, it's perhaps surprising that they didn't make better use of Chaney. However, this was probably due to the actor's drink problem and increasing unreliability. Karloff and Rathbone may have been getting on in years, but they were still on good form and could be counted on to turn up on time and do their work without a word of complaint. The same was true of Peter Lorre, who was in extremely poor health at this time. They could all still be relied on to give it their best shot. Chaney on the other hand found himself out on a limb.

Chaney took a step into TV nostalgia in 1963 by guest-starring alongside Boris Karloff and Peter Lorre, all playing themselves, in the weirdly-titled episode 'Lizard's Leg and Owlet's Ring' in the popular road series *Route 66*. Chaney had already guest-starred in a couple of earlier episodes of the series. This time, the theme of the story was the three titans of terror discussing whether or not their old monsters could still frighten audiences, and testing this out by scaring a women's convention. The action saw Chaney recreating the Mummy, the Wolf Man and his father's Hunchback of Notre Dame. Also involved in the show was the formidable British actress Marita Hunt, best known as Miss Havisham in *Great Expectations* (1946) and Baroness Meinster in Hammer's *The Brides of Dracula* (1960). The episode was fun but very out of step with the times; and even though Chaney made a convincing hunchback, it wasn't enough to bury his father's shadow.

For all his success, and a résumé that any actor would be thrilled with, Chaney was definitely not a happy man. Nor was he happy at the way horror films had dwindled in his eyes. 'I used to enjoy horror films,' he said, 'when there was thought and sympathy involved. Then they became comedies. Abbott and Costello ruined the horror field: they made buffoons out of the monsters. Then the cheap producers came along and made worse buffoons of them, because they killed for the sake of killing, there was blood for the sake of blood. There is no thought, no true expression of feeling. We used to make up our minds before we started that this is a little fantastic, but let's take it seriously. And they were sold seriously. But all this foolishness today, it isn't sold seriously. It's made as a joke, a laugh, for the kids to go in and have a ball.'

Chaney obviously never saw the Hammer films, which were taken very seriously by the cast and crew. The scares were real, and in colour. Did Chaney come across as an embittered man who resented the way his career had gone? 'I don't think he was particularly bitter about the way his life had turned out,' said Forrest J Ackerman, who still saw Chaney as an affable guy, but one reluctant to discuss his career. 'He just wanted to talk about fishing and other subjects that were not in the least bit rewarding in trying to find out anything about his career. At any time I attempted to talk about his own career or his father's, he would become very vague and uninterested. I asked where his father was buried and he said, "Oh, over there somewhere." He didn't even know where he was pointing.' Chaney Snr's desire for private obscurity had remained until the end; he was buried in an unmarked grave.

Chaney's comments about how cheap producers were exploiting the old monsters were also ironic, given that he was being exploited in the same way. The horror boom was once again in full swing, and low-budget independent producers were taking full advantage of his name, horror reputation and alcohol dependency. *The Black Sleep* and *The Alligator People* weren't great films, but they were classics compared with *Face of the Screaming Werewolf.*

There was at least one more decent horror film for Chaney to appear in; the British-made *Witchcraft* (1964). By this time he was deep, deep, deep into the bottle. This was noticeable during the shooting of *Witchcraft*. His face was bloated from his constant drinking and he carried around a briefcase full of booze, which he consumed throughout the twenty-day shoot, to such an extent that he often could not remember the night before. According to the film's director Don Sharp, 'We had to make sure that Lon's dialogue scenes were completed by lunchtime. The more quickly we got through the scenes, the less time he had in his dressing room with his bottle. Wardrobe staff said he would drink a bottle of vodka before lunch. I don't know if he did, but he certainly was of very little use in the afternoon.' Such behaviour could come only from a man hell-bent on self-destruction.

Witchcraft is a very stylish low-budget horror with an unusually complex plot. Despite his star billing, Chaney appears only intermittently, chanting and ranting for all he's worth. This being a British chiller, he looks out of place. While he makes the most of his few scenes and is still a formidable presence, he remains the film's weakest link. Still it was a high-class production and one of the final highlights of his declining career.

The Haunted Palace and *Witchcraft* should have led to better things, but with television work drying up, Chaney had to make do with appearing in a string of ultra-low-budget Westerns for A C Lyles Productions. *Law of the Lawless* (1964), *Stage to Thunder Rock* (1965), *Young Fury* (1965), *Black Spurs* (1965), *Town Tamer* (1965), *Apache Uprising* (1965) and *Johnny Reno* (1966) were all below-average efforts that featured Chaney, despite his high billing, playing a tiny role such as sheriff or bartender. These roles didn't amount to much and did nothing for his career.

In between these Western bit parts were further appalling exploitation horror films that cashed in on his name. Either he was drunk when he made them or needed the money to get drunk. *House of the Black Death* (1965), *Hillbillies in a Haunted House* (1967) and *Dr Terror's Gallery of Horrors* (1967) all represented the sort of pitiful garbage that the intoxicated Chaney was reduced to appearing in. *Hillbillies in a Haunted House* especially is a perfect example of the depths the actor had descended to. It is basically a showcase for a dreadful country music band, and Chaney wanders around in a complete daze alongside a bemused John Carradine and a frail Basil Rathbone.

Spider Baby (1967) is even worse. Also known as *The Liver Eaters* (no livers get devoured) and *Cannibal Orgy* (none actually takes place), it opens with Chaney singing a song about vampires and werewolves (none of which feature). Against all odds, the actor's performance drew praise, critic Jim Morton commenting: 'Lon Chaney Jnr, whose acting was usually somewhat substandard, is brilliant as Bruno, giving the character the right qualities of compassion and desperation.' Did this moving performance is such a dreadful movie sum up Chaney as a man at the end of his tether?

Chaney passed up the chance to play another werewolf in the Spanish-made horror flick *La Marca del Hombre* (1967). Under his real name Jacinto Molina, actor Paul Naschy wrote the script for this after being approached by his friend, director Enrique Lopez Eguiluz. 'I told Enrique about my intention to write a script for a horror film about a werewolf,' said Naschy, 'and his immediate reaction was to accuse me of insanity. The truth is that there was no tradition of this genre in Spanish cinema.' The werewolf in question is not Larry Talbot but Waldemar Daninsky. 'Daninsky is a Polish name I gave to my werewolf,' said Naschy, 'thinking of the oppressed people of Poland. My character is bitter, persecuted and misunderstood, the bearer of a curse he cannot shake off. In the end he is forced to kill without wanting to.' It was a typical Lon Chaney role, and being a lifelong fan of the actor, Naschy was desperate to use him in the film. However, a combination of poor health and not wanting to travel to Europe prompted Chaney to turn down the offer. After trying out other actors, Naschy hired himself instead. Renamed *Frankenstein's Bloody Terror*, even though Frankenstein doesn't appear, the film was a huge box office hit on the continent, and one that made Naschy the undisputed king of Eurotrash horror. 'I was the pioneer of the Spanish horror cinema,' he said of his success. Naschy went on to play Daninsky in a slew of gory sequels / prequels / remakes / variations throughout the '70s.

Had Chaney agreed to appear in Naschy's opus, it might have paved the way for him to be cast in better British- and European-made horror movies on the lines of *Witchcraft*. His well-worn features would have been ideal for leading roles in several Italian 'spaghetti' Westerns; the kind that struggling American actors Clint Eastwood and Lee Van Cleef were making their names with. It would have been interesting to see Chaney working with Sergio Leone in films that would have been a marked improvement on the tepid Westerns he did for A C Lyles Productions.

As it was, he had to make do with whatever work came his way. This included a bit part in the larger-budget Western *Welcome to Hard Times* (1967) starring Henry Fonda. It was the last film he made of any note. So then it was back to low-budget cowboy adventures in *Buckskin* (1968) and *A Stranger in Town* (1969), and a venture into '60s LSD antics with *Fireball Jungle* (1968).

'They don't know how to make good horror films in Hollywood,' Chaney once lamented of the state of the genre. 'Boy, they really need me!' Well, inept zero-budget filmmakers like Jerry Warren and Al Adamson certainly needed him, and Chaney's association with Adamson produced the most humiliating films of his career. The infamous Adamson stinker *Dracula versus Frankenstein* (1970) features Chaney as Groton the mad zombie, opposite a frail J Carrol Naish (in his last movie) as Dr Frankenstein. Adamson also used the famous laboratory set designed by Kenneth Strickfaden for *The Bride of Frankenstein*.

Chaney spends much of his time in this film chasing the actresses around with an axe and being menacing. Playing mute zombies helped compensate for his inability to remember (or speak) his lines due to the amount of booze he consumed by the minute; it seems unlikely he even knew where he was! Chaney may have done the film out of financial necessity, but the wheelchair-bound Naish, who was comfortably off financially and long retired from the big screen, played his role out of choice, making this film the nadir of his otherwise brilliant career.

Chaney's co-star Anthony Eisley recalled the terrible state of the once-great horror star. 'He was very, very ill, and had to lie down in between every take. But to talk with him and hear his stories was just incredible. Such a wonderful, lovely and interesting man.'

Also appearing in the film was Forrest J Ackerman. 'I had been slightly involved with the movie, and he had frankly warned the director and producer about his drinking. He told them, "Get everything you can out of me before 1.00 pm, because after that I can't guarantee anything." He carried a hip flask that supposedly contained iced tea but was actually liberally laced with alcohol.'

Ackerman also observed the pathetic figure of Chaney during a meeting of the Count Dracula Society. 'They had him as guest of honour at their annual banquet. I was sitting opposite him, and I saw he didn't eat a morsel of food at the banquet, he just sat there drinking. It worried me, because I knew from experience that he was only good until the afternoon, and from then on he was blotto.

'When his name was announced at the banquet I made the introductory speech about him. He then appeared on stage, and he got a standing ovation, and that really turned him on. He said, "Would you like me to do Lennie?" Everyone said yes, and he did Lennie. And he really had it down pat. He stood up there and he became that powerful figure from *Of Mice and Men*, and it brought tears to everybody's eyes to see how great he could be when he tried.'

But Chaney had long given up trying, and his final humiliation came with Al Adamson's inept Western *Time to Run* (1971). Cruelly billed as 'Lon Chaney Jnr' for the first time in 25 years, he was more or less finished with life. During the making of the film, the dazed and confused actor wandered off into the desert in a drunken stupor and remained out there, completely out of his head on booze, for several days. Considering the poor man's state of mind, it seems odd that no-one bothered to look for him when he went AWOL. This being a no-budget movie, production would have continued on, with Adamson making use of whatever footage he had of Chaney. The actor eventually returned to the set surrounded by buzzing fruit flies, obviously attracted to the strong smell of alcohol coming from him.

Chaney wanted to return to Broadway in *Arsenic and Old Lace*, but the throat cancer had destroyed his voice. Now broke, he planned a horror comeback in two films, *Curse of the Gila Man* and *Night of the Werewolves*, both of which he had a hand in writing. 'He had personally written a script,' said Ackerman, 'called *Gila Man*, which was somewhat like another film he was in called *The Alligator People*. He had written in roles for his two sons.' Neither film saw the light of day, so Chaney concentrated on a biography of his father and himself. 'He had started work on a book called *A Century of*

Chaneys,' said Ackerman, 'which was going to go back earlier than his father and tell something about his grandfather. He asked me to participate in some way. I was going to supply some of the stills and write the captions for them.' That too fell by the wayside because of his poor health.

There was one potential high point at the start of the '70s: Woody Allen considered Chaney for the role of mad scientist Dr Bernado in his anthology comedy *Everything You Always Wanted to Know About Sex** *(*But Were Afraid to Ask)* (1972). 'I felt like a fan sitting across from the Wolf Man,' said an enthusiastic Allen when he first met Chaney. But, despite serious talks, the actor was simply unable to take on the role due to his serious health problems. (He was replaced by John Carradine, who gives a hilarious performance.) With his voice gone, he was now experimenting with a throat microphone; in fact he was so ill that he resorted to acupuncture to ease his pain.

Loyal friend Forrest J Ackerman described Chaney's final months: 'Like his father, he died of cancer of the throat. I had known [that he had] this for some time, but it was a closely-guarded secret and I wasn't going to put it in print even when it looked like he might die. He had clung to at least half a voice. He should have had all his vocal chords removed, but they went halfway. I was told privately that the cobalt treatments were killing him faster than the cancer. I guardedly called it to the attention of his fans that he was in serious shape, and that it might be wise to let him know right away if they cared for him. I asked them please not to pester him for pictures or ask him to tell stories; but if they wanted to send get well cards or expressions of appreciation, now was the time. I was surprised and flattered when one day I picked up the telephone and heard a very rough, gruff voice say, "Say, young fellow, you sure been doing a great job for me. Want to thank you for all them letters I been getting. Really makes me feel good."

'I don't know whether it is was just bravado or whether he didn't know he had terminal cancer, but he was preparing to go 3,000 miles east to appear live on stage in a revival of *Arsenic and Old Lace*. I couldn't believe it when I received a phone call from someone in New York, very excited, who had heard the announcement on the radio. So I called his wife and she said, "Yes, he's learning his lines and will be using a throat mike." And two weeks later he was dead.'

After years of alcohol abuse, personal trauma and cinematic humiliation, Creighton Tull Chaney aka Lon Chaney Jnr died on 12 July 1973 in San Clemente, California aged 67 (quite an achievement considering his drunken lifestyle). He wanted no publicity at his deathbed and asked his wife Patsy not to reveal the cause of death or the funeral arrangements to the press. She abided by his wishes, but it was later reported he had suffered a fatal heart attack. Riddled with throat cancer, arthritis, gout, hepatitis, beriberi and cataracts, Chaney's screwed up corpse was donated to the University of Southern California Medical School as an anatomical specimen. After dissection, his liver and lungs were kept in jars, illustrating the damage alcohol and tobacco can do to human organs. There isn't a grave to mark his final resting place.

Shortly before his death, Chaney was asked which of his film roles he had found most rewarding. 'I guess it was the Wolf Man … since at the time it was totally new. [Universal] received more fan mail for me during that period than any other star.' His popularity remained high, even when he was admitted into hospital a few months before he died; he received hundreds of cards from fans wishing him well. No matter how traumatic life had been, his fans had always been there for him. But for Chaney, the Wolf Man was more than just a wonderful role; it was a personal triumph, maybe over his father in some way. '[The Wolf Man] was someone I felt really proud of. He was my baby!'

Chaney was a prime example of a minor actor with limited range, who reluctantly made his fame on his father's excellent reputation, only to be typecast in unsuitable horror roles that got steadily worse with his advancing years. With the childish pranks, belligerent attitude and endless boozing undermining and eventually destroying his film career, Chaney never came close the 'Master Character Creator' persona created for him by Universal as a way of promoting him as their new horror star.

But the sad thing for Chaney was his failure to escape the shadow of his father and those demons that blighted his life: drink, insecurity and the inability to enjoy the success he had. Lon Chaney 'Jr' remains one of the movie world's great tragedies, as much a cursed human being as he was a cursed horror star.

Lon Chaney Jnr Filmography

Heart of a Wolf (1922), *The Galloping Ghost* (1931), *Girl Crazy* (1932), *Bird of Paradise* (1932), *The Last Frontier* (1932), *Lucky Devils* (1933), *Scarlet River* (1933), *The Three Musketeers* (serial – 1933), *Son of the Border* (1933), *Sixteen Fathoms Deep* (1934), *The Life of Vergie Winters* (1934), *Girl O' My Dreams* (1934), *Woman of Destiny* (1935), *Uniform Lovers* (1935), *The Shadow of Silk Lennox* (1935), *A Scream in the Night* (1935), *The Singing Cowboy* (1936), *Undersea Kingdom* (serial – 1936), *Ace Drummond* (serial – 1936), *Killer at Large* (1936), *O'Riley's Luck* (1936), *Texas Serenade* (1936), *Cheyenne Rides Again* (1937), *Love is News* (1937), *Midnight Taxi* (1937), *Secret Agent X-9* (1937), *That I May Live* (1937), *His Affair* (1937), *Angel's Holiday* (1937), *Slave Ship* (1937), *Born Reckless* (1937), *Wild and Woolly* (1937), *The Lady Escapes* (1937), *One Mile from Heaven* (1937), *Lovely to Look At* (1937), *Wife, Doctor and Nurse* (1937), *Charlie Chan on Broadway* (1937), *The Joy Parade* (1937), *Second Honeymoon* (1937), *Checkers* (1937), *Love and Hisses* (1937), *Happy Landing* (1938), *Sally, Irene and Mary* (1938), *Walking Down Broadway* (1938), *Mr Moto's Gamble* (1938), *Alexander's Rag Time Band* (1938), *Josette* (1938), *Speed Burn* (1938), *Passport Husband* (1938), *They're Off* (1938), *Submarine Patrol* (1938), *Road Demon* (1938), *Jesse James* (1939), *Union Pacific* (1939), *Frontier Marshal* (1939), *City in Darkness* (1939), *Off Mice and Men* (1939), *One Million BC* (1940), *North West Mounted Police* (1940), *Man Made Monster* (1941), *Too Many Blondes* (1941), *Billy the Kid* (1941), *San Antonio Rose* (1941), *Riders of Death Valley* (1941), *Badlands of Dakota* (1941), *The Wolf Man* (1941), *North of the Klondike* (1942), *The Ghost of Frankenstein* (1942), *Overland Mail* (1942), *Eyes of the Underworld* (1942), *The Mummy's Tomb* (1942), *Frankenstein Meets the Wolf Man* (1943), *Frontier Badmen* (1943), *Crazy House* (1943), *Son of Dracula* (1943), *Calling Dr Death* (1943), *Weird Woman* (1944), *Follow the Boys* (1944), *Cobra Woman* (1944), *Ghost Catchers* (1944), *The Mummy's Ghost* (1944), *Dead Man's Eyes* (1944), *House of Frankenstein* (1944), *The Mummy's Curse* (1944), *Here Comes the Co-Eds* (1944), *The Frozen Ghost* (1944), *Strange Confession* (1944), *The Daltons Rides Again* (1945), *House of Dracula* (1945), *Pillow of Death* (1945), *My Favorite Brunette* (1947), *Silver City* (1948), *The Counterfeiters* (1948), *Abbott and Costello Meet Frankenstein* (1948), *16 Fathoms Deep* (1948), *There's a Girl in My Heart* (1949), *Captain China* (1950), *Once a Thief* (1950), *Inside Straight* (1951), *Only the Valiant* (1951), *Behave Yourself* (1951), *The Rebel* (1951), *Bride of the Gorilla* (1951), *Flame of Araby* (1951), *Thief of Damascus* (1952), *High Noon*

(1952), *Springfield Rifle* (1952), *Battles of Chief Pontiac* (1952), *The Black Castle* (1952), *Raiders of the Seven Seas* (1953), *A Lion is in the Streets* (1953), *Lost Treasure of the Amazon* (1954), *The Boy from Oklahoma* (1954), *Casanova's Big Night* (1954), *Passion* (1954), *The Black Pirates* (1954), *Big House USA* (1955), *The Silver Star* (1955), *Not as a Stranger* (1955), *I Died a Thousand Times* (1955), *The Indian Fighter* (1955), *Manfish* (1955), *The Indestructible Man* (1956), *The Black Sleep* (1956), *Pardners* (1956), *Daniel Boone, Trail Blazer* (1956), *Cyclops* (1957), *The Defiant Ones* (1957), *Money, Women and Guns* (1958), *The Alligator People* (1959), *La Casa del Terror/Face of the Screaming Werewolf* (1960), *Rebellion in Cuba* (1961), *The Devil's Messenger* (1961), *The Haunted Palace* (1963), *Law of the Lawless* (1964), *Witchcraft* (1964), *Stage to Thunder Rock* (1965), *Young Fury* (1965), *Black Spurs* (1965), *Town Tamer* (1965), *Apache Uprising* (1965), *House of the Black Death* (1965), *Johnny Reno* (1966), *Dr Terror's Gallery of Horror* (1967), *Welcome to Hard Times* (1967), *Hillbillies in a Haunted House* (1967), *Cannibal Orgy* (1967), *Buckskin* (1968), *Fireball Jungle* (1968), *A Stranger in Town* (1969), *Dracula versus Frankenstein* (1970), *Satan's Sadists* (1970), *Time to Run* (1971).

The Curse Of Holmes: Basil Rathbone

'When you become the character you portray, it's the end of your career as an actor.'
– Basil Rathbone

Had it not been for a prophetic dream his mother once had, Basil Rathbone might never have graced theatre and film. We might never even have heard of Sherlock Holmes. So providence spared the brilliant actor even as a child. It happened this way …

To many, Basil Rathbone *is* Sherlock Holmes. Long after his death, the actor's identification with the Great Detective has remained with him. His films, readily available on DVD and often shown on TV, have produced generations of fans impressed by his definitive performance. Sadly this association eventually caused the same resentment in him that Sir Arthur Conan Doyle had experienced toward his immortal creation. Rathbone felt that Holmes, in the words of Conan Doyle, 'kept his mind from better things!'

Typecasting for film actors is not rare, and those strongly identified with a particular character (such as Christopher Lee and Bela Lugosi) have dealt with this dilemma by either battling against it or accepting it for what it is and making the most of the perks that come with it.

But Basil Rathbone wasn't just any actor. He was a brilliant performer of immense versatility. As one of Hollywood's success stories, he achieved everything he could have wanted, but was always itching to stretch himself as an actor. So it is easy to imagine how his identification with Holmes became a hard thing for him to stomach, especially when it pushed his classic early work into the background. The shadow of Holmes proved so strong that it made him an extremely bitter man in his later years.

Basil Rathbone was born Philip St John Basil Rathbone in the bustling industrial city of Johannesburg, South Africa on 13 July 1892. South Africa of the late 19th Century was split into four districts: Cape Colony and Natal were under British rule, while the Orange Free State and the South African Transvaal were Boer Republics. Although the districts were strongly linked, relations between the British and the Boers had been extremely tense since 1834, when the British had abolished slavery.

While the Boer Republics were comprised of farming and religious communities, the Cape became a bustling industrial area with a large population of Europeans immigrants. In 1870 large diamond fields were discovered in Griqualand West. Although it was under Orange Free State control, the Cape, backed by the British Government, successfully took over the fields. When gold was discovered near Johannesburg in 1886, an influx of British immigrants, known as Uitlanders, came to South Africa in search of work. They included a well-travelled mining engineer named Edgar Philip Rathbone.

Edgar Rathbone was a scion of the Rathbones of Liverpool. The family origins can be traced back to Gansworth, near Macclesfield, where the first William Rathbone was born in 1669. His son William left Gansworth for the bustling port of Liverpool, where he successfully set up a timber business. Now an important part of Liverpool's social and business circles, the Rathbones were non-conformist merchants, ship owners and philanthropists, with shares in Liverpool, London and Globe Insurance, Holt and Company Shipping and Rathbone Brothers' Cotton. Basil's great uncle, William of Greenbank, became famous for sponsoring and subsidising the arts. A family friend and regular visitor to the Rathbone residence of

Greenbank Cottage was the distinguished actor Sir Henry Irving.

The family also had strong political connections. One of Basil's cousins, Herbert Rathbone, was a former Lord Mayor of Liverpool, and another, Eleanor Rathbone, became the first female MP. Her nephew John Rathbone became a Conservative MP (he was killed in action during World War II), as did his son Tim.

There were strong family links with America. Perry T Rathbone was director of the St Louis Art Museum and Boston's Museum of Fine Arts. Henry Riggs Rathbone was a congressman whose father, American Civil War veteran Major Henry Rathbone, was a member of Abraham Lincoln's celebrated theatre entourage that witnessed the President's assassination by John Wilkes Booth. Major Rathbone got stabbed trying to prevent Booth from fleeing the theatre, but survived to marry Clara Harris, another member of Lincoln's party. However his failure to save the President brought about mental deterioration that led to him murdering his wife in 1883. Declared insane after insisting there were people hiding behind the pictures on the walls of their home, Rathbone spent his last years in an asylum in Hildesheim, Germany, where he died in 1911.

A born adventurer, Edgar Rathbone arrived in Johannesburg with his Irish-born second wife Anne Barbara George, an accomplished violinist and descendent of King Henry VI. The discovery of gold made the Transvaal the richest and potentially the most powerful nation in South Africa. It also attracted more Uitlanders than the country could handle, and brought about increased friction between the British and the Boers. Fearful of the Transvaal becoming a British colony, the Boer government imposed heavy taxes on gold mining, and working restrictions on the Uitlanders. The Rathbones' arrival came at a time when unrest quickly escalated, culminating in the infamous Jameson Raid and the Second Boer War.

'The Jameson Raid was an abortive venture,' wrote Basil Rathbone in his autobiography *In and Out of Character*, 'and my father had been a friend of Dr [Leander Starr] Jameson, and also Cecil Rhodes, who was "the power behind the throne" in South Africa.' As Governor of the Cape, Rhodes had commercial interests in the De Beers Mining Corporation. It was his intention to incorporate the Transvaal and the Orange Free State under British rule and control the Johannesburg mining industry. To do this, he sanctioned an armed column of Rhodesian and Bechuanaland police, led by British colonial Statesman Dr Jameson, to invade the Transvaal over the New Year weekend of 1895. British Uitlanders were supposed to organise an uprising in Johannesburg and seize the Boer armoury in Pretoria. Jameson's forces would show up, restore order in the city and take control of all gold mining interests. By cutting all communications, Jameson's men could invade the Transvaal before the Boer government knew what was happening. Unfortunately they failed to cut the telegraph wires to Pretoria.

With Jameson surrounded by Boer militia, the uprising never took place and the Raid was a failure.

Edgar Rathbone's involvement with the Raid is unknown, but his life and those of his family were in danger. Basil Rathbone was only three years old when they fled Johannesburg. 'There was a price on my father's head,' he recalled of the incident, which was related to him by his mother. 'He was accused by the Boers of being a British spy. Whether he was or not I shall never know. I never asked him about it, and he never gave the slightest indication at any time that he would be interested in satisfying my curiosity!' In any case, Edgar Rathbone was a wanted man. 'It became necessary for my father and family to seek sanctuary. Heavens alone knows what further complications to all our lives might have ensued had my father been captured by the Boer forces.'

Fearful of Boer reprisal following the failure of the Jameson Raid, British Uitlanders made a mass exodus from Johannesburg. Forced to leave everything behind, the Rathbones found sanctuary at the Sister of Nazareth Home. With only a few essentials, they then boarded a freight train heading for Durban, Natal. It was a 300-mile journey and fraught with danger. Edgar Rathbone was forced to hide under his wife's wooden chair, while Basil and two-year-old sister Beatrice were seated either side of their mother.

The train journey was complicated by the arrival of a suspicious Boer trooper who questioned Anne Rathbone. She used her maiden name and explained to the trooper that she was on the way to Durban to visit her husband. 'At this moment,' recalled Rathbone, 'my mother, who had been pinching me vigorously, obtained the results she had been anxiously waiting for. I let forth a hideous scream, and could by no means be consoled.'

The distraction worked, and the Boer allowed the family to go on their way. Although they were now safe from danger, the journey was further complicated by Anne contracting typhoid. Upon arrival in Durban, mother, son and daughter were rushed to hospital. 'All three of us,' said Rathbone, 'lay at death's door.'

Once the family had fully recovered from illness, they were due to set sail for England on a Union Castle liner. However, as Basil recalled, 'My mother begged my father to postpone our sailing for a week because of a dream she had had.' Edgar Rathbone agreed to this, as his wife's dream had, in his son's words, 'concerned him deeply.'

The dream was a vivid and disturbing one. The ship the family were due to sail on encountered a storm at the Bay of Biscay. The storm proved so fierce that the lifeboats were useless. As the waves hit the deck with increasing ferocity, a band of the Seaforth Highlanders, in full dress uniform, played 'Flowers of the Forest' as the ship went down with all hands.

Anne Rathbone's dream turned out to be an accurate premonition. The Union Castle Line even confirmed that the Seaforth Highlanders had played

'Flower of the Forest' as the ship capsized in stormy weather at the Bay of Biscay. How Anne was able to foresee this tragedy will never be known, but Basil Rathbone had his own view. 'My mother's strange participation in this terrifying story you must accept, and bring to it such an answer as you may. So often in one's life a situation or a circumstance can be best epitomised by turning to Mr Shakespeare, "There are more things in heaven and earth than are dreamt of in your philosophy."' The incident of the dream made Rathbone a firm believer in ESP and a devoted follower of spiritualism.

'We reached England aboard the Walmer Castle, unaware of the fate that had been in store for us. And so, as a boy of four, I had already defied the stars three times.'

His cheating death on three occasions at such a young age must surely have been an indication of his future destiny as an adult. Was Sherlock Holmes already calling out to him ...?

'Childhood was sweet – very sweet,' wrote Rathbone of his life once the family had settled in England. 'The days were long, but not long enough for all the dreams and adventures we envisioned and planned and experienced, my brother [John], my sister and I.'

It was a financially secure environment, although one important family member was missing for very long spells. Always the adventurer and forever travelling the world to make his fortune, Edgar Rathbone went to Canada following the Klondike Gold Rush of 1896. But with a close assortment of relatives around him, and regular trips made to Liverpool and Greenbank Cottage, Basil's early years were happy ones.

In 1906, Rathbone informed his parents of his decision to attend Repton College, a public school with a long and distinguished tradition of sporting excellence. (It produced 130 top-class cricketers.) 'My father and mother had been somewhat at a loss to know why I was so insistent upon going to Repton School. My reasons were lame, but never lost their insistence. I had private reasons, which, if they had became known, I felt would cast some doubts upon my intent to work hard like a good boy and pass my exams.'

It was Repton's sporting history that had attracted the tall, spindly 14-year-old. He excelled at cricket, rugby and athletics but showed very little interest in academic study. 'Repton School was possibly the most renowned public school in England for its accomplishments in the field of sports, ' wrote Rathbone. 'Not that we didn't turn out great scholars. But I had no intention of competing for these honours. I enjoyed essay writing, Greek, Latin and history, but I had little time for swotting, owing to my concentration on sports.'

Rathbone, or 'Ratters' to his school friends, scraped through his exams and avoided finishing in last place. 'But I made one serious mistake,' he added. 'I won first prize for an essay on *Was Shylock the Villain of a Melodrama or Hero of a Tragedy?*' Not that he was bothered, considering his continued achievements on the field, but clearly young Rathbone had developed a passion for drama, music and theatre. Being a masculine place, Repton never prided itself on the arts. Instead of doing his homework in the evenings, Rathbone spent his time writing his first play, *King Arthur*, which he kept quiet from his tutors and classmates to avoid being labelled effeminate.

'My father, who was suffering from a severe financial setback, and my mother had made considerable sacrifices to send me to Repton. Sacrifices that my brother and sister shared, in that they received, materially, a little less all round in order to enable me to have the maximum of opportunity. They knew this and gave their tithe willingly and affectionately. And so at times I could not help but feel an uneasiness in the face of my meagre academic accomplishments.'

On graduating from Repton in 1910, Rathbone determined to become an actor – a decision that was greeted with disapproval from his father. 'I told my father I wanted to make the theatre my profession. The theatre had recently taken its rightful place among the arts, following the knighthoods of Sir Henry Irving, Sir Herbert Beerbohm-Tree and my cousin Sir Frank Benson. My father asked me to compromise by going into business for one year, at the end of which time I might do as I please. It was a generous compromise.'

Using the family connection, young Rathbone secured a post as junior clerk at the London-based branch of the Liverpool, London and Globe Insurance Company. Edgar Rathbone, although himself an amateur actor, singer and writer in his day, hoped the steady employment would be enough to make his son change his mind about his future career.

To vindicate his father's decision, Rathbone worked hard, and within a few months was moved to the company's accounts department at the West End branch. He also kept up with his sports, playing cricket and soccer for the LL&G first teams. But his love of the theatre never diminished. In fact it increased after he met the office cashier Mr Howell, who took him to many concerts at the Queen's Hall. Rathbone also spent his lunchtime in the office attic learning Shakespeare – and with good reason, too. He had an important appointment with a distinguished gentleman who would change the course of his life.

It was 1911, and on his final day at LL&G, Rathbone arrived at an office in Henrietta Street, London for his scheduled appointment. It was an audition for one of the English theatre's most powerful figures. He also happened to be Rathbone's cousin.

Sir Francis Robert Benson had begun acting with Sir Henry Irving at the Lyceum. His successful career as an actor-manager included touring the provinces, managing the Globe Theatre and founding his own drama school. A dedicated Shakespearean scholar, he founded the Stratford-Upon-Avon Shakespeare Festival and the actors' union Equity. In 1916, King George V knighted him for his services to the British theatre.

'I had written to him asking for an interview and informing him of my intention to become an actor,' Rathbone recalled of his audition. 'I went well prepared and without the slightest doubt that the theatre was about to receive into its arms one the future's true "greats". Such is the sublime confidence of youthful inexperience.'

Rathbone was asked by Benson if he had anything prepared that he could recite. 'Anything prepared!' He was almost beside himself. 'Now the time had come to prove that those long hours of study and rehearsal in the attic at the office had not been wasted.

'I chose a scene between Shylock, Salarno and Salerino from *The Merchant of Venice* – shades of Repton. Mr Benson listened attentively as I coloured each role with what I considered to be brilliant characterisations. When I had finished, there was a long pause as he looked at me quizzically.'

What were Frank Benson's thoughts of this young aspiring actor? Was the audition a success for Basil Rathbone? Benson's reply was, 'A young actor is like a horse. As a yearling or even as a two-year old, it is not easy to estimate his future capabilities. But if his breeding and conformation are good, one is inclined to go along with him, for a while at least.' It was clear that Benson liked what he saw, and in a decision echoing Rathbone's father's, he told the young man, 'I'm going to give you a chance with my No 2 Company, and then we'll see what you look like at the end of a year.'

It was a dream come true for young Basil Rathbone. However, though they may have been cousins, Benson bestowed no favours on his protégé. If Rathbone was to succeed, he had to work hard. 'He always referred to me as "Mr Rathbone" and I always addressed him as "Sir", as did all the other members of his company'.

In April 1911, Rathbone made his professional stage debut as Hortensio in *The Taming of the Shrew* at the Theatre Royal, Ipswich. Starting out in bit parts, he found his time with the No 2 Company, under the direction of Henry Herbert, beneficial. 'At the end of a year I had toured all over England, Scotland and Ireland, playing in a repertory of Shakespearean plays. Small parts, but an invaluable experience. Add to this, instruction in diction, the use of swords, period dancing, deportment and make-ups.'

In October 1912, Rathbone went to America for the first time with the Company, playing Fenton in *The Merry Wives of Windsor*. He proved himself to Benson, and in the summer of 1913 his cousin promoted him to the No 1 Company. He then quickly progressed to juvenile leads in several major Shakespearean productions. In August 1913, while performing at the Stratford-Upon-Avon Festival, he met Marion Foreman. 'She was an excellent actress,' he recalled, 'with a beautiful speaking and singing voice.' They were cast as second leads Lorenzo and Jessica in *The Merchant of Venice* and as Silvius and Phoebe in *As You Like It*. They married in October 1914 following a brief courtship. Their son Rodion was born the following year.

Rathbone's stage career was progressing nicely. In July 1914 he made his first appearance at the London Savoy Theatre as Finch in *The Sin of David*. He also played Dauphin in *Henry V* at the Shaftesbury Theatre London. Returning to Benson's No 1 Company, he rounded off the year as Lysander in *A Midsummer Night's Dream* at London's Court Theatre.

By 1914, increased tensions between Britain and Germany meant war was not only inevitable but also imminent. Rathbone, like many young men, had to put his promising career on hold to fight for his country. Not that he was enthusiastic about it. 'I was pondering how long I could delay joining up. The very idea of soldiering appalled me, and to think of it, there were men who did these things by their own free choice.' Nor was the thought of killing a fellow human being high on his wish list. 'The whole thing was monstrous, utterly and unbelievably monstrous, irrational, pitiable, ugly and sordid.'

Despite his obvious reluctance, Rathbone finally enlisted in 1916 as a private with the London Scottish Regiment ('as per my request'). Also serving in the same regiment were future Hollywood actors Claude Rains, Herbert Marshall and Ronald Coleman. Private Rathbone trained at a camp in Richmond Park, London before applying for a commission, which he did 'purposely and with grim intent in order to avoid an early baptism of fire in the battlefields of Northern France.' The application was accepted, and Rathbone was sent to the officers' training camp at Gailes in Scotland. Once again the officer cadet spent more time playing rugby than studying for his exams. His commandant, Captain Smith, saw potential in his leadership skills but insisted the young cadet studied hard. Rathbone finally received his commission and was sent (again as per his request) to the Liverpool Scottish 2nd Battalion.

Saying goodbye to his parents at Victoria Station prior to his journey to France was difficult for 2nd Lieutenant Rathbone. But being conditioned by his training, the officer, resplendent in his uniform, kept the British stiff upper lip as he embarked on an unknown destiny that many of his comrades-in-arms would not come back from. 'There was the train whistle,' he said of his departure, 'some wry smiles, and a final "Goodbye dear". I was never to see my mother again.' Anne Rathbone died the following year, while her beloved son was on active service.

As the regiment's intelligence officer, Rathbone sneaked behind enemy lines in broad daylight, under heavy camouflage, with his trusted sniper Corporal Tanner. They usually retrieved information about German machine gun positions (destroyed later by British artillery), but on one occasion Rathbone noted how sparse the enemy lines were. To try to find out why this was, he was ordered by his commanding officer Colonel Monroe to capture one of the German soldiers.

Rathbone and Tanner went out under heavy disguise, hoping their appearance in the German trenches during daylight would be enough to disorganise the enemy and accomplish their mission. From the air came a squadron of German planes that opened fire on the British. 'Each plane had a different colour,' said Rathbone. 'The leading plane was black, and its pilot was the famous Baron von Richthofen; the second plane was painted red, and its pilot was Hermann Goering. The other planes were painted blue, green, yellow, but their pilots, as far as I know, never became as famous as their leaders.'

With German troops cheering their airborne comrades, Rathbone and Tanner sneaked behind enemy lines and cut the wires from trench to trench. They encountered a German soldier whom Rathbone shot dead with his revolver. Tanner took the dead man's identification tags, a diary and some papers that provided information wanted by British High Command. Then they had to make it through the barbed wire (which left permanent scars on Rathbone's right leg) while avoiding German machine gun fire.

To confuse the enemy further, Rathbone would up and run to the left, as Tanner did the same to the right. 'Tanner and I arrived back to our trenches at approximately the same time, and at about half a mile distance from one another. The information we had brought back was of much value. There seemed no doubt that a German retreat all along the line was imminent. All this came from the diary of the dead soldier. What a mania the Germans have always had for keeping detailed records!'

Rathbone and Tanner met again in 1934 when the actor was appearing in *Romeo and Juliet* in Toledo, Ohio. Tanner had moved to America and become a policeman; after finding out that his former commanding officer was in town, he got touch, and together they enjoyed a happy reunion.

Thanks to his amazing death-defying missions, Rathbone got promoted to captain and was awarded the British Military Cross for bravery under fire. With typical modestly, he said of his achievements on the battlefield, 'All I did was disguise myself as a tree – that's correct, a tree! – and cross no man's land to gather a bit of information from the German lines. I have not since been called upon to play a tree!' Perhaps not, but his flair for disguise would turn out to be equally useful when he came to play Sherlock Holmes. Was the actor's future destiny taking shape? Not yet; the Great War had still not ended, and there were further changes in store for Rathbone.

There came more family tragedy with the death of Basil's brother John, who was also serving in France. 'On 4 June 1918, I was sitting in my dugout in the front line. Suddenly I thought of John, and for some inexplicable reason I wanted to cry, and did immediately. I wrote him a letter to which he never replied, and in due course I received news of his death in action at exactly one o'clock on 4 June. We had always been very close.' A tragic as it was, it further confirmed his belief in ESP.

Summing up the war and John's death, Rathbone wrote a private letter revealing his emotions during the conflicts: 'Out here we step over death every day. We stand next to it while we drink our tea. It's commonplace and ordinary. People who had lives and tried to hold on to them and didn't, and now slump and stare and melt slowly to nothing. You meet their eyes, or what used to be their eyes, and you feel ashamed. And Johnny is one of them. That's the end of it. Grieving is only ridiculous in this place. It could be me today or tomorrow and I shouldn't want to bother grieving over that.'

With the Great War officially over, the Liverpool Scottish Regiment boarded a ship leaving Le Havre for England. The return to home was fraught with mixed emotions for Rathbone: 'It was a curious silent group of men that stood on the upper deck watching the coastline of England come into focus on that morning of our demobilisation. As I remember it now, we had boarded the ship in high spirits. We were still very young, and memories fade with merciful ease at that age. The war was already a long way behind us. And much of the fear and the filth and the smell were drifting into a healthy forgetfulness. Why then had we suddenly become silent? There were those who should, but could not, come back to us, who rested forever silent and forever still in graves of French soil that they had made "forever England," my brother John being one of them.'

Heavily traumatised by his experiences and deeply overshadowed by the deaths of his brother and mother in such a short space of time, Rathbone found his world had changed. 'My father had aged considerably, I thought, since I had last seen him. He seemed completely lost without my mother, and to the day of his death he was to cling to me desperately, loving me more in his uncertain loneliness. My sister was lost to us both. Her spirit had been deeply wounded by my mother's and brother's deaths during the war, and year after year after year even to this day she mourns them in an ever-increasing solitude of prayer and contemplation.

'In all this I was the most selfish, for a strong sense of moving forward was already trembling within me, while they had decided to live in the past. Then there was my wife and son. He was now nearly four years old.'

By August 1919, Rathbone and his wife were living separate lives, although they remained amicable for the sake of Rodion. Rathbone was going through a period of reflection, self-analysis and self-imposed loneliness prompted by the guilt of his marriage ending. He made sure his wife and son were looked after financially, but maintaining two households – he resided in a one room flat in Kensington – proved a big financial struggle. 'My father was hurt and my sister was shocked by the break-up of our marriage. Marion refused to believe that we would not be in due course coming back together again, and my son was missing his father.'

It was the autumn of 1919 when Rathbone received a call from W H Savery, former general manager to Sir Frank Benson and current manager of the Stratford-Upon-Avon Shakespeare Festival, offering him the part of Cassius in *Julius Caesar* and that of Romeo in *Romeo and Juliet*. It was a dream come true! He returned to Shakespeare once more.

After his spell in Stratford, Rathbone joined the new Shakespeare Company. He played Ferdinand in *The Tempest* and Florizel in *The Winter's Tale*, and spent the following year touring in *Henry IV Part II* and *The Merchant of Venice*. There was a change of direction when he played the aide-de-camp in *Napoleon* at London's Queen's Theatre in October 1919. Other non-Shakespeare plays included Sadou's *Fedora* and Philipe Moeller's *George Sand*. Around this time, Rathbone was romantically involved with actress Eva Le Gallienne.

The start of the new decade brought Rathbone's first big success in the English theatre. *Peter Ibbetson* was Samuel Raphaelson's adaptation of George Du Maurier's celebrated novel, and Rathbone was in competition with Henry Daniell and George Relph for the title role. Meeting his friends at a pub in London's Haymarket, Rathbone jokingly told them he had got the part for £10 a week compared with Daniell's demand of £20 and Relph's of £25. 'Nobody laughed,' said Rathbone, 'and I paid for the drinks.'

Peter Ibbetson opened at the Savoy Theatre on 20 February 1920. Rathbone recalled, 'The play was a great success, and in one night I was launched from obscurity to the limelight of unlimited adulation. Sir Johnston Forbes-Robertson and Sir John Hare came backstage to congratulate me, as did Sir Gerald Du Maurier, whose father wrote the original story. Society, titles, statesmen, authors and actors, all of whom presented themselves at my dressing room. For that moment I was the toast of the town.'

Making his movie debut as Amadis de Jocelyn in *Innocent* (1921), Rathbone followed it up with a supporting role as Don Cesare Carelli in *The Fruitful Vine* (1921), but he remained firmly committed to the stage, successfully mixing Shakespeare with contemporary roles. Flushed by his amazing success in Britain, and tempted by the artistic and financial rewards, Rathbone's next ambition was to conquer Broadway.

Rathbone boarded the *SS Olympic* on 21 December 1921, full of new hopes and dreams. During his cruise he befriended the much-travelled American theatre impresario Gilbert Miller. Spending Christmas and New Year crossing the Atlantic, the ship arrived in New York in the early hours of one morning. Rathbone's first impressions of the great city were vivid. 'The New York sky line rose majestically with the dawn, like a drawing by Arthur Rackham. I was emotionally stunned by its beauty, and every time since that I have left or returned to New York by sea, I have had this same reaction.'

Checking in at the Algonquin Hotel, Rathbone met actress Tallulah Bankhead, 'one of the most beautiful women I have ever met.' He made his New York stage debut in *The Czarina* at the Lyceum. 'There is nothing much to relate about *The Czarina*, which was only a modest success.' Shortly after the play closed its run, Gilbert Miller loaned Rathbone out for a London production of Somerset Maugham's *East of Suez*. Then in quick succession he appeared in Karel Čapek's *R.U.R.* at the St Martin's Theatre, before Miller called him back to New York to appear in Ferenc Molnar's *The Swan*.

Rathbone described *The Swan* as, 'The most memorable play of my life. I loved it passionately, and it made me a star in America.' However, it turned out to be something of a baptism of fire for all concerned. Prior to its New York opening at the Court Theatre on 23 October 1923, the play had try-out weeks in Detroit and Toronto, which turned out to be such dismal failures that Gilbert Miller was all for abandoning the production. Even when it made its New York debut, the first act played to a half-full theatre as people slowly came in from the bad weather outside. Even the cast agreed with Miller, until the second act brought the house down with a standing ovation at the end. The matinee performance the following day brought in a packed house, and the play was a huge success.

The success of *The Swan* was instrumental in Rathbone meeting the screenwriter and actress Ouida Bergère. It was November 1923 and Rathbone was invited to a party hosted by Ouida and her actor friend Clifton Webb. The party itself was described as being like Grand Central Station. Rathbone's first impressions of his beautiful hostess were vivid: 'She was indeed young and very petite, with the most beautiful natural red hair I have ever seen. And eyes that danced with the joy of living, and a skin texture of alabaster.' Rathbone made an equally good impression, as he was invited with other friends to spend the weekend at Ouida's Long Island home.

Born Ouida DuGaze in Madrid, Spain on 14 December 1886, she was of English, French and Spanish origin. Moving to America in her early teens, she started out as an actress with the Schubert Stock Company. Following extensive vaudeville experience, she appeared on Broadway in *The Stranger* at the Bijou Theatre in 1911. During World War One she set up her own talent agency. In 1915 she started writing stories for the *New York Herald* before moving into screenwriting. In addition to providing the script for the film version of *Peter Ibbetson* (1921), she designed the costumes. She later worked as a writer with MGM and Pathé before joining Famous Players Lasky, which later became Paramount Studios. Her niece Ouida Branch was married to David Huxley, brother of American writer Aldous Huxley.

It was love at first sight. 'By the time Ouida and I met,' recalled Rathbone, 'we both lived full lives and had much valuable experience, beyond the average, that should enable us to live together until death us do part.' They loved literature, theatre and movies, but more importantly it was a spiritual union that connected them, despite opposition from friends who knew about Ouida's incredible extravagances; she spent money as fast as she earned it.

Rathbone was still performing on Broadway in *The Swan* and Ouida was still contracted to Paramount. She requested a release from her contract so they could marry as soon as possible. The studio wasn't happy, but she persisted until they reluctantly agreed. The couple got engaged, but were initially thwarted in their plans, as Basil was unable to obtain a divorce from Marion. The actor was philosophical about Marion's feelings about his new relationship and her reasons for not granting a divorce: 'Be it said on Marion's behalf that she was waiting to see if this time I was really serious.'

It was June 1924 and *The Swan* closed for the summer holidays, giving Rathbone a chance to return the England. 'I was determined that Ouida and I should be free to marry as soon as possible, and to do so I need both legal advice and the opportunity to convince Marion that our long separation should be terminated.'

There was a less pleasant factor facing Rathbone on his return home. His father, who had never fully recovered from the death of his wife, was very ill. He was recuperating in the country, where Rathbone had sent him a letter. After reading the letter aloud, Edgar died peacefully in his sleep, with a smile on his face and the letter still in his hand. It seemed Edgar Rathbone had forgiven his son for treading the boards as an actor.

During his time in England, Rathbone squeezed in a few film roles. He played Sir Joseph Surface in *School for Scandal* (1924) and, though this is unconfirmed, is believed to have made an appearance in *Loves of Mary Queen of Scots* (1924). Marion agreed to a divorce, and by the time Rathbone was on his way back to New York, proceedings were under way. He toured America with *The Swan* from September 1924 to the spring of 1925 and continued his Broadway success by repeating his role of Sir Joseph in *School for Scandal*. With the divorce finalised, he married Ouida on 18 April 1926.

In between his extensive stage commitments, Rathbone made his American movie debut as Tony Winterslip in *Trooping with Ellen* (1924). *The Masked Bride* (1925) and *The Great Deception* (1926) followed, but the massive success of *The Swan* made him a hot stage commodity. Commuting between London, New York and San Francisco, Rathbone starred in several contemporary plays with equal success. He was cast mainly in sophisticated womaniser roles. Not surprisingly, he became very popular among female fans.

As an actor happy to push the boundaries of theatre, Rathbone got into some controversy when he starred in *La Prisonniere*, or *The Captive*, a semi-autobiographical piece by Edouard Bouret, which had enjoyed a huge success in Paris. This French social drama covered the taboo subject of lesbianism, and in a role against type, Rathbone played Jacques Vieieu, a young Frenchman who finds out his fiancée Irene, played by Helen Menken, is having an affair with a woman. Produced by Gilbert Miller, who translated the play into English, *The Captive* premiered at the Empire Theatre, New York on October 1926. 'The play was produced without any pre-production publicity,' said Rathbone. 'Of course there were rumours as to what it was all about, since a limited number of Americans had seen the play in Paris, but our first night audience was completely ignorant of its theme. They were stunned by its power and the persuasiveness of its argument.'

Despite its sensitive nature and stark permissiveness, *The Captive* struck a chord with the public, much to Rathbone's delight. 'We were an immediate success, and for 17 weeks we played to standing room only at every performance.' Clearly proud of his involvement in *The Captive*, he never felt the play exploited its taboo subject. 'At no time was it ever suggested that we were salacious or sordid or seeking sensation. It was a modern Greek tragedy in the tradition of such Greek tragedies as *Medea* and *Oedipus Rex*, and as in Brieux's *Damaged* and Ibsen's *Ghosts*, we were helping to educate a public to a better understanding of a social sickness that could not be ignored. Such matters have always been the prerogative of the theatre when approached seriously and in good taste. And Gilbert Miller and his company were doing just that. These were challenging days for us in the theatre and we accepted them gladly.'

Perhaps too challenging for some people. During one evening performance of *The Captive*, Rathbone noticed that all wasn't well. 'As we walked out onto the stage to await our first entrances we were stopped by a plainclothes policeman who showed his badge and said, "Please don't let it disturb your performance tonight, but consider yourself under arrest!" Incredible but true.' The performance went off without a hitch, despite the audience being more preoccupied by the strong police presence. 'At the close of the play,' said Rathbone, 'the cast were all ordered to dress and stand by to be escorted in police cars to a night court.' The entire cast were then charged with offending public morals.

Thanks to the intervention of theatre impresario Horace Liveright, the charges were dropped, but the play never reopened – much to the actor's disgust. The incident made headlines, with every sensation-seeker turning up to see the cast and crew answering to their charges. A humiliating experience for all concerned.

With *The Captive* closed for good, Rathbone appeared the following year in the French bedroom farce *Command to Love*. 'But once again, we were to encounter the uncertain hand of local censorship; which, however, expressed itself this time without viciousness, only to expose the pathetic immaturity of "The Guardian of the Public Morals." As with *The Captive*, we had already run on Broadway for several months before someone's "sensibilities" became suspicious of our innocuous fun. We were severely "edited", but continued our successful stay at the Longacre Theatre for a year, to be followed by another year on tour, during which time we put back much that had offended New York!'

The time was now right for Rathbone to bring his own play to the stage. 'I think I was still in my teens when the relationship between Jesus of Nazareth and Judas Iscariot first troubled me. Over the years the thought pursued me and eventually became an obsession. If Judas was the mean, despicable betrayer, why did Jesus choose him to be one of his disciples?' This fascination about the two biblical characters prompted Rathbone to write *Judas*, which focused on their intense relationship and the reasoning behind their motivations.

But there was the possibility that the play's subject matter could be considered blasphemous and offensive to the Roman Catholic and Jewish communities. 'I attempted to discuss the subject with friends, but I got little response,' Rathbone recalled of his attempts to rally support for his ambitious venture. 'I talked with Ouida, and found her interested but extremely sceptical of a play based on such subject matter. She was fearful there might be considerable adverse criticism from churches, the press and public opinion. However, I talked with a few people of the Jewish faith and found them intrigued with the idea.'

Undeterred, Rathbone took religious instruction from a rabbi for accuracy. Ouida remained supportive, albeit reluctantly. With *Command to Love* close to finishing its successful tour in January 1929, Rathbone was determined to get *Judas* out on stage.

Rathbone had already met writer Walter Ferris, who agreed to collaborate on the play. 'To Walter I talked of my idea, and he caught fire immediately. In my mind I had the play completely constructed for a long time, but I knew its writing required a very special quality. This was a job for a "man of letters", and I was no "man of letters" and Walter Ferris was. He seemed to me the perfect collaborator.'

Rathbone took the play to Dwight Wiman and William Brady Jnr, producers of *Command to Love*. 'Wiman had reservations, but Bill Brady had none. His enthusiasm was most encouraging, especially since he was a devout Roman Catholic, and it was obvious to us all that we might be in for some considerable opposition from Roman Catholics. The Protestant churches we felt would offer a lesser problem, and the Jewish rabbis I had contacted were quite positive in their approval.'

The production of *Judas* quickly gained momentum. 'Richard Boleslawski was approached to direct the play and Jo Mielziner to designed the sets. Both accepted immediately.' *Command to Love* had ended its run and Rathbone returned to New York to devote his energies to his pet project.

Judas opened in February 1929 and ran for three weeks, to mixed reviews and public indifference. Rathbone remained philosophical. 'Failure refers to box office receipts. Within this context then we were a failure. But many

Catholics and Protestants and Jews wrote letters and came backstage to see me. Some were much moved by our play, others were disturbed, and a few were offended.'

Despite the failure of *Judas*, Rathbone remained proud of his work. 'After 33 years the play is all but forgotten, except by a few of us who played in it and some of our audience who remember it, not alone in their minds but in their hearts. I myself have never been able to escape the ethical and religious problems posed.'

Rathbone had little time to dwell on the relative failure of *Judas*. He went to Hollywood to star in *The Last of Mrs Cheyney* (1929) with Norma Shearer. '*Mrs Cheyney* was, I think, the second talking picture ever to be made at MGM,' he said of the film. 'It was a most interesting experience. It was directed by Sydney Franklin, one of the most sensitive directors I have ever worked with. The whole picture was rehearsed for three weeks on the sound stage and the sets that were eventually to be photographed. Every minute detail was carefully planned and rehearsed over and over again. Consequently we shot the picture, a big and expensive production, in a mere three weeks.'

Like many early talking pictures, the film suffers from static scenes, stage-bound settings, ponderous dialogue and stilted acting. Although Rathbone, as Lord Arthur Dilling, comes off best, the slow delivery of his dialogue shows his inexperience on screen. 'Sound,' he said, 'being very new, was naturally far from perfection.'

With Hollywood going through a radical change with the coming of sound, stage actors, tempted by the financial rewards, were heading to Tinsel Town. Rathbone had been offered a role in the Broadway production of *Death Takes a Holiday*, but still bitter about the failure of *Judas*, he felt that the next phase of his career should be directed toward filmmaking.

Ouida, who was also her husband's business manager, was not too keen on returning to Hollywood, and voiced her feelings to him. Tearing up the original MGM contract offered, she struck a deal with the studio's representative Robert Rubin that doubled Rathbone's salary. 'She threatened not to go with me if I accepted the contract offered! She felt I would gain stature by waiting and joining the crowd that was being herded into the talking picture market.' The gamble paid off.

Rathbone's next film was a prophetic forerunner to his later career. As detective Philo Vance in *The Bishop Murder Case* (1930), he could well have been the Great Detective using his powers of deduction to solve a murder. Co-star Roland Young's character even refers to him jokingly as 'Sherlock Holmes' several times in the movie.

So began the curse of Holmes – although it didn't happen immediately. In fact, the Great Detective's suffocating presence couldn't have been further away from the actor's life.

Even though his Philo Vance is Holmes in all but name, Rathbone gives an incisive performance that shows how much his acting had improved since *The Last of Mrs Cheyney*. Now completely at home with sound, Rathbone had a modern approach and natural screen presence that made him perfect for talking pictures, his smooth voice and impeccable diction further exemplifying his cinematic style.

And the film work rolled in! Another romantic lead followed as Paul Pariscot in MGM's wartime drama *This Mad World* (1930). For First National Pictures he was miscast as Italian violinist Paul Gheradi in *A Notorious Affair* (1930), but fared slightly better as Colonel Smith in the drawing room drama *The Flirting Widow* (1930). He then played Edward in *The High Road* (1930), back with MGM; Carl Vandry in Universal's drama *Blind Wives* (1930); and the romantic lead Reggie Durant for Pathé's *Sin Takes a Holiday* (1930) – all this in the space of a year! These efforts gave Rathbone valuable experience and provided a good springboard for better films.

After appearing in the RKO musical *A Woman Commands* (1932), Rathbone, British to his core, wanted to return home. 'I was very homesick for my motherland, and Ouida, who has always been patient with me in these moods, encouraged me to return to the London theatre.'

However, his homecoming in 1932 was greeted with typical British indifference. 'I was received in London with a sort of "Oh, you're back again, are you?" attitude, as though I were doing something unethical! I had been away too long, and my Broadway successes in *The Swan*, *The Captive* and *Command to Love* did not have the effect I had anticipated they would.' At least he was still popular enough to get starring roles in the British films *After the Ball* (1932), *One Precious Year* (1933) and *Loyalties* (1933).

Staying only a few months in London, Rathbone accepted an offer from Katharine Cornell to return to America for a tour. This included productions of *Romeo and Juliet*, *The Barretts of Wimpole Street* and later, once the first two plays got established on Broadway, George Bernard Shaw's *Candida*.

'I was to play Romeo, Robert Browning and Morrell [in the three productions]. Miss Cornell invited Ouida and me to visit with her at her local chalet near Garmisch, Bavaria, so I might work with her, particularly on *Romeo and Juliet*.' However, Europe was going through a tense and unsettled period – a fact not lost on Rathbone. 'And so it was in the shadow of the Jungfrau and of Adolf Hitler that I restudied Romeo for the last time.' But it was an enjoyable time in Bavaria. 'A gentle people these Bavarians,' he said with great affection, 'with a smile and a warm greeting of welcome for any stranger to their spacious valley.' Nevertheless, with Munich only a few miles away, the rise of the Third Reich was far too close for comfort.

It was October 1933 and both *Romeo and Juliet* and *The Barretts of Wimpole Street* opened in Buffalo, New York. 'We were to have several dress rehearsals and open with *Romeo and Juliet*, to be followed the next night by

The Barretts.' Unfortunately Rathbone encountered terrible health problems. 'No sooner had we arrived in Buffalo than I promptly lost my voice. I had a throat infection that was to persist throughout this arduous seven-month tour and was to cause me considerable physical and mental distress. Thanks to Ouida's tender and selfless attention, I recovered sufficiently to open in both plays, and we were off in a blaze of glory. We played 86 cities, 24 of which were consecutive one-night stands, and as far as I know there was never a seat to be had at any performance.'

Rathbone also had the greatest praise for the work of Katharine Cornell. 'Miss Cornell has contributed as much to the theatre of her time as any living actor or actress. It seems to me to be a most grievous oversight that a theatre in New York has not as yet been named after her, to honour her as other worthy stars of her generation have been so honoured. Her Elizabeth Barrett was not only the greatest performance of her life, it was also the greatest performance by an actress that I have ever seen.

'I have always disliked Shaw's *Candida*,' he said of the third play. 'It is such a pompous, ultra women's rights play, with both Morrell and Marchbanks unnecessarily sacrificed to Candida's annoying self-righteousness and her smug sense of superiority.' Rathbone also felt the play suffered because of a 'fatuously unpleasant performance' by Orson Welles as Marchbanks. 'Orson Welles had come to our company via Dublin, Ireland, and was supposed to be a boy wonder verging on the phenomenon of genius. With this type of advance publicity much should be forgiven of him, especially since he was only 19 years old. But these early impressions mean little today, for Mr Welles has proven himself an actor of considerable talent.'

The tour continued, stopping off at Texas, Seattle, Washington and Minnesota before closing in May 1934 at the Brooklyn Academy of Music. The throat infection made touring an exhausting experience for Rathbone. In June 1934 he had his tonsils removed. During his recovery he received an offer from David O Selznick to return to Hollywood to play his most important film role to date, the abusive Murdstone in *David Copperfield* (1935).

'David Selznick has always surrounded himself with the finest talent available in every department of his business, regardless of cost,' noted Rathbone. This lavish MGM adaptation of the Charles Dickens classic gave the actor the ultimate role of the handsome, debonair villain. The film also had a cast to die for – Lionel Barrymore, Elsa Lanchester, Roland Young and W C Fields (an incomparable Micawber). Rathbone, as the title character's stepfather, personified the civilised sadist. It set the pattern for his future film career.

But his performance was achieved with a great deal of difficulty. 'The director [George Cukor] told me I had to express no emotion whatsoever, but merely to thrash the child [Freddie Bartholomew as David] to within an inch of his life!' Rathbone, who had always loved children, added, 'I had a vicious cane with much whip to it, but fortunately for Freddie and me, under his britches and completely covering his little rump, he was protected by a sheet of iron rubber. Nevertheless Freddie howled with much pain. As Mr Murdstone I tried to make my mind blank, thrashing Freddie as hard as I could but like a machine.'

At least this unpleasant scene had no effect on the relationship between the actors. 'Freddie and I became great friends, and he was often at our house for a swim in the pool and dinner.'

Rathbone's performance, although positively received by critics, had a negative effect on the audience. 'When the picture was released I received good reviews and a very heavy fan mail – all of it abusive!'

The curse of Holmes was slowly becoming reality as Rathbone found himself pigeonholed in a certain kind of role. 'I had done my job so well that for some considerable time I was to become [beset by] one of motion pictures' worst curses, "typing." I was now typed as a "heavy" of villain, a category that often did not do justice to the role it was supposed.'

Following his stint in *David Copperfield*, Rathbone returned to the stage in November 1934 for Katharine Cornell's Broadway opening of *Romeo and Juliet*. Despite being limited to a 12-week run, it was a tremendous success. It was also Rathbone's last performance as Romeo. The success of *David Copperfield* led to another offer from Selznick, to play Karenin in the big-budget movie adaptation of Tolstoy's classic novel *Anna Karenina* (1935).

Having achieved his success on stage, Rathbone was now ready to tackle cinema full time, and his positive approach to the medium exemplified his adaptability, which he put to great effect in all forms of popular entertainment. 'Although any well-equipped actor should be able to adjust his technique to all four media of the theatre, motion pictures, radio and television, he should bear in mind that each of these media is distinctly individual and must be approached as such.'

By the time he appeared in *Anna Karenina*, Rathbone had decided to move permanently to the West Coast. He rented a house for three months but ended up living there for 'three of the happiest years of my life.'

With the mysterious Greta Garbo in the title role, *Anna Karenina* is another lavish MGM costume drama. Once again Rathbone provides superb support as Anna's repressed husband. Although the character is dark and cruel, his magnetic, multilayered performance evokes more sympathy than the script suggests.

But the problem of typecasting persisted, and Rathbone's feelings were pretty obvious. 'Here, in the making of this picture, is the almost perfect example of a loss of integrity that becomes inevitable when a single label is tabbed to a character of many dimensions. Karenin is not "a heavy" – a motion picture term that Tolstoy would have shuddered to hear defined.'

Rathbone makes a good point – after all, Anna marries Karenin of her own free will, but falls in love with someone else because she's bored. The fault with Karenin is that he is dull, not that he is cruel, so any bitterness he shows toward Anna is understandable.

'He had not been cruel or unkind,' Rathbone insisted. 'Rather he had been insensitive and possessive, and without much imagination. His faults are evident, but surely this does not make him a villain!'

Returning to MGM to give an excellent performance as Pontius Pilate in *The Last Days of Pompeii* (1935), Rathbone had the pleasure of meeting the aviator Amelia Earhart during the making of the film. 'The producer of this picture was Merian Cooper, and one Sunday he invited me to lunch at his beach house in Santa Monica. There were several guests to lunch, I remember none of them but Amelia Earhart. To say it was love at first sight would be both unseemly and utterly ridiculous. And yet with that first glance there was a tug at the heart.'

Rathbone was obviously captivated by the lady. 'Of medium height and slight of build, she had those faraway eyes that travel the seas and the heavens above. Her hair was short, a mass of curls. She was wearing a trim pair of trousers and a turtleneck sweater. She was the only woman I have ever seen of whom one can say that this mode of dress graced her sex. Her composure was sublime, her speech soft, and her manner detached yet not impersonal. I have met no traveller on this earth who is so completely ethereal.'

For Columbia Pictures, Rathbone gave a good account of himself as alcoholic aristocrat Captain Courtney in the drama *A Feather in Her Hat* (1935). Returning to MGM, he played suave beggar Henry Abbott in *Kind Lady* (1935). Then came a reunion with producer David O Selznick.

'Selznick,' said Rathbone, 'in his determination to accomplish the absolute limit of perfection in his work that is humanly possible, has always driven himself and all those who work with him with a fierce and implacable resolution.'

The association continued with two more successful classics. The first of these was *A Tale of Two Cities* (1935). Starring Ronald Colman, the film deserves a place in cinema history for its incredible sequence of the storming of the Bastille. And it had yet another plum role for Rathbone. 'The part that I play in *A Tale of Two Cities*, the Marquis St Evremond, could rightly be called "a villain" or "a heavy". Charles Dickens purposely uses the Marquis to demonstrate the arrogance and cruelty of the French aristocracy of that time. The Marquis is the symbol of the conditions that were the major causes of the French Revolution, but not necessarily the epitome of the French aristocrats.' Rathbone's memorable performance was a landmark one that paved the way for similar screen villainy.

The final film for Selznick was *The Garden of Allah* (1936), a romantic melodrama starring Marlene Dietrich and Charles Boyer as doomed lovers. As Count Ferdinand Anteoni, Rathbone was given a rare chance to play a sympathetic role. 'I was looking forward to this picture as a possible break for me in getting away from "villain" roles. Also I was very thrilled to be playing opposite Marlene Dietrich, whom I admired for a long time and considered one of the world's great beauties. Marlene is an extremely generous artist to work with, and she knows her business.'

Relishing the opportunity to play a nice guy, Rathbone milks the role for all it's worth. It's dated tosh but, with a cast that includes C Aubrey Smith and John Carradine, provides solid entertainment.

Rathbone can't have been unduly concerned about typecasting at this point, as it was bringing the money in. 'I soon found out that I was much in demand and consequently had the security of continuous work that came as a very pleasant surprise after my life in the theatre.' Away from Selznick, the actor earned another high-profile supporting role as Wroxton in 20th Century Fox's *Secret Interlude* (1936). 'Win lose or draw,' he added, 'one is paid in the movies irrespective of the results of a picture's release. It's like getting three months' salary in advance in the theatre before the play opens! Also a picture star's salary is at least triple that one receives in the theatre.'

Rathbone entered the next phase of his career with a role in the classic pirate yarn *Captain Blood* (1935). This was notable for introducing a new swashbuckling hero in the shape of Tasmanian-born adventurer Errol Flynn. According to Rathbone, '[Flynn] was under contract to Warner Brothers at I believe $150 a week when he was literally propelled into his first starring role as Captain Blood, owing to an emergency, the nature of which I forget. A couple of years later he was negotiating a contract that would pay him £7,000 a week.' Although Flynn gives an awkward performance (he hadn't quite ditched his Australian accent), it was enough to make him a star.

Captain Blood was a career-defining film for all concerned. It provided archetypal roles for Flynn, Rathbone and Olivia de Havilland, a teenager who became Hollywood's favourite maiden fair. For Rathbone, the villainous image took a step further as he showed off both his athleticism and his skills as an expert swordsman when his evil Levassur engages in a duel to the death with Flynn's dashing Peter Blood. Of course we all know who wins.

'We crossed swords but never words,' said Rathbone of Flynn. 'He was generous and appreciative of my work. I liked him and he liked me. He was one of the most beautiful male animals.' But Rathbone was equally aware of Flynn's limitations as an actor. 'He could not compare to Valentino, John Gilbert or Clark Gable. I think his greatest handicap was that he was incapable of taking himself seriously. I don't think he had any ambition other than living up every moment of his life to the maximum of his physical capacity, and making money. He had talent, but how much we shall never know; there were flashes of this talent in the three pictures we made together.

'He was monstrously lazy and self-indulgent, relying on a magnificent body to keep him going, and he had an insidious flair for making trouble, mostly for himself. I believe him to have been quite fearless, and subconsciously possessed of his own self-destruction. I would say that he was fond of me, for what reasons I shall never know. It was always "dear old Bazz", and he would flash that smile that was both defiant and cruel but, for me, always had that tinge of affection in it.'

Rathbone also became lifelong friends with the film's leading lady. 'Captain Blood was also Olivia de Havilland's first picture. I understand she was about 18 or 19 years old at the time, and a more enchantingly beautiful young girl it would be impossible to imagine. She has developed into a very talented actress.'

Rathbone's love of Shakespeare continued when he returned to Romeo and Juliet for the 1936 film version produced by MGM. Now too old for Romeo, he settled for the role of Lady Capulet's nephew Tybalt. However, Leslie Howard's Romeo looks older than Rathbone! The cast included Norma Shearer (as an equally over-aged Juliet), C Aubrey Smith and the great John Barrymore, whose distinctive profile was as famous as Rathbone's.

The 'profiles' engaged in a ferocious sword fight, and once again Rathbone showed off his excellent fencing skills. It was also the only time his character won on screen! Making the most of his limited role (cut down from the original text), he earned a well-deserved Oscar nomination for Best Supporting Actor. He lost out to Walter Brennan.

'Irving Thalberg was one of the most sensitive men I have ever met,' said Rathbone of the film's producer. 'Most certainly his production of Romeo and Juliet had a physical beauty, an integrity and inspiration that place it among the all-time greats.' Perhaps that's not really the case, considering the miscasting of the tragic lovers, but for Rathbone it was another excellent role in a high-profile movie.

Summing up this phase of his career and his association with two of Hollywood's legendary moguls, Rathbone said, 'I can only speak of those I know and for whom I have worked, and Irving Thalberg and David O Selznick stand head and shoulders above any other producers of my time. I have no heart to talk of any others, however excellent they may be.'

Rathbone made his first excursion into the horror genre as the Bluebeard-inspired killer Gerald Lovell in Love From a Stranger (1937), a psychological thriller based on an Agatha Christie story. It was the first of three parts he would play for director Rowland V Lee, his first starring role since The Bishop Murder Case, and his first British film since Loyalties. He gives an excellent performance, adding flare, polish and depth to what is a stereotypical maniac killer role.

'The storm clouds were gathering over Europe,' the actor recalled of his time back in England. 'We had felt them at the end of 1936 when we visited Paris, Berlin and Budapest on a trip after completing *Love From a Stranger*. There were ominous evil things in the air about us, which grew more ominous and evil as King Edward VIII deserted his country in its hour of need, and Neville Chamberlain failed to understand that peace at any price had never led to anything but war.'

Returning to Hollywood, Rathbone added another villainous role to his increasing portfolio, playing Michael Michailow in *Confession* (1937). Then, in a welcome change of pace, he had a sympathetic part as struggling composer Johnny Seldon in the delightful children's drama *Make a Wish* (1937) – this time his character even gets the girl!

Rathbone's next role was as Commissar Dimitri Gorotchenko in *Tovarich* (1937), a big-screen adaptation of Jacques Deval's play about a royal Russian couple (played by Charles Boyer and Claudette Colbert) fleeing to post-revolutionary Paris, where they work as servants to a wealthy household. Rathbone is in fine form as the villain of the piece.

'*Tovarich* was a good picture made from a very successful Broadway play,' recalled the actor. 'In it we were all extremely health-conscious, because dear Claudette Colbert, who is married to a doctor, had a passion from administering medicines. She would watch us all closely for symptoms. A vagrant sneeze or mild clearing of the throat and she was at one's side in a moment. She had a thermometer, aspirin, cough drops, eye wash, iodine and a Red Cross kit in a special bag that was always with her on the set. Claudette is also a very accomplished actress.' Ironically, the actress fell ill during the making of *Tovarich*, holding up production for several weeks.

Rathbone then returned to historical adventure, providing elegant villainy as Ahmed the Saracen in *The Adventures of Marco Polo* (1938), a fictionalised account of the exploits of the famous Italian adventurer, improbably played by Gary Cooper. Although a lavish production, the film is strictly comic book stuff, featuring white actors made up to look Asian! Not politically correct, but it adds to the unintentional fun, and Rathbone rises above the material with a sly performance.

Rathbone's next film for Warner Brothers stands as classic cinema. Eighty years on and *The Adventures of Robin Hood* (1938) is still the swashbuckler to end all swashbucklers. In the title role, Errol Flynn became the prototype for all subsequent movie interpretations of the character, none of which has come close to his career-topping turn. And in Rathbone you could not have asked for a better actor to play Sir Guy of Gisbourne, a classic villain who is an equal to Flynn's heroic outlaw in terms of intelligence and bravery.

Rathbone, handsome and sinister throughout, plays it to the hilt and beyond. With an amazing cast that includes Olivia de Havilland (Maid Marion), Claude Rains (Prince John), Alan Hale (Little John) and Eugene Pallette (Friar Tuck), *The Adventures of Robin Hood* has the mark of brilliance stamped all over it.

Rathbone moved from medieval England to medieval France for Paramount's *If I Were King* (1938). Starring Ronald Colman as French poet Francois Villon, this is a fictionalised account of the Burgundian army's invasion of France and Villon's relationship with the steadfast but doddery King Louis XI, best known as 'the Spider King' because of his unique skills at scheming and deception. In a welcome departure from his usual screen villainy, an unrecognisable Rathbone is in fine cackling form as the hated monarch. His performance earned him a second Oscar nomination for Best Supporting Actor. Once again he lost out to Walter Brennan.

Returning to Warners, Rathbone worked with Errol Flynn one last time in *The Dawn Patrol* (1938). Set during the Great War, it tells the story of several British RAF pilots dealing with the harsh realities of war. It gave Flynn a chance to show the flash of acting talent Rathbone saw very briefly during their three collaborations. For Rathbone, it was a case of art imitating life as he relived his early wartime experiences. As Flynn's commanding officer Major Brand, he gives an excellent account of a man cracking under the pressure of sending his inexperienced young pilots to almost certain death in action.

'Those four pictures I made at Warner Brothers were not great pictures,' recalled the actor, 'but they were very good pictures and excellent entertainment. In their category I do not see their like being as well made today.' Sadly a falling out with Jack Warner ended his association with the studio.

The following year, Rathbone's career took another distinct turn. The horror genre had been dormant since 1936, but all that was to change in 1938 when film distributor E Mark Umann made a fortune following his cinema screening of Universal's *Dracula* (1930) and *Frankenstein* (1931). Flushed by this success, Universal produced 500 new prints of both films for future screenings. The financial return was enough to put a second sequel to *Frankenstein* into production.

Pre-production on *Son of Frankenstein* (1939) commenced in October 1938 with Willis Cooper providing a new script and Rowland V Lee assuming directorial duties. In addition to Boris Karloff returning as the Monster, Bela Lugosi joined the cast as Ygor the hunchback, along with Lionel Atwill as the one-armed Inspector Krough. But it was the casting of Baron Wolf Von Frankenstein that was pivotal to the film. Claude Rains was seriously considered before the studio settled on Peter Lorre; when Lorre dropped out due to illness, Lee brought in Rathbone to complete a strong male cast.

86

Originally intended to be made in Technicolor, which Lee vetoed, *Son of Frankenstein* is an excellent production featuring magnificent art deco sets by Jack Otterson. Lee effectively captures a strong gothic atmosphere, even if his pacing occasionally slacks. Karloff still dominates the film despite his lack of screen time – although the Monster make-up is less impressive. On the plus side, Lugosi is in fine form, and Lionel Atwill steals the acting honours as the embittered policeman, making the most of memorable lines such as 'One doesn't easily forget, Herr Baron, an arm torn out by the roots.'

Playing the new Baron, Rathbone is immaculate as always. But he disliked horror films and considered his role something of a comedown from his previous work. There are times when he goes over the top, especially during the scenes when the Baron plays darts with the Inspector. He gives the impression that he is going through the motions just to get the film finished. The end result makes him the least interesting of the impressive star quartet.

Despite going over budget by $420,000, *Son of Frankenstein* was a box office smash on both sides of the Atlantic, taking in well over $1 million and reviving Universal's monster cycle. It also marked the start of Rathbone's horror career, even though that wouldn't really take off until much later. Shortly after he completed *Son of Frankenstein*, another form of typecasting was awaiting him, and one that would have a profound effect on his life.

So began the curse of Holmes.

'Ever since I was a little boy and first got acquainted with the Great Detective I wanted to be like him. My desire to be an actor also began when I was a youngster, so it was only natural to combine the two – to play such a character means as much to me as ten Hamlets.' Such was Rathbone's enthusiasm when 20th Century Fox first offered him the role of Holmes in *The Hound of the Baskervilles* (1939). Pre-production began in November 1938 following a party attended by producer Darryl F Zanuck, director Gregory Ratoff, writer Gene Markey and several executives who were involved in bringing Holmes to the big screen. 'When the executives asked me who could possibly play Holmes,' Markey recalled, 'I replied "Who? Basil Rathbone."'

The Hound of the Baskervilles remains the most popular screen adaptation of Sir Arthur Conan Doyle's often filmed novel. And the casting of Rathbone is inspired. The sharp profile is obvious, but it's the actor's incisive approach that makes it work so well, despite the character being absent for much of the film's running time. Rathbone's Holmes is both alert and charismatic. Not only does he play the part with typical consummate professionalism, he adds more – a great deal more. The nervous energy and authoritative manner that epitomise the Great Detective are put across with such skill and confidence by Rathbone, he virtually becomes the character he plays. The script even gives him a nice oblique reference to Holmes's cocaine addiction when he casually says, 'Oh Watson, the needle.'

Surprisingly, Rathbone has second billing after Richard Greene as Sir Henry Baskerville. There's nothing wrong with Greene's performance – he is the romantic lead, with more screen time – but the part is rather bland, and although Greene does a decent enough job, he suffers badly in comparison with his excellent co-star. The film has its fair share of flaws, notably that the direction lacks pace and that the hound is disappointing – a factor that has also marred subsequent movie and television versions of the story.

And then there's Nigel Bruce's Dr Watson. Conan Doyle's character is a no-nonsense former army surgeon, but the film depicts Watson as a bumbling comic relief – a trait that Bruce would overplay in the later films. Rathbone however was always supportive of his friend, and defended his portrayal. 'There is no question in my mind that Nigel Bruce was the ideal Dr Watson, not only of his time but possibly of and for all time. There is an endearing quality to his performance that to a very large extent, I believe, humanised the relationship between Dr Watson and Mr Holmes. It has always seemed to me more than possible that our adventures might have been met with a less kindly public acceptance had they been recorded by a less lovable companion to Holmes than was Nigel's Dr Watson.' Rathbone makes a good point, but time hasn't been kind to Bruce in light of the far more effective way Watson has since been portrayed by other actors.

Whatever the flaws, the critics sang the film's praises. Rose Perwick of Hearst newspapers said of Rathbone's performance, 'Smoking the traditional pipe and playing the violin, but otherwise making the character credible rather than eccentric, Mr Rathbone is vastly superior to the previous screen impersonators of the Baker Street genius.' The British *Kinematograph Weekly* commented, 'This new Holmes is undoubtedly Holmes. What seemed to please and impress was that the authenticity of the movie was a refreshing change after Clive Brook's and Arthur Wontner's modern Holmes.'

But it was Rathbone who had the last word on the film. 'Of all the adventures, *The Hound* is my favourite story, and it was in this picture that I had the stimulating experience of creating, within my framework, a character that has intrigued me as much as any other I have ever played.'

Rathbone returned to Universal for *The Sun Never Sets* (1939), which cast him and Douglas Fairbanks Jnr as brothers working as diplomats in South Africa – echoes of Edgar Rathbone's adventures. With a solid cast that also includes C Aubrey Smith and Lionel Atwill, the film is a well-mounted drama filled with good performances. But with *The Hound of the Baskervilles* storming the box office, 20th Century Fox already had plans for a sequel.

Rushed into production in June 1939, *The Adventures of Sherlock Holmes* (1939) is a screen adaptation of William Gillette's famous play, first performed in 1889. The film version actually bears little resemblance to

Gillette's original, but it hardly matters, because it's classic Holmes all the way. And this time Rathbone takes both top billing and centre stage, and has a chance to develop the character with a complex case to solve. More importantly, Holmes crosses swords with archenemy Professor James Moriarty, played with equal brilliance by that ubiquitous screen villain George Zucco; their scenes together in a horse-drawn carriage positively crackle. If anything Rathbone plays it to the hilt with a more effective performance. He even gets a chance to disguise himself as a music hall singer. Dressed in a pin-stripe blazer and wearing a walrus moustache and boater, he performs a jolly rendition of 'Oh I Do Like to be Beside the Seaside'.

The Adventures of Sherlock Holmes is not as effective as *The Hound of the Baskervilles*. It suffers from an unconvincing plot, a lack of pace and bland romantic leads. And there's Nigel Bruce's Watson. His comic antics were kept under control in the first film, but here he moves away from the original concept of Watson to become the familiar fool that would characterise the later ones.

Many years afterwards, Rathbone shared his misgivings about the film. 'It would seem our timing was bad. 1939 was far too late for a serious presentation of *The Adventures of Sherlock Holmes*. In the early years of the present century, theatre audiences were chilled to the marrow by William Gillette's famous portrayal of Sherlock Holmes, in a play I have read and been invited to revive. This play, believe me, is so ludicrously funny today that the only possible way to present it in the '60s would be to play it like *The Drunkard*, with Groucho Marx as Sherlock Holmes. Time marches on! Even the witticisms of Oscar Wilde are already somewhat dated.'

Despite Rathbone's reservations, *The Adventures of Sherlock Holmes* did well at the box office on its release in September 1939. Once again the critics praised the star's performance. According to *Variety*, 'The Holmes character is tailor-made for Rathbone. It was in *The Adventures* that he gave us one of his finest disguises – that of a music hall singer.'

With two successful Holmes films behind them, Fox considered two more entries in the series, but by 1940 they had scrapped their plans. According to writer Amanda Field, 'There was a complicated stand-off with the Conan Doyle estate, which attempted to bludgeon Fox into purchasing rights in further Doyle stories by threatening to sell instead to MGM and later Warners.'

The series was put on hold for a while. Rathbone was nevertheless on a cinematic high. To him, Holmes was a great role: 'For once I get to play the good guy instead of the bad guy.' And although Fox had dropped the series, Rathbone and Bruce happily recreated their signature roles in some 200 radio plays for the Music Corporation of America.

During the making of *The Adventures of Sherlock Holmes*, Rathbone still kept abreast of the worsening situation in Europe. 'War was declared in August 1939,' he observed, 'and I wrote to the War Office in London offering my services. In due course I received an official letter of interminable length in reply. It began "Dear Sir" and ended with "Your obedient servant." I waded through it, and all it said was: "You are too old!" Politely but firmly.' Despite his many years in America, Rathbone retained his British citizenship (and remained a strong supporter of the Conservative Party) out of respect for his country and admiration for his late brother.

Released at the same time as *The Adventures of Sherlock Holmes*, *Rio* (1939) is a Universal thriller starring Rathbone as Paul Reynard, a Parisian swindler who escapes from Devil's Island to kill his wife's lover. Following the success of Holmes, the film is a bit of a comedown, but it is solid enough, and the actor gives another impeccable performance.

As this tremendous decade of his career came to a close, Rathbone remained at Universal for his next film. He had been due to play Frollo in *The Hunchback of Notre Dame* (1939), but had to pull out as the production schedule conflicted with that of *Tower of London* (1939). In the hands of Rowland V Lee, this loose screen adaptation of Shakespeare's *Richard III* got the horror treatment. Rathbone is in fine Machiavellian form playing the Bard's most enduring villain. His hawk-like profile – enhanced by a false nose – is as ideally suited to Crookback Dick as it was to Holmes.

Being a horror film, *Tower of London* centres on Richard murdering his way to the English throne with the aide his loyal henchman Mord, the club-footed executioner, memorably played by Boris Karloff. With his severe bald head and heavy beetle brows, Karloff makes a scary and formidable servant, ready to kill at a moment's notice, but showing his all too human soul when he reluctantly carries out Richard's orders to kill the young princes in the Tower.

Once of Richard's victims is Lionel, Duke of Clarence, who gets dispatched in a large vat of wine. Cast as Clarence was a 28-year old Hollywood newcomer, Vincent Price. Price enjoyed working with Rathbone and Karloff, and found his death scene especially memorable. 'We had the scene where Basil and I had to drink to the kingdom of England,' he recalled. 'Rowland V Lee didn't like the dialogue, and neither did we, because the more we drank, the less we could remember. It was only Coca-Cola, but Coke is stimulating too. Well, over in one corner was a huge vat of malmsey wine in which I was to be drowned. Boris and Basil, knowing I was new to the business, thought it was great fun to throw everything they could into that vat of wine, which was actually just water. You know, old Coca-Cola bottles, cigarette butts, anything they could get into it. There was a handrail at the bottom of the vat, so I could dive down and hang onto it. I had to stay under for a full ten counts, and then I was yanked out by my heels. Well, when I came out I got a round of applause from the crew, but was disappointed not to see Boris and Basil. Then, a few minutes later, they reappeared and they were very nice to me. They congratulated me on playing the scene so well for a newcomer, and then presented me with a case of Coca-Cola!'

Tower of London wrapped in September 1939, in ten days and $80,000 over budget. The film enjoyed positive reviews and good box office receipts, even though it is far from perfect. The pace is a little slow to make the film completely effective – but this is a minor quibble, as the production design and first-rate acting hold the interest, with Rathbone giving one of his best screen performances.

Playing Richard III gave Rathbone a nostalgic reminder of his early days with Sir Frank Benson. It must have been a bitter-sweet experience for him, as 1939 was the year of his cousin's death, in circumstances ill befitting a great actor. 'The last time I saw Sir Frank he was lying on an iron cot in a rooming house in the Holland Road, London. He was dying – alone – and he was penniless, except for a government grant of £100 a year. His marriage had broken up, and after his dismissal from Stratford-Upon-Avon, he never had any further success. No businessman, he gradually fell into poverty, and then into virtual penury.' Rathbone was with Benson when he passed away on 31 December 1939. 'There was a shadow of a smile in his eyes. He just said one word, "Basil." Then he lapsed into semi-consciousness.' Among the treasured possessions Benson left to his loyal protégé was the sword used by King George V to honour one of the great figures of the English theatre.

By the time he was 43, Rathbone was one of Hollywood's highest paid freelance actors – no mean feat, as most foreign actors received a lot less for their work. The money allowed him and his wife to take it easy. 'Above and beyond everything, Ouida and I were free to enjoy a long postgraduate honeymoon. Many were the sacrifices she had made for me in this journeying we had planned together and in the directing of my professional life, and we fell in love again, as it were, in this Garden of Eden. Not that we had ever fallen out of love. But our loving one another was deserving of this time we earned together, and we were in need of the time to enjoy one another again, released as it were, at last, from the pressures and burdens that are inherent in the building of any successful career.'

The Rathbones were thoroughly settled in their new Tudor-style mansion home situated in the Hollywood Hills. In addition to a kennelful of dogs – they owned seven at one time – they also adopted two cats. 'The house was small but extremely comfortable. It had a large and lovely garden with a kidney-shaped swimming pool. We were rarely indoors. We lived in the garden and in the pool. And what a haven it was for our dogs! Ouida was divinely happy. At last we had the home she had hoped for all her life. We loved each other very much and we loved our dogs, and our dogs loved us and the cats!'

The Rathbones also became proud parents when they adopted their daughter. 'Cynthia was born on 13 April 1939,' he said, 'and took up residence with us some few days later.' They were very devoted parents, and Cynthia had a loving and happy upbringing; she travelled with them when they toured provincial theatres in between his film commitments. Rathbone described the new arrival as having, 'a fierce independence and that Irish trait of needling a weak spot wherever she could find one.' With Cynthia, the dogs and their home, life was complete.

With the leisure time at their disposal, the Rathbones pursued many interests together – their joint hobbies included baseball, music, boxing, spiritualism and reading. They attended all the major sporting events, although Ouida never understood her husband's love of golf.

Rathbone remained an avid cricket fan and a keen player. Hollywood had a very strong community of British ex-pats, among them C Aubrey Smith. Described by Peter Cushing as 'That grand old stalwart of British theatre, empire and cricket,' Smith founded the Hollywood Cricket Club. Rathbone, Boris Karloff, Laurence Oliver, Robert Coote, Nigel Bruce, Ronald Coleman, Cary Grant and David Niven were among the British members, with Errol Flynn representing Australia, Louis Hayward representing South Africa and Douglas Fairbanks Jnr representing America (!). Shortly after arriving in Hollywood, the starstruck Cushing was invited to play. 'I was bowled out first ball,' he recalled, 'and missed several easy catches when being so distracted by all those luminaries surrounding me. My services were not called upon again!'

In addition to her own happy family life, Ouida made every effort to bring her husband closer to his son Rodion. She became firm friends with Marion and even invited Rodion to live with them. During his two years in Hollywood, Rodion enjoyed his time with his father; he even acted in a couple of his films under the name John Rodion. However, with the outbreak of World War II, he left Hollywood to serve in the British army.

The Rathbones remained strictly home birds. 'We deliberately made few friends and dined out rarely,' he said. 'There were David Niven and the Richard Boleslawskys with their son, and Freddie Bartholomew and Jack and Phyllis Morgan, Newell Vanderhoef and John Roche and friends from New York. I think we were somewhat frowned on by "the industry" for our apparent exclusiveness. And I was the despair of the studio's publicity department, because I would not dine out with their starlets or get into some kind of trouble. But Ouida and I had waited a long time for this sort of life, and no increase in salary could buy us off!'

That said, the Rathbones were an extremely popular couple in Hollywood. His quiet wit, humour and way with a story meant Basil could make friends easily. Only the extremely suspicious Bela Lugosi disliked him, but then Lugosi mistrusted everyone in Tinsel Town!

There was one downside to the marriage, although it was not apparent at the time. Ouida had a tendency to spend money on increasingly elaborate parties at their home. These were expensive affairs attended by influential and prominent people both in and out of the industry. On one occasion when they hosted a Christmas party, Ouida made it more festive by importing real snow! Her extravagances inspired a joke in the Bob Hope comedy *The Ghost Breakers* (1940), where Hope, observing a massive thunderstorm in New York, concludes, 'Basil Rathbone must be throwing a party!'

But Rathbone's love and devotion to his wife were so strong, he overlooked her extravagances; they both had a zest for life and were willing to live it to the full, thanks to his high earning power. 'We lived well but not luxuriously, walking and reading and talking, [enjoying] my new collection of classical records and the beautiful new player that Ouida had given me. Tennis with Jack Morgan, golf with David Niven and Nigel Bruce, archery lessons from Howard Hill. And the races!' Rathbone's view of his Hollywood life seems to overlook Ouida's spendthrift ways. Because they never saved for their old age together, their later years would prove financially hard.

The new decade kicked off with another swashbuckling villain role for Rathbone: Captain Esteban Pasquale in *The Mark of Zorro* (1940). This 20th Century Fox action adventure has the actor getting out-fenced by Tyrone Power as Don Diego Vera, aka Zorro. It's rip-roaring stuff, with Rathbone oozing evil in every scene. And his final fencing scene with Power is considered one of the best produced by Hollywood. Although an expert fencer, Rathbone never cared for the sabre, which is used in the action, but he did all his own stunts on the film, with Power doing just a handful. During their duelling scenes, Rathbone commented, 'Tyrone Power could fence Errol Flynn into a box!'

For Paramount, Rathbone appeared in the Bing Crosby musical *Rhythm of the River* (1940) as slimy songwriter Oliver Courtney – a nice enough time-passer that gave the actor a pleasant change from screen villainy and a chance to do a bit of comedy. Later, from the same studio, came the role of prolific wife killer Dr George Sebastian/Dr Frederick Langamain in the intriguing thriller *A Date with Destiny* (1941). Because of Rathbone's part-time association with horror, the film was released overseas as *The Mad Doctor*.

Horror continued with the spooky house mystery *The Black Cat* (1940). Despite top billing as Montague Hartley, Rathbone is merely a red herring. There is a nice gag where co-star Broderick Crawford says, 'He thinks he's Sherlock Holmes.' Was this a prophecy? If it was, it would return to Rathbone sooner than he, or anyone else, expected.

The early years of the new decade saw Rathbone's movie output severely curtailed because of the renewed hostilities between Britain and Germany. 'After the swift conquest of Poland, the war seemed to drift lazily along, and a number of our friends began referring to it as "the phony war" – but not for long. I remember it all so well. It was Kentucky Derby Day in May 1940, and the German armies were pouring into Belgium and France. Things grew worse hourly, and we lived constantly within hearing of the radio. Then came Dunkirk and Britain's year alone against the united Axis powers.'

Despite being too old to enlist, Rathbone wanted to 'do his bit' for Blighty by putting his energies into promoting British support in America. 'Ouida organised her first benefit, the proceeds to be shared by the RAF Benevolent Fund and the Red Cross. She organised it absolutely alone at the Beverly Wilshire Hotel and netted some $100,000. It was a staggering job, attended by everybody in the motion picture industry.'

Rathbone became President of the Los Angeles Chapter of the British War Relief Committee. 'I wrote to all the top executives at MGM asking them to contribute. Not one of them so much as answered my letters. But with the Warner brothers it was very different. They were terrific Anglophiles and supported us with both their time and their money.'

With the Japanese coming into the war following the bombing of Pearl Harbor, Rathbone was elected President of the War Chest Executive Committee. There was also extensive work for the United Nations War Relief.

The Rathbones organised parties at their home for servicemen of the Eighth Army, the Tank Corp and the RAF; leading military dignitaries Lord Halifax and Admiral Halsey were guests. 'Such wonderful boys,' said Rathbone about his time with the young British soldiers. 'They all wrote to us afterwards, but very few of them came home again. Most of them were killed in the great air raids over Germany. They would eat, drink, sleep, talk, laugh and play golf. Some took it in their stride, others were moody and disturbed. Either way I think we were of much therapeutic help to them all.'

Ouida Rathbone earned the title Hostess of Hollywood; she was even offered a radio show of her own under that name. She organised the Hollywood Canteen, a club offering hospitality to American servicemen now fighting, and brought in big stars to entertain them. Rathbone himself entertained American troops in California and visited many army hospitals in between his work commitments.

A great deal of this effort was personally financed, and Rathbone still had to earn a living. His first foray into wartime drama came with *International Lady* (1941) as Scotland Yard Inspector Reggie Oliver – again jokingly referred to by co-star George Brent's character as 'Sherlock Holmes'. Next it was back to Universal, as French Resistance leader Andre Benoit in *Paris Calling* (1941). Then Rathbone signed with agent Jules Stein at MCA Inc, and thanks to him secured a five-year contract with MGM – a deal that would enable him to meet his ongoing financial needs and contribute more to the Hollywood war effort.

Now committed to the studio, Rathbone starred in the efficient crime thriller *Fingers at the Window* (1942) as Dr Santelle, a disfigured hypnotist who uses his powers to turn his patients into axe murderers. The villainy continued with *Crossroads* (1942) as Henri Sarou. These films kept the actor's career ticking over in between his extensive charity work. However, MGM were by now involved in plans to revive a character Rathbone had not played in four years.

After the situation with Warners and 20th Century Fox, the Conan Doyle estate had gone elsewhere with the Sherlock Holmes movie rights. According to Amanda Field, 'They began negotiating a deal with independent producer Lester Cowan to produce two to four pictures a year, released through Columbia or Paramount, with William Cameron Menzies set to direct.' Rathbone and Nigel Bruce were still playing Holmes and Watson on radio, so it looked an obvious move to have them repeat their roles on screen. And with Menzies scoring a huge hit as production designer on *Gone With The Wind* (1939), the idea looked good on paper. The deal fell through, but Universal then stepped in, striking a seven-year arrangement with the estate, purchasing 21 stories and extended rights to the characters. The estate walked away with a tidy $300,000. Finally Universal secured an arrangement with MGM for them to loan out Rathbone for the proposed series of two films a year.

Unlike the Fox films, the new series were going to be low-budget second features set in modern day London. 'The stories we did were modernised, but the characters of the famous detective and his biographer were kept more or less as originally written by Conan Doyle,' recalled Nigel Bruce. 'To begin with, Basil and I were much opposed to it, but producer Howard Benedict pointed out that the majority of youngsters that would see our pictures were used to fast-moving gangster pictures.'

It was a sound argument, and to a modern viewer, Rathbone's Holmes doesn't look the least bit out of place in his new setting. As Holmes is a timeless character, he can be transferred effectively to a modern setting – as recently seen in the BBC series *Sherlock* starring Benedict Cumberbatch and Martin Freeman.

Modernising the series had one significant attraction for Rathbone – it would allow for the films to highlight the war in Europe. So the early entries in the Universal run had the Great Detective exposing Nazi spies, and London was depicted with blackouts, sandbags, ration books and bombings. However, the 221B Baker Street residence remained unchanged, as did Holmes's dressing gown, pipe and dreaded violin, although the famous cape and deerstalker were replaced by a tweed overcoat and matching fedora hat.

The first of the series, *Sherlock Holmes and the Voice of Terror* (1942), seamlessly transfers the Victorian Holmes to modern London. However, one less successful change is visible in Rathbone's appearance. To give Holmes a Bohemian look, the actor opted for an untidy comb-over hairstyle that unfortunately removes the emphasis from his finely-chiselled features. Nigel Bruce's appearance as Watson has also changed. His hair and moustache are no longer dyed, giving him a much older look. (He was actually three years younger than Rathbone.) Also retained from the Fox series is Scottish character actress Mary Gordon as 221B's housekeeper Mrs Hudson.

Directed by John Rawlins, *Sherlock Holmes and the Voice of Terror* is supposed to be based on the Conan Doyle tale *His Last Bow*, but the link is tenuous to put it mildly. It is the first film to see Holmes exposing Nazi spies. Rathbone, despite his hair being at odds with the character, plays Holmes with the same intensity and gusto as ever, and he retained the praise of most critics, although reviews were generally mixed. Nigel Bruce's performance however shows the beginnings of the comic caricature that became associated with the series. His Blimp-inspired Watson may have been popular with cinema audiences but was hardly a companion Holmes could have tolerated for long.

Sherlock Holmes and the Secret Weapon (1942) continued the flag-waving, with Holmes exposing more Nazi spies. It marked the directorial debut of Roy William Neill, who went on to helm the remaining films. Rathbone felt it was Neill – known as 'Mousie' on the set – who made the series what it was. 'There was a nominal producer and some writers, but Roy Neill was the master and final hand in all those departments.' Thanks to Neill's suspenseful and economic direction, the series kept a high level of consistency to the very end.

Sherlock Holmes and the Secret Weapon once again has only loose connections to the Conan Doyle canon (it's supposed to be based on his story *The Adventure of the Dancing Men*), but the solid writing remains in tune with the Holmes universe. It brings back Moriarty, played with suave menace by Lionel Atwill, as a Nazi sympathiser and marks the debut of British actor Dennis Hoey as bumbling Inspector Lestrade, whose endearing idiocy provides a perfect foil for Holmes. The film also gave Rathbone a chance to try out a couple of disguises – as a Swiss inventor and an old German bookseller – and although these seem to have been included mainly for comic effect, he acquits himself well with them. Reviews were positive, the Hollywood Reporter stating, 'Basil Rathbone assumes the part of Sherlock Holmes with the suavity that is his stock in trade.' Could this have been a prophetic comment that sealed the actor's typecasting?

Sherlock Holmes in Washington (1943) is the third and least interesting of the flag-wavers. For a welcome change, the Nazi spy exposed by Holmes is American. The film also welcomes back George Zucco, playing a character that is Moriarty in all but name. Although the end result is enjoyable, the espionage angle has run thin; how many times can Holmes win the war? The reviews here were less positive than before, but Rathbone, as always, came out on top. The New York Post summed it up best: 'You can practically see the mighty muscles of his mind tense, grab and get to the heart of the toughest mystery.' As usual, the public lapped it up.

But Rathbone soon realised the drawbacks of repeatedly playing Holmes. 'Had I made but the one Holmes picture [*The Hound of the Baskervilles*], I should probably not be as well known as I am today. But within myself, as an artist, I should have been well content.' As much as he loved Holmes, the series began to compromise his artistic leanings. The films were popular, but his frustrations grew with each one. 'The continuous repetition of story after story after story left me virtually repeating myself each time in a character I had already conceived and developed. The stories varied but I was always the same character merely repeating myself in different situations. *The Hound* was, as it were, a negative from which I merely continued to reproduce endless positives of the same photograph.'

With the espionage angle exhausted, *Sherlock Holmes Faces Death* (1943) returned to the traditional gothic mystery formula. Thankfully Rathbone went back to his familiar back-combed hairstyle for this one; and Roy William Neill assumed the role of producer, leaving him in full charge of the series. Loosely based on Conan Doyle's *The Musgrave Ritual*, the plot has Holmes and Watson arrive at Musgrave Manor, currently being used as a convalescent home for wounded soldiers – the wartime theme hadn't been completely abandoned. Watson's voluntary work gives Nigel Bruce a chance to show the character's serious side, and the confines of Musgrave Manor provide plenty of atmosphere, with Holmes solving the mystery via a massive chessboard. By reverting to the familiar Victorian trappings, the series works much better, with Rathbone and Bruce looking more at home in spookier surroundings, so the changes were good for all concerned, and the reviews were positive all round.

If *Sherlock Holmes Faces Death* was a step in the right direction, then *Sherlock Holmes vs the Spider Woman* (1943) is the best of the series, with Rathbone giving his finest Holmes performance since *The Hound of the Baskervilles*. The film also boasts one of the character's most convincing disguises – that of distinguished Indian prince Rahjul Khan – but unfortunately he throws in an obnoxious cockney postman for good measure. Nigel Bruce gives his most serious performance as Watson, and even Dennis Hoey's Lestrade is less of a dimwit than before. Abandoning all references to the war, the film benefits from a tight script that borrows elements from several Conan Doyle tales, and Neill's first rate direction doesn't slacken for a minute on suspense, building up to a brilliant climax at a fairground.

Not surprisingly, the film received some of the best reviews of the series. Its success owes a great deal to the excellent performance of Gale Sondergaard as the killer Andrea Spedding, aka the Spider Woman, inspired by Conan Doyle's Irene Adler character. As Hollywood's sinister housekeeper or a femme fatale, Sondergaard was always value for money, and is so good here that it's a shame Universal didn't make use of the character in further films – although she would play Zanobia Dollard in the unrelated *The Spider Woman Strikes Back* (1946). Sondergaard's film career was wrecked by the McCarthy witch-hunt of the '50s; her second husband, writer/director Herbert Biberman, was one of the 'Hollywood 10' who got blacklisted for alleged communist sympathies.

During the making of *Sherlock Holmes vs the Spider Woman*, Rathbone and Bruce made a gag appearance as Holmes and Watson for *Crazy House* (1943), a Universal comedy starring Ole Olsen and Chic Johnson. In their brief scene, Watson queries why everyone is running to the air raid shelter, to which Holmes replies that Olsen and Johnson have arrived. When Watson asks how he knows this, he gets the reply, 'I am Sherlock Holmes. I know everything.' It was meant to be a gag, but there is something unnerving about the punchline that echoed Rathbone's negative feelings toward Holmes. 'Could he not fail just once and prove himself a human being like the rest of us!' he exclaimed in frustration. 'His perpetual seeming assumption of infallibility; his interminable success; his ego that seems to verge on the superman complex.'

Sherlock Holmes vs the Spider Woman was a hard act to follow, and the series slowly experienced the law of diminishing returns, a situation made all the more obvious by Universal adding horror elements with each film. With a few changes, *The Scarlet Claw* (1944) would look no different from a standard Universal chiller. Directed with atmospheric flare by Neill, it is reasonably effective, and if Rathbone was starting to tire of the series, he didn't show it in his performance. 'Everybody involved was very excited about this film,' recalled editor Paul Landres. 'I think it was because we all knew it was far superior to anything else in the series.' Perhaps the commercial and artistic high of *Sherlock Holmes vs the Spider Woman* had given everyone involved a renewed confidence. Critical evaluation of the film was positive, and *The Scarlet Claw* became one of the most popular films in the series.

The high confidence continued with *The Pearl of Death* (1944). Based on Conan Doyle's *The Six Napoleons*, and the last really good film of the series, it is notable for two screen villains on a par with Moriarty and Andrea Spedding. Series regular Miles Mander's low-life killer Giles Conniver is an interestingly ambiguous figure who matches Holmes' own intellectual powers; it's a shame the character was never used again. The other villain comes in the grotesque shape of Rondo Hatton as the Hoxton Creeper. Due to an intake of gas during military service in World War I, Hatton suffered from the terrible condition acromegaly, which distorted his facial features. Universal were quick to tastelessly cast the poor man in a succession of monster roles, which would include reprising his Creeper role in *House of Horrors* (1943) and *The Brute Man* (1946), before the disease claimed him at 51.

Rathbone remains good value in *The Pearl of Death*, donning some excellent disguises, including those of an elderly vicar and a surgeon. He also effectively imitates Mander's voice for one scene. Holmes was still very much in the hearts of his public, but now Rathbone and Bruce were effectively becoming the characters they played.

The resentment had set in for Rathbone as he grew tired of both the film series and the radio shows that were being broadcast at the same time. He appeared in a few non-Holmes films – *Above Suspicion* (1943), *Bathing Beauty* (1944), *Frenchman's Creek* (1944) and *Heartbeat* (1946) – but these weren't enough to keep his creative mind active. 'I think these endless repetitions forced me into a critical analysis of Holmes that was often disturbing and sometimes destructive. Toward the end of my life with him I came to the conclusion that there is nothing lovable about Holmes. He seemed capable of transcending the weakness of a mere mortal such as myself. It would be impossible for such a man to know loneliness or love or sorrow, because he was completely sufficient to himself.

'One was jealous of Holmes. Jealous of his mastery in all things both material and physical. He was a sort of god in his way, seated on some Anglo-Saxon Olympus of his own design and making! Yes, there was no question about it, he had given me an acute inferiority complex!'

Rathbone made every effort to distance himself from Holmes, personally if not professionally. In between films he invariably grew his trademark moustache as a way to assert his own personality. Sadly the treadmill of making one Holmes film after another had exhausted his creative mind. Professionally, Holmes limited his choice of roles and increased his frustration.

Even with the usual atmospheric touches from Roy William Neil, *The House of Fear* (1945) gives a clear indication that the Holmes series was flagging. Rathbone looks tired. Not that his disillusionment ever affected his performance – he remained professional throughout – but by this time he had simply lost his spark.

Woman in Green (1945) continued the downward trend, despite having, in Rathbone's words, 'a delectably dangerous Moriarty in Henry Daniell.' *Pursuit to Algiers* (1945) was pretty much on the same level, with the actor looking uninterested – as he had good reason to be.

Rathbone's frustration with Holmes came to a disagreeable head when he lobbied hard for the role of Mephistophelean Lord Henry Wotton in *The*

Picture of Dorian Gray (1945), a big-budget MGM adaptation of Oscar Wilde's famous novel. He lost out to George Sanders, who went on to give one of his most memorable performances, although it was really just an extension of the familiar cad persona he had created so well on screen. Had Rathbone played the part, especially with the excellent dialogue allotted to Sanders, he could have got Holmes out of his system with an enthusiastic and unforgettable performance. It wasn't to be, and losing out on an excellent role in a high-profile film served as a clear indication to Rathbone that he needed to break away from Holmes.

'When you become the character you play, it is the end of your career.' Rathbone's famous words echoed the resentment all too well. 'My 52 roles in 23 plays of Shakespeare, my years in the London and New York theatre, my scores of motion pictures, including my two Academy Award nominations, were slowly but surely sinking into oblivion. There was nothing I could do about it, except to stop playing Mr Holmes, which I could not owing to the existence of a long-term contract.'

Terror by Night (1946) was at least a cut above the previous film. Being set on a train and obviously inspired by Alfred Hitchcock's *The Lady Vanishes* (1939), the story could move at a faster pace. Even Rathbone himself seemed livelier – and with good reason, as writer David Stuart Davies observes: 'Basil Rathbone had made the momentous decision to say goodbye to Holmes. He had been handcuffed to the character because of long-term contracts with MGM – who loaned him to Universal – and with the Music Corporation of America – with whom he had signed years earlier for the radio series. But by 1946 his contracts were due to expire, and Rathbone decided he was not going to renew them.' It seems the chance to break away from Holmes made the actor's performance in *Terror by Night* all the more enthusiastic, even though there was still one more film left to go.

Dressed to Kill (1946) was a lacklustre entry that brought the series to a quiet but dignified end. The film featured another evil femme fatale, but Patricia Morrison in the role was no match for Gale Sondergaard. Now going through the motions, Rathbone knew he had to move on. But his refusal to sign another contract left Hollywood in a state of shock.

Whereas Sir Arthur Conan Doyle had opted to kill off Holmes with his celebrated death at the Reichenbach Falls, only to resurrect him following a public outcry from angry fans, Rathbone found himself in very different circumstances. 'I could not kill Mr Holmes, so I decided to run away from him. However, to all intents and purposes I might as well have killed him. My friends excoriated me for my dastardly behaviour, and for a while my long-term friendship with Nigel Bruce suffered severe and recurring shocks. The Music Corporation of America, who represented me at the time, treated me as if I were sick.'

The friendship between Rathbone and Bruce was never the same again.

Being a jobbing actor unconcerned about typecasting, Bruce would have been quite happy to continue playing Watson on film. This being denied him, he carried on playing the good doctor on radio, with Tom Conway taking over as Holmes. But despite Conway's sterling work, his performance was greeted with public indifference, and the show lasted only two more seasons before finally getting cancelled in 1947.

Rathbone had grown tired of filmmaking altogether. 'I had accomplished as much as was coming to me in motion pictures at that time. Los Angeles had become a very cosmopolitan city during the war, and our war work had been most stimulating for us both. Without it, and no longer meeting continuously with interesting people from all over the world, we felt the community would slip back into a conventional pattern that might prove to be a tremendous letdown.'

Despite protests from close friends, and seven old Cynthia, who was 'deeply upset about leaving her home,' Rathbone was adamant. 'It wasn't instinct but just luck that we decided to return to New York in June 1946. Most of our friends considered us mad and pleaded with us not to throw away my career and home. I needed another springboard in order to return successfully. I had had seven years of Sherlock Holmes and was not only tired and bored with the series but felt myself losing ground in other fields of endeavour. I was literally aching to get back to my first love, the theatre.'

Friends and colleagues still harboured hopes that Rathbone would change his mind. 'It was in August 1946, that Jules [Stein] phoned me in Philadelphia, where I was appearing in a play and headed for a New York opening. A new seven-year Sherlock Holmes radio contract had been negotiated by MCA. Was I about ready to return to the Coast? The climax was reached in a long distance telephone call from Jules in Los Angeles – *No!* I was not coming back. I had sold my house in Bel Air and was heading to the Plymouth Theatre in New York.'

For Rathbone, there was no turning back, but as hard as he tried, putting Holmes behind would not be easy, and the character would remain a part of his persona. 'Ever since I said goodbye to Mr Sherlock Holmes,' he admitted, 'there has lingered somewhere inside of me a sentimental attachment for this character.' Over the next decade, however, that sentiment would evaporate in the face of increasing frustration and bitterness.

Rathbone returned to the stage with *Obsession*, a character drama rewritten and modernised by Ouida. 'We met with considerable success to begin with,' he said, 'but as the very hot summer developed we were less successful as we toured the Middle West. Coming to the Plymouth Theatre in New York in September of 1946, we received mixed reviews and managed to run only three weeks. In spite of Ouida's work on the play it was generally considered too old-fashioned and audiences were not particularly interested. Had we brought the play into New York at the end of the season we might have got away with it.'

The Rathbones bought an apartment overlooking the East River. Unfortunately further theatre roles were not forthcoming. 'I could not find a play or anyone willing to consider me for one. One well-known playwright came to see me. I wanted to do his play about King David. There was no question he wanted me. But the producer decided against it because of my seven-year identification with Sherlock Holmes. They felt this identification would be a hazard to them.'

By the end of 1946, Rathbone's output was limited to radio guest spots. The following year he starred in the radio series *Scotland Yard* as Inspector Burke, a policeman with an obvious Holmesian bent – the Great Detective would not go away.

Salvation came the following year when producer Jed Harris offered Rathbone the role of Dr Austin Sloper in a Broadway production of *The Heiress*, an adaptation by Augustus Goertz of the Henry James novel *Washington Square*. 'I shall be ever grateful to Jules Stein, his acceptance of my decision [to quit Holmes] and his most generous attentions to my wellbeing on my return to New York, which eventualised in a contract he made for me in 1947 to appear as Dr Sloper.

'I read the play and loved it. Then I gave it to Ouida, and for one of the few times in our lives, we did not agree. I have never been able to pinpoint her reasons. Leading man or villain, my roles previously, in all media, had a certain amount of glamour. Dr Sloper was in his late fifties, a difficult, complex man, and as with all doctors of his time, he wore a beard!'

Selling both their Hollywood home and their New York apartment, the couple bought a new house, and while Rathbone was in rehearsals, Ouida carried out the costly renovations in her usual extravagant style. 'Our furniture and effects were transported from California across the country by road. One day two colossal vans arrived at our front door, and the bill was back-breaking. It was essential that *The Heiress* be a success.'

The play opened in September 1947 at the Baltimore Theatre to tremendous success – although it very nearly had to close on its opening night after Rathbone, while walking his dogs, suffered a blackout, breaking his wrist in the process. Having been rushed to hospital to get his hand fixed, he actually played his part while still under the effects of the anaesthetic!

Undeterred, Rathbone continued, and the successful New York run of *The Heiress* was followed by an equally successful year-long tour. The play ran on Broadway for three years, and Rathbone's critically acclaimed performance won him the Tony Award for Best Actor.

But then the curse of Holmes reared its ugly head once more. Rathbone lobbied hard for the role of Dr Sloper in the 1949 film version of the play, which would have reunited him with Olivia de Havilland. This time he lost out to Sir Ralph Richardson, whose performance in the finished film is merely adequate; had Rathbone got the part, it would surely have been all the better, both for his incisive manner and for his knowledge of the role. Not surprisingly, Rathbone blamed Holmes once more for his failure to secure a high-profile part.

1949 was however the year the actor made his first known television appearances, for the *Ford Theatre Hour* and *The Chevrolet Tele-Theatre*. He also lent his voice as narrator to *The Wind in the Willows* segment of Disney's *The Adventures of Ichabod and Mr Toad* (1949).

After *The Heiress* closed, Rathbone began the new decade touring America with an acclaimed one-man show, *An Evening with Basil Rathbone*. There were also several television drama anthologies that kept him busy throughout 1950-51, which included a return to the horror genre as the title character(s) of *Dr Jekyll and Mr Hyde* in a television adaptation for the popular CBS thriller series *Suspense*. Then, toward the end of 1951, and in an amazing change of mind, Rathbone suggested to his wife an idea for bringing Holmes back on Broadway.

After discussing the idea closely with her husband, Ouida agreed to write a play based on five classic Holmes stories while he was away touring. As a major Broadway production starring the definitive big-screen Holmes, it looked certain to succeed. Rathbone may have been 61 years old, but he still looked fit enough to tackle the role once more. Ouida even invited Sir Arthur Conan Doyle's youngest son Adrian over to their home for advice and approval. 'We met with him and his charming Dutch wife and they were most enthusiastic about the play,' said Rathbone. 'Adrian told us he was sure it would have had his father's approval. It pleased him that his father and mine had known each other in South Africa.'

With Adrian Conan Doyle's support, the script was presented to several producers before being accepted by Bill Doll, who, in Rathbone's words, 'read the play and fell for it hook, line and sinker.' With the Rathbones putting up a $25,000 share, generously provided by close friends, Stewart Chaney constructed the sets and Reginald Denham took on the directorial duties. Rehearsals were followed by a three-week try-out at the Schubert Theatre in Boston before the play made its Broadway debut. This was a shrewd move, as there was plenty of support from the Boston chapter of the Sherlock Holmes aficionado group the Baker Street Irregulars.

There was another, more personal reason for Rathbone wanting to return to Holmes: he saw it as a way to smooth things over with his old friend Nigel Bruce, who was also scheduled to return as Dr Watson. Unfortunately, though, Bruce suffered a stroke before rehearsals began and was unable to take part. The role went to Jack Rains instead.

During preparations for the play, Rathbone received an offer to play Holmes on television, in another episode of *Suspense*. In addition to helping

Ouida with the play, Adrian Conan Doyle adapted his story *The Adventures of the Black Baronet* for the episode. He wanted Rathbone to play Holmes with the hope that a television series might be forthcoming. Nigel Bruce's poor health again prevented him from taking part, so British stage actor Martyn Green took over as Watson. There is no known recording of the episode in existence, but it would seem that the critical evaluation was negative. The *New York Times* felt, 'Mr Rathbone did not seem too happy with a part with which he could never really come to grips.' Plans for a further six Holmes adaptations starring Rathbone failed to come to fruition.

Ouida's play turned out to be beset by problems, as Rathbone sadly recalled: 'The first warning that all was not well came when I went down to the Schubert Theatre in Boston. There was no line-up at the box office, only desultory buying.' The first dress rehearsal was a disaster. The stage manager suffered a heart attack; the stage crew turned out to be hopeless; and tempers quickly frayed. The opening night was worse for poor Rathbone. 'Shattered with nerves and tiredness, I blew up badly in the very first scene! I never quite recovered, and gave a hesitant performance.

'Business in Boston had been bad, very bad,' Rathbone added. 'Even the reviews had not helped us much. As the star of the play, in a character I was so indelibly associated with, I was aware of an added burden of responsibility.'

The play finally opened at the Majestic Theatre, New York on 10 October 1953, but the omens were bad, as Rathbone observed. 'The opening night in New York had seemed listless, and only modest applause had greeted our efforts.

'Try as I would, my heart was not really in it. I hoped to be carried by the volume of public opinion that had supported me enthusiastically from 1939 to 1946. But this was 1953. Seven years had passed, we were seven years too late! I believe it possible that had I returned to New York from the West Coast in this play in 1947 the results might have been very different.'

Rathbone's dejection was exacerbated by the death of Nigel Bruce two days prior to the Broadway opening. 'We had been close personal friends for many years,' he commented sadly, 'and his sudden death in 1953 was a painful shock to all of us who had experienced him with great joy with his Elizabethan humour.'

But still, he had a play to perform in and had to take the brunt of this impending disaster. 'It was up to me to be the optimist, until the curtain dropped with a sickening thud on the opening night in New York.' With bad reviews, the play's run finally ended on a sour note. 'The notice was on the board as I went to my dressing room for the matinee. We were closing after three performances.'

Rathbone's last word on Holmes was given in February 1955 to columnist Aline Mosby: 'Youngsters are hooked on the subject of sex, and there's no sex in Sherlock Holmes. That, combined with their desire for blood and thunder stories, has killed Holmes. I will never play him again.

'Dated, that's the word,' he added. 'The Sherlock Holmes stories are dated and their pattern and style, generally speaking, unacceptable to an age where science has proven that science fiction is another outdated joke. The only possible medium still available to an acceptable present-day presentation of Sir Arthur Conan Doyle's stories would be a full-length Disney cartoon.'

Despite Rathbone's blunt words, he did make one final television appearance as Holmes, in an edition of *The Milton Berle Show*. And, of course, Holmes could never really die. 1955 saw the first full television series of Holmes adventures, starring Ronald Howard. Howard's young-looking and rather laid back Holmes spends a great deal of time slouching with his hands in his pockets. 'In my interpretation,' he said, 'Holmes is not an infallible, eagle-eyed, out-of-the-ordinary personality, but an exceptionally sincere young man trying to get ahead in his profession.' Rathbone was far from happy with Howard's interpretation. 'All I can say is, I think he's too young for the role. I never thought of Holmes being too young.' Although it was very successful when originally shown, time has not been kind to the series. The 39 episodes vary in merit from interesting to dire. The speed with which they were made also took its toll on Howard. 'You must realise,' he said, 'we were churning these films out at a rate of one every four days; it was really breakneck speed. It was a terribly concentrated effort to keep going at all. After about six months I was becoming deadbeat. There was scarcely time to learn the lines.'

That first series may have faded into obscurity, but the Great Detective has continued to be depicted in film and television in one form or another. And just when it seemed that the definitive Jeremy Brett-starring ITV series of the 1980s and 1990s had taken Homes and Watson as far as they could go, in the 21st Century Robert Downey Jnr and Ian McKellen (for the cinema), and Benedict Cumberbatch and Johnny Lee Miller (on television) have managed to make their adventures as fresh and exciting as they were in Rathbone's day.

Throughout the '50s Rathbone concentrated on the theatre. *The Heiress* was his last big Broadway production, and although he worked steadily, the less rewarding roles were limited to off-Broadway, summer stock and vaudeville productions. He was also earning less money, and with Ouida continually spending his weekly pay cheque, he had to go on working to make ends meet.

He remained busy on radio, and narrated the works of Nathaniel Hawthorn, Edgar Allan Poe and Sir Arthur Conan Doyle for several spoken word recordings. His work in this capacity on the Sherlock Holmes novels confused many fans, because he actually played Dr Watson!

Rathbone also continued to appear on television, acting in drama anthologies for *The Broadway Television Theatre* and *The Lux Video Theatre*. His output included four different versions of Charles Dickens' *A Christmas Carol*. The first two were adapted in 1954 and 1956 for the television series *Shower of Stars* and had Rathbone playing Jacob Marley. 1956 saw another adaptation for *The Alcoa Hour*, entitled *The Stingiest Man in Town*, with Rathbone as Ebenezer Scrooge. He repeated this role two years later for the series *Tales of Dickens*. Away from Dickens, he appeared in an episode of *The Science Fiction Theatre* in 1955 and acted as compere on the CBS television game show *Your Lucky Clue*.

Having moved to another New York apartment in 1954, Rathbone returned to films with the Bob Hope comedy *Casanova's Big Night* (1954). As Casanova's disgruntled butler Lucio, he has a reasonable amount of screen time. But things flag early on, and Hope's performance clearly strains as he delivers some mistimed gags.

Rathbone's next film was *We're No Angels* (1955), starring Humphrey Bogart, Peter Ustinov and Aldo Ray as three Devil's Island convicts who escape and hide out in a nearby store owned by a family who take them in. The convicts repay the family's kindness by disposing of their nasty landlord Andre Trochard, played with customary relish by Rathbone. It's a broad, agreeably performed but forgettable movie.

More satisfactory was Rathbone's return to swashbuckling action with the enjoyable Danny Kaye medieval comedy *The Court Jester* (1955). Playing the evil Sir Ravenhurst, Rathbone enjoyed working with Kaye. 'There is one actor whose exceptional talents have always made a deep impression. Danny's success does not lie alone in his natural God-given talents but in a quality that few beginners seem to realise is probably a determining factor in any successful career, *work*! He has an indefinable quality we all call "class".'

Rathbone also got the chance to return to sword-fighting once more in an effective duelling scene with Kaye. Despite being in his sixties, he was as fit and athletic as ever, and found a worthy opponent in Kaye. 'Our instructor was Ralph Faulkner,' noted Rathbone, 'a very well known swordsman on the coast, who had specialised in the sabre. After a couple of weeks of instruction, Danny could completely outfight me!'

But despite these impressive film appearances, Rathbone found himself increasingly out of favour. Hollywood was undergoing radical changes at this time, with the arrival of new-wave filmmakers, mostly from television, and kitchen sink drama gaining favour over period drama. There was also a new acting style inspired by Lee Strasberg called 'the Method,' as exemplified on film by Marlon Brando in *On The Waterfront* (1954) and James Dean in *Rebel Without a Cause* (1955).

Rathbone's classical style became redundant in the face of these changes. 'He had been a great Shakespearean actor,' observed Vincent Price, who faced the same problem, 'a great star in the theatre and movies. And he suddenly found himself [outdated] – as we all did when Jimmy Dean and Marlon Brando and those people came out, and there was a kind of speaking in the vernacular. And all of us spoke with trained accents and trained English, and theatrically we were different in our approach to acting – that if you wanted to stay in the business, you bloody well went into costumes pictures.'

But there was still a demand for classical actors in another genre: horror! Hammer had successfully spearheaded a cinematic revival, and with the classic Universal chillers being screened on television, low-budget American film producers were quick to hire the surviving horror veterans. Rathbone had been only a part-time horror star, but it was enough to get him the starring role as Victorian scientist Sir Joel Cadman in *The Black Sleep* (1956), a mundane affair directed by Reginald Le Borg and featuring Bela Lugosi, Lon Chaney Jnr and John Carradine, whose presence added gravity to a chiller that would have looked more at home as a '40s second feature. And despite these stellar names, only Rathbone emerges from this dull chiller with any credit. He gives a credible performance as a scientist whose attempts to find a cure for his catatonic wife leave him up to his neck with mad mutants, including one played by Edward D Wood Jnr regular Tor Johnson. Lugosi and Chaney are cast as mutes, while Carradine turns up toward the end as a patient who thinks he's Bohemund of Antioch!

Shot in 12 days for $400,000, *The Black Sleep* grossed $1,600,000 at the box office. If there was one good thing to come from it apart from this profit, it was that the very frail Lugosi patching up his (real or imagined) differences with Rathbone. Although it enabled him to make some fast money, Rathbone had scant regard for the film. He refused to join Lugosi, Chaney, Carradine and Tor Johnson in a promotional tour across America; instead he remained in New York, where he continued his television and theatre work.

In between his various acting commitments, Rathbone found a great deal of satisfaction touring colleges across America, giving recitals and lectures on Shakespeare. He felt students unfamiliar with the Bard learnt a great deal, and he enjoyed the positive response he got from his young and appreciative audience.

It was only a matter of time before the stress, overwork and financial responsibilities took their toll on Rathbone's health. In 1957 he collapsed during an American tour of *Witness for the Prosecution*. He recovered after a week and returned to the tour, being well aware he could not afford to take a break. Keeping up the workload, he also returned to film with *The Last Hurrah* (1958), a well-received political drama that was an improvement on *The Black Sleep*. His role was secondary, but at least he was part of an excellent ensemble cast that included Spencer Tracy, Jeffrey Hunter, Donald Crisp and John Carradine.

Rathbone next received an offer to appear in a play entitled *J.B.*. This had a biblical theme akin to that he had previously dabbled with during his own brief spell as a playwright. 'From *Judas* in January 1929 to my association with Archibald MacLeish's *J.B.* in May 1959 is a leap of thirty years,' observed the actor. 'I became involved in *J.B.* for somewhat the same reasons that impelled me toward my collaboration in the writing of *Judas* and my playing of the name part.' *J.B.* had already had a successful New York run in November 1958, and producer Alfred Liagre offered Rathbone the part of Nickles. However, director Elia Kazan wanted to make a major change. According to Rathbone, 'He contended that the part of Nickles should be played by a younger man who should be something of a beatnik.' Kazan won out and replaced Rathbone with Christopher Plummer, who, in Rathbone's words, 'gave a very exciting and completely convincing performance.'

So it was back to arduous summer stock theatre for Rathbone, with a production of *Dark Angel*. Unfortunately the hot weather took its toll on the actor, who found touring exhausting. 'A new play like *Dark Angel* presented added problems,' he noted. 'Summer audiences are hesitant to support an unknown property.' Not surprisingly, *Dark Angel* closed after a few weeks, leaving Rathbone looking for further stage roles.

Luckily the producers of *J.B.* then changed their minds and offered Rathbone another role in the play, as a man named Zuss. Joining the production in May 1959, he played the part for the next ten weeks. 'During this period,' he said, 'Christopher Plummer would sit with me in my dressing room during intermissions and tactfully and most stimulatingly endeavour to help me in the development of my performance. It was hard work, because Mr Zuss and I had nothing in common. I even came to dislike him!'

By August 1959, Plummer had left the production, and Rathbone stepped in as Nickles, the role he had been originally offered. 'I had watched Chris closely for weeks and had studied the part carefully at home. Nickles I found tremendously stimulating. The tour of *J.B.* was a tremendous success. In Boston at the Colonial Theatre we broke the house record.'

Unfortunately Rathbone's health suffered another terrible setback during a sold out performance at the Hartman Theatre in Columbus, Ohio in January 1960. That morning he had felt extremely dizzy. 'I ate a light breakfast and struggled to pull myself together,' he recalled. 'I proceeded to the Hartman Theatre feeling despondent and ill. The dizziness recurred at intervals.' His performance that night turned out to be a struggle. 'As the second act progressed, I became more and more unsteady on my legs. During the last few minutes of the play I was holding on desperately; my knees were going to give way and I was afraid of falling.'

Once the curtain went down, Rathbone was promptly escorted to an ambulance – he had suffered a heart attack. Once again, after just a week's convalescence, he went back to the play.

Rathbone returned to swashbuckling adventure in *The Magic Sword* (1962), a cheesy low-budget effort from director Bert I Gordon that had the actor top billed as evil sorcerer Lodac. The film is fun, despite its poor special effects, bad acting and intrusive American accents. Next came a trip to Italy to play Caiaphas in *Pontius Pilate* (1962), a typical sword-and-sandal epic but for the fact that it features the interesting idea of John Drew Barrymore playing both Jesus and Judas in the same narrative. Both these films were a comedown compared with Rathbone's earlier work in the same genres.

In 1962 Rathbone published his memoirs, *In and Out of Character*. Although this was a brilliantly-written book full of funny anecdotes about his early life, war years and illustrious stage and screen career, he devoted too much of it to writing about his undying love for Ouida. The sales were only modest; the public were apparently more interested in sleazy books about scandal than in pleasant ones containing funny stories and romantic musings.

The early '60s marked a permanent revival of Rathbone's film career. After many years of producing cheap science fiction films, American International Pictures (AIP), under the leadership of Samuel Z Arkoff and James H Nicholson, gambled on a £300,000 horror production called *The Fall of the House of Usher* (1960). The film's success prompted a series of gothic chillers based on the short stories of Edgar Allan Poe. These films, directed by Roger Corman, established Vincent Price as the new king of American horror.

Apart from Price's chest-thumping melodramatic ham, *The Fall of the House of Usher* and *The Pit and the Pendulum* (1961) suffered from weak casts. James H Nicholson decided to improve things by giving Price the kind of reliable back up previously denied him. Rathbone, Boris Karloff and Peter Lorre were signed up to star alongside Price in several chillers, giving them all one final burst of film stardom.

Rathbone marked his return to horror with the Poe anthology *Tales of Terror* (1962). Appearing in the final tale, 'The Facts in the Case of M Valdmar', he gives an excellent performance as Carmichael, a reptilian mesmerist who puts his patient Valdmar (Price) into a deep sleep so he can get his hands on the poor man's wife. This being a horror film, Carmichael meets a nasty end at the hands of a melting Valdmar! Price stars in all three tales, but despite being in fine form, he's upstaged by Peter Lorre (in the second tale, *The Black Cat*) and Rathbone, who is commanding throughout his appearance.

Ever since Rathbone's Richard III had drunkenly dispatched Price's Duke of Clarence in *The Tower of London* all those years before, the actors had remained good friends who enjoyed working together. 'Basil was an intelligent person and a brilliant actor,' Price recalled. 'He was rather unhappy toward the end of his life about having been stuck in the Sherlock Holmes pictures. He had been a great Shakespearean actor in the theatre, but most people thought of him as Holmes or as a villain.'

Tales of Terror did good business, grossing $1.5 million on its initial release. The box office takings were down from the previous films, but it was still a decent return for all concerned. More importantly it helped increase Rathbone's profile, even if it was limited to the horror genre.

Rathbone continued the horror phase of his career with *The Comedy of Terrors* (1963), an uneven but thoroughly enjoyable movie, which again cast him alongside Vincent Price, Peter Lorre and Boris Karloff. Karloff was due to play Shakespeare-spouting landlord John F Black, but the physical demands of the action prompted him to swap roles with Rathbone, who gives an energetic and amusing performance. When Black is killed off by his impoverished tenant Waldo Trumbull (Price), he refuses to stay dead and periodically turns up at inopportune moments. Despite being in his seventies, Rathbone performed his own stunts with the skill of a much younger man.

'The premise for *The Comedy of Terrors* was really very funny,' said Price. 'It shows you how simple comedy is. It's about a family of out-of-work undertakers. Now what do you do? You kill somebody! So you kill the richest man in town – who was played by Basil – and you have the most expensive funeral. That's all the plot was.'

'Working on *The Comedy of Terrors* was a lot of fun,' said Richard Matheson, who wrote the screenplay. '[Rathbone, Price, Lorre and Karloff] were all very charming, marvellous people, and it was really a delightful experience just talking with them on the set. They loved doing the film.'

It was a view shared by Vincent Price. 'They were all divine people, with great senses of humour. We used to sit around and say very seriously [of the audience], "How can we scare the little bastards!" We had a wonderful time.'

They may be a long way from Rathbone's early Hollywood classics, but *Tales of Terror* and *The Comedy of Terrors* are enjoyable efforts. The warm, happy atmosphere, the consummate professionalism and the working relationship Rathbone enjoyed with his co-stars added up to a positive experience for him – although Lorre did rub him up the wrong way on numerous occasions. 'Peter always threw out little shockers for him,' recalled Lorre's agent Lester Salkow, 'which he didn't realise were for him. "For a while it was very tough making films in Germany," said Peter. "Of course, after Hitler came to power, may he rest in peace."' The remark deeply offended Rathbone, who stormed off the set in disgust.

Unfortunately *The Comedy of Terrors* did poor business at the box office when it opened in December 1963. President John F Kennedy had just been assassinated the previous month, and American audiences were in no mood for laughing at death. The fact that Rathbone's character was called *John F Black* turned out to be an unhappy coincidence.

Rathbone was also unhappy at being labelled a horror star, but financial necessity and being too old for mainstream tastes left him with no choice but to make these films. 'I still felt that he was playing other kinds of roles a bit,' said Sam Arkoff. 'My guess is that he was doing horror films for the money, not because he really loved it. I always had a feeling about Basil that he would just as soon have been in a different kind of picture.'

Unfortunately *Tales of Terror* and *The Comedy of Terrors* were Rathbone's last really notable efforts. He rounded off his film career with a slew of worthless tripe. *Voyage to the Prehistoric Planet* (1965), *Queen of Blood* (1966), *The Ghost in the Invisible Bikini* (1966), *Hillbillies in a Haunted House* (1967) and *Autopsia de un Fantasma (Autopsy of a Ghost)* (1968) are all unworthy of such a great man. The last two are especially bad. *Hillbillies in a Haunted Hose*, a showcase for a third-rate country music band, has a frail, embarrassed looking Rathbone as a spy alongside a bemused John Carradine and a drunk Lon Chaney Jnr. *Autopsia de un Fantasma* is even worse, with Rathbone donning a hippie wig opposite Carradine's comic-book Satan. The actor was clearly at the end of his tether when he appeared in this trash.

At least television offered more rewarding roles. As the Duke of York in the NBC TV drama *A Soldier in Love*, Rathbone gave his last memorable performance. The rest of his time was taken up touring America with his one-man show and his various college lectures.

In 1967 Rathbone received an offer from the BBC to return to England and reprise the role of Sherlock Holmes in a new series of radio adaptations. Ever since the Broadway fiasco he had stayed firmly away from the character. Now he felt the time was right to give it one more go. It had been many years since he last played Holmes, and with his confidence dented by his last few film appearances, he was unsure if he could carry it off. To get the encouragement he needed, he contacted Anthony Howlett, president of the Sherlock Holmes Society of London.

'Rathbone had this idea of reviving Holmes, but admitted he was far too old to do it on film,' Howlett recalled from the various letters and phone calls he received from the actor. 'He wanted to do a different approach from the American radio plays, and the BBC offered that. Plus his wife Ouida used to spend money like water and he was probably a bit hard up.'

Rathbone's return to London also brought the welcome prospect of some decent film work in *The Blood Beast Terror* (1967). This would be a step up in quality from his previous horror movies and, as a British period chiller, would perfectly suit his impeccable Shakespearean delivery. The actor was extremely enthusiastic about the film and signed up in early July 1967, specifying requirements for costumes and expressing hope that there would no last-minute script changes. Ever the perfectionist, Rathbone said of his preparations for the film, 'I like to get the part under my belt, as I find it difficult to unlearn.'

Rathbone's renewed enthusiasm may have had something to do with the fact that the project offered him an opportunity to work alongside another actor who had portrayed Holmes, namely Peter Cushing. Rathbone's role as Professor Mallinger, inspired by that of Sir Joel Cadman in his earlier film *The Black Sleep*, was standard mad scientist stuff. Cushing, as the Holmes-inspired Scotland Yard officer Inspector Quennell, had the more interesting part (and this would be the only time he played a policeman on film).

There were many similarities between Rathbone and Cushing. Both men were classically-trained actors with very distinctive features that made them ideal for playing Holmes. (Cushing loved the role and regretted not getting the chance to play the Great Detective more often.) Both had family members who had performed with Sir Henry Irving. Both had had administrative jobs before starting their acting careers at the bottom. Both had been exceptional sportsmen with little time for academic pursuits. Both had worked extensively on the Shakespearean stage. And Cushing was as devoted to his wife Helen as Rathbone was to his beloved Ouida.

Sadly film fans never got to see this historic teaming of the two great Sherlocks. On 21 July 1967, Rathbone returned to New York after completing a tour of his one-man show. His doctor gave him the all-clear for his flight to England. Back in his apartment, he played a record he had just bought on his gramophone, and while quietly listening to the music suffered a fatal heart attack, only two weeks before production on *The Blood Beast Terror* was due to begin. He was 75 years old.

With Robert Fleming replacing Rathbone, *The Blood Beast Terror* was a box office hit. 'Production was over in three weeks,' said Fleming. 'It was a "quickie" but it was quite successful. I think we were in it for the money!' Cushing himself said it was his worst ever movie. However, had Rathbone lived long enough to star in it, it might have led to better acting roles for him in higher quality British horror films.

Devoutly Catholic, Rathbone was given a funeral at the St Jane Episcopal Church in New York. His body is interred in a crypt in the Shrine of Memories Mausoleum at Ferncliff Cemetery, Hatsdale, New York.

Rathbone's estate totalled $20,000, which he left to Ouida, Rodion and Cynthia. It was a paltry sum considering his past earning power in Hollywood. Ouida's knack for spending everything had finally caught up with her.

And worse was yet to come. Cynthia, who after leaving convent school had become an art buyer and consultant for Hockaday Associates in New York, never got over her father's death, and she herself died suddenly in

1969, following a short illness, at the age of only 30.

Ouida Rathbone lived her final years in dire poverty. Such was her financial distress that close friends took a collection on her behalf. Now close to blindness and suffering from complications following a broken hip, she died on 29 September 1974. She is buried beside her husband.

Rodion died in 1996.

Rathbone once said, 'Never regret anything you have done with a sincere affection: nothing is lost that is born of the heart.' However, that statement is contradicted by the fall-out from his association with Holmes. Rathbone had the kind of acting career many could only dream of, but the Great Detective's presence eroded everything he had achieved, and eventually it all evaporated because of that one fictional character's refusal to go away.

But the curse of Holmes was only part of the story. The decline of Rathbone's fortunes was just as much due to major changes in film and theatre that signified the end of the classical actor. With his advancing years, he was unable to adapt to those changes, so his career ended with routine stage roles and bad movies. It comes as no surprise that he spent his final years feeling bitter about his decline.

And yet Holmes carries on living, in the hearts and minds of the public as well as on television and in the cinema. Among the many other actors who have played Holmes since 1946, it appears that only Jeremy Brett has encountered problems with the character. Brett researched the role extensively, but the dark, depressive nature of Holmes seems to have affected his own mindset, and before long mental illness took hold, contributing to an early death in September 1995.

But as brilliant as Brett was, Basil Rathbone remains the definitive Sherlock Holmes, as well as being the most stylish of horror villains. Playing every role with total conviction, he was a one-of-a-kind actor and a man of unique qualities.

Basil Rathbone Filmography

Innocent (1921), *The Fruitful Vine* (1921), *The Loves of Mary, Queen of Scots* (1923), *The School for Scandal* (1923), *Trooping with Ellen* (1924), *The Masked Bride* (1925), *The Great Deception* (1926), *The Last of Mrs Cheyney* (1929), *Barnum was Right* (1929), *The Bishop Murder Case* (1930), *A Notorious Affair* (1930), *The High Road* (1930), *This Mad World* (1930), *The Flirting Widow* (1930), *Blind Wives* (1930), *Sin Takes a Holiday* (1930), *Once a Lady* (1931), *A Woman Commands* (1932), *After the Ball* (1932), *One Precious Year* (1933), *Loyalties* (1933), *David Copperfield* (1935), *Anna Karenina* (1935), *The Last Days of Pompeii* (1935), *A Feather in Her Hat* (1935), *Captain Blood* (1935), *A Tale of Two Cities* (1935), *House of Menace* (1936), *Secret Interlude* (1936), *Romeo and Juliet* (1936), *The Garden of Allah* (1936), *Confession* (1937), *Love From a Stranger* (1937), *Make a Wish* (1937), *Tovarich* (1937), *The Adventures of Marco Polo* (1938), *The Adventures of Robin Hood* (1938), *If I Were King* (1938), *The Dawn Patrol* (1938), *Son of Frankenstein* (1939), *The Hound of the Baskervilles* (1939), *The Sun Never Sets* (1939), *The Adventures of Sherlock Holmes* (1939), *Rio* (1939), *Tower of London* (1939), *Rhythm on the River* (1940), *The Mark of Zorro* (1940), *The Mad Doctor* (1940), *The Black Cat* (1941), *International Lady* (1941), *Paris Calling* (1941), *Fingers at the Windows* (1942), *Crossroads* (1942), *Sherlock Holmes and the Voice of Terror* (1942), *Sherlock Holmes and the Secret Weapon* (1942), *Sherlock Holmes in Washington* (1943), *Crazy House* (1943), *Above Suspicion* (1943), *Sherlock Holmes Faces Death* (1943), *Sherlock Holmes and the Spider Woman* (1943), *Sherlock Holmes and the Scarlet Claw* (1944), *Bathing Beauty* (1944), *Sherlock Holmes and the Pearl of Death* (1944), *Frenchman's Creek* (1944), *Sherlock Holmes and the House of Fear* (1945), *Sherlock Holmes and the Woman in Green* (1945), *Sherlock Holmes and the Pursuit to Algiers* (1945), *Sherlock Holmes and the Terror by Night* (1946), *Heartbeat* (1946), *Sherlock Holmes and the Secret Code* (1946), *The Adventure of Ichabod and Mr Toad* (narrator only) (1949), *Casanova's Big Night* (1953), *We're No Angels* (1955), *The Court Jester* (1955), *The Black Sleep* (1956), *The Last Hurrah* (1958), *The Magic Sword* (1961), *Pontius Pilate* (1961), *Red Hell* (1962), *Two Before Zero* (narrator only) (1962), *Tales of Terror* (1962), *The Comedy of Terrors* (1963), *Queen of Blood* (1966), *Ghost in the Invisible Bikini* (1966), *Voyage to the Prehistoric Planet* (1967), *Dr Rock & Mr Roll* (1967), *Autopsy of a Ghost* (1967), *Hillbillies in a Haunted House* (1968).

The Curse Of M
(Morphine, Money And Misuse):
Peter Lorre

'That picture M has haunted me everywhere I've gone.' – Peter Lorre

In 1931 director Fritz Lang began work on a controversial new film. Controversial because its central character was based on a recently apprehended serial killer who had terrorised the streets of Dusseldorf. Searching for an actor to play fictional child killer Hans Beckett, Lang set his sights on a talented but strange-looking young man who had become the toast of the Berlin stage. Adamant that this unique individual should be his

115

star, Lang persuaded him to turn down all other film offers.

The actor in question was Peter Lorre, and his disturbing performance in Lang's thriller *M* (1932) brought stardom, critical acclaim and notoriety in equal measures. 'I was a murderer,' he recalled, 'but I was also a star.' Even when Lorre later achieved Hollywood success, Hans Beckett proved impossible to shake off. 'People just demand it over and over again. That picture *M* has haunted me everywhere I've gone.'

So began the curse of *M*.

Lorre was born Laszlo Loewenstein on 26 June 1904 in Rozsahegy (now Ruzomberok), a small Austro-Hungarian (now Slovakian) town situated on a high plateau of the Carpathian Mountains, not far from the Transylvanian Alps. The Loewenstein family originally came from the city of Arad. The centre of Hungary's economic stability, Arad's railway junction provided a lucrative transport system for importing and exporting goods. With the countryside used for agricultural production, the discovery of gold, silver and copper established a wealthy mining industry.

Thanks to the railway link, 40,000 people lived in Arad at the start of the 20th Century, among them Lorre's father, an office worker and assistant rabbi named Alajos Loewenstein. Born in Csene, Hungary in 1877, he moved to Arad to work as a bookkeeper following graduation from a business academy in 1897.

Loewenstein's devotion to Emperor Franz Joseph of Austria prompted him to join a volunteer infantry regiment in 1897. Rising to the rank of field sergeant, he received a commission to second lieutenant in 1901. The threat of war with Russia prompted heavy investment in the military by the Austro-Hungarian government. Because Loewenstein spoke German and Hungarian, his standing as a reserve officer increased.

While carrying out military manoeuvers in Grosswardein, Loewenstein met Elvira Freischberger. They married on 8 September 1903, and the following year they moved to Roszahegy, where Laszlo came into the world. His brother Ferenc (later Francis) was born in 1906 and Andras (Andrew) in 1908. Shortly after the birth of Andrew, Elvira died from blood poisoning.

Loewenstein later married Elvira's best friend, Melanie Klein. They had two more children, daughter Liesl and son Hugo. With Loewenstein constantly away on manoeuvers, Melanie brought the children up single-handedly.

In his later years, Lorre related that he had had a strained relationship with his stepmother. He reportedly said that Melanie never forgave him for hiding under the bed when they first met. Although his brothers accepted Melanie as a disciplined but loving mother who treated them equally, Laszlo kept his distance. 'He never joined in any play,' according to Francis's daughter Kathy, 'and never helped with the household chores.' The rebellious Laszlo usually stayed in his room painting watercolours.

In 1910 the family moved to Braila, a bustling harbour town situated near the Danube River, where Alajos took up the position of inspector at the Textil Industrie Akteingesellschaft. Unrest in Europe and the start of the Second Balkan War in August 1913 then prompted a move to Vienna, where they stayed with family friend Oskar Taussig.

With the outbreak of World War I, the newly promoted Lieutenant Loewenstein got posted to the Eastern Front with the Third Army. Following bitter fighting against Russian forces in the Carpathians during the winter of 1915, Loewenstein, who converted to Catholicism, got pulled out of active duty because of heart problems and was placed in charge of a Russian prisoner-of-war camp.

In March 1915, shortly after Alajos left the army, the family moved to Moeadling, a fashionable rural community village ten miles south of Vienna. He had acquired three thousand acres of farmland near to the Sava River in Carinthia. It was an ideal existence for the boys, as they helped with the farming chores and furthered their equestrian skills by horse-riding regularly. Young Laszlo regarded this period of his life as 'the nicest time of our youth.'

Alajos's estate became part of the Kingdom of the Serbs, Croats and Slovenes (renamed Yugoslavia in 1929) and his prior service in the Austro-Hungarian army classified him as an enemy. His land got placed under state supervision, with a government commissar appointed to oversee production. Alajos sold the estate to Oskar Taussig, who, not being a serving soldier, could operate without state interference.

In May 1917 the family returned to Vienna, where Alajos worked as a sales director for a car company. The boys attended a private school, where study came easy to Laszlo, who sailed through his classes while his brothers had to work hard. Tired of the dull classroom atmosphere and stern teachers, Laszlo immersed himself in art and literature. He later claimed that one of his teachers was Sigmund Freud.

In September 1918, Laszlo's excellent grades enabled him to take the second year of a four-year business course at Werner Handels-Akademie. Doing well in business law and bookkeeping, he was set for a financial career. 'I did not say to myself I was going to be an actor,' he admitted, 'because I did not know what an actor was. Acting is a ridiculous profession, unless it is the very part of your soul.'

Han Winge, a casting director at the Vienna Kammerspiele theatre, was looking for someone to play a criminal in a three-act play. From a recommendation by one of his professors, Laszlo got the part. 'Somewhere in my subconscious being,' he said, 'the root stirred and motivated me.' This marked the start of a long friendship with Winge. Winge later stated that Laszlo 'had no interest in the theatre,' but the director 'dragged him into the theatre and into the movies and further from his business career, which he had intended to pursue.'

After he graduated with honours in June 1921, Laszlo's wish to become an actor met with family disapproval. Austria being in the grip of an economic downturn, Alajos expected more from his son. Thanks to Oskar Taussig, Laszlo was found a job at the foreign exchange department of the Anglo-Ostereichischen Bank in Vienna.

Laszlo was an efficient clerk, and by October 1922 he headed his own department. But the boredom set in as, he said, 'counting people's money is a thankless business.' Developing a passion for experimental theatre, Laszlo and several other would-be actors built a stage inside a barn, where they created characters and plays by improvising dialogue and movement. 'We acted out these plays we concocted. They were bad, very bad, but we were acting.'

Because the plays were staged late at night, Laszlo's timekeeping at work suffered. When he failed to show up at the bank one day, his boss contacted his parents, who knew nothing of his nocturnal antics. When Melanie eventually confronted Laszlo, he told her in no uncertain terms that he wanted to act. She persuaded him to return to work, where his boss lectured him about his tardiness. It was to no effect, and Laszlo got fired. It was November 1923. 'From that time on,' said Andrew Lorre, 'he just devoted his entire attention to the stage.'

Although Laszlo continued living with the family, Melanie made it clear that if he didn't make it home by nine o'clock sharp, he would be locked out for the night. The same applied if he failed to attend meals on time. Ever the rebel, he walked out.

Vienna was going through a serious depression, with poverty and unemployment running rampant. Laszlo moved from lodging house to lodging house on a daily basis, and his siblings often gave him their school lunches and pocket money to help him out. Alajos also gave him some financial support, but with high inflation consuming every penny, he often came home broke and hungry. Alajos eventually arranged with the family's lawyer a weekly allowance for Laszlo to collect until he found work.

This gratuity still wasn't enough. Unable to afford even the cheapest hotels in Vienna, Laszlo slept on park benches, in doorways and among packing crates. He took to begging, stealing and selling newspapers to buy food, or queuing up at soup kitchens. 'For a long while I went hungry and friendless and cold. I am the only actor, I believe, who really had scurvy.'

Vienna's theatre scene remained surprisingly busy. Laszlo and struggling actor-writer Walter Reisch regularly visited the Burgtheatre, where they worked for no pay as clappers – their job being to prompt audience applause. According to Reisch, 'Peter's great obsession and ambition was the theatre. He spent practically every night there.' Francis Lorre agreed. 'I know once he became an actor, he stuck to it and spent all his time either going to the theatre or learning.'

Vienna saw the rise of a new wave of young Bohemian intellectuals who embraced the kind of bourgeois thinking that appealed to Laszlo. They frequented the city's street corner coffeehouses, which as well as being venues for actors and writers also provided warmth and shelter. Laszlo's favourite haunts were the Café Central and the Café Herrenhof, as both had a strong Jewish influence.

It was in one of these coffeehouses that Lazslo met William Moreno. Fascinated by the strange young actor and his exaggerated tales of his life (he claimed that his family banished him for getting a maid pregnant), Moreno told his brother Jacob of this odd individual. In 1922 Jacob had founded the experimental Stregreifitheater, because he felt that traditional theatre had lost its spark. Also known as Theatre of Spontaneity, this new form of theatre appealed to actors with a talent for improvisation. 'Jacob was always fond of mavericks,' said William Moreno, who felt Laszlo would be perfect for the Stregrefitheater.

Jacob Moreno put Laszlo in a particular situation, where he had to express himself through gesture and movement. Impressed with his skills at improvising and intrigued by his unique appearance, Moreno made him a member of his company.

'It was an ideal school of acting,' said Lorre. His ability to get to the psychological root of a role made him a favourite of Moreno, who introduced him to his social circle at the Café Herrenhof. Moreno was also instrumental in changing Laszlo's name, as he felt it needed to be more professional. He decided on Peter Lorre, the surname allegedly taken from an unruly character from the German fairytale *Struwwelpeter*. The first name was taken from Moreno's friend Peter Christian.

As beneficial as the Stregrefitheatre was to Lorre, he admitted that, 'after certain period of Bohemianism, you've had enough.' In 1924, Leo Mittler, director of the Lobe Theatre and Thaila Theatre in Breslau, Germany (now Wroclaw, Poland), gave Lorre a part in a play he was directing. With a monthly salary of 100 Deutschemarks, the ecstatic actor still had to provide his own basic costume of a dark suit, hat, shoes and a white shirt. His father gave him an old suit along with the train fare to Germany.

'Peter was very intelligent, well read and ambitious,' said writer Hans Sahl. 'He was very eager to become somebody, but he was not a faker, he was very, very serious about it.' Sahl was studying at Breslau University when they met, and he freely admitted that he never expected this odd individual to be successful. 'We often walked all night through the little streets of Breslau and spoke about our future fate and about the difficulties of making something of yourself.'

Lorre once said, 'I would rather stay a little actor who plays small parts big than a big actor who plays big parts small.' His time with the Lobe

Theatre was spent touring the provinces with *Die Bremer Stadtmusikanten* – a Grimm Brothers' fairytale that cast him as a donkey! – Shakespeare's *Romeo and Juliet* and Henrich von Kleist's *Die Hermannsschlacht*. His stage appearances were brief, but he always made an impression. During a performance of *Die Hermannsschlacht*, Lorre's Teutonic warrior dropped his spear. He started flapping around like a bird, reducing the audience to laughter. Not surprisingly, he got fired!

Lorre balanced the serious, high-brow stuff at the Lobe with comic roles at the Thalia that included a servant in Shakespeare's *The Merry Wives of Windsor*. 'He loved to parody himself and to scare others,' said Hans Sahl. However, one day Lorre developed severe stomach cramps caused by a ruptured appendix. Rushed to hospital for emergency surgery, he took a large quantity of prescribed drugs to ease the pain.

The director of the Lobe Theatre production of *Die Bremer Stadtmusikanten* was former actor Hans Peppler. When Zurich's Schauspielhaus Theatre offered Peppler the post of director, he took Lorre with him.

Working extensively with Peppler, Lorre played supporting roles in John Galsworthy's *Loyalties*, George Bernard Shaw's *St Joan* and (as a black man!) Leon Gordon's *White Cargo*. These were interspersed with comic performances in Shakespeare's *As You Like It*, Johann Nestroy's *Die Schlimmen Buben in der Schule* and another Grimm fairytale, *The Brave Little Tailor*. Lorre used his physical and facial movements to give each role a life of its own, and the audience loved it!

While touring the provincial towns of Switzerland, Germany and Austria, Lorre maintained his high standard of work, but at a cost to his health. The persistent and painful stomach cramps resulted in vomiting and diarrhoea. Alajos sent his son to Geneva, where old friend and fellow Freemason Dr P Clairmont operated on Lorre's gallbladder, removing any obstructions that had resulted from his appendix operation. Dr Clairmont administered morphine to ease the pain. 'I had been given great amounts of narcotics,' Lorre recalled. 'I was not addicted at the time.' However, the good intentions of Dr Clairmont initiated a long-term drug problem for Lorre. Whenever he needed morphine he obtained it from the doctor treating him. His brother Francis expressed his own concerns about the drug use. 'It seemed to be the beginning.'

In September 1926, Lorre signed a one-year contract with the Kammerspiele Theatre in Vienna. He acted in over thirty productions, working with the German actor and director Hans Peppler in *Die Madchen auf dem Diwan*. Thanks to his macabre sense of humour and his ability to turn a dull role into an impressive one, he often saved a dreadful production from disaster. He also kept busy as chairman and secretary of a local chapter of the Austrian Theatre Union, and remained a popular face around the

Vienna coffeehouses.

The health problems continued. Rushed to hospital after collapsing on stage one day, Lorre woke up in a ward full of alcoholics and addicts. His father arranged for him to stay in a private ward, where he remained in intensive care for several months. After several unsuccessful attempts to cure his drug habit, the doctors ended up prescribing more morphine. Once discharged from hospital, Lorre forged prescriptions and falsified doctors' names to get his regular shots.

In February 1927 Lorre's appeared in Franz Csokor's play *Die Stunde des Absterbens* at the Max Reinhardt Theatre. Impressed by his performance, Csoker felt the actor was ready for Berlin. Despite its own economic problems, Berlin was a hotbed of Bohemian decadence that made Vienna's coffeehouses seem conservative in comparison. An exciting and dynamic metropolis filled with artistic splendour, Berlin was described by Csokor as 'the most immoral city in Europe.' And a perfect place for Peter Lorre.

On Csokor's recommendation, Lorre reported to Gustav Hartung, director of Berlin's Renaissance Theatre. Hartung then introduced him to general manager Rudolph Joseph. 'He didn't look too healthy,' recalled Joseph. Despite a pleasant enough meeting, Joseph saw nothing new in this young man, and felt his unusual looks might work against him. Joseph told Lorre he needed to think over the idea of employing him, and suggested another meeting to discuss his final decision.

The follow-up meeting never took place, because Lorre suffered an internal haemorrhage. After being diagnosed with pulmonary tuberculosis, he spent three months in hospital before being transferred to a sanatorium for further treatment. 'I was given big amounts of morphine, as a result of which I became addicted,' he later said – although by that point he was already a regular user of the drug. In the meantime, Csoker contacted Joseph to smooth things over for when the actor was fit enough to work.

Discharged from hospital and armed with a letter of introduction from Csokor, Lorre arrived at the Theatre am Schiffbauerdamm, where he met Ernest Aufricht, the entrepreneur who leased the theatre. Aufricht, who described Lorre as 'a small, comical man, who looked like a tadpole,' told the actor that playwright Bertolt Brecht was producing *Pionere in Ingolstandt* and that the part of the village idiot was still available. When Lorre reported for work on Brecht's play, it began a long and tumultuous friendship with one of Germany's greatest theatre mavericks.

The meeting between Lorre and Brecht could be best described as the meeting of two unique minds. When Lorre first saw Brecht rehearsing *Pionere in Ingolstandt*, he found this tall, thin, scruffy man had an air of overpowering fascination. Charismatic as he was intellectual, and never short of admiring women at his side, Brecht was equally taken by this odd individual, because 'he did not look like an actor.'

They chatted for an hour, but to Lorre, 'It was as if we had known each other for twenty years.' As a man attracted to offbeat individuals, Brecht saw great potential in Lorre; he even had him pencilled in for a lead role in his next play and a possible three-year contract. In the meantime, Lorre played the role in *Pionere in Ingolstandt*.

Now frequenting the Berlin coffeehouses, most notably the Romanisches Café, Lorre visited Germany's legendary theatre entrepreneur Max Reinhardt, founder of Berlin's Deutsche Theatre. This didn't lead to anything, so Lorre decided that his best option was to stay with Brecht at the Schiffbauerdamm.

Lorre didn't need Reinhardt to further his career. The progressive plays performed at the Schiffbauerdamm struck a chord with audiences. Brecht's 1928 production of *Die Dreigroschenoper* had pushed the boundaries of theatre with a new and exciting use of language, and the public wanted more. With its premiere scheduled for March 1929, *Pionere in Ingolstandt* marked Peter Lorre's German stage debut.

Written by Mareiluise Fleisser, *Pionere in Ingolstandt* had been performed in Dresden a year earlier. Brecht had optioned the play to give him time to complete one of his own. Determined not to pull any punches, he had reworked the original in his own unique style. 'Brecht was aiming for scandal,' said Fleisser, 'because it guaranteed success.' The play tells the story of how a company of soldiers arrive in Ingolstandt to build a bridge, and how their involvement with the local girls destroys the village. The play's frank sexual nature made it perfect for Brecht, whose principal goal was to shock.

And he did just that! Brecht's willingness to exploit bad taste and the human condition prompted a mixed audience reaction, where the booing equalled the applause. On several occasions, an uncomfortable silence from the auditorium made the play even more effective. During one performance, a member of the Nazi SA, outraged at the way the army was portrayed, threw a stink bomb in protest. Even Ernest Aufricht had doubts as to whether or not the play could survive the backlash.

A proposed ban on *Pionere in Ingolstandt* prompted an edited version of the play for a special private performance for Berlin's leading theatre critics. The reaction from those in attendance was split down the middle. However, Brecht saw the negative reaction from shocked and disgusted critics as a good thing. On that level, the play worked.

Lorre's performance as Fabian earned good reviews. Putting his emotions into full swing, he made the most of a small role. 'Peter was completely uninhibited when it came to acting,' said co-star Lotte Lenya. 'His talent came out. It came natural to him.' The audience reaction was incredible. 'These people are really cheering me,' said Lorre. 'It is heady wine. Now I can buy a new suit.'

During the play's run, Lorre was rushed to hospital after suffering another haemorrhage. Prescribed enough morphine to carry on working, he continued attracting rave reviews and admiring fans. 'I was the hottest thing on the Berlin stage.' Aufricht immediately put him under contract with an option to loan him to other theatres.

One of Lorre's new fans was the popular Austrian actress Celia Lovsky. After watching his performance, she went backstage to congratulate him. 'There were women all over him,' she recalled, so she left without introducing herself. Some time later she saw Lorre eating lunch in a nearby pub and came over to congratulate him properly. After chatting for a while, Lorre asked to walk her home.

Lorre was already besotted with Celia after seeing her as Desdemona in Shakespeare's *Othello* – so much so that as they walked home he openly told her that he loved her. 'I laughed,' she said of his outburst. Celia, who was seven years older, quickly got over the shock, and before long the couple became inseparable. Within a brief period she moved into Lorre's apartment. She also put her career on hold to devote her energies to her new man.

Lorre made his film debut in *Die Verschwundene Frau* (1929). His uncredited appearance as a dentist's patient is tiny, but his round face and bulging eyes are unmistakable. Long considered 'lost' until its rediscovery in 1984, the film, now fully restored, is a curiosity piece for fans.

Pionere in Ingolstandt was one of the Schiffbauerdamm's most successful plays. Brecht's next production was Dorothy Lane's *Happy End*. With Kurt Weill providing the music and Brecht the lyrics, Lorre was cast along with Oscar Homolka and Helene Weigel. Opening in August 1929, the play began well enough, but audience grew restless during the third act. The end came when Weigel read an anti-capitalist statement full of Marxist propaganda, causing a near riot in the theatre. *Happy End* closed after three performances.

At the same time, Lorre took part in Karl Heinz Martin's ambitious production of Georg Bluchner's *Danton's Death* at the Volksbuhne Theatre. Set in 1794 in post-revolutionary France, this four-hour epic covers the events leading to Georges Danton's execution. Lorre's character, Governor Saint-John, is killed off in the first act – handily for the actor, because he could then go to the Schiffbauerdom for his performance in *Happy End*, which opened on the same night. When *Happy End* closed, Lorre continued in *Danton's Death*, to critical acclaim and audience approval.

Martin retained Lorre for his production of Frank Wendekind's controversial tragedy *Fruhlings Erwachen*. Playing a teenage misfit coming to terms with puberty only to commit suicide, Lorre was singled out for praise, although the play's frank treatment of teenage sex divided critics.

Fruhlings Erwachen attracted the attention of another fan who wanted to meet Lorre – Fritz Lang. Celia introduced Lang to Lorre during a dress rehearsal of the play, and in between the backstage chat, Lang made an intriguing offer to the actor. 'I will do my first sound picture. I do not know yet what it will be. You will receive many offers from pictures. But if you accept no other offers, this picture will be written for you. You will be the star of it.'

'I never paid any attention to it,' said Lorre, who didn't consider motion pictures high on his career plan. But nevertheless he kept to his word not to take any other screen roles and waited for Lang's call. 'I must have waited 14 months, and couldn't accept film offers.'

In October 1929 Lorre appeared in another play, the Karl Kraus satire *Die Unuberwindlichen*. With overwork taking it toll, he started coughing blood. Franz Csoker arranged – and paid – for him to stay at a sanatorium in Badenweiler, where he made a full recovery. Rounding off a tremendous 1929, Lorre and Celia got engaged. At the start of the new decade, Lorre then returned to the stage in Carl Sternheim's *Der Kandidate* at Berlin's Kammerspeile Theatre.

Taking a break from stage work, Lorre acted on radio for the first time in Jacques Offenbach's operetta *Die Seufzerbrucke* for the *Berlin Radio Hour*. Then it was a welcome return to Rudolph Joseph at the Renaissance Theatre for the comedy *Voruntersuchung*; among those who watched the play were Albert Einstein and the Crown Prince of Austria.

Back at the Schiffbauerdamm for Ernest Aufricht's production of *Die Quadratur des Kreises*, Lorre was reunited with Lotte Lenya. 'Peter loved the play,' she recalled, 'because he was very funny when he did it. He loved anything that furthered his talents.' However, despite the play's initial success, ticket sales tailed off due to the city's financial recession and political unrest that resulted in youths from the Nazi and Communist Parties fighting in the streets. The play's scheduled six-month run was curtailed after only a few weeks.

'The only compliment I've had about my acting that meant anything to me was from Brecht,' Lorre said of their friendship. February 1931 saw the opening of Brecht's *Mann ist Mann* at Berlin's Staatstheatre, with Lorre playing Galy Gay, an Irish dockworker dragged into a shady business deal by British soldiers. Brecht's powerful use of language confused both critics and audiences. The play nearly shut down during one matinee performance when Nazi party members started heckling the actors. *Mann ist Mann* finally closed after six performances.

The failure of *Mann ist Mann* was perfectly timed. Fritz Lang arrived at the Schiffbauerdom with a script of the film he wanted Lorre do. Lang was so confident that the actor would be perfect for the role that he didn't even give him a screen test. Originally called *Morder unter Uns*, the film would eventually be given the shortened title *M*.

As previously mentioned, *M* was based on the real-life case of serial killer Peter Kurten. An intelligent, impeccably-dressed bisexual who had brutally murdered forty men, women and children by axe, knife or strangulation, Kurten had been dubbed the 'Vampire of Düsseldorf' and had made the front page of every German newspaper. Lang had read about Kurten in the Berliner Tageblatt and become intrigued by his compulsive urge to kill. Having been given access to police files and interviews with members of the criminal underworld who had assisted the police in catching Kurten, by January 1931 Lang and his wife Thea Von Harbour had a completed script ready and scheduled for production.

Having confessed to his crimes, on 22 April 1931 Kurten was sentenced to death, and on 2 July 1931 was consequently beheaded. Certain rewrites to Lang's script were made following the execution, the main one being that Kurten's fictional counterpart Hans Beckett became a child murderer. Another marked difference between Kurten and Beckett is the deep regret Beckett feels for his actions. To give *M* added authenticity (and controversy), Lang hired real criminals to play supporting roles.

From his first (off-camera) scene, where he befriends a little girl, Lorre *is* Hans Beckett. 'I put myself into this character until I begin to display his symptoms,' the actor admitted. Portraying Beckett as a pathetic misfit, Lorre gave Lang the emotional edge he wanted from him. 'Lang wrung him out like an old towel,' said editor Paul Falkenberg. The stress of playing Beckett took its toll on the actor physically as well as emotionally. 'Peter fainted,' said writer Curt Siodmak, who visited the set but was refused an audience with Lorre because Lang wanted him in total isolation.

The human qualities Lorre gives to the role, coupled with the raw emotion brought out by Lang, are disturbing, especially during the film's climax when Beckett is put on trial by the criminal underworld. 'Lang was a perfectionist,' said actor Gerhard Bienert. 'He liked to stir up actors, to keep them off balance. He felt more creative in an atmosphere of tension.' Lang didn't force a performance out of Lorre; he beat it out of him through sadism and sheer physical torment!

M premiered on 11 May 1931, and while critical reaction was mixed, the cinema queues stretched onto the Berlin streets. Reviews for Lorre's performance were favourable. Lang felt the actor 'gave one of the best performances in film history,' although Lorre himself felt indifference toward the movie. During the Berlin premier of *M*, some of the audience actually thought Lorre was Kurten and pelted him with rocks. 'A success can be too great,' he lamented.

Shortly after completing *M*, Lorre returned to the Schiffbauerdamm for Alfred Savoir's *Der Dompteur*. Film offers pursued the reluctant star, but typecasting as a villain caused problems. 'Once you are typed,' Lorre said, 'your field is limited and your screen life is apt to be short.'

Despite the financial advantages of film work, Lorre needed to show his versatility. His next film was the comedy *Bomben auf Monte Carlo* (1931). The film was a success, but his supporting role as a sailor failed to eradicate the memory of *M*.

After appearing in *Koffer des Herrn O. F.* (1931), Lorre returned to the stage, working with director Karl Heinz Martin in Georg Kaiser's *Nebeneinander: Volksstuck in fünf Akten* at the Volksbühne. Then he went to the Deutches Theatre for Max Reinhardt's production of Odon von Horvath's *Geschicten aus dens Wiener Wald: Volksstuck in Drei Teilen*. His final Berlin stage appearance was in Louis Verneuli's *Die Nemo Bank* at the Komodienhaus. He had been cast in Brecht's production of Nikolai Wessovschikow's *Die Mutter* at the Schiffbauerdamm but, fed up with the low wages, he didn't turn up for rehearsals. Perhaps he had also grown tired of Brecht.

Lorre's next film, *Funf von der Jazzband* (1932), was a musical comedy about a group of struggling musicians, with the actor cast as a car thief. It received a mixed reaction from the critics and public alike, as did *Schuss im Mongengrauen* (1932), a crime thriller produced by Germany's major film company UFA. Cast as a thug, Lorre actually changed his small, thankless role into that of a sex maniac. 'He played it like that,' recalled screenwriter Rudolf Katscher.

Lorre's next film brought him closer to international attention. Directed by Karl Hartl, the UFA-produced *F.P.I. Antwortet Nicht* (1932) is a screen adaptation of a Curt Siodmak science fiction novel. Adapted by Walter Reisch, it was filmed by Hartl simultaneously in German (starring Hans Abler), French (starring Charles Boyer) and English (staring Conrad Veidt). Hartl chose Lorre to play the hero's photographer sidekick for the German version, and Reisch tailored the part especially for him. 'We decided to have this character played by the smallest actor in Berlin,' said Reisch. 'Peter was very happy to get the part, in which he could show his sense of humour.'

Lorre and Veidt became good friends. 'Veidt always died laughing whenever Peter Lorre did,' observed Reisch. 'Peter could tell the most incredible stories. He had an enormous sense of humour and was the happiest man on Earth when people laughed.'

Despite a mixed critical reaction, *F.P.I Antwortet Nicht* was a box-office hit, selling out at the Apollo Theatre in Vienna and the UFA Palast in Berlin. Lorre made the most of a small role and once again received favourable reviews. There was however a negative reaction from some Jewish audiences, who felt his character was anti-Semitic. Ironic, considering that Lorre, Walter Reisch, Curt Siodmak and the film's producer Erich Pommer were all Jewish!

Lorre remained under contract with UFA for his next film, *Der Weisse Damon* (1932). His role being that of a hunchback drug addict, it was a case of art imitating life, but Lorre's performance received good critical reviews. UFA later shot additional footage to give the film an anti-drug message. The role itself was little different from the other bad guys Lorre had played. 'Once typed,' said Lorre, 'the public just demand it.'

Another comedy, *Was Fauen Traumen* (1933), followed, but by the time it premiered in April 1933, Adolf Hitler had become Germany's new Chancellor. With political and social unrest further exacerbated by the rise of anti-Semitism, Lorre's future in Berlin looked uncertain.

For now, things were on an even keel. Lorre had been collaborating with writer Axel Eggebrecht on a script for *Ein Kasper Hauser von Heute*. This was based on the famous story of a mysterious boy who turned up in Nuremberg with no memory of his existence, and whose subsequent murder sparked endless conspiracy theories. Lorre, who wanted to direct the German, French and English film versions, approached actor Fritz Kortner with the project. UFA took up the option, but everything stalled as the Nazi terror campaign escalated in the streets of Germany.

Lorre showed little interest in current events, but Fritz Lang followed them closely. Following the arrest of Jewish actress Helene Weigel and the appointment of Dr Joseph Goebbels as Minister of Propaganda and Popular Entertainment, it was made illegal to employ Jewish actors and technicians for future film productions.

With German movie legends Emil Jannings, Paul Weggener and Werner Krauss embracing Nazism, Lorre could avoid the situation no longer. Even Lang's wife Thea Von Harbour and her former husband Rudolph Klein-Rougge joined the New Order. (Lang was Jewish but had converted to Catholicism.) Lorre's friendship with the overtly Marxist Brecht only made matters worse.

'They were friends,' Lorre said of Jannings and Weggener, 'who have boozed with us and who would stick a knife in our back with the same charm.'

Lorre himself helped news editor Egon Jacobson burn potentially incriminating official documents at a secluded beach-house, assisted by, of all people, the police!

It was rumoured that Joseph Goebbels, an alleged a fan of *M*, instructed Lorre to leave Berlin. In reality, it was producer Sam Spiegel who told him to get out of Germany. With a completed script for the film *Unsichtbare Gegner* (1933) under his arm, Spiegel joined Lorre, Oscar Homolka and director Josef Von Sternberg on a train bound for Vienna. Celia Lorre was already in the city, where she was appearing in a play.

Unsichtbare Gegner was completed in Vienna, but the critical reaction was negative, with Lorre getting the brunt of the criticism. Shortly after the film's completion, he took the role of Judas in V O Ludwig's *Golgotha* at the Zirkus-Renz Theatre – his first appearance on the Austrian stage since making it big in Berlin.

Soon after arriving in Vienna, Lorre received a telegram from Joseph

Goebbels requesting that he return to Berlin and make films for the Third Reich. Lorre's sudden exit from Germany had also left UFA with a few legal problems over the *Kasper Hauser* project. The studio asked Lorre to sign over the German rights, in exchange for which he could keep the English and French. Sensing a possible trap if he returned, Lorre sent a telegram, not to Goebbels, but to the general manager of UFA, famously saying, 'There is no room in Germany for two murderers like we are, Hitler and I!'

Lorre's Austrian sojourn didn't last. Hitler set about damaging the country's economy by imposing massive fees on anyone travelling from Germany to Austria. In the summer of 1933 he instigated a series of bombs attacks across the country. With fighting on the streets of Vienna between Nazi and socialist groups, a proposed general strike and the threat of civil war, Austria's Christian Socialist Chancellor Engelbert Dollfuss dissolved Parliament and placed the country under martial law.

With the coffeehouses and theatres officially closed, the lively Bohemian existence Lorre had previously enjoyed had gone. It was a city he no longer knew. Staying at the Hotel Kranz-Ambassador in Vienna, Lorre and Celia had to consider their options. With anti-Semitism on the increase, they fled to the small Czechoslovakian town of Vranov.

The strong possibility of Hitler invading Czechoslovakia prompted a further exit, this time for Paris. Lorre spoke fluent French, and with *M* on general release in France under the title *Le Maudit*, the possibilities of stage and film work looked promising. Even his *Kasper Hauser* project might get off the ground, since he owned the French rights.

With the train fare paid for by Andrew Lorre and a loan from friend Karl Kraus, the Lorres arrived in Paris, where they booked a cheap room at the Hotel Ansonia on the Rue de Saigon. They were not alone, as Fritz Lang and Billy Wilder were among the many German and Austrian Jews who had fled to Paris. Obtaining a work permit proved difficult. Whiling away their days inside the various Parisian cafes, Lorre and fellow exiles Fredrich Hollaender, Billy Wilder, Franz Waxman and Jan Lustig worked on a film project that never materialised.

'I went to various doctors and got prescriptions for morphine,' the actor later recalled. 'I kept using it for longer than I had a medical need for it.'

Concerned about Lorre's health, fellow exile Paul Falkenberg found a sanatorium on the outskirts of Paris. 'Lorre was at a terrible stage,' recalled Rudolph Joseph, who had also fled to Paris and regularly visited the actor. Another visitor was the German film director G W Pabst. Aware of Lorre's financial situation, Pabst paid toward his treatment (as did Falkenberg) and wrote a part for him in his forthcoming film *Du Haut en Bas* (1933).

In October 1933, a few days after completing his stint on the film, Lorre checked back into the sanatorium. Financially things were extremely difficult, with Celia doing her best to keep the creditors happy. Lorre's few days on Pabst's film had earned him some money, but it all went on medical bills, along with his life insurance policy. Celia assured Karl Kraus and others that as soon as Lorre could work again, the debts would be paid.

Even when he could work, Lorre faced the same problems the other refugees had. He may have been a star in Berlin, but in Paris he was just another washed up foreign actor. And with Hitler's constant presence on French radio and cinema newsreels, he knew he had to move on.

One of Lorre's many admirers in the UK was Alfred Hitchcock, who was about to start filming *The Man Who Knew Too Much* (1934) for Gaumont-British. Assistant producer Ivor Montague found out from his German associate Otto Katz that Lorre was scraping a living in France. He reminded Hitchcock of Lorre's performance in *M* and suggested that he would be perfect for a role. 'We wanted him at once,' Montague recalled. 'There was never any question about his coming over to be tested.' Nor was Lorre's limited English considered a barrier. Michael Balcon, head of production at Gaumont-British, cabled Lorre with an offer that included covering his expenses and sorting out immigration. The expenses could not be finalised straightaway, however, so Lorre asked for further financial assistance from loyal brother Andrew.

Lorre was initially considered for the small part of hired gunman Levine. Introduced to Hitchcock on his arrival in London by his old friend Sidney Bernstein, Lorre admitted, 'All I knew in English was yes and no. I couldn't say no because I would have had to explain it, so I said yes to everything.'

'As soon as Hitch saw him,' said Montague 'we developed his part in the picture.' Hitchcock then decided that Lorre would be perfect for the role of sexually perverse criminal mastermind Abbott. It may have been *M*-inspired, but it was a bigger role, which came with second billing.

To help Lorre get over the language barrier, Hitchcock hired interpreter Joan Harrison. Knowing his future lay in British and American films, Lorre insisted she spoke to him in English. He then spent three months mentally translating his script into German and then memorising the dialogue – he felt that, had he just learnt it parrot fashion, this would have come across as too mannered. Not only did he get to grips with the English, his approach helped him to tone down his strong German accent.

Lorre's time in London introduced him to a nicer existence. Sidney Bernstein invited him to stay at his luxury apartment in Albermarle Street, complete with butler and maid service. He was overwhelmed by the new surroundings, in which he met famous intellectuals and movie stars. It was a dream come true, and even better things were not far away.

Working with Hitchcock, Lorre found a man intellectually on a par with Brecht and Lang. Hitchcock understood the actor's improvisational approach, and Lorre responded to the director's suggestions. They even shared the same sense of humour. 'Hitch loved and frequently played practical jokes,' recalled Montague, 'but only on people who liked them equally.'

Lorre worked harder on *The Man Who Knew Too Much* than on any other movie he had previously appeared in. It was a happy shoot, and if he had problems with his English, they never showed. 'Lorre would concentrate attention by his timing,' said Montague.

The Man Who Knew Too Much was successful on both sides of the Atlantic. During a press party, Rufus LeMaire, a casting director for Columbia Pictures, sent word to studio head Harry Cohn about Lorre, and within a few days the actor signed a five-year contract, on a weekly salary of £500 and a six-month renewal option. He sent word to Celia in Paris, and she immediately set sail for London. Once there, she made sure Lorre's new success didn't go to his head, as he owed money to a lot of people. Moving into a nice apartment in Pall Mall, she set to work sorting out their meagre finances.

After five eventful years together, Lorre and Celia married on 22 June 1934; she had to rehearse the wedding vows because she couldn't speak English. On 18 July 1934, the couple obtained visas from the American Consulate in London before boarding the Cunard Liner *The Majestic*, which sailed from Southampton to New York, and to a new life.

M had had some success in America, so the Lorres' arrival in New York on 25 July 1934 was greeted by a wave of photographers and journalists expecting to see Hans Beckett. Instead they met on the gangplank a round-faced, good-humoured young man. The following day the couple boarded a train for Chicago, and then to Los Angeles, where the actor's arrival was planned well in advance.

Lorre's introduction to Hollywood was a happy one. He was reunited with old friends Fritz Lang, G W Pabst and Conrad Veidt and made new ones. He attended lavish parties and met important movie people. His intellect and sense of fun made him popular with his new friends, among them Charlie Chaplin. 'He is endowed with such intuitive, emotional and imaginative powers that impress me,' recalled the comedian. 'I look forward to seeing him make a genuine contribution to the art of acting on the screen.'

Unlike many Hollywood émigrés who clung to the old remnants of Europe, Lorre embraced America. 'As long as Hollywood wants me, I want Hollywood. I am convinced my future definitely rests here. I love everything about it,' he said. With memories of Berlin and Vienna having no place in Hollywood, he seldom mixed with other émigrés.

Lorre rented a beach-house near the ocean, and took in the fresh air and bright sunshine of Los Angeles. 'I'm here,' he said, 'as free as the wind, the font of extraordinary knowledge, splendidly corrupt, and eager to be of profitable service.' Celia also loved it, and with a new career in the making, she continued devoting her energies to her starstruck husband.

Shortly after his arrival in Hollywood, though, Lorre began coughing up blood. He was rushed to hospital with an internal hemorrhage brought on by suspected pulmonary tuberculosis. There, Dr Joel Pressman made further tests that revealed he had bronchiectasis, a disorder of the large bronchi. The actor was prescribed Dilaudid to ease the pain.

Harry Cohn had no suitable projects lined up for Lorre. It seemed that Columbia had signed up this great, if unconventional-looking, actor but had no idea what to do with him. Kept hanging around for several months, on full salary (enabling Celia to pay off a few debts), Lorre spent his time tending his garden, reading Edgar Allan Poe and Carl Jung, and waiting with bated breath for his breakthrough film.

Taking matters into his own hands, Lorre presented Cohn with a possible project in the form of a two-page summary of Leon Tolstoy's *Crime and Punishment*. Instead, however, Cohn decided to loan the actor out to MGM to star in *Mad Love* (1935), a remake of the German horror classic *The Hands of Orlac* (1924). (When lacking work for a contract player, one studio could loan him out to another for a fee higher than his salary, pocketing the difference.) Lorre reluctantly accepted the role of obsessive Dr Gogal on the condition that *Crime and Punishment* got made. After a year on the Columbia payroll, he would finally be able to show America his talent with *The Hands of Orlac*; and if the film was a success, it could eventually lead to better-paid work – a pressing concern, as Celia could hold off the creditors only for so long.

As well as being his Hollywood debut, *Mad Love* started Lorre's horror career. The director was Karl Freund, an excellent cinematographer who made his name as a pioneer of Germany's expressionist cinema of the '20s, and who had been cameraman on the original 1924 version. Lorre wasn't the only member of the cast on loan to MGM – Frances Drake came from Paramount and Colin Clive from Warner Brothers.

Because of their similar backgrounds in German films, Lorre found a kindred spirit in Freund. The director gave the actor full reign to improvise his role, enabling Dr Gogal to go beyond one-dimensional villainy. 'He was careful that his character had a sense of reality and vitality,' observed co-star Keye Luke.

'I imagine I'm the character, figure out what he would do, and thus live the role,' said Lorre himself. With his shaven head emphasising his expressive eyes, Lorre's Gogal is a sad villain, because his unrequited love for Drake's Yvonne Orlac is genuine. He's a real person with good qualities and we feel for him when she spurns his advances. But he is also a flawed mortal as his obsession becomes destructive. Few villains could inspire sympathy the way he could, with Lorre's sensitive portrayal. 'Peter was a very complex man,' recalled Drake. 'My impression was that he was a very sensitive person, easily hurt.'

Mad Love premiered on 2 August 1935 to good notices but public indifference. The levels of perverted eroticism and overt sadism were a bit strong for '30s sensibilities. The film made a domestic gross of only $170,000, and although it did better overseas, with takings of $194,000, it still made a net loss of almost $40,000. It came close to being banned in the UK by the Secretary of the British Board of Film Censors, the Rt Hon Edward Short, who had previously banned *Freaks* (1931) and *Island of Lost Souls* (1932).

Although *Mad Love* is a visually striking film, it is a cold, cynical effort that suffers from a weak climax and the stolid casting of Drake and Clive – both fine actors, but unappealing romantic leads. Its true centre is Lorre as Gogal.

Lorre himself considered *Mad Love* a poor movie. Worse still, with typecasting rearing its ugly head, he then found himself pigeonholed in horror roles, a situation he was unhappy about. 'I had never played a single horror picture [before then]. I somehow got into that category, but it's psychological terror I used to play.'

Initially, however, with *Mad Love* behind him, Lorre had an opportunity to build his reputation by starring in a film version of a literary classic close to his heart. As promised, Harry Cohn gave the go-ahead to *Crime and Punishment* (1935), with the autocratic Josef von Sternberg directing. Although generally unpopular with the actors on his set, von Sternberg got on well with Lorre, who regarded him as a 'fluid and straightforward director. Everybody warned me about him before we started the picture, but I found him helpful and sincere.'

Von Sternberg equally respected Lorre, and although the actor did not physically suit the part of killer Roderick Raskolnikov, the director knew his performance would be excellent. After his false start in *Mad Love*, Lorre could live the part once more. He achieved this, but not without some difficulty. *Crime and Punishment* began production immediately after *Mad Love* wrapped, so the strain of making the two films back to back increased Lorre's drug use. Aware of the actor's fragile state, von Sternberg made sure he rested as often as possible in between takes.

Crime and Punishment wrapped in 28 days. Unfortunately the film met with a negative response following its premiere in November 1935, most critics agreeing that Lorre was miscast. It also paled in comparison with the French version released a week earlier. With two films based on the same book on general release at the same time, box office takings suffered.

Columbia loaned Lorre out again, this time to Gaumont-British to return to London and appear as a villain called the Mexican Hairless in Alfred Hitchcock's *Secret Agent* (1936). Lorre appreciated the help Hitchcock had given him in kick-starting his film career, so he returned the favour by giving a committed performance. 'Hitch and Lorre understood each other,' said Ivor Montague. 'There were no directing or acting problems between them.'

Lorre kept a tight lid on his drug use during the production to avoid any harmful publicity. At the end of each day's filming, he left the Shepherd's Bush studio to visit a Harley Street doctor to get his regular morphine shots.

Shortly after the completion of *The Secret Agent* in January 1936, the Lorres went to the American Consular Service in London, where they successfully applied for American citizenship. Once again however the actor's health problems recurred, and he got admitted to the Wellback Nursing Home, with Gaumont-British covering the cost of his treatment. Celia's stayed at the Mayfair Hotel in London, where she used her husband's weekly salary to settle a few more long-term debts.

Lorre recovered sufficiently to attend the London premier of *Crime and Punishment* in March 1936 before making a trip with Celia to Vienna, and then to Budapest to visit family and friends. With the ominous rumblings of Hitler just around the corner, it was his last trip to Europe for some time. Returning to England, the Lorres boarded the *SS Washington* bound for America.

Back in Hollywood, Lorre waited once more for his next film. He was denied the opportunity of being offered Gogal-inspired roles by other studios, as censorship restrictions, a slump in demand and financial problems facing horror specialists Universal meant that by the end of 1936, the horror genre was temporarily finished.

But even with America's government debt of $4 billion and the reduction of public spending imposed by President Franklin D Roosevelt, Hollywood remained unaffected by the downturn, with audience figures of 75 million keeping everyone happy. Everyone, that is, except Lorre, who was still kept hanging around for his next film. Not tall or good-looking enough to play a romantic lead, he was also too specialised for conventional character roles. He aspired to do comedy, but nothing was forthcoming. If there was a conclusion to be drawn, it was that Lorre was too talented for Columbia.

Making his American radio debut in May 1936 in Rudy Vallee's anthology show *Fleishmann Yeast Hour* for NBC Studios in Washington, Lorre found his distinctive tones were perfect for the airwaves, where casting proved less of a problem. Following his well-received performance in the drama *Doctor Mallaire* for NBC, he recited his climatic monologue from *M* for the *MGM Radio Club*. Over the next few years he made further sporadic radio appearances for *The Lux Radio Show* and *The Royal Gelatin Hour*, switching effortlessly between comedy and drama.

There then came a golden opportunity for the actor to play Napoleon on stage. During his final visit to Vienna, Lorre had met his old friend, poet and playwright Ferdinand Bruckner, and they had discussed in detail the possibility of bringing the life of the French emperor to the theatre. When Columbia scrapped a proposed film about Napoleon (test footage of Lorre in costume had been shot by Josef von Sternberg), the realisation of a stage version took shape, with an intended Broadway premiere scheduled for the end of the year.

With fellow playwright Sidney King brought in on the production to assist Bruckner, the script for *Napoleon the First* focused on the Emperor's psychological nature. Money was spent on costumes and set designs, but when Lorre arrived in New York, he found out that King had been unable to find a suitable actress to play Josephine, Tallulah Bankhead and Gladys George having both declined the role. Despite all the combined efforts – especially from Bruckner, who worked on the play in his spare time – King cancelled the production, leaving Lorre with a great sense of frustration in view of the amount of time he had invested.

The trip to New York wasn't a total waste though. Lorre took time out to file a Certificate of Alien Claiming Residence in the United States, putting him one step closer to becoming an American citizen.

Other than *Crime and Punishment*, which he instigated, Lorre's films had come from other studios. He realised that if he was to progress, he needed to go elsewhere. Not surprisingly, Harry Cohn released him from his contract. Away from acting, Lorre wasn't completely idle. In March 1936 he joined the Screen Actors Guild (SAG) and regularly attended the bimonthly meetings.

In November 1936, studio boss Darryl F Zanuck offered Lorre a long-term contract at 20th Century Fox. Keen to make use of the actor's services, Zanuck agreed to his request to play comedy roles – in fact a whole variety of screen roles to showcase his talents.

Lorre wasn't about to be duped by false promises; he had lived in America long enough by now to understand that movie contracts were not always what they seemed. By mutual agreement with Zanuck, he took on the comic role of an eccentric master criminal in *Crack-Up* (1937). However, not about to be walked over by the studio, he also had a clause inserted into his contract allowing him to complete his proposed stint on *Napoleon the First*. This made him unavailable for film work until the play ended its intended run, and was in preference to appearing in a film version of Napoleon's story produced by Fox.

'I'm not a superstitious man, but I'm beginning to think to think insofar as Napoleon is concerned, I'm a jinxed man,' the actor noted ruefully. It may have been an effective bargaining tool, but once *Napoleon the First* got cancelled, Zanuck recalled Lorre to Hollywood to play an extortionist in the prison drama *Nancy Steel is Missing* (1937).

Did the curse of *M* follow the actor to Fox? Filming *Nancy Steel* proved difficult for Lorre, who had previously gone to Culver City for treatment of his morphine addiction and was hardly in the best of health. After collapsing on the set shortly before the film's completion, he withdrew from his next intended role, in the period drama *Slave Ship* (1937), and on the advice of his doctor checked into the West Hill Sanatorium in New York.

Hollywood had developed a fascination for all things Oriental, with Boris Karloff playing Sax Rohmer's criminal mastermind Dr Fu Manchu in *The Mask of Fu Manchu* (1932) and Warner Oland scoring a hit as Earl Derr Biggers' inscrutable Chinese detective Charlie Chan. As producers of the Chan series, Fox were eager to continue the winning formula in a slightly different format, so Zanuck decided to try out a similar character created by John P Marquand.

After travelling extensively across China, Korea and Japan, Marquand had returned to America with a notebook filled with stories, anecdotes and observations, all of which had formed the basis of his 1935 novel *Ming Yellow*. The following year he had written *No Hero*, his first novel to feature Japanese agent Mr Moto. Marquand never took his Moto novels seriously, but they proved very popular with the public.

Zanuck bought the movie rights to two Marquand stories and developed a third with the intention of producing a series of second features to run alongside the Chan films. The first story became *Think Fast, Mr Moto* (1937), with Sol Wurtzel producing and Norman Foster directing. 'The first Moto script given to me was terrible,' recalled Foster, who was unhappy with Wurtzel's decision to cast Peter Lorre as Moto.

Having an Austro-Hungarian playing a Japanese character was hardly politically correct – but then the faintly Asian-looking Warner Oland, who played Chan so convincingly, was Swedish! 'Peter was so unlike the Japanese,' said Foster. 'Everything was wrong with him, except the eyes.' Lorre's poor health made it equally doubtful that he could pull off the role. The Moto of Marquand's novels is a rugged G-man, far removed from Lorre's diminutive stature.

With the aide of the make-up artists, Lorre became Japanese. Although happy to play a good guy, he creditably refused to pander to racial stereotyping. 'All Chinese do not clasp their hands and run about in a jumpy step. There is a typed idea of nationality, and actors think they must imitate that idea. Mr Moto is a Japanese detective, a clever, swift-thinking man.'

Released in July 1937, *Think Fast, Mr Moto* did well at the box office. Seven further films followed – *Thank You, Mr Moto* (1937), *Mysterious Mr Moto* (1938), *Mr Moto's Gamble* (1938), *Mr Moto Takes a Chance* (1938), *Mr Moto Takes a Vacation* (1939), *Mr Moto's Last Warning* (1939) and *Mr Moto on Danger Island* (1939). *Mr Moto's Gamble* was originally called *Charlie Chan at the Ringside*. It became a Moto film after Warner Oland pulled out due to ill health (he died shortly afterwards) but retained Lorre's *Mad Love* co-star Keye Luke as Chan's No 1 Son.

To keep the series as fresh as possible, Foster endeavoured to maintain quality, authenticity and atmosphere by constantly rewriting scripts, even if the stories bore little resemblance to the novels on which they were supposedly based. Gone too were Marquand's political references. Lorre meanwhile tried to keep a sense of realism by visiting Japanese restaurants, reading Japanese novels and practicing Buddhism. 'I made the Moto series purposely,' he said. 'I wanted to get the flavour of *M* out of the cinema palate of the American fan.'

Because Moto was a more physical character than Chan, Lorre was claimed to have studied jujitsu with martial arts expert Haiku Watsutu. This is doubtful, however, because his health prevented him from performing difficult stunts. In fact, the hectic shooting schedule and the physical demands soon took their toll. During the making of *Mr Moto Takes a Vacation*, Lorre seriously damaged his shoulder; the injury allegedly cost him the title role of *The Son of Frankenstein* (1939).

Lorre's regular morphine shots in his dressing room didn't help, and Foster felt his addiction affected his performance. 'He did his best to be Japanese,' he recalled, 'though he didn't make Moto as believable as [Warner] Oland made Chan. Peter was very sick during the making of these films.'

Lorre initially enjoyed making the films. He earned good money – $10,000 a picture, although this was still low for a contract player – and was grateful to play the hero. But he grew tired of Moto, as he felt repeating the character on screen diminished his abilities. 'Moto was fine for a while, but the role is really childish.' Foster was very understanding and wasn't surprised when Lorre told him he wanted out. The anti-Japanese feeling that spread across America allowed the detective to bow out at the right time.

With Moto finished, Fox had problems finding Lorre suitable screen roles. His non-Moto films *Lancer Spy* (1937) and *I'll Give a Million* (1938) hadn't advanced his career, and the actor made no secret of the fact that he was unhappy at Fox. He wanted to do comedy but got only B-movie villainy that diminished his standing. Gone too were the promised salary increases. After six months of no work, Lorre's contract ran out, and he left the studio.

There were pressing financial issues facing the actor. The debts to friends and associates had escalated into legal threats that Lorre could ignore no longer. But the amounts he could pay back fell short of what was owed. Even when some of the debts were properly settled, long-term friendships came to a bitter end.

Following his release from Fox, Lorre went freelance, but what came his way were further routine B-movies. He auditioned for the role of Quasimodo in *The Hunchback of Notre Dame* (1939) but lost out to Charles Laughton. A bout of pneumonia also prevented a return to the horror genre with the Ritz Brothers' spoof *The Gorilla* (1939): his role went to Bela Lugosi.

Lorre returned to MGM to play a villain opposite Clark Gable and Joan Crawford in *Strange Cargo* (1940). Then it was back to Fox for an enjoyable comic performance as a jewel thief opposite the formidable Erich von

Stroheim in *I Was an Adventuress* (1940). After completing his stint on *Island of Doomed Men* (1940), Lorre signed a non-exclusive contract with Columbia for two films on $3,500 per week. He then made a trip to RKO to play the title role in the film noir thriller *Stranger on the Third Floor* (1940), his 'Stranger' owing a great deal to Hans Beckett.

Remaining with RKO, he starred in the comedy murder mystery *You'll Find Out* (1940), a film notable for the teaming of Hollywood's three 'horror men' – Lorre, Boris Karloff and Bela Lugosi – although they all played second fiddle to the popular NBC radio star Kay Kyser. It hardly proved a big stretch for any of them, and a proposed musical number to be performed by the actors never materialised.

By the time *You'll Find Out* went on general release, Lorre had made an unwitting and decidedly unwelcome appearance in *Der Ewige Jude: Ein Dokumentarfilm uber das Weljudentum* (1940), or *The Eternal Jew: A Documentary about World Jewry*. This despicable anti-Semitic film was produced by Dr Fritz Hippler, head of Goebbels' film division at the German Propaganda Ministry. Mainly comprised of news footage, it preaches a message that Jews are responsible for all the evil in the world. Lorre's uncredited appearance comes in footage taken from *M* (long banned by the Nazis), and is supposed to give the impression that Jews are child killers.

Lorre returned to Columbia to play the lead in Robert Florey's *The Face Behind the Mask* (1941), a neat little thriller that casts him as a Hungarian immigrant in New York, who is scarred for life in a hotel fire. Unable to work and close to suicide, the character dons a rubber mask and becomes a crime lord. The film centres on his relationship with a blind woman (played by Evelyn Keyes) who becomes his wife. When she dies at the hands of rival gangsters, he loses his remaining humanity and takes revenge.

For once Lorre was able to give a moving performance that expressed his full range as an actor. Oddly enough, though, he had scant regard for the film. 'I don't think Peter was very much impressed by *Face Behind the Mask*,' said co-star Don Beddoe. 'His other successes made him pretty blasé about this particular venture.' The critics responded favourably to his performance, and the film proved a huge box office hit, so much so that it was re-released to further financial success two years later – rare for a B-movie potboiler.

Lorre rounded off his freelance period with *Mr District Attorney* (1941) for Republic and a cameo appearance in *They Met in Bombay* (1941) for MGM. With the notable exception of *Face Behind the Mask*, Lorre's output from this period was unremarkable. But with the start of a new decade, another film of the stature of *M* came his way, and one that would have a very positive effect on career – John Huston's *The Maltese Falcon* (1941).

A successful scriptwriter at Warner Brothers, the ambitious Huston took a risky career decision to direct *The Maltese Falcon*. With complete control over the film, he determined to keep it close to the atmosphere of the Dashiell Hammett novel on which it was based. Once Jack Warner gave him the green light for the project, he set about casting. When first choice George Raft turned down the role of the central private eye character Sam Spade, Huston hired Humphrey Bogart. The rest of the cast soon fell into place – Mary Astor (as femme fatale Brigid O'Shaughnessy), Gladys George (Ivy Archer), Lee Patrick (Effie Perine) and Elisha Cook Jnr (Wilmer Cook). When it came to the two principal villains, to call Huston's casting decisions inspired is something of an understatement.

As the jovial but sinister fat man Casper Gutman, Huston picked the massive, husky-voiced British actor Sydney Greenstreet. With his hefty build and impeccable diction, Greenstreet was a star of the British and American stage. He was 'discovered' by Huston following his appearance in *There Shall Be No Night* at the Biltmore Theatre, Los Angeles. *The Maltese Falcon* marked the 61-year old actor's big screen debut.

As the slimy, effeminate, curly-haired Joel Cairo, Huston needed an actor with special qualities. From a list of 24 candidates, he opted for Peter Lorre. He had seen *M* and was greatly impressed by the actor's versatility. 'Peter could do anything,' Huston said. 'The flight of his talent is just unlimited.' Lorre signed up on a $2,000 a week salary – the minimum for a freelance actor under Screen Actors' Guild (SAG) regulations – and was guaranteed five weeks' work. Being short of money, he managed to secure a $500 advance.

Lorre described working on *The Maltese Falcon* as 'One of my happiest memories.' John Huston kept a strong family atmosphere throughout, and this camaraderie between the cast and crew made for a wonderful time, with Huston looking after everyone like a father figure. This only added to the effectiveness of the performances.

Lorre gives a career defining turn as the vicious, ineffectual toady who gets knocked around by everybody, especially Bogie's Sam Spade. ('When you're slapped, you'll take it and like it!') This was the kind of dark comical role he would often be associated with throughout the '40s, and Lorre was very happy with the material.

The Maltese Falcon began Lorre's lifelong friendship with Huston and Bogart. They all shared a similar sense of humour and a love of practical jokes. 'The combination of Huston, Bogart and Lorre was a very fast company in the wit department,' said Mary Astor. 'You joined in at your own risk!'

The Lorre/Bogart friendship went beyond fun and games. 'I like Bogie because he is 100% what he is, and that is very rich,' said Lorre. Bogart was going through a stormy marriage with Mayo Methot, so he spent a lot of time with his new friend. It was Lorre who convinced Bogart to marry Lauren Bacall despite the age gap between them. 'It's better to have five good years than none at all,' he reportedly told Bogart. Separated from Celia and cut off from his family as war raged in Europe, having Bogart around lifted Lorre's spirits.

The Maltese Falcon wrapped in July 1941, under budget and ahead of schedule. The film premiered in October 1941 to huge critical and commercial success that included Academy Award nominations for Best Picture, Best Supporting Actor for Sydney Greenstreet and Best Screenplay for John Huston. They lost all three, but it hardly mattered.

At Warners, Lorre enjoyed the intimate family atmosphere. Although he was still a freelance, he became a permanent fixture at the studio. Extremely popular with the actors and technicians, he was described by set designer Harper Goff as 'a font of knowledge.' It was a perfect studio to work in. There were no stars at Warners, only actors: seasoned professionals who turned up on time and worked to a very high standard – no room for slackers or over-inflated egos!

Lorre was also in better shape than he had been in a long while. On the advice of fellow actor Gilbert Roland, he went on a strict diet. The svelte new look and new life coincided with a permanent change of name. On 8 August 1941, the US District Court officially declared that Laszlo Loewenstein would be permanently known as Peter Lorre.

As Lorre lived the American Dream, Bertolt Brecht came back to haunt him. Stripped of his German citizenship, Brecht was on the run, along with his family and agent/mistress Ruth Berlau. Although he had no desire to go to America, the playwright applied for US immigration in 1939, but it fell through when he was forced to flee to Sweden. When Hitler's forces invaded Scandinavia, he moved to Finland. Finally securing US immigration, he arrived in America shortly after Lorre completed *The Maltese Falcon*.

Because Lorre distanced himself from the other European émigrés, how much he knew of Brecht's arrival is uncertain. However, he welcomed his old friend to his home, where they talked for hours. As Hollywood was the place a man of his reputation could earn good money, Brecht established important contacts with Orson Welles, John Huston and Charlie Chaplin.

Brecht knew Lorre would be his ticket to success. In a way they needed one another. Lorre's celebrity was a springboard for Brecht to establish a writing career, and Brecht could provide Lorre with that all-important film role. The financial assistance Brecht got from Lorre was also a big help.

Despite their reputations, few European filmmakers equalled their early success in Hollywood; and Brecht, being Brecht, was never going to pander to Hollywood, especially when his Marxist views were guaranteed to close many doors and open very few. He found America intellectually bankrupt and corrupt. The method of alienation in his plays may have worked in Germany, but Hollywood was something else entirely. So he was astonished when he saw how Americanised had Lorre became. 'Peter immersed himself with all things American, or rather Western,' noted actor Tony Martin. Lorre loved the outdoors, the open ranges, horse riding, and could speak slang as well as any native American. His high earning power meant he could live well. To a baffled Brecht, it was incomprehensible excess. But then Lorre had never embraced Marxism; he had always been liberal in his political views.

Lorre returned to Universal for another heavy role, in the wartime thriller *Invisible Agent* (1942), starring Jon Hall as the grandson of the character played by Claude Rains in *The Invisible Man* (1933). Thanks to John P Fulton's excellent special effects, the film rang the box office tills despite being pretty obvious, and quite politically incorrect in its depiction of racial stereotypes.

Returning to Columbia for the silly horror spoof *The Boogie Man Will Get You* (1942), Lorre worked once more with Boris Karloff, who had resumed making films following his Broadway hit *Arsenic and Old Lace*. In one of the weirdest roles of his career, Lorre is a Stetson-wearing small-town sheriff who acts as justice of the peace, doctor, coroner and loan shark. The mixture of comedy and horror never worked well, and hamming it up wasn't the forte of either actor, both of whom took it all a little too seriously.

All Through the Night (1942) was a more satisfactory effort that had Lorre back at Warners with Humphrey Bogart and Conrad Veidt. He also met on this production the woman who would become his second wife. Playing the small role of a nightclub singer was a pretty blonde German actress named Kaaren Verne.

Born in Berlin on 6 April 1918, Kaaren studied at the Berlin Staatstheater in 1934. Working in small theatre productions, her taste for notoriety began when she refused to swear a loyalty oath to Adolf Hitler. In 1936 she fell in love with British pianist Arthur Young. Because her uncle was acting as her guardian following her father's death, she was barred from marrying until her twenty-first birthday. However, the couple eloped to Denmark, where they married in August 1936. Their son was born the following year.

The couple split in 1939, with Kaaren's husband gaining custody of the boy. Kaaren then pursued her career in England, first as a model and then as an actress opposite Rex Harrison in *Ten Days on Paris* (1939). This led to an MGM screen test and a trip to Hollywood. Following a bit part in the B-movie *Sky Murder* (1940), Kaaren got the lead in the propaganda movie *Underground* (1941). Because she could speak perfect English with a slight accent, Warners saw the potential of using her in their wartime movies and put her on a contract.

As a child, Kaaren had heard of Peter Lorre but had been forbidden to watch his films because of his villainous image. Thanks to her new contract, she was able to visit the set of *The Maltese Falcon* to see him at work. 'Kaaren admired him greatly,' said friend Naomi Yergin. The couple quickly became inseparable. Lorre represented adult sophistication to Kaaren's young

Hollywood glamour. They excited each other and the chemistry showed on screen in *All Through the Night*. Away from the film they headed for the beach, played tennis and acted like a couple of lovesick teenagers.

Shortly after the completion of *All Through the Night*, the Japanese bombing of Pearl Harbor prompted the American government to mobilise its dormant war machine and fight alongside the Allies. Prior to joining the armed forces, however, noted director Frank Capra watched the Broadway production of *Arsenic and Old Lace* and decided he wanted to bring it to the big screen. Although the play's writers, Howard Lindsay and Russell Crouise, had already sold the rights to Warners, the film was not supposed to be made until the play closed its Broadway run. Determined to take it forward more quickly, Capra set up the film's budget, sorted out the production estimates and negotiated salaries. He got Cary Grant involved as the male lead and brought in Josephine Hull, Jean Alexander and John Alexander to recreate their stage roles. Only Boris Karloff was unable to take part due to work commitments. Capra made his sales pitch to Jack Warner. Highly impressed, Warner agreed, and Capra began work the following day.

Peter Lorre was Capra's first choice for the role of alcoholic plastic surgeon Dr Einstein, and the actor relished the chance to play real comedy. Capra was also willing to let Lorre and Cary Grant ad-lib as much as possible, allowing both actors to give fluid performances without resorting to eye rolling.

Arsenic and Old Lace is a delightfully anarchic black comedy filled with Capra's typically whimsical touches and an outstanding cast in exceptionally good form. The only fault is the casting of Raymond Massey in Karloff's role. Although there is nothing wrong with Massey's performance, he looks too serious alongside the fun-fuelled antics of the other actors. If Karloff had been able to take part, the film would have been elevated to classic status.

Hollywood was now obsessed with the war, especially with the increase of Europeans coming to America. The situation helped produce one of the greatest films ever made, and one that secured Lorre's reputation.

Inspired by his travels across Europe, Murray Burnett wrote with Joan Alison a play called *Everybody Comes to Rick's*. Set in a café where people can forget the horrors of war, it impressed theatre producers Martin Gabel and Carly Wharton, who optioned it for Broadway, only to abandon it following creative differences with the writers. Burnett and Alison then sold the film rights to Warners for $20,000. The play was renamed *Casablanca* (1942), after the Moroccan city where the central setting of Rick's Café is situated.

From this unlikely start, *Casablanca* emerged as a timeless classic with career-defining performances from a perfect cast. What makes it work is not the simple love story at its heart, but the political intrigue going on around it, all of which is overseen by the cinema's ultimate antihero, Rick Blaine, expertly played by Humphrey Bogart. Bogie is so good as Rick that it's impossible to imagine anyone else in the role. It's even more surprising that he wasn't the original choice – George Raft turned it down and Ronald Reagan was considered (seriously!)

Casablanca features more émigré actors than any other Hollywood movie, singer/drummer Dooley Wilson being the only American other than Bogart in the cast. Austrian Paul Henreid (who plays resistance leader Victor Laszlo) and German Conrad Veidt (SS officer Major Strasser) were both outspoken in their hatred of the Nazi party. The much-loved Austrian comedy star S Z Sakall (bumbling headwaiter Carl) had been forced to flee Germany because of his Jewish background. Britain is represented by Claude Rains (taking the acting honours as Free-Frenchman Captain Renault) and Sydney Greenstreet (donning a fez as Sr Ferrari), while Swedish actress Ingrid Bergman plays Rick's lost love (and Lazlo's wife) Ilse Lund.

Keeping the strong European link was formidable Hungarian director Michael Curtiz, whose autocratic style and ability to get a film finished on time and on budget made him Warners' most successful director.

As doomed black marketeer Ugarte, Lorre was a late addition to the production, on a $1,750 a week salary. The story of his own exit from Germany made good studio publicity. Although the part is small, Ugarte is pivotal to the story. (He holds priceless letters of transit, which he entrusts to Rick following his arrest.) Little is said about his background, but this adds to Ugarte's mystique, and Lorre plays up to this, presenting a well-rounded character. What makes this all very surprising is his apparent reluctance to appear in the film. According to director Buzz Kulik, 'Lorre, Bogart and Bergman thought it was a horror, an awful thing.'

Whatever the stars felt about the film at the time, *Casablanca* is cinema brilliance. Its release coincided with the Allies landing in North Africa and capturing Casablanca. No-one could buy that kind of publicity! Not surprisingly *Casablanca* picked up eight Oscar nominations, winning Best Picture and Best Screenplay.

The making of the film had other advantages for Lorre. The roulette wheel featured in Rick's Café was actually used by the cast and crew for gambling, and Lorre claimed he earned more from playing roulette than from his performance in the film.

Although he was generally unpopular among the cast and crew, Michael Curtiz got on well with Lorre, who basically gave him what he wanted. A notorious womaniser, Curtiz took his latest conquest to a secret bordello he had set up on the set of *Casablanca*. He had no idea that Lorre knew of this place, or that the actor had hidden a microphone in the room so that the entire cast and crew could hear Curtiz having sex with this woman.

Remaining with Warners, Lorre returned to standard villainy as a Russian agent in *Background to Danger* (1943). A change of pace followed with the role of a romantic playboy in *The Constant Nymph* (1943), although most of his contribution ended up on the cutting room floor.

Radio kept the actor busy, with regular appearances in the anthology show *Suspense* for CBS in New York. He recited Edgar Allan Poe's *The Cask of Amontillado* for *The Kate Smith Show* and entertained servicemen at home for CBS and overseas for *The Armed Forces Radio*. He also attended a variety of charity events to raise money for the war effort. Early in 1943 he became one of the big names to sign up with the Music Corporation of America.

Lorre's next film was *The Cross of Lorraine* (1943), an MGM adaptation of Hans Habe's French Resistance novel *A Thousand Shall Fall*. Starring Gene Kelly, the film gives an uncompromising depiction of Nazi brutality toward demobilised French soldiers. In his most evil role to date, Lorre, the only freelance actor in the cast, is brilliant as the sadistic Sergeant Berger. 'For such a small man he was so much more menacing than anyone we have today,' recalled director Tay Garnet. 'I thought he was magnificent.'

On 2 June 1943, Lorre signed a five-year contract with Warners, which included the standard renewal options. Lorre would make two films a year at a salary of $1,750 a week. The contract permitted him to undertake further radio work as long as it did not conflict with the studio schedules. This was a good move, as Lorre gave over forty radio performances during this period, most notably for *Suspense* and *The Inner Sanctum Mysteries*. He also pulled enough weight to have a clause inserted allowing him to work for other studios, making two films a year, along with the option to direct one feature.

The contract had its drawbacks though. Keeping a tight reign on his services, Warners rushed Lorre from one film to another, forcing him to turn down work from other studios because of conflicting schedules. Warners also had a tendency to pigeonhole an actor into a certain persona. Lorre knew the pros and cons of this arrangement. Character roles would always be there, but at the expense of creativity and artistic development. It was his estranged wife Celia who gave the best description of Lorre's tenure at the studio: 'Happily unhappy!'

Bertolt Brecht hoped that Lorre's new contract could help him too to secure a foothold in the movie industry. But Lorre had no real connections at Warners; the studio had their own writers, who always played by the rules. Brecht came to realise that American movies were little more than a moneymaking business, with art having little to do with it. This only fuelled his increasing contempt for all things Hollywood.

Working again with Humphrey Bogart, Sydney Greenstreet, Claude Rains and Michael Curtiz, Lorre starred in Warners' flag-waver *Passage to Marseilles* (1944), one of the first films to use the flashback-within-a-flashback-within-a-flashback technique. The end result is a confusing mess that fails to match the quality of *Casablanca*. As convicted safecracker Marius, Lorre excels in a sympathetic role full of sardonic humour, even though performing in the movie's smoky battle scenes triggered off a dust allergy from which he suffered.

Warners intended Lorre and Greenstreet to star in a proposed sequel to *The Amazing Dr Clitterhouse* (1938). However, writers Alvah Bessie and Leonhard Frank instead turned to Eric Ambler's interesting spy novel *A Coffin for Dimitrios*; and, on the advice of John Huston, director Jean Negulesco convinced Jack Warner that this was a more interesting vehicle for the studio's 'Laurel and Hardy of crime'.

The Mask of Dimitrios (1944) is an important film, because it relies entirely on character actors to carry the dramatic weight instead of a handsome romantic lead. 'It was a great gamble,' recalled Negulesco, a talented artist who was making his debut as director. It also marked the incredible screen debut of American stage actor Zachary Scott. However, excellent as Scott is in the role of Dimitrios, it is Lorre's and Greenstreet's film all the way.

Lorre is cast as Dutch mystery writer Marius, whose research into the life of master criminal Dimitrios drags him into the sleazy world of espionage in the Middle East. Negulesco directs with a stimulating feel for the film noir material, making good use of the evocative sets and backdrops and getting excellent performances from his cast, especially Lorre. 'If you watch Dimitrios,' recalled Negulesco, 'you'll find the whole picture, its entire mood, is held together by Lorre. Without him you're a little bored by it.' Lorre however did not share this feeling. 'I can't control my leers,' he said. 'My glowers get out of hand. I snarl when I should be wincing with fear.'

If Lorre was being too hard on himself, it was probably because a general disenchantment with Hollywood had started to set in. 'He felt a kind of cynicism about his career and life in general,' said director Vincent Sherman. 'I think he found that instead of being regarded as a very serious actor he was regarded as a freak.'

Sydney Greenstreet's role in *The Mask of Dimitrios* is as the jovial but deadly blackmailer Mr Peters, who befriends Lorre's lost little man. The two actors complement each other on film – Greenstreet, jaunty but evil, and Lorre, impulsive but insecure. It is a creepy alliance brought to unsettling life by two versatile actors who generate a darkly menacing chemistry. Fittingly, Greenstreet and Lorre referred to each other as 'The Old Man' and 'Puck'!

For two men who worked so well together, they were total opposites as actors. Greenstreet was the trained thespian, and Lorre the improviser. But they gelled on screen even when Greenstreet sometimes found Lorre's antics hard to take. '[Peter] used to drive Sydney Greenstreet up the wall,' said writer Richard Matheson. 'Greenstreet was this theatre-trained perfectionist and he would deliver a line, and Lorre would just throw something back that seemed to have no relationship to the picture.'

Despite their different backgrounds, they respected each other and remained good friends. 'Sydney Greenstreet was not only one of the nicest men and gentlemen I've ever known,' said Lorre, 'I think he was one of the truly great, great actors of our time. It's fun to work with Sydney. The only problem is staying out of his shadow.' Actress Joan Lorring summed up the professional relationship best: 'They were both on the same wavelength.'

However, Greenstreet was earning a lot more than Lorre, even though he had never made a film prior to *The Maltese Falcon*, whereas Lorre had ten years' experience behind him. For *The Maltese Falcon* itself, Lorre got paid $2,000 a week to Greenstreet's $1,000 and received higher billing than him; but in their subsequent collaborations, Greenstreet had the fatter pay cheque and the higher billing. Although this never caused any problems between them, Lorre felt it undermined his position at Warners.

After making guest appearances in *Hollywood Canteen* (1944), Lorre and Greenstreet reunited with Paul Henreid and Jean Negulesco for the wartime thriller *The Conspirators* (1944). Set in Lisbon, the film is not up to the standard of either *Casablanca* or *The Mask of Dimitrios*, although Lorre and Greenstreet are in typically good form.

Lorre and Kaaren had been living together for a while by this point, so the time was right for them to make things legal. Kaaren had already filed for divorce in November 1944, so Lorre began his own divorce proceedings in March 1945. Celia was happy to let her husband live his life. The divorce was finalised, with Celia receiving $200 a week alimony until she either remarried or passed away.

Coinciding with Warners agreeing a one-year extension of his contract, Lorre married Kaaren in a private ceremony on 25 May 1945. Returning to Hollywood, the couple enjoyed a double celebration with Humphrey Bogart's marriage to Lauren Bacall. After touring several army hospitals across California, the couple spent their honeymoon at Big Bear Lake. Celia came with them!

Returning to Hollywood, Lorre played the sympathetic part of an alcoholic professor in Warners' wartime drama *Hotel Berlin* (1945), set during the Reich's final months in power. Once again Warners got the timing right, releasing the film just prior to Russian forces invading Berlin. Unfortunately most of Lorre's role ended up on the cutting room floor.

More intriguing was Jean Negulesco's *Three Strangers* (1945), starring Lorre, Greenstreet and Joan Lorring as strangers who meet during the Chinese New Year and buy a lottery ticket with the hope of wealth and good fortune. When the ticket is drawn, it becomes a clue linking Lorring's character to murder. Deserting Greenstreet's pompous lawyer and Lorre's disenchanted drunk, she ends up being responsible for their downfall. The critics found *Three Strangers* less film noir and more art house before art house became fashionable, although Lorre and Greenstreet, playing roles against type, were singled out for praise.

Lorre's final wartime move for Warners was *Confidential Agent* (1945). May 1945 signalled the end of the fighting in Europe, and America's conflict with Japan ended three months later. The majority of the actor's Warners films having been wartime dramas or thrillers produced to bolster audience morale, the end of the war marked an uncertain future for him. And at 42, he was now too old to play the romantic lead type roles that had in any case always looked out of his reach.

Lorre's next film with Sydney Greenstreet would be his last. Adapted from Israel Zangwell's classic novel *The Big Bow Mystery* (1892), *The Verdict* (1946) was a crime thriller that marked Don Siegel's directorial debut. Greenstreet was cast as a Scotland Yard detective investigating a murder case with enough red herrings to sink a ship. Lorre's role was as suspect Victor Emmeric, while Joan Lorring was recruited from *Three Strangers* to be the female lead.

The Verdict proved a difficult shoot for all concerned. To give the film a Victorian period feel, fog was created by using dry ice, burning cans of charcoal and vaporising mineral oil. Too much of it, apparently. When Lorre inhaled the fumes, he developed respiratory problems, headaches and a severe attack of the liver. To ease the pain, he was prescribed Dapyrin and then Dilaudid. When Greenstreet went down with pneumonia, production had to be halted.

To make matter worse, Warners' union employees staged a mass walkout over low pay and poor working conditions. This resulted in an ongoing feud that descended into violence between the union members and hired studio heavies. Not only was Siegel the only director working on the lot, he had to fight his way to the studio, not knowing if his cast or crew would be present. This sordid incident became known as the Battle of Burbank.

Although Lorre was not directly threatened with violence if he crossed the picket line, he sided with the union, causing a serious rift with Jack Warner. He may not have realised it at the time, but Lorre had burnt his bridges with Warners, giving the studio a good reason to terminate his services when his contract next came up for renewal.

Although it was hardly his best work, Siegel directed *The Verdict* with a strong visual style that belied the troubled production. By mutual consent, Lorre and Greenstreet decided to terminate their own association at this point. It had been fun while it lasted, but according to Lorre, 'We didn't want to end up like Abbott and Costello.' *The Verdict* marked a quiet but dignified end to an electric partnership.

With no further use for Lorre, Warners loaned him out to Nero Films for *The Chase* (1946) and to Universal for *Black Angel* (1946). The actor did however made one final film for Warners, which ironically turned out to be one of his finest screen performances.

The Beast with Five Fingers (1946) is a handsomely mounted chiller that features excellent special effects to complement Lorre's superb turn as Hilary Cummins, a deranged bookworm tormented by a severed hand. Curt Siodmak wrote the script with Paul Henreid in mind, but Henreid actor did not want to play opposite a hand. 'I would love to have shot it with him,' said Siodmak, 'because I thought a man looking so debonair was much more interesting than the freakish Lorre.' The writer wasn't too happy with Warners' decision to cast Lorre. 'A threatening Paul would have more impact then bug-eyed Peter, whom everyone suspects is the monster.' Siodmak also found Lorre a strange person to work with. 'He was really a sadistic son-of-a-bitch. Liked to look at hospital operations. He really was a very weird character.'

Aware of Lorre's declining reputation at Warners, director Robert Florey decided to shoot *The Beast with Five Fingers* through the eyes of Cummins, so that he could give Lorre free reign to improvise. Siodmak wasn't happy about that idea either. He might have been right, but it doesn't detract from the fact that Lorre is excellent in the role, especially in the final scenes when he confronts the hand. Florey's fluid expressionist style complements Lorre's improvisational skills.

Unfortunately the studio decided to edit the film, which spoilt a good climax. The original ending had Cummins strangled by the hand. That scene was cut, however, leaving the audience with the impression that Cummins imagined the whole thing and strangled himself! A total cop-out of an ending, which wastes Lorre dedicated acting. Florey was so incensed by the studio interference that he disowned the final cut.

The Beast with Five Fingers did decent business at the box office. More horror roles could have followed for Lorre, but the genre was in decline once more. On 13 May 1946 he parted company with Warners, leaving him with an even more uncertain future.

For Bertolt Brecht, this was a chance to get Lorre out of Hollywood. A return to theatre was the solution. 'I think Brecht to Peter was a form of friendship,' according to fellow friend Ralph Greenson. 'Brecht represented some of Lorre's idealistic views that he was unable to carry out.' Brecht encouraged Lorre to re-immerse himself in the arts. Fellow European exiles Lotte Lenya and Elizabeth Bergner were also on hand to boost his flagging confidence. But taking Lorre away from the celebrity lifestyle would be difficult.

Although he was now free from the shackles of Warners, the cessation of his weekly salary was less pleasant. Someone had to take care of the money, and salvation came courtesy of a manager named Sam Stiefel, who promised to sort out Lorre's finances. Confident that he was the right man, Lorre signed a contract with Stiefel, who formed the business Lorre Incorporated. Stiefel now had power of attorney over all of Lorre's business and personal affairs.

Lorre got a good supporting role as knife-throwing heavy Kismet in the Bob Hope comedy *My Favorite Brunette* (1947). Although he plays second fiddle to Hope's typically sharp wisecracks, he more than holds his own. Nevertheless, this venture into full-blown comedy was an uncomfortable forerunner to the later phase of his career, when he would resort to self-parody.

In February 1947, Stiefel booked Lorre a three-week engagement at the Roxy Theatre in New York with a one-man show. It was to finance another cure for his addiction. Placed in the care of Dr Max Gruenthal, Lorre underwent insulin shock therapy. When that failed, he checked into the New York State Psychiatric Institute to undergo electric shock therapy. He recovered sufficiently to give a drug-free rendition of Edgar Allen Poe's *The Tell-Tale Heart* to an enthusiastic young audience at the Roxy. But the cure didn't work, and Lorre, who was suffering from depression, buckled under the strain. With his system unable to cope with any more drugs, he informed the Federal Bureau of Narcotics (FBN) of his condition. Reporting to the FBN, Lorre was examined and certified an addict. Aware of the bad publicity this could bring, his old friend and journalist Irving Yergin managed to keep the press quiet.

FBN's district supervisor Garland Williams wanted to arrest Lorre, but Commissioner Harry Anslinger took a sympathetic view. Aware that Lorre wanted to kick the habit, Anslinger allowed him to complete his engagement on condition that he committed himself to a state-run facility where he could be treated. If successful, all drug charges would be dropped.

Lorre agreed, and on 3 March 1947 he checked into the US Public Health Service Hospital in Fort Worth, Texas, using his real name to avoid bad publicity. His treatment was a slow withdrawal of the Dilaudid and morphine in his system. He slept well, ate well and even lost weight, but there were still mood swings and psychosomatic headaches.

Responding well to the treatment, on 16 April, after a month off drugs, Lorre got discharged, although he would have to make regular visits to the facility. Unhappy with Lorre's discharge, Anslinger ordered agents to keep a close eye on his every movement.

Looking fitter and healthier than he had in a long time, Lorre returned home to Kaaren. He decided to take a complete break from film work and concentrate on radio, which was less stressful.

Brecht had received an offer from a Berlin theatre to produce a series of plays for the 1947-48 season consisting of classics and originals. The playwright accepted the offer with the intention of taking Lorre with him. 'I need Lorre unconditionally, if I'm going to get my theatre together again.

Without him I can hardly imagine the whole thing.'

Brecht wanted Lorre to play all the lead parts, tailored to his individual style. With the actor's health restored, all that was needed was for him to sort out his debts and get money together, which meant him taking other work for the early part of the season. That way he could re-establish his position as Germany's great stage actor but still remain firmly rooted in America.

In the meantime, Lorre returned to radio with a new crime anthology series for NBC called *Mystery on the Air*. He played a different role in each episode, and the series ideally suited his macabre style. *Mystery on the Air* ran from June to September 1947. Following its cancellation, the actor continued giving three to four radio performances a year in other shows.

With Lorre ready for his return to the theatre, Brecht searched for backers for his play *Galileo*. Despite the initial enthusiasm, potential investors pulled out following pressure from the Vatican. Lorre loved the play and acted as advisor. A proposed film version to be made in England never materialised. *Galileo* eventually played on the New York stage in December 1947 to unfavourable reviews. It closed after four weeks.

While Brecht made plans for his return, Lorre received a surprise visit from the FBI. The agents provided a list of movie people and asked if the actor knew any of them. Lorre happily cooperated with them. Because his political views were at best naïve, he did not realise this was the start of Senator Joseph McCarthy's infamous communist witch-hunt that engulfed Hollywood in the '50s. Lorre also failed to realise that his friendship with Brecht was damaging to him. The pair saw each other frequently, but it had more to do with Brecht's theatre plans than with his politics. Brecht however remained a staunch Marxist, and Lorre's support for the union strike at Warners had incensed Jack Warner enough for the actor to be labelled a communist agitator.

With FBI files handed over to the House Un-American Activities Committee (HUAC) in May 1947, a total of 41 actors, directors, producers and writers were subpoenaed to testify in Washington. Lorre came close to being summoned. The FBI files included extensive information about his relationship with Brecht.

Subpoenaed to appear before the HUAC as an 'unfriendly witness,' Brecht denied under oath that he had been a member of the Communist Party. It was an unusual move for a self-confessed maverick, but one he made on Lorre's advice. Brecht hated betraying his associates, but the witch-hunt had started, and Lorre told him to leave America. Brecht complied and left for Germany the next day. As for Lorre, his friendship with alleged communists Orson Welles, Humphrey Bogart, Charlie Chaplin and Vincent Price only spelt trouble.

Film work still came his way. There was a scene-stealing turn in

Universal's *Casbah* (1948) and a cameo in Paramount's *Rope of Sand* (1949). Other than that, Lorre spent most of 1948 and 1949 on the New York stage with his one-man show. With Hollywood wrapped up in the witch-hunt, the best thing for him to do was stay away.

In addition to provincial tours of Baltimore and Philadelphia, Lorre made his first television appearances. Financially however he struggled. He lived and spent money as if he was still at Warners – he had dogs, horses and expensive tastes to maintain. He was so desperate for cash that the Music Corporation of America were able to hire him for a mere $350 to appear in Spike Jones' *Spotlight Revue*.

Lorre rounded off the decade with *Quicksand* (1949), a comedy starring Mickey Rooney as a car mechanic who gets into debt while trying to impress his rich girlfriend. In the role of a creepy blackmailer, Lorre has a whale of a time on screen, playing alongside Rooney with the aplomb of a comedy double act, although the humour is very dark.

Lorre's marriage ran into problems at this time. Being the wife of a big star proved too much for Kaaren. She was a modern young woman, and having given up her career had added to her frustration. Lorre never talked about his work at home and often chastised his wife for not looking after things. This made her even more unhappy.

Already jealous of her husband's enduring friendship with Celia, Kaaren felt alone. Lorre's friends and associates had little time for her, and she didn't quite fit in. The age gap also added to her isolation. 'She's absolutely miserable,' said her friend Rhoda Riker. 'A poor, forlorn, lost soul.'

Perhaps having a child could have helped the situation, but Kaaren was unable to conceive. While Lorre enjoyed night outs with Bogart, she stayed at home fighting loneliness. Now taking solace in alcohol to combat her depressive moods, she made the first of several suicide attempts.

Happily settled back in Berlin, Brecht waited for Lorre's return. He organised a revised production of *Mann ist Mann* and new versions of *Faust* and *The Caucasian Chalk Circle* and sorted out a possible film role for the actor. With the movie work drying up, Lorre was ready to return to Germany. But to turn away from Hollywood would not be that simple.

Things at Lorre Incorporated fell apart. Lorre had trusted Sam Stiefel and paid no attention to what he was doing behind his back. In a nutshell Stiefel robbed him blind. To salvage something from this financial mess, Lorre hired a reliable young attorney named Robert Shutan.

Shutan had his work cut out. In addition to a list of unpaid bills, Lorre owed three years' back taxes amounting to $16,000, and $9,675 in maintenance to Celia. He was even summoned before the Labor Commission for $1,202.28 owed to Elizabeth Hauptmann. He sorted things out with Celia when she agreed to reduced alimony of $4,450 a month.

On the advice of old friend Jonas Silverstone, Lorre filed for bankruptcy in May 1949. Auditors assessed all his debts, including $5,000 for his horses, $56,561.08 to a variety of creditors (for medical bills, restaurants, clothes, dog food!) and a variety of subscriptions ranging from the Screen Actors Guild dues to a couple of tennis clubs. Allowing time for the creditors to file their claims, Lorre was declared bankrupt on 18 August 1949.

Now discharged from all debts, Lorre could return to Germany. Before doing that, however, he went to London with Kaaren to start a ten-week theatre tour. During his time in England, Lorre reprised one of his one-man show character pieces as *The Man with the Glass Head* for BBC TV and got inducted into the Grand Order of Water Rats, one of the world's oldest theatrical fraternities.

Lorre was still popular in England, and the tour led to a film role in director Ken Annakin's *Double Confession* (1950). Annakin saw him as 'a great screen actor with that inborn gift of making himself stick out on screen.' Happy to earn some extra cash, Lorre upstaged everyone, much to the annoyance of William Hartnell, who played the film's chief villain. The strained interaction between the two actors was obvious to the other cast and crew. Hartnell was old school like Sydney Greenstreet, but not as good-humoured about Lorre's improvisational approach.

With the tour ending, Lorre returned to Germany in September 1949. Kaaren had left beforehand to look after her sick mother in Eggelkofen, South Bavaria; she then travelled to the resort town of Garmisch-Partenkenkirchen to stay with her sister Barbara and arrange for her husband to stay at the nearby Wiggers-Kuenheim Sanatorium, where he could relax. Although he had been drug-free for a while, he was still on codeine for his sinus problems. On his arrival in Munich to meet Kaaren, he suffered a relapse in his addiction. What should have been a relaxing holiday at a health farm became another attempt to cure him. At least this modern facility offered up-to-date methods, with the added bonus of great weather. It also led to hopes that the marriage could survive.

Lorre spent a year at Wiggers-Kuenheim trying to get off the morphine. The doctors gave him substitutes that included sweets – which increased his weight – and there was electrotherapy and hypnotherapy, but nothing worked. In fact the treatments rendered him unable to do anything.

Kaaren stayed at the sanatorium with the financial support of a friend she borrowed money from. But the marriage was over. After having a brief affair with a doctor at the clinic, she checked out and moved to East Berlin to look for work, before returning to America with Lorre's remaining cash and whatever else she could earn.

Lorre's poor health prevented him from taking part in the November 1949 opening of Brecht's Berlin ensemble. Disappointed but not defeated, Brecht harboured hopes of a glorious return to the German theatre, and offered Lorre the lead in *Hamlet* and the part of Death in *Salsburger Totentanz*.

But the actor, reluctant to be at Brecht's beck and call, had other plans.

Lorre had recovered sufficiently at Wiggers-Kurnheim to undertake a tour of refugee camps and American military hospitals. While reconnecting with his past, he saw a country shattered by the horrors of World War II, with over twenty million Germans homeless. Genuinely disturbed by this, he took a decision that became the biggest gamble of his career.

Returning to Wiggers-Kuenheim, Lorre received a visit from old friend Eon James, who told him about the attempted suicide of a doctor from one of the refugee camps he had visited. The doctor had been linked to the murder of one of his medical assistants. With Europe rebuilding itself after the war, the case remained unsolved. The doctor in question was Carl Rothe. Lorre's interest in Rothe's life gave him the idea for a movie reflecting post-war Germany.

Setting up Lorre Incorporated Films, he converted his room into an office and began working on his project. 'If my film helps to enlighten the conscience of only a single man, then it will not be made for nothing,' he said. Not only did Lorre see the film as a way of asserting his independence, he also wanted to use it to help Germany rise from the ashes. And it wasn't enough for him just to star in it; he wanted to direct on his own terms. 'I'd be a better director than an actor,' he said, 'but I can't live without acting.'

Joining Lorre as producer was old friend Arnold Pressburger, who had also returned to Germany from Hollywood. Pressburger sorted out partial finance with Hamburger Filmfaninazierungs-GmbH, with producer Friedrich Mainz footing the rest of the bill. Pressburger also arranged studio facilities with Jung Film Union in Benedesdorf and distribution with National Film GmbH. With filming set for the autumn of 1950, Lorre assembled his production team, which included cinematographer Vaclav Vich. In the meantime he took up several speaking engagements across Germany.

The film being set in Hamburg, Lorre hired local theatre talent for the leading roles. The cast included Karl John, a veteran from the Deutsches Theatre, screen actor Helmut Randolph and, lower down the cast list, an attractive young brunette called Annemarie Brenning.

Born in Cruxhaven in 1922, Annemarie graduated from Hamburg's Staatlichen Schauspeilschule in 1940. She moved to Berlin to establish herself as an actress, but her career was put on hold by military service. She appeared on stage in Hamburg and later worked as a script editor. After sustaining a leg injury, she was admitted to Wiggers-Kurnheim, where she met Lorre, who hired her to work on the script of his film.

In Pressburger words, Annemarie was 'absolutely devoted to Peter.' She never left his side during the production, much to the actor's bemusement, since he could never understand the attraction. But then Lorre adored the opposite sex and they adored him!

Now titled *Der Verlorene* or *The Lost One* (1951), the film began production in November 1950. Assuming duties of director, producer and writer, Lorre reluctantly cast himself as Dr Karl Rothe, a Nazi scientist who murders his wife after finding out she has sold his secret research to the Allies. Tracing the events of Rothe's life prior to his suicide, the film is a character study of how a good man can be corrupted by the sinister power. Lorre described *The Lost One* as a story of psychopathology under Nazi control.

The narrative is told in flashback, and Lorre's knowledge of film noir is evident. His experience as an actor gives *The Lost One* an intimate style. Seeing his work as an artistic endeavour, he left his crew to handle the technical side. He wanted freedom of expression and did his best to avoid the kind of tight schedules imposed by the studios. He began shooting around midday and held daily script conferences and discussion with his actors concerning every aspect of the production.

Lorre maintained a team spirit. He felt a great responsibility for his actors, who appreciated his sensitive approach. 'Working under Peter was hard, but wonderful,' said actress Renate Mannhardt. It was a feeling shared by editor Carl Bartning: 'He had a very strong personal radiance about him. There were people who talked with him for the first time, and they loved him at once.'

The Lost One was nevertheless a difficult production in some respects. Buckling under the stress of directing, Lorre resumed his drug-taking, while the constant need for money drove Pressburger over the edge. To help out with the technical side of things, Lorre hired Hans Grimm as his assistant director. Despite his efforts to finish the film on time and within budget, the incomplete script and Lorre's penchant for improvising quickly soured Grimm's relationship with him.

When Arnold Pressburger died from a cerebral hemorrhage in February 1951, his son Fred took over as producer, but he found Lorre's constant demands for cash frustrating. The actor claimed heavy expenses and sold non-existent foreign distribution rights to Friedrich Mainz. Production halted for a while when Karl John broke his leg, and the film ran into financial problems despite Fred Pressburger doing his best to secure additional funding.

Thanks to his drug use, Lorre underwent mood swings that were apparent to the cast and crew. He was bristling with enthusiasm one minute, introverted the next. His performance as Rothe was distant, as if he had other things on his mind. Looking tired, thin and older than his 46 years, he was a troubled man with the weight of the world on his shoulders.

Once production wrapped, *The Lost One* was placed in the hands of Carl Bartning for a final edit. Unfortunately a fire destroyed the editing room at Harvestehuder Weg Studio, leaving him to have to re-edit an existing negative left in storage.

Due to the amount of debt he had racked up throughout filming, Lorre fled to Hamburg, leaving bills from Jung Film Union and National Film GmbH unpaid.

The Lost One received a special screening in Munich in March 1951, but adverse publicity surrounding the making of the film, plus Lorre's erratic behaviour, did it no favours. When it went on general release in September 1951, audiences and critics alike reacted with indifference. Lorre blamed National Film GmbH for the lack of advance publicity, but at the end of the day, no-one enjoyed the film.

The main problem was timing. *The Lost One* was a gloomy reminder of World War II. Thousands of servicemen were returning home from Europe, many of them physically and mentally scarred by six years of fighting. Adapting to civilian life would not be easy for them, so a film like *The Lost One* was never going to be popular. Not surprisingly, the film bombed at the German box office – although it did well in France.

The making of *The Lost One* turned out to be a bitter experience for Lorre. He had put everything into the film but received little positive benefit. However, even with his spirit crushed and his creative energy drained, he harboured hopes of a new career as a film director. He remained in Germany for the rest of the year waiting for film offers. None was forthcoming, and this added to his depressive state. Even Bertolt Brecht had nothing lined up for him.

Broke, depressed and unemployed, Lorre realised his only option was a return to America, where he still had an admiring public. Transportation back to the States came courtesy of the American Air Force, who agreed to take him home in exchange for a free showing of *The Lost One*. The actor finally arrived back in America on 16 February 1952 to begin the next phase of his chequered career.

Arriving in New York in March 1952, he re-established contact with a few friends before getting a job on NBC Radio's *The Big Show*, where he sent up his bogeyman image alongside Tallulah Bankhead. Annemarie arrived in New York a few months later.

Unable to get work on a Broadway production, Lorre joined a summer stock tour of Edwin Mayer's *A Night at Madame Tussaud's – A Shocker in the Grand Guignol*, in which he was cast as Brutus. The play opened at the Norwich Summer Theatre in August 1952. The audience response was positive; the play took seven curtain calls at the Boston Summer Theatre.

Unfortunately Lorre and actress Miriam Hopkins, who played Ninon, hated each other. The ill feeling between them was so bad that when the curtain fell after a performance at York Theatre, Pennsylvania, Hopkins kicked Lorre. According to Edwin Mayer's son John, 'Peter took his bow hopping on one foot, certainly more for effect than pain.'

The play was scheduled for a lengthy Broadway run that never happened. The financiers wanted to keep Lorre and dispense with Hopkins, but Hopkins owned the rights to the play and refused to release them unless Lorre dropped out. She held out long enough for the producers to concede to her demands, but the play never reached Broadway.

By the time Lorre returned to Hollywood, Kaaren had gone to the New York Supreme Court of Justice in December 1952 to file for divorce, citing a list of reasons, including giving up her own career. With health problems hampering her attempts to re-establish herself as an actress, she demanded monthly $250 alimony payments, claiming that despite his own money woes, Lorre continued living a lavish lifestyle.

Salvation came from agent Paul Kohner, who represented John Huston. When Kohner found out about Lorre's return, he wrote a letter to the actor congratulating him on his work on *The Lost One* and offering his services to represent him. The possibility of decent film work was enough for Lorre to sign on the dotted line. John Huston even had something lined up for him: a movie that would reunite Lorre with Humphrey Bogart, who acted as co-producer.

Based on Claud Cockburn's novel of the same name, *Beat the Devil* (1953) was a comedy about several international criminals planning to defraud British East Africa out of their rich uranium deposits. With Truman Capote hired to rewrite Cockburn's original script, Bogart and Huston brought in Jack Clayton as cinematographer and cast Lorre, Gina Lollobrigida, Jennifer Jones and Robert Morley in the lead roles.

Huston initially had high hopes that the film could be another *The Maltese Falcon*, but various problems occurred before shooting that almost caused him to abandon it altogether. Although funny in parts, the finished film is an incoherent mess full of unexplained situations and an assortment of characters that are too weird for an audience to take in all at once.

For Lorre, though, *Beat the Devil* was a return to form, with a nice performance as O'Hara the Chilean toady. With his dyed blond, cropped hair and rotund shape, Lorre looks like Joel Cairo in befuddled middle age! Capote got on well with Lorre, so much so that he expanded the role and gave him an immortal line: 'Time, time is, what is time? The Swiss manufacture it. The French hoard it. The Italians squander it. The Americans say it is money. Hindus say it does not exist. You know what I say? I say time is a crook.'

Still in touch with his improvisational side and wanting spontaneity from his cast, Huston let Lorre do his own thing. The humorous elements of *Beat the Devil* enabled the actor to play it tongue-in-cheek. If anything, he saved the film from being completely tedious.

Bogart and Lorre hadn't worked together for some time, and they had great fun during filming. Capote also took part in their hard drinking antics.

As tempers frayed between the other cast members – the company were staying at a hotel in Ravello, Italy, where the location work was filmed – Lorre acted as counsellor to smooth things over, while Huston and Jack Clayton sorted out the troubled production.

Freddie Francis, who worked as camera operator, enjoyed his time on the film but was aware of the internal problems. 'Working on *Beat the Devil* was fun. The situation was that Bogart owned the rights to it and Huston agreed to direct in a weak moment. Right up to the last moment, I'm pretty sure that John didn't want to do it. He tried all sorts of ways to get out of it, but he couldn't, and all of a sudden there we all were in Italy.'

Huston wanted Sydney Greenstreet to take part, but the retired actor was unable to do so due to poor health. (He died the following year.) Robert Morley assumed the Greenstreet role but was too jovial to make an impact. Because the British actor kept to himself, Lorre did his best to annoy him throughout the production. 'I have always thought him an intensely tiresome little chap,' said Morley, obviously not amused by Lorre's antics.

Freddie Francis on the other hand enjoyed Lorre's presence. 'Peter Lorre was great to work with, he had a great sense of humour; though I didn't particularly like Humphrey Bogart.'

Beat the Devil didn't do well on its initial release, the comedy being too personal for some tastes, although it became a cult film several years later. 'I'm sure that when it was released, people were expecting another *The Maltese Falcon*,' said Francis. 'A lot of people hated it, but a lot liked it. It could have been a disaster, but I don't think it was entirely.'

Although Annemarie was heavily pregnant, Lorre could not marry her until his divorce from Kaaren was finalised. On 20 June 1953, two days before his daughter Catherine was born, a Las Vegas court granted him a divorce that included a cash settlement of $13,750 to Kaaren. Once production on *Beat the Devil* wrapped, Lorre flew to Hamburg in July 1953 to see his month-old daughter and marry Annemarie.

The arrival of Catherine sparked a new Peter Lorre – an adoring and devoted father. Returning to Hollywood, the Lorres rented a house in Benedict Canyon, Beverly Hills, which was ideal for the family. Annemarie loved California and happily gave up her career to be a housewife and mother.

Next for the actor came *20,000 Leagues Under the Sea* (1954), Walt Disney Studios' first live action movie. Directed by Richard Fleischer and starring James Mason, Kirk Douglas and Paul Lukas, it has all the typical Disney hallmarks. The fourth-billed Lorre plays Conseil, assistant to Lukas's Professor Arronax, with Douglas as harpoonist Ned Land.

20,000 Leagues Under the Sea is a rollicking adventure complete with hidden treasure, cannibals, and a memorable giant squid that attacks *The Nautilus*, itself a remarkable design. Thrills galore! All held together by an excellent production and James Mason's unforgettable turn as Captain Nemo. The film's only fault is Kirk Douglas, whose surprisingly belligerent performance as Land makes Nemo seem both sympathetic and heroic! Ned Land is no hero. In fact he's incapable of helping anyone, and often gets himself and everyone else into trouble.

The only time Douglas is worth watching is in his scenes with Lorre. They make an enjoyable comedy double act, with Douglas constantly rubbing his hand over Lorre's cropped hair. Lorre himself is in splendid comic form; and despite having to work in extremely hot conditions, he had a lot of fun on the film. 'When I first met Peter,' recalled Douglas, 'I think he felt it was all over and he was just making a living.'

Lorre also embraced the new medium of television. Although not apparent at the time, he made history by being the first ever James Bond villain when he played Le Chiffre in a television adaptation of *Casino Royale* for the CBS anthology series *Climax!*. Playing 007 – as an American CIA agent! – was Barry Nelson, who didn't want to do it until he heard about Lorre's involvement. Broadcast live in October 1954, and long believed lost from the archives until its rediscovery in the '80s, *Casino Royale* is a curiosity piece, complete with fluffed lines, missed cues and claustrophobic sets that were part and parcel of the era's live television. Nelson gives a decent performance, while Lorre adds memorable menace.

From 1955, Lorre worked on nine television productions. He repeated his role of Dr Einstein in *Arsenic and Old Lace*, with Boris Karloff returning as Jonathan Brewster. He made appearances in *The Eddie Cantor Comedy Theatre*, *Studio 57*, another episode of *Climax!* – this one based on Oscar Wilde's *Lord Arthur Saville's Crime* – and an episode of *Rhinegold Theatre*. In between these television assignments, he regularly turned up on quiz shows and talk shows.

Lorre's movie roles from this period were generally inferior to his television ones. After making an unbilled appearance as himself in the MGM musical *Meet Me in Las Vegas* (1956), he turned up briefly as a Japanese steward in *Around the World in Eighty Days* (1956), and followed that up with a larger role as a director in *The Buster Keaton Story* (1957). As one of the many guest stars in Irwin Allen's dreadful fantasy *The Story of Mankind* (1957), he looks so ill that it seems unlikely his Emperor Nero could even manage to play the fiddle while Rome burns! The only highlight from this output was a good supporting role as a local chief of police in the jungle adventure *Congo Crossing* (1956).

On a personal level, Lorre had to deal with the loss of two close friends. 1956 saw the death of Bertolt Brecht, while the following year Humphrey Bogart passed away. On top of this, Lorre's father, who had moved to Australia in 1949, died in 1958. Brecht had never been happy with Lorre's career decisions and had probably never forgiven him for returning to

Hollywood, but whatever Lorre felt about his friend's death, he kept to himself. With Bogart, though, Lorre made his feelings known. As throat cancer took hold of Bogie, Lorre remained loyal to him, and his death left the actor with a profound sense of loss.

There was another loss that deeply affected Lorre when Annemarie miscarried. This tragedy put a strain on the marriage, with Annemarie drinking heavily and Lorre suffering high blood pressure. Devastated by the loss of his unborn son, Lorre turned to the one person he could rely on, Celia. Relations had also improved between Lorre and Kaaren, who had since remarried. Celia often babysat Catherine, but her continued role in Lorre's life quickly angered Annemarie.

With horror films making a comeback, Lorre got offered the part of Odo the gypsy in *The Black Sleep* (1956), but did not take it as he wanted more money than the producers could afford. He also turned down *The She Creature* (1956), because he refused to act in what he called 'a cheap pile of junk.' Despite his financial troubles, Lorre drew the line at these trash efforts.

Lorre's television career continued through 1957 with a production of F Scott Fitzgerald's *The Last Tycoon* for *Playhouse 90* and another episode of *Climax!*, this time an adaptation of *The Amazing Dr Clitterhouse*. Then came a sizable film role as corrupt Russian official Branlov in *Silk Stockings* (1957), a musical remake of *Ninotchka* (1939), starring Fred Astaire and Cyd Charise. Partnered with Jules Munshin and Joseph Buloff, Lorre gave a funny performance that included a couple of dance routines. Realising he would never be taken seriously as an actor anymore, he played his comic self to full advantage. 'Peter would do whatever job you hired him for,' said actor Keenan Wynn. 'He would do it well, but he knew it was shit.'

As the '50s drew to a close, Lorre appeared briefly as an Arab in the Jerry Lewis comedy *The Sad Sack* (1957) and made a partial return to form with a bit of welcome screen menace in *Hell Ship Mutiny* (1957). The following year he made his final radio appearance, in the CBS series *Easy as ABC*, after which this type of work just dried up.

Lorre continued his Irwin Allen association with the all-star extravaganza *The Big Circus* (1959). This lavish production about drama and intrigue under the big top starred Victor Mature, Rhonda Fleming and Vincent Price. Lorre's casting as Skeeter the clown was, in Irwin Allen's mind, the coup of all time. 'I thought it was simply marvellous to have this man, this great villainous face, to play a clown.'

Of course, playing a clown, one who inspires laughter but hides sadness behind the make-up, held great dramatic possibilities for Lorre, even if his poor health prevented him from taking part in the physical slapstick. He brought lots of suggestions to Irwin Allen and co-producer Victor Mature, and usually met with approval. *The Big Circus* proved a popular hit, with Lorre making the most of his few scenes.

Lorre began the new decade with *Scent of a Mystery* (1960), an odd thriller starring British actor Denholm Elliott. The first film to credit the manufacturers of the brand of shoe polish used in the action, it also offered audiences the gimmick of Smell-o-Vision, which comprised of a variety of odours released throughout the cinema! Directed by Jack Cardiff, it boasted vivid Spanish locations that are more impressive than the actual film. Lorre turns in a nice comic performance as a sardonic taxi driver who drives Elliott's character around the countryside. 'I play a very nice man,' he noted. 'On one hand I can count the times I've been a nice man. I enjoy being normal.'

Unfortunately the intense Spanish heat on location gave Lorre a bad case of sunstroke. Jack Cardiff was having dinner at a local restaurant when his frantic assistant director rushed in screaming, 'Peter Lorre is dying.' The actor was found unconscious in his hotel room, his breathing erratic. Five heart specialists were brought in, but none could accurately diagnose the problem until a local doctor used leeches and Lorre responded without any problem. While recovering in hospital, he received a welcome visit from Lauren Bacall. Annemarie and Catherine arrived in Spain later. Within a few days Lorre returned to the set.

Scent of a Mystery didn't create a stir at the box office – only bad smells! Because many cinemas had poor ventilation, the various odours quickly built up, causing nausea among the audiences. A scentless version of the film never materialised, and *Scent of a Mystery* disappeared into smelly obscurity!

Lorre returned to television with a guest appearance in an episode of the popular anthology series *Alfred Hitchcock Presents*. Hitchcock was not involved in the series except as presenter. Lorre's *Casablanca* co-star Paul Henreid directed this macabre episode entitled 'The Diplomatic Corpse'. It features Lorre as a mysterious stranger who meets a character played by Steve McQueen and bets a brand new convertible against his little finger that the young man's cigarette lighter will not light up ten times in a row.

Lorre almost followed Hitchcock with his own anthology series, *The Peter Lorre Playhouse*, in 1961. It was to be produced by Moffett Enterprises, with Lorre acting as host and occasional star. Production facilities were arranged, but Moffett were unable to secure finance, so the series was scrapped. In the meantime, Lorre continued to appear on quiz shows and in commercials, mainly for the money.

Lorre next starred in his third fantasy film for Irwin Allen. *Voyage to the Bottom of the Sea* (1961) has Lorre and Walter Pidgeon as naval scientists investigating a high level of dangerous radiation. The film also features Hollywood villain Henry Daniell as mad scientist Dr Zucco. At least Lorre plays a good guy this time, and his performance lifts a rather plodding affair that suffers badly in comparison with the slightly later spin-off television series of the same title starring Richard Basehart.

Lorre always flirted with the ladies. According to co-star Barbara Eden, 'He had a little bit of the devil in him, with kindness, and every square inch of him laughed when he laughed, every round inch.' Another co-star, Frankie Avalon, also saw Lorre's funny side: 'He was having fun with himself. He would do little things that weren't in the script and add little things to his character.'

Eden also noted a brittle sadness in Lorre, especially when he looked back on his career. During one of these moments of candour he told her, 'Whatever you do, don't let anyone sign your cheques.' Lorre's participation in *Voyage to the Bottom of the Sea* was strictly for financial reasons. 'It was just a job,' said Avalon. 'He was just there. Peter was definitely a frustrated man at that point, knowing he had to do this film and there was really nothing for him to do.'

Lorre rounded off his Irwin Allen association with a comic role in *Five Weeks in a Balloon* (1962), a lumpy film version of Jules Verne's novel, which cast the actor as affable slave trader Ahmed. Unfortunately this lacklustre affair wastes a decent cast of Cedric Hardwick, Paul Lukas, Richard Haydin and Henry Daniell. Like everyone else involved, Lorre walks through the film for his all-important pay cheque.

Lorre's weight problem is certainly evident on screen in *Five Weeks in a Balloon*; and it was alluded to shortly after the film's completion when the actor appeared on Groucho Marx's popular quiz show *You Bet Your Life*, and the anarchic comedian asked him if he was playing the balloon!

The '60s brought a horror comeback for Lorre. Following the box office success of *The Fall of the House of Usher* (1960) and *The Pit and the Pendulum* (1961), Samuel Z Arkoff and James H Nicholson of AIP continued the Edgar Allan Poe series with the horror anthology *Tales of Terror* (1962). By the time this got made, director Roger Corman and writer Richard Matheson had grown tired of the series; to lighten the tone, Matheson decided to write a humorous screenplay, while Nicholson brought in Peter Lorre and Basil Rathbone to provide solid support to their contract star Vincent Price. Lorre's agent Lester Salkow, who also represented Price and Boris Karloff, negotiated a one-picture deal for him with AIP.

Appearing in the film's second tale, 'The Black Cat', Lorre steals the show with a remarkable performance as alcoholic Montressor Herringbone. Looking pickled throughout, Lorre's layabout souse shows a nasty side in his brutal treatment of his long-suffering wife Annabel (played by Joyce Jameson) by stealing her sewing money to blow on booze. In his drunken stupor Montressor stumbles on a wine tasting where he meets mincing fop Fortunato Lucresi (Price). He challenges Fortunato to a wine tasting, and even in his inebriated state manages to match every wine, vintage for vintage. It's a brilliantly timed comic scene, with Price exaggerating the correct method of wine tasting while Lorre consumes bottle after bottle without missing a drunken beat. 'That one scene of wine tasting was really something that remained in people's minds,' recalled Price. 'Peter and I played two drunks, but before we did it they brought in this famous wine taster to show it how it was done. We got very drunk in the afternoons.'

After carrying Montressor home, Fortunato begins an affair with Annabel, taking full advantage of Montressor's drunken state. However, in a rare moment of lucidity, the souse finds out about the affair, kills them both and entombs the bodies behind a brick wall. Unfortunately, he also walls up his wife's hated cat, whose constant meowing attracts the attention of the police and brings about Montressor's well deserved downfall.

'The Black Cat' is the best of the anthology's three tales thanks to the excellent comic performances of Lorre and Price. To add spontaneity, Corman allowed the actors do their own thing as long as they stuck to the story. Understanding this approach, Richard Matheson, who dubbed Price and Lorre 'the Laurel and Hardy of black humour,' tailored the script accordingly.

But despite the fun on set, Lorre was not a well man. Walking and moving more slowly than before, he got tired very easily. Although it never affected his performance, it's obvious from *Tales of Terror* that the actor was grossly overweight and ill.

The horror link continued with Lorre, Boris Karloff and Lon Chaney Jnr guest-starring in an episode of the television series *Route 66*. Entitled 'Lizard's Leg and Owlet's Wing', this had the three actors playing themselves. But the episode is rather silly, and the actors are wasted.

On the strength of his performance in 'The Black Cat', AIP offered Lorre a four-year contract that included eight films and a television series – quite a coup, considering that Karloff and Rathbone had only short-term contracts. The deal included a couple of back-to-back comedy chillers he would make with Price and Karloff. With his teaming with Price recalling his time with Sydney Greenstreet, the potential for making more comedy horror looked promising.

But with his film career on the rise again, Lorre's marriage broke down and the couple separated in October 1962. Unlike with his previous marriages, there was the complication of a child. Annemarie's heavy drinking and Catherine's diabetes weighed heavily on Lorre. He left the family's rented house and moved to a small one-bedroom apartment not far from where Celia lived. Concerns about Catherine made him increasingly reclusive. He enjoyed the isolation of his new home and immersed himself in books. He had few visitors and often turned down party invitations and dinner engagements. The ever-devoted Celia made sure he ate properly and sorted out his debts.

Lorre's next film with Price is their most memorable collaboration. Although it has little to do with the Poe poem from which it takes its title,

The Raven (1963) is a wonderful horror spoof described by Richard Matheson as 'tongue in cheek from the very beginning.' The cast also includes Boris Karloff, Hazel Court and a young Jack Nicholson, whose wooden performance adds to the film's camp value! 'I don't think it was meant to be a comedy,' said Court, 'but it evolved into one on the set. Roger [Corman] just let the thing roll.'

The story centres on medieval sorcerer Dr Craven (Price) and his encounter with Dr Bedlo (Lorre), who first appears as a talking raven. Restored to human form by Craven, Bedlo travels with him to the castle of fellow sorcerer Dr Scarabus (Karloff). Craven wants to retrieve his statuesque wife Lenore (Court), while Bedlo wants revenge on Scarabus for turning him into a bird. Forget the plot, though, because there really isn't one! It just serves the purpose of seeing three great actors play off one another with magnificent aplomb, the action all building up to a well-staged wizard duel between Craven and Scarabus. Matheson's comic script supplies a good number of gags, with the rest improvised by Lorre. Matheson actually wrote the part of Bedlo especially for Lorre, explaining, 'He's the only actor who sort of winged my lines.'

Lorre's improvisational skills worked well in contrast with the classical approach taken by Price and Karloff, although it often caused tension with the latter. 'Boris frankly didn't like Peter's way of doing things,' said Corman. 'It threw him off his memorised reading of his lines.' With Lorre the improviser and Karloff the traditionalist, Price fell in between, as Corman observed: 'Vincent was the one who could walk both ways. He understood Boris, he understood Peter, and I think that helped bring unity to the film.'

Hazel Court came away from *The Raven* with fond memories of Lorre, both as a person and as an actor. 'Peter was absolutely fascinating, although he was very sick at the time. You would rehearse a scene and it wouldn't be quite the same when you did the take. You had to be one jump ahead of him, knowing that he might do something different. Once the camera started to roll, there was no sign of his being ill.'

Made for $350,000, *The Raven*, thanks to its slapstick fun and enjoyable performances from the leads, won favour with the critics and with the American public, who lapped up the comic elements – although it was sold as a straight horror film, complete with X certificate, in the UK. The comic teaming of Lorre and Price makes the film, and with Karloff in equally fine form, it is one of those rare horror spoofs that actually works.

A few months after the release of *The Raven*, Lorre's life took a bizarre but not very amusing turn with a court case best described as Peter Lorre vs Peter Lorre! Born in Karlsruhe, Germany, Eugene Weingand moved to New York in 1954 and then to California in 1958. There he sold real estate before enrolling at the Loretta Young Acting School. Subsequently working in summer stock theatre, the actor allegedly bore a vague resemblance to Lorre and was quick to exploit this by adopting the name Peter Lorie or Peter Lorre Jnr. In July 1963 he applied for a change of name to Peter Lorie, because everyone called him that and his real name was too hard to pronounce. There was just one problem – the real Peter Lorre! The actor was not amused by Weingand's antics: 'I have never sued anybody who imitated me, but it's a different story to use my name.' Lorre was under contract with AIP and therefore in a position to fight the claim, as a bogus namesake could affect his earning capacity.

In August 1963 Annemarie filed for divorce, citing mental cruelty and failure to provide adequate financial support for her and Catherine. She asked for a monthly sum of $1,150 in alimony and an additional $525 in child support. Although Lorre had landed a good contract with AIP, he was hardly a rich man.

By September 1963, the Lorre/Lorie fiasco made it to court. Lorre called upon his old friend Robert Shutan to represent him. When questioned about the motivation for his proposed name change, Weingand claimed it would avoid confusion with Lorre, but Shutan insisted that it would be a lot less confusing if he kept his real name.

In October 1963, the case went to the Supreme Court of Los Angeles. Judge Burnett Wolfson was unconvinced by Weingand arguments – especially his contention that his real name was hard to pronounce. He asked him 'What's hard to pronounce about Eugene Weingand?' Weingand could not answer, and the Judge denied the application, citing it as an attempt to cash in on the real Lorre's name.

Weingand later claimed that he had applied for the name change as a publicity stunt to advance his own acting career. If anything, however, it had blown up in his face. Judge Wolfson not only denied the application, but he issued a restraining order preventing Weingand from calling himself either Peter Lorre Jnr or Peter Lorie without the actor's written consent. The real Peter Lorre had won his case, but Weingand wouldn't give up so easily.

Lorre's next venture was in a similar vein to *The Raven*, only this time the chills took a back seat to the laughs. *The Comedy of Terrors* (1963) again focused on the Price-Lorre double act, with Karloff recruited once more, along with *Tales of Terror* stars Basil Rathbone and Joyce Jameson. With the tag-line 'Your Favorite Creeps Together Again' it was obvious how the film would turn out.

The plot of *The Comedy of Terrors* centres on crooked undertaker Waldo Trumbull (Price), who, in the face of bankruptcy and eviction, drums up some illegal business of his own with the help of his put-upon assistant Felix Gillie (Lorre). Also on hand is Waldo's decrepit father-in-law Amos Hinchly (Karloff) and wealthy Shakespeare-spouting landlord (and first victim) John F Black (Rathbone). In a reverse twist from *Tales of Terror*, Joyce Jameson's character is the wife of Price's no-good drunk, but harbours feelings for Lorre's ineffectual little man!

Author Denis Meikle described *The Comedy of Terrors* as the *Some Like It Hot* (1959) of the horror genre; it even has Joe E Brown as a cockney cemetery keeper! The plot is merely a device to let the gags, both improvised and scripted, flow freely. Price and Lorre had honed their double act to macabre perfection. 'Their comic instincts formed an easy complement,' noted scriptwriter Richard Matheson, who knew that much of Lorre's improvising was down to failing memory. The actor's poor health was obvious to the cast and crew, who noticed how tired he got with the smallest amount of physical exertion. But although being in a great deal of pain and distress (he carried a briefcase full of prescribed drugs), Lorre maintained his good humour and professionalism throughout.

Despite spirited performances and inspired comic moments, *The Comedy of Terrors* doesn't quite come off. Matheson's script is far from being consistently funny, although that hardly matters with Price and Lorre in such brilliant form. The main problem is the approach taken by director Jacques Tourneur, whom Matheson had persuaded AIP to hire. 'I think he is a marvellous director,' said Matheson, 'but with a two-week shooting schedule you can't spend too much time on anything. That's all the time AIP ever spent on any of those pictures. That's how they made their money.'

Unlike Corman, who let the actors just do their thing, Tourneur was a perfectionist whose subtle approach was at odds with the broad script and broader acting, especially from Lorre. 'It probably bothered Tourneur,' said Matheson, 'but I think he quickly saw that it wasn't something Lorre was doing to be nasty.' As on *The Raven*, there was a stark contrast to the stars' acting styles; the traditionalists Karloff and Rathbone following the script, the improviser Lorre given a free reign to improvise, and the jack-of-all-trades Price providing the all important link between the two styles.

While valuable as a record of the once-in-a-lifetime cast, *The Comedy of Terrors* performed poorly at the box office. Its release on Christmas Day 1963 came only a month after the assassination of US President John F Kennedy, so cinema audiences were in no mood to laugh about death, even though the film features Joyce Jameson's Amerylis walking hand-in-hand into the sunset with Lorre's Felix.

Although he never made it back to the top, Lorre's performances in *Tales of Terror*, *The Raven* and *The Comedy of Terrors* consolidated his reputation as a leading genre icon. But even with those inspired comic turns, he felt a deep sadness about his career. 'Making movies used to be fun in the old days,' he lamented. 'It isn't any longer. It's a cold-hearted business.'

The Comedy of Terrors should have been Lorre's swansong. Sadly his final appearances were wasted cameos in the Jerry Lewis clinker *The Patsy* (1964), where he played a Hollywood director, and AIP's *Muscle Beach Party* (1964).

Lorre was still under contract with AIP, and another teaming with Vincent Price was proposed for an adaptation of the Edgar Allen Poe story *The Gold Bug*. Richard Matheson also provided a new script that would have reunited Lorre, Price, Karloff and Rathbone. Another black comedy, entitled *It's Alive*, was on the cards, to be directed by Roger Corman's art director Daniel Haller, along with a role in *John Goldfarb, Please Come Home* (1965), and a further cameo in *Bikini Beach* (1964). There was even a bit of radio work on the horizon. But fate would intervene to prevent any of these roles coming to fruition.

On 22 March 1964, Celia Lovsky drove to Lorre's Los Angeles apartment to prepare lunch. Lorre was due to attend his divorce hearing the next day but wasn't feeling well. Celia contacted his doctor, who found nothing wrong. She stayed with her ex-husband until late in the evening before going home.

The following day, Lorre's housekeeper Beatrice Lane discovered his body on the bedroom floor. She telephoned Celia, who rushed over immediately. His doctor arrived and pronounced him dead; the cause of death was a stroke. He was 59 years old.

Lester Salkow contacted Vincent Price with the sad news. 'I was doing a Red Skelton show,' recalled Price. 'I wrote the eulogy and I went to Red and said, "Red, you know Peter died yesterday morning. Would you mind if I took an extra hour for lunch, because I'm going to his funeral to read his eulogy." So Red said, "Peter's dead? We'll all go!" So the entire company went to Peter's funeral, which was marvellous.'

Lorre's funeral took place on 26 March 1964 at Pierce Brothers' Hollywood Chapel. Rabbi William Sanderson conducted the service, and the honorary pallbearers were Vincent Price, Lester Salkow, Robert Shutan, Samuel Arkoff, James H Nicholson, Burl Ives, Irwin Allen and Jonas Silverstone. As Lorre's oldest living friend, Price delivered a moving eulogy before the body got interred privately at Abbey of the Psalms at Hollywood Memorial Park Cemetery.

There was little dignity for Lorre after his death. A few days after the interment, his body was stolen by some over-zealous fans. It was later recovered and cremated. The financial settlement from his pending divorce was rescheduled to April 1964. His total estate was valued at $13,000, but because he still owed backdated income taxes and never made a will, he died insolvent, leaving Catherine with nothing.

A few months after Lorre's death, Weingand once again adopted his name. Not only did he insist he was Peter Lorre's sole surviving son, but his driving licence and social security number both bore the name Peter Lorre Jnr. In November 1971 Weingand initiated another petition to have his name legally changed; however, his lawyer suddenly filed for dismissal, no doubt caused by the Lorre estate threatening legal action. Nevertheless, he continued to use the Lorre name for his film appearances in *Fragel, The Sensuous Lion* (1973), *The Cat Creature* (1973) and *The Son of Sassou* (1975), in which he even tried to imitate that famous voice. A decade later he was impersonating Lorre for a series of television commercials for General Mills' cereals, until Andrew Lorre threatened legal action. Weingand moved to Houston, Texas, where he spent his remaining years in obscurity. He suffered a fatal heart attack in 1986.

Kaaren Verne was now married to critic James Powers, but her career never regained its earlier footing. The mental health problems and alcoholism took their toll on her looks. On 23 December 1967, she died suddenly and mysteriously. There was speculation that she had committed suicide, although the likely cause was heart failure.

Celia Lovsky was a little more fortunate. Working steadily in film and television until her retirement in 1974, she gained an amazing piece of television immortality when she played T'Pau, ruler of the Planet Vulcan, in an episode of *Star Trek*. Still Lorre's one true soul mate, when she died on 12 October 1979, her ashes were combined with those of her beloved ex-husband.

For the tragic Catherine Lorre, worse was to come.

Catherine grew into a very pretty young woman with the same expressive eyes as her father. Left with nothing when her mother died a few years later, it was Celia who came to her rescue. Shortly after Kaaren's death, her widower James Powers was allowed to move into Celia's house as a lodger on the condition that he adopted Catherine. He agreed to the request and the girl also moved in. Catherine always looked upon Celia as her grandmother.

Plague by diabetes all her life, Catherine made the headlines in 1977 when she got kidnapped in Los Angeles by the so-called Hillside Stranglers Kenneth Bianchi and Angelo Buono, posing as policemen. They changed their minds about the abduction when they found out who she was, and let her go, because, in Catherine's telling of the incident, Peter Lorre was their movie hero. She herself did not realise who they were until their arrests, two years later.

Catherine was admitted to the Harbor General Hospital in Los Angeles with serious problems regarding her vision and blood circulation on top of her diabetes. She died on 7 May 1985 at the age of 32, the causes of death being sepsis, encephalomalacia and complications brought on by diabetes. What made her death more tragic was the fact her family and friends had no idea she had died; she remained in the morgue for a month before they found out. (Her husband had been killed in a motorcycle accident some time earlier.) She was laid to rest at Inglewood cemetery on 4 June 1985. The only people who attended her funeral were Robert Shutan, his son Peter, Catherine's cousin Larry Lorre, her nurse, and biographer Stephen D

Youngkin, author of *The Lost One: A Life of Peter Lorre*.

After years of special screenings in a variety of German film clubs, *The Lost One* finally got its American premiere in 1983 to a belated but positive critical response.

Was Peter Lorre a cursed horror star? He had a successful career, was always in demand, and continued working to the end. The biggest tragedy was that Hollywood never made full use of his unique talents. He was always the outsider looking in. Always on the edge, never part of a clique. A sinister figure, even when he played comedy. Being on the fringe meant his career was destined never to reach the prominence it really deserved. His life always seemed to have a touch of sadness about it.

But compared with another Hungarian actor, who also achieved Hollywood success, Lorre was a very lucky man.

Peter Lorre Filmography

Die Verschwundene Frau (1929), *Bomben auf Monte Carlo* (1930), *M* (1931), *Die Koffer des Herrn O.F.* (1931), *Der Weisse Damon* (1932), *F.P.I. Antwortet Nicht* (1932), *Funf vin der Jazzband* (1932), *Schuss im Morgengrauen* (1932), *Was Frauen Traumen* (1933), *Unsichtbare Gegner* (1933), *Du Haut en Bas* (1933), *The Man Who Knew Too Much* (1934), *Mad Love* (1935), *Crime and Punishment* (1935), *Secret Agent* (1936), *Crack-Up* (1936), *Lancer Spy* (1937), *Nancy Steele is Missing* (1937), *Think Fast, Mr Moto* (1937), *Thank You, Mr Moto* (1937), *Mysterious Mr Moto* (1938), *I'll Give a Million* (1938), *Mr Moto's Gamble* (1938), *Mr Moto Takes a Chance* (1938), *Mr Moto Takes a Vacation* (1939), *Mr Moto's Last Warning* (1939), *Mr Moto on Danger Island* (1939), *Island of Doomed Men* (1940), *I Was An Adventuress* (1940), *Strange Cargo* (1940), *You'll Find Out* (1940), *Stranger on the Third Floor* (1940), *Mr District Attorney* (1941), *The Maltese Falcon* (1941), *The Face Behind the Mask* (1941), *They Met In Bombay* (1941), *Invisible Agent* (1942), *All Through the Night* (1942), *The Boogie Man Will Get You* (1942), *Casablanca* (1942), *In This Our Life* (1942), *Background to Danger* (1943), *The Constant Nymph* (1943), *The Cross of Lorraine* (1943), *Arsenic and Old Lace* (1943), *Passage to Marseilles* (1944), *Hollywood Canteen* (1944), *The Mask of Dimitrios* (1944), *The Conspirators* (1944), *Hotel Berlin* (1945), *Confidential Agent* (1945), *Three Strangers* (1946), *The Chase* (1946), *Black Angel* (1946), *The Verdict* (1946), *The Beast with Five Fingers* (1946), *My Favorite Brunette* (1947), *Casbah* (1948), *Rope of Sand* (1949), *Quicksand* (1949), *Double Confession* (1950), *The Lost One* (1951), *Beat the Devil* (1953), *20,000 Leagues Under the Sea* (1954), *Seidman and Son* (1956), *Congo Crossing* (1956), *Viva Las Vegas!* (1956), *Around the World in Eighty Days* (1956), *Operation Cicero* (1956), *The Story of Mankind* (1957), *The Buster Keaton Story* (1957), *Silk Stockings* (1957), *The Last Tycoon* (1957), *The Jet-Propelled Couch* (1958), *Hell Ship Mutiny* (1958), *The Sad Sack* (1958), *The Big Circus* (1959), *Thin Ice* (1959), *The Cruel Day* (1960), *Scent of a Mystery* (1960), *Voyage to the Bottom of the Sea* (1961), *Tales of Terror* (1962), *Five Weeks in a Balloon* (1962), *The Raven* (1963), *The Comedy of Terrors* (1963), *The Patsy* (1964), *Muscle Beach Party* (1964).

The Curse Of Dracula:
Bela Lugosi

'I can blame it all on Dracula.' – Bela Lugosi

An impeccably-dressed but frail old man, wearing a black hat and cape and carrying a walking stick, steps slowly out of a modest-looking bungalow. He takes in the air of the day and inspects the flowers in the garden. He sniffs one of the roses before stepping out of view of the camera filming his movements. There is great sadness in his ravaged, once handsome face. It's as if his life, like the rose he smells, has but a short time left.

Two versions of the film exist. The most recent comes from Tim Burton's biopic *Ed Wood* (1994), featuring Martin Landau perfectly acting out the slow movements of the old man. The other is a home movie, and the gentleman in question is the once celebrated horror legend Bela Lugosi. Whereas Landau acted out the emotions, Lugosi was living them, a dying man with nowhere else to go.

Bela Lugosi's rise and fall is Hollywood folklore. His star-making performance as *Dracula* (1930) gave him world fame but also became an albatross around his neck, and one that followed him to the grave. Did Dracula curse Lugosi? If so, it remained the most vivid and tragic of all the curses.

So began the curse of Dracula.

Bela Lugosi's life has always been closely associated with the legend of Dracula, and as with the vampire himself, his background is shrouded in mystery. What is actually true and what was simply made up for the Hollywood tabloids is highly debatable. He was born Bela Ference Dezso Adelbert Blasko on 20 October 1882 (or 1888 according to Lugosi himself) in Lugos, a heavily fortified city in Timis County, Hungary. Lugos is fifty miles from the western border of Transylvania and Poenari Castle, the famous home of Vlad the Impaler, the tyrant who inspired Bram Stoker's immortal villain. 'I was not a very brave child while I was growing up in Hungary,' Lugosi recalled. 'I grew up in Transylvania where the legend of Dracula comes from, and never did I go down into our cellar. It was full of bats!'

Lugos had experienced the rise and fall of the Ottoman Empire and become a military stronghold against the Turkish occupation during the Battle of Vienna in 1683. It was situated on both banks of the River Timis, and the influx of German immigrants following the Treaty of Passarowitz in 1783 and the expulsion of the Turks split it into two distinct halves; the Romanians occupying the right bank of the river and the Germans occupying the left. In the mid 19th Century, it was the final centre of the Hungarian Revolutionary Government. At the time of Lugosi's birth, however, it was part of the Austro-Hungarian Empire, a constitutional monarch union between the Austrian Empire and the Kingdom of Hungary. As a county seat of Caras-Severin, it had very strong links to the Roman Catholic Church. With the dissolution of the Empire following the end of World War I, Lugos, renamed Lugoj, became part of Romania.

'The writers ask if my parents were hypnotists,' Lugosi said of his father Istvan Blasko and mother Paula de Vojnich, 'or if I commune with ghosts, and whether or not I practise the supernatural in my private life. They say my eyes have an expression unlike the eyes of any human being! As a matter of fact, my childhood in the Black Mountains was the usual husky, healthy everyday life of any country boy. My father, Baron Lugosi, was a banker by trade and there was nothing weird or extraordinary in my family background.' These comments about his early life were probably written by a press agent trying to give Lugosi an aristocratic image. Istvan Blasko was actually neither a baron nor a banker. In reality he came from a long line of Hungarian farmers but broke with tradition to work as a baker, although later he did become a director at a local bank in Lugos.

The youngest of four children, Lugosi had a very strict upper middle class Roman Catholic upbringing. 'I was very unruly as a boy,' he said, 'very out of control. Like Jekyll and Hyde, except I changed according to sex. I mean, with boys I was tough and brutal. But the minute I came into the company of girls and women, I kissed their hands. With boys, I say I was a brute. With girls, I was a lamb.'

After attending a local grammar school in Lugos, Lugosi went to the Superior Hungarian State Gymnasium in 1893. Still rebellious by nature, he hated the strict discipline there and showed little interest in academic study. He did however develop an interest in theatre. 'I wanted to be an actor right from being a child.' But after one miserable year in higher education, he quit school and ran away from home.

Lugosi became a wanderer, travelling across the country, working whenever he could to earn a bit of cash and relying on the help of strangers for food, money and lodgings. Arriving at the small mining town of Resita, he got regular work as a miner and later became a machinist's assistant.

Resita often played host to travelling repertory companies, and the stagestruck but inexperienced Lugosi always got involved in their productions. 'They tried to give me little parts in their plays,' he recalled, 'but I was uneducated, so stupid. People just laughed at me. But I got the taste of the stage. I got also the rancid taste of humiliation.' Knowing that his lack of a formal education could hinder his prospects, Lugosi embarked on a strict self-improvement regime that made him extremely well versed in literature.

Remaining in Resita until 1897, Lugosi then moved to Szabadka to live with his sister Vilma. His mother had also moved there following her husband's death and the loss of the family income. He returned to school but dropped out after a few months. Taking a job as a railroad labourer, he still continued acting in amateur theatre. Vilma's husband then used his influence to get his brother-in-law a job in the chorus line of a travelling repertory company. Thanks to his natural enthusiasm, Lugosi progressed to more serious acting roles as he toured Hungary with the troupe.

'In Hungary,' Lugosi once said, 'acting is a career for which one fits himself as earnestly and studiously as one studies for a degree in medicine, law or philosophy.' In 1900 he got accepted into Hungary's most prestigious drama school. 'I was very fortunate in being able to get a place in the Budapest Academy of Performing Arts. There is only one place in the world where it is worthwhile to be an actor – Hungary. For there you have a four-year training course, and once you have passed through you have nothing to worry about. Even in your old age you still get a pension. In America and the rest of the world there is always the fear of unemployment.' Realising the necessity of formal training, he studied acting theory and method with total conviction. With hard work and commitment, he became extremely proficient in Shakespeare.

Lugosi's earliest stage appearances were around 1900 or 1901. In 1902 he joined the National Actors Company, which toured provincial towns in Hungary and Transylvania. His first notable stage role was as Count Konigsegg in a 1902 production of *Ockskay Brigaderos*. The following year he had his first brush with horror as Svengali's sinister servant Gecko in *Trilby*. Throughout the company's 1903-04 repertory season, he acted in several plays and put his fine singing voice to good use in a handful of operettas. A prolific actor during the early part of his career, he averaged around thirty to forty stage roles a year. It is unlikely these roles were large, but it kept him in steady employment.

It was around this time that he adopted the stage name Bela Lugossy to honour his hometown, adding the 'y' to make it sound aristocratic. It was later altered to the more familiar Lugosi.

Lugosi spent the next few years touring the provinces of the Austro-Hungarian Empire. Graduating to Shakespearean roles, he performed in productions of *Romeo and Juliet* (which earned him good reviews), *Hamlet*, *Richard III* and *The Taming of the Shrew*. Moving to Budapest in 1911, he joined the National Theatre of Hungary. Now an established actor, he moved on to the Budapest National Theatre in 1913 and appeared in high-profile productions of *Cyrano de Bergerac*, *Faust* and *Tovarich*, in the latter of which he played Commissar Dimitri Gorotchenko.

On his later arrival in Hollywood, Lugosi (or rather a studio press release) would claim that he had been 'the idol of the Royal National Theatre in Budapest.' Research into his past however casts doubt on the suggestion that he had been a big star. American writer Robert Bloch noted: 'Several people I know have tried to verify that. They've tried to find out to just what degree he was famous in Hungary and how much of it was a product of his press agent.' Writer and biographer Arthur Lennig shared Bloch's scepticism: 'Lugosi was never a great actor in Hungary nor was he ever a leading one at the National Theatre.'

Whether or not he was a star, Lugosi was successful enough to stay in full employment, and on a good salary with the Budapest National Theatre. According to Lennig, 'His very presence showed he was among the best.' Robert Bloch agreed that it was 'undoubtedly true that he played some of those classic roles he later talked about; but he was not, so far as those cast and credit listings that have been unearthed show, a great matinee idol of the stage prior to World War I.' Nevertheless, from his existing early photos, the handsome, impeccably dressed Lugosi looks every inch a star, showing the same presence and noble bearing as Olivier or Gielgud.

Although actors from the National Theatre were exempt from military service during World War I, Lugosi's deep sense of duty to his country prompted him to join the Hungarian Army in June 1914 as a lieutenant. He later rose to the rank of infantry captain with the ski patrol. The stories he later told of his wartime exploits carried that same elusive grandeur as his alleged matinee idol reputation. He was allegedly decorated for bravery after being badly wounded on three separate occasions while fighting on the Russian front. He also told a story about how he hid amongst corpses in a mass grave to escape capture by enemy forces, and claimed that one of his many duties was hanging deserters. In 1916 he managed to obtain a discharge from the army by feigning insanity caused by concussion.

Whatever the truth of these stories, one thing that is certain is that the injuries Lugosi received in battle led to chronic sciatica in his later years. When various remedies such as asparagus juice and opiates failed to ease the pain, the doctors prescribed morphine, which did the trick but led on to the actor's future drug problems.

Returning to the National Theatre, Lugosi played Jesus Christ in a well-received production of *The Passion*. Motion pictures had by this time become a new form of entertainment, and capitalising on Hungary's pioneering film industry, he made his screen debut, under the name Aristid Olt, in *A Leopard* (1917). His first brush with the horror film came in *Az Elet Kiralya* (1917), a screen adaptation of Oscar Wilde's *The Picture of Dorian Gray*, in which he played the role of Dorian's Mephistophelean mentor Lord Henry Wotton.

Lugosi worked in a variety of films over the next two years, apparently reprising the role of Jesus in one production, and would later claim that he had been successful as a romantic lead. However, because so little visual evidence of these productions survives, that claim is hard to verify. Since he wasn't the big stage star he made himself out to be, chances are that his absence from the theatre during wartime would have had a negative effect on his film career; so the best screen work he could have got would probably have been supporting roles. It is also possible that he made a lot more films during this period than those currently credited to him, the others now lost and their titles unknown.

But it was undoubtedly a good time for Lugosi, and one that he looked back on with great nostalgia. With film and stage work regularly coming in, his career ticked over nicely, and before long his personal life went through several important changes.

In 1917 Lugosi married Ilona Szmik, daughter of a local banker, following a brief courtship. The marriage was rocky from the start, however, because her parents disapproved of his strong Marxist views. An outspoken political activist and trade unionist, Lugosi became a fierce supporter of communist revolutionary leader Bela Kun; he felt that Kun would give actors a better deal if he took power in Hungary. Lugosi was also instrumental in organising Hungary's first actors' union.

Turn-of-the-century Hungary had been Europe's prominent trade centre thanks to its industrial, agricultural and mining industries. But following the rise of communism in Russia, political unrest swept the country. Influenced by the romance of the Russian Revolution of 1917, Bela Kun founded the Hungarian Chapter of the Russian Communist Party and travelled extensively across Europe promoting radical left wing politics. After fighting for the Bolsheviks during the Russian Civil War of 1918, Kun decided it was time to bring a communist regime to Hungary. With the backing of several hundred followers and financial support from Russia, he returned to Hungary in March 1919 to set up the Hungarian Soviet Republic, the second communist government to be established in Europe.

Kun's first act as leader was to nationalise all private property in Hungary. Instead of redistributing land to the peasantry, which was his intention prior to taking power, he converted agricultural land into collective farms overseen by former landowners, a decision that alienated many of his loyal supporters. To try to redress the balance, he cancelled all rural taxation; but the internal tensions had already undermined a fragile government that was split down the middle over the choice of party name!

After a failed anti-communist coup in June 1919, Kun used strong-arm tactics to root out 'undesirables', with over 600 people being executed by the secret police. By July 1919, tensions with neighbouring Romania escalated into war. Having already sustained heavy casualties fighting in the Ukraine, Russia was either unable or unwilling to give Kun additional support, and on 1 August 1919 Romanian forces and their allies seized power. The Hungarian Soviet Republic had lasted just 133 days.

The collapse of Kun's government left many left-wingers and trade unionists at the mercy of the new ruling Social Democratic Party. Lugosi's own life was in jeopardy. 'After the war,' he recalled, 'I participated in the revolution. Later, I found myself on the wrong side.' He left Hungary for Vienna with a price on his head, and would later claim that he had hidden under a pile of straw in a wheelbarrow to escape the authorities. 'I left my country in 1920 and have never been back,' he recalled with deep sadness. 'I do not like to live under a dictatorship.'

Lugosi didn't stay in Vienna long. The arrest of Bela Kun while in exile in Austria prompted a further exit to Germany. He had to do this alone. Although Ilona had accompanied him to Vienna, the marriage was over. By the time he fled to Germany, she had returned to Hungary to divorce him.

Lugosi made his German film debut in *Nachenschur des Tot* (1920). Other films included *Auf den Trummerin des Paradieses* (1920) and *Die Todesskarawane* (1920), both screen adaptations of Karl May's popular

Western novels. Lugosi's association with this most unlikely of genres continued when he played Chingachgook in two films based on James Fenimore Cooper's *Leatherstocking* stories, *Lederstrumpf 1: Teil – Der Wildtoter und Chingachgook* (1920) and *Lederstumpf 2: Teil – Der Letze der Mohikaner* (1920). He also played Andre Fleurot in *Der Fluch der Menschheit* (1920) and *Der Fluch der Menschheit 2* (1920). In total he played supporting roles in sixteen German movies made in 1920.

This prolific output included the horror films *Die Teufelsanbeter* (1920) and *Der Januskopf* (1920). The latter of the two is notable for having been part of an exciting new form of cinema known as expressionism, which was perfected by German filmmakers following the success of *The Cabinet of Dr Caligari* (1919). *Der Januskopf* is an unauthorised screen version of Robert Louis Stevenson's *Dr Jekyll and Mr Hyde*, starring Conrad Veidt as Dr Warren and Mr O'Connor. Lugosi's part of Dr Warren's butler Dienan is secondary, but he regarded *Der Januskopf* as 'one of the first true horror films. But to someone like me who concentrated on drama and romance it was just another part.'

Although an influential film on its release, *Der Januskopf* has long been considered lost. It does however have a strong link to Lugosi's most famous role. The cinematographer was Karl Freund, one of the key figures of German expressionist cinema, who would later work with Lugosi on *Dracula*; and Veidt himself would be considered for the role of the Count when Universal Studios began pre-production on the film. The director of *Der Januskopf* was F W Murnau, the man who would soon be responsible for one of the finest screen adaptations of *Dracula*, *Nosferatu: Eine Symphonie des Grauens* (1922), a truly unique film featuring an unforgettable performance by Max Schreck as vampire Graf Orlock. Unlike many film versions of the novel, *Nosferatu* hasn't dated with time; after ninety years, its dreamlike quality still has the power to fascinate.

'What I didn't know was that Murnau was planning to film Bram Stoker's book and call it *Nosferatu*,' Lugosi recalled. 'I don't suppose I would have got the part if I had stayed in Germany, but one can never tell!' It was also around this time that the actor first read Stoker's novel. 'It made quite an impression on me. Although it is a fanciful tale of a fictional character, it is actually based on a story that has many elements of truth. I was born and raised in almost the exact location of the story, and I came to know that what is looked upon merely as a superstition of ignorant people, is really based on facts, which are literally hair-raising in their strangeness – but which are true.' The impact of the novel was powerful enough to influence Lugosi's future decision to play Dracula on stage or film.

Whether or not Lugosi could have played the part in Murnau's version will never be known. Despite his regular film appearances at the turn of the decade, which included a rare romantic lead in *Der Tanz auf dem Vulkan*

(1920), the work soon dried up. He consequently decided to emigrate to the USA, a land of acting opportunities, whether on Broadway or in Hollywood. In October 1920, after a brief spell in Italy, he boarded a cargo ship bound for New Orleans. Working as a deck hand, he came close to death when his identity was discovered by several of the Hungarian crew, but fortunately he survived.

Docking in New Orleans in December 1920, he worked his way to New York, finally arriving at Ellis Island in March 1921 to be legally inspected for immigration. He was granted political asylum and allowed to work in the States. With the exception of three visits to England, Lugosi would never return to Europe. America became his permanent home.

Though unable to speak English, Lugosi was welcomed with open arms by New York's large Hungarian immigrant community, many of whom knew him from the stage. After working as a labourer, he resumed his acting career at a theatre within the community. With a group of out-of-work Hungarian actors, he then set up a small repertory company and assumed the role of lead actor and director. The company toured the various Hungarian communities across the east of America, but the venture failed and Lugosi returned to New York. To succeed as an actor in the States he would have to learn English. Meanwhile, in September 1921 he married fellow Hungarian Ilona Von Montagh de Nagybanyhegyes.

Professionally, things improved with an offer of the lead role in a Broadway production of *The Red Poppy*. It would be his English-language stage debut – but the actor still couldn't speak a word of it! To overcome the problem, he learnt his role phonetically. It seemed to work. *The Red Poppy* opened at the Greenwich Village Theatre in December 1922, with Lugosi's performance getting favourable reviews. Described by critic Alan Dale as 'the greatest actor to come to America,' Lugosi got a better reaction than the play itself, which closed after six weeks.

Lugosi's well-received performance led to his Hollywood film debut as a villain in *The Silent Command* (1923). This being a silent film, there were no problems with his English. In Hungary he had played (so he said) the romantic lead, but in Hollywood, his sinister persona made him ideally suited to play the villain – a foretaste of things to come.

The Silent Command did not lead to further Hollywood offers, so it was a return to New York, where Lugosi's next few movies were made. Cast mainly as a European continental type, he had sixth billing as Frenchman Jean Gagnon in *The Rejected Woman* (1924) and apparently (though this is unconfirmed) appeared as a clown in *He Who Gets Slapped* (1924). In October 1924, his marriage came to an end.

Lugosi continued to work steadily in a variety of films without making much impact. After playing wealthy but amoral entrepreneur Nicholas Harmon opposite silent star Lila Lee in the romantic melodrama *The*

Midnight Girl (1925), he returned to standard villainy in *Daughters Who Pay* (1925) as communist agent Romonsky, a role that reminded him of those early years with Bela Kun.

In 1925 Lugosi returned to the stage with the comedy/fantasy *The Devil in the Cheese*, which enjoyed a five-month run. He followed that up with a role as an Arab sheik in *Arabesque*. The play opened in October 1925 at the Teck Theatre in Buffalo, New York before successfully transferring to Broadway. Film-wise he made an appearance as Harlequin in the short *Punchinello* (1926) and made use of his distinctive voice for the first time in the early talkie *The Last Performance* (1927), when he dubbed his *Der Januskopf* co-star Conrad Veidt for the Hungarian version of the film. His next stage role, however, would turn out to have a lasting impact on both his career and his life. Ultimately it would follow him to his grave.

'When I first came to Broadway I was still playing romantic parts – the Spanish lover in *The Red Poppy* and the Valentino-type sheik in *Arabesque*. Then in 1927 the New York stage producer Horace Liveright acquired the rights to the play and began looking for someone to play Dracula.'

Dracula was originally adapted for the stage in 1924 by Irish actor-manager Hamilton Deane. The Dublin-born Deane lived close to the families of Bram Stoker and Florence Balcomb, whom Stoker married; and like Lugosi, he too read Stoker's famous work. The novel had such a profound impact on him that his decision to bring *Dracula* to the theatre turned into an obsession that stuck with him throughout the early part of his career. He first tried to write a stage version in 1897, but soon dropped the idea at that time.

Deane eventually wrote the play while convalescing from a severe cold. Although he successfully secured the dramatic rights to the book from Florence Stoker, the finished work was viewed with scorn by London's sophisticated theatre set. Undeterred, he included the play as part of his company's repertoire at the Grand Theatre in Derby after another production fell through at the last minute.

It was Deane who first presented Dracula as a handsome, immaculately dressed character complete with evening clothes and opera cape. This shrewd move had a lot to do with cost-cutting, because the play was written in the style of a low-budget drawing-room murder mystery, and Dracula had to fit into this environment. The gamble worked, even if the play owed more to the over-the-top, blood-soaked gothic melodramas of Tod Slaughter's infamous stage productions than to Stoker's original. *Dracula* opened at the Grand Theatre in 1924 to tremendous critical disdain but massive commercial success.

When the other plays in the repertoire were abandoned, Deane took *Dracula* on a well-promoted UK tour that lasted four years. For an extra bit of lurid publicity, he made sure a Red Cross nurse was present for each performance. Deane wanted to play Dracula himself, but eventually opted for the larger role of Dr Van Helsing. The part of the Count went instead to Edmund Blake, who is thus notable for being the first actor to play Dracula on stage. Almost nothing is known about this actor other than that he had a prominent gold front tooth!

With Raymond Huntley replacing Blake, the play then met with surprising success in London's West End. Huntley, a familiar face of British stage and screen, holds the record for playing Dracula the most times on stage, working non-stop in England and America between 1926 and 1930. However, the actor admitted to being embarrassed by the role, which he felt limited his future career options. The production was so threadbare that Huntley had to wear his own evening clothes!

With *Dracula* breaking all UK box office records, Deane became an extremely happy and wealthy man. Having grown jealous of him receiving all the income, Florence Stoker commissioned Charles Morell to write a new, rival adaptation, which opened in 1927 with the mysterious Edmund Blake returning as Dracula. But with Deane's play being so successful, the new version never stood a chance, and flopped badly. As for Edmund Blake, he, like a vampire, vanished without trace!

It was perhaps inevitable that *Dracula* would meet with equal success in America. Producer Horace Liveright purchased the American rights to the play – Florence Stoker successfully negotiating a deal that gave her a slice of the royalties – and hired flamboyant American playwright John L Balderston to carry out extensive rewrites to satisfy the more sophisticated Broadway audiences. Brought in as director was John D Williams, who had previously worked with Lugosi on stage.

The part of vampire hunter Van Helsing went to Dutch-American character actor Edward Van Sloan. Liveright had seen Van Sloan in a New York production of Hans Werfel's drama *Schweiger*. 'I was usually cast as romantic leads,' recalled the actor, 'so it was a bit of a surprise that I was offered a part in *Dracula*. One day the producer Horace Liveright attended a show I was appearing in and suddenly shouted out "That's him! That's the man to play Van Helsing!" Of course I had no idea what he was talking about until we met and he showed me the script for the stage production.'

Van Sloan, who had never read the novel, had doubts about *Dracula* having a long stage run. 'I had been in five plays, none of which lasted more than three weeks.' He accepted the role with the philosophical view, 'It would at least buy cakes and ale!'

Now it was time to find the actor to play Dracula. When Raymond Huntley turned down the chance to reprise the role, Liveright opted for his second choice – Bela Lugosi. 'In America,' Lugosi said, 'they have the type system of casting. And there was no male vampire type in existence. Someone suggested an actor of the continental school who could play any type, and mentioned me. It was a complete change from the usual romantic characters I was playing, but it was a success – *such* a success!'

Despite Edward Van Sloan's reservations, *Dracula* opened at the Fulton Theatre, New York on 2 October 1927 to audience approval. Even with Balderston's rewrites, the play still had the air of a second-rate Victorian murder mystery, but the trick effects of flying bats, Dracula disappearing in a puff of smoke at various intervals and changing into a skeleton when he gets staked thrilled everyone. 'When *Dracula* was first presented on Broadway,' Lugosi said, 'there were members of all audiences who took it literally. People screamed and fainted. The first aid staff were kept busy all the time. I did not dare pretend to bite my victims' necks for fear of the hysterical reaction from the public.'

Dracula proved so successful it stayed on Broadway for forty weeks, playing a total of 261 performances. 'It was a wonderful play,' said Lugosi. When the Broadway run ended, several companies successfully took the play on the road. Edward Van Sloan ended up playing Van Helsing for two years – and that bought him a lot of cakes and ale!

As for Bela Lugosi, *Dracula* put him on the map in a role tailor-made for his distinctive persona. The vampire's every move and gesture are so well defined that it was as if Balderston had rewritten the play with Lugosi in mind. 'On the stage, the actor's success depends wholly on himself,' said Lugosi. 'He goes onto the stage and gives the performance in what to him seems the most effective manner.'

Lugosi's level of commitment was amazing: 'It takes me about half and hour to warm up before the curtain rises. I never eat a meal before a performance. I like to go on thirsting for blood! I really have to get in the mood. I don't like to be spoken to for an hour before each show – and even half an hour after we've finished, I'm *still* Dracula.'

Dracula may have been a big success, but the curse had taken root. From 1927 onwards, Lugosi walked alongside the haunting spectre of Dracula for the rest of his life.

After successfully applying to the New York Supreme Court for a Certificate of Alien Claiming Residence in United States in 1928, Lugosi toured the West Coast and California with *Dracula*. This led to several films roles for him, starting with an uncredited appearance as a diplomat's aide in *How to Handle Women* (1928) and the part of a murdered suitor in *The Veiled Woman* (1928) – the latter production being notable because one of his co-stars, the statuesque Mexican actress Lupita Tovar, would play Mina in the Spanish-language film version of *Dracula* (1930), which would be made back to back with the Lugosi version. His next film, *Prisoners* (1929), marked his official sound debut.

Working as director on the *Dracula* tour was future horror movie maestro William Castle. He found Lugosi a shy but intelligent, interesting and delightful man to know. 'He seemed strange and moody at first,' he recalled, 'very quiet, very morose, but when you got to know him he opened up and became warm and gracious. Many people thought he was a snob because he kept very much to himself, but he was actually a shy and introverted man. He always seemed ill-at-ease, but when you pierced the armour he surrounded himself with, you found a very likeable human being.'

Lugosi's next film, for MGM, is the most distinguished of his prolific but generally routine output of this period. *The Thirteenth Chair* (1929) marked the first time he worked with director Tod Browning (who was making his first sound film). It is a stale drawing-room murder mystery with all the hallmarks of an early talkie – stage-bound settings, static direction, lack of pace, too much dialogue and melodramatic acting. Although he is seventh-billed, Lugosi's scenery-chewing turn as the mysterious detective Inspector Delzante stands out from the wooden performances of the other actors.

With a major stage success behind him and a film career slowly but surely gathering momentum, Lugosi's personal life not only improved, it saw him entering Hollywood's elite social circle. On 28 September 1929 he married the wealthy San Francisco-born socialite Beatrice Weeks following a brief courtship. Unfortunately, though, the curse of Dracula reared its ugly head again when he experienced his first serious taste of bad luck. The marriage was only three days old when his wife filed for divorce, citing adultery – the 'other woman' being actress Clara Bow, described by the Hollywood tabloids as 'the Hottest Jazz Baby in Films.'

Bow's sexual exploits were legendary; the Chinese Den of her Beverly Hills home had an endless stream of 'gentleman callers,' among them Eddie Cantor, Gary Cooper and Lugosi. It was even rumoured that she had 'entertained' the University of Southern California football team that included the then unknown John Wayne, although this turned out to be an exaggeration. The Brooklyn-born redhead has seen Lugosi as Dracula at the Biltmore Theatre in 1928 and subsequently picked him up. From all accounts, Bow was the sexual aggressor. The actress also received regular visits from society physician Dr William Pearson. When the good doctor's wife began suspecting that her husband's trips to Bow's home had little to do with administering aspirin, she hired a private eye to tail him. The scandal made unsavoury press headlines, and before long, Lugosi's name got dragged through the mud.

The divorce caused a media sensation that launched Lugosi into national notoriety. For an actor trying to establish himself in Hollywood, this type of scandal was even more harmful than the horror typecasting he would eventually suffer. The situation got even worse when Bow's former private secretary Daisy DeVoe, whom she had fired when she threatened blackmail, sold the story of her former employer's exploits to the sleazy tabloid *Graphic*. DeVoe had kept a detailed account of all the men, including Lugosi, who had visited the actress and of the sordid sexual activities that had taken place. With Lugosi's marriage effectively over before it began, the couple divorced on 2 October 1929.

With her career in ruins, Clara Bow left Hollywood, but she always spoke about Lugosi with warm affection. It was a feeling shared by the actor, who kept a large nude portrait of her on display in his bedroom. The painting remained with him for the rest of his life.

Lugosi began the new decade, in between touring, with a supporting role as surgeon Dr Goodman in *Such Men are Dangerous* (1930), a bizarre romantic melodrama produced by 20th Century Fox about a rich but ugly man who fakes his suicide and undergoes plastic surgery to win back his selfish wife. Although his role is sympathetic (he runs a clinic that helps World War I veterans rehabilitate to civilian life), there is an air of mad science about the character. Next came an uncredited bit part in Universal's follies-inspired musical revue *King of Jazz* (1930), which is notable for being Lugosi's first colour film and crooner Bing Crosby's big-screen debut.

Further film work came in steadily, even though the actor was invariably cast in supporting roles. Lugosi returned to 20th Century Fox for *Wild Company* (1930), a creaky melodrama in which he plays the small role of doomed nightclub owner Felix Brown, and *Renegades* (1930), a Myrna Loy-starring French Foreign Legion adventure. The latter once again has Lugosi shunted aside in a small supporting role, but as the cape-waving Sheik Muhammed Halid he looks like an Arab version of Dracula!

The next film on the agenda was Lugosi's second in colour (or rather a two-colour Technicolor process), a Warner Brothers musical called *Viennese Nights* (1930). Considering Lugosi's fine operatic voice, it would have been interesting to see him perform a musical number. As it was, though, he merely made an uncredited appearance as Russian Ambassador Count von Ratz. He fared slightly better, however, with a small role as music impresario Frescatti in the Fox-produced *Oh, for a Man!* (1930).

Although he was commanding regular film work, Lugosi's Hollywood career wasn't amounting to much, his roles still being mostly sinister continental types. But the new decade would bring about a massive change to his life, as the character he had played so well on stage was about to make an impact on the big screen.

It was inevitable that Hollywood would consider a film version of *Dracula*. With their notorious lack of originality and imagination, most of the Hollywood majors were busy remaking their silent classics to lesser effect as talkies. They were also snapping up popular stage plays with the intention of producing movie versions. Among the plays bought by Universal from the previous year's repertory season was *Dracula*. However, the Count's transition to the big screen came about almost by accident.

Despite having given one thousand stage performances in the role over a four year period, Lugosi wasn't first choice to play Dracula on film. His lack of movie fame and the recent scandal of his divorce were two prominent reasons for this, but there was one other – Carl Laemmle Jnr, the head of Universal, had his mind set on using silent movie star Lon Chaney.

Although he had paid Deane $40,000 for the movie rights to the play, Laemmle wanted to adapt Stoker's original novel for the big screen, so he negotiated another deal with Florence Stoker. With *Dracula* going into pre-production, Laemmle tried to get Chaney, who had just signed a lucrative new deal with MGM, to play the Count. It looked highly unlikely that MGM would agree to loan Chaney out, because of the cost involved, but in any case Chaney died from throat cancer that year, shortly after Laemmle completed his negotiations with Florence Stoker, so the question became academic.

Dracula turned out to be Universal's baptism of fire in the horror genre. Its original director was Paul Leni, the German-born avant-garde painter, designer and leading light of the country's expressionist cinema of the '20s. Under contract as a director with Universal, he had scored a big hit with *The Man Who Laughs* (1925). His striking use of visuals would have made him a perfect choice to direct *Dracula* – had he not died on 2 September 1929 from blood poisoning caused by an infected tooth.

With Leni dead, Universal hired Tod Browning as a last-minute replacement. Although he had had a very successful career in the '20s, Browning was essentially a competent journeyman who made only a partly successful transition to sound films. As he had frequently worked with Lon Chaney, he may have been hired originally in order to bring Chaney onto the project, but with the actor now dead, the lead part was vacant.

Universal's next choice to fill the vacancy was Conrad Veidt, who had played the lead in *The Man Who Laughs* (1928) and was originally linked to the project with Paul Leni. Veidt however was returning to England, so the studio then turned to America's Shakespearean master John Carradine, who had just started out in films and had the type of gaunt looks ideally suited to the role. But Laemmle did not want to risk using a generally unknown actor for a major role, so he opened it up to several better-known candidates. Paul Muni, Ian Keith, John Wray, Chester Morris, Arthur Edmund Carew, Joseph Schildkraut and William Courtney were all serious contenders to play the Count.

Lugosi probably felt quite insulted at not being considered in the first place. But he wasn't going to go down without a fight! Undeterred, he lobbied hard to win Laemmle over; he even acted as unpaid intermediary during Universal's negotiations with Florence Stoker. Thanks to his efforts, Laemmle successfully got Mrs Stoker to lower her asking price from $200,000 to $60,000. Laemmle may have been unaware of it at the time, but Lugosi's presence during these negotiations was a further indication of his desperation to secure the coveted role of Dracula.

There were other, more practical factors in the actor's favour; not only did he know the part backwards, but he was actually touring Los Angeles with the play at the time the film went into production. Thanks to the Wall Street Crash of 1929, the Great Depression and Universal's own financial problems, the film's production budget got scaled down considerably, which meant that the expensive adaptation of the novel was dropped in favour of the much cheaper play version.

Of course Lugosi was also cheap to hire. When he finally got the role, his fee was a paltry $3,500 for seven weeks' work – $500 a week to be exact. Bland romantic lead David Manners earned $2,000 a week for his time on the film, but because he was under contract with First National Pictures, his payment went to the studio, and he was paid just his usual weekly rate.

The production was fraught with problems. Louis Bromfield's abandoned original script, which closely followed the novel, had posed censorship problems as well as budgetary ones; the novel's strong erotic content was considered unacceptable by the strongly conservative Catholic League of Decency and similar groups. The play version, on the other hand, was at least (on paper) guaranteed box office material, judging by its Broadway success.

Production began in September 1930, but somehow the making of the film was rather disorganised. Depressed by the death of Chaney, Browning lost interest in the project early on; he became extremely aloof and unprofessional toward the cast and crew. He was never fully at ease with sound, and his fascination with horror remained fixed firmly to the grotesque; gothic melodrama simply wasn't his forte. He would tear out pages of the script that he felt were redundant and ignored most of the suggestions made by cinematographer Karl Freund. A chronic alcoholic for most of his life, he often walked off the set in a drunken blur, leaving Freund to direct certain scenes, including the opening ones set in Dracula's castle.

Because the haphazard seven-week shooting schedule ran over by a week, several scenes were hastily shot to keep costs down. This may explain the film's rushed-looking second half. Footage of sailors struggling with a vicious storm while taking Dracula to Whitby was actually reused from the silent film *The Storm Breaker* (1925); it got speeded up and spliced with scenes of Lugosi and Dwight Frye as the fly-munching Renfield. Budget cuts also meant that Dracula's transformation into a bat had to take place off-camera. The finished film features plenty of fog, lightning effects and rubber bats taken from the stage play, along with the usual static close-ups of actors' faces and long silences – the art of background music having not yet been perfected.

Despite the production problems and his insultingly small fee, Lugosi grabbed the role with both hands and made it work in his favour. Despite his own lack of interest in the film, Browning graciously helped him tone down his theatrical approach. 'In playing in the picture,' the actor said, 'I found that there was a great deal I had to unlearn. In the theatre I was playing not only to the spectators in the front rows but also to those in the last row of the gallery, and there was some exaggeration in everything I did, not only in the tonal pitch of my voice but in changes of facial expression. But for the screen, in which the actor's distance from every member of the audience is equal to his distance from the camera, I have found that a great deal of repression is an absolute necessity. Tod Browning had to "hold me down." Having played Dracula a thousand times on stage I found that I had become thoroughly settled in the technique of stage and not the screen. But thanks to director Browning. I unlearned fast.'

If Lon Chaney's death had been a great negative on Browning's life, working closely with Lugosi and improving the actor's performance on screen had a positive effect on his mindset.

Lugosi probably worked harder on *Dracula* than on any other movie he had previously made. He believed in the role and played it to the hilt. '*Dracula* is a story that has always had a powerful effect on the emotion of an audience,' he said, 'and I think that the picture will be no less effective than the stage play. In fact, the motion picture should even prove more remarkable in this direction, since many things that could only be talked about on the stage are shown on the screen in all their uncanny detail.'

Lugosi's romantic opinion may have hidden a more practical reason for his enthusiasm. He had previously played supporting parts, and now approaching the age of 48 he was a little too old for starring roles. So playing the Hollywood lead for the first time in his career, he knew he had to work hard to win over both the studios and the public. It is fair to say that *Dracula* was his final chance to make it in Hollywood.

Dracula premiered at the Roxy Theatre in New York on 12 February 1931, but despite the novel being a literary classic and the play having conquered Broadway, the Universal executives were unconvinced that the film would succeed. Those doubts quickly disappeared when *Dracula* became the unexpected hit of 1931. Within 48 hours of its New York opening, 50,000 tickets were bought. Reports that members of the audience had fainted during the screening only added to the impact – although these were really down to the Universal publicity people trying to attract more cinemagoers.

Sadly *Dracula* has not stood the test of time. Because it is based on a stodgy play, the film is boring, overlong and ponderous, hampered by a dialogue-driven script and little action. The brilliant sets are a plus, but the lack of music makes it a strain to watch. The opening scenes in Dracula's castle have a surreal, evocative atmosphere, but this owes more to Karl Freund's outstanding camerawork (and uncredited direction) and less to Browning's flat, uninspired handling. Overall *Dracula* is far too slow and static to be completely effective.

The melodramatic acting varies from stilted to over-the-top, although this has a lot to do with the fact that the silent movie actors were adapting to the still-new medium of sound. Edward Van Sloan and Herbert Bunston, recreating their stage roles as Van Helsing and Dr Seward, give commendable performances, and Dwight Frye's hysterical turn as Renfield sets the tone for cinematic madmen, loonies and nut-jobs for the next ninety years. The juvenile leads however are extremely weak. Helen Chandler (Mina) and Frances Dade (Lucy) lack that all-important sexual allure, and David Manners (John Harker) is the equivalent of a well-dressed, flawlessly-manicured tailor's dummy.

As for Lugosi, well there is no denying his hard work, but audiences today will wonder what all the fuss was about. His somewhat mannered performance is heavily stylised and overtly theatrical, especially with the slow delivery of his dialogue. He may look every inch the distinguished, well-dressed European aristocrat, but with his youthful good looks fading in middle age, the sexual attraction he tries to project on screen looks unintentionally laughable to a modern viewer. Lugosi also lacks the dangerous raw edge that would later make Christopher Lee's animalistic interpretation so magnetic.

To make matter worse, the film suffers badly when compared with the Spanish-language version that Universal made back-to-back. Fearing the loss of foreign-language markets with the introduction of sound, the Hollywood studios would often at this time shoot German, Spanish and/or French versions of their latest films alongside the English version. Many of these forgettable efforts have long since vanished without trace. But in some rare cases the 'remake' turned out to be a vastly superior movie. Considered lost for many years, the Spanish *Dracula* was rediscovered in the '90s and restored to its original form. It now has a belated cult following, and has somewhat undermined the classic status of the famous original, on which it is a big improvement.

The Spanish version was the brainchild of Universal's new head of foreign language production Paul Kohner, who devised the remake as a way of keeping Mexican actress Lupita Tovar in Hollywood. (He later married her.) It was shot in the evenings and at weekends on the same sets and using the same script as the English version, but with a different cast and crew. George Melford, best known for his work on the Rudolph Valentino film *The Sheik* (1925), was assigned as director.

Because Melford was able to see Browning's rushes, he was able to improve on several scenes even though he couldn't quite overcome the dialogue-heavy script. Despite being half an hour longer, the tightly-constructed Spanish version moves at a slightly faster pace. The stronger juvenile leads, Lupita Tovar (Mina) and Carmen Guerrero (Lucia), look far sexier than their English equivalents. Both sport very revealing nightdresses; Tovar nearly falls out of hers on several occasions. Barry Norton's Juan Harker looks less like a tailor's dummy than David Manners, and Pablo Alvarez Robio's Renfield may not be as memorable as Dwight Frye's famous interpretation but is far less melodramatic and more realistic.

And then we have Dracula, in the shape of Spanish actor Carlos Villarias. Sporting Lugosi's hairpiece, Villarias may not be completely convincing in the role (his attempts at being hypnotic are laughable), but his feral intensity makes Lugosi look ineffectual.

Even Lugosi himself was a fan of the Spanish version, regarding it as 'beautiful, great, splendid.'

Shortly after completing *Dracula*, Lugosi made an uncredited appearance as Orizon the Magician in *50 Million Frenchman* (1931), a zany Warner Brothers musical farce starring comedy duo Ole Olsen and Chic Johnson. The film was released at the same time as *Dracula*, and Lugosi's presence adds camp value to the proceedings.

In May of the same year there was another uncredited turn, as Prince Hassan in the Fox melodrama *Women of All Nations* (1931), an awful film that allegedly featured Humphrey Bogart until he decided at his own expense to have his part removed to avoid harming his film career.

Lugosi returned to Warners with a supporting role in the comedy *Broadminded* (1931), starring Joe E Brown and Thelma Todd. As the temperamental Mexican Pancho Arango, Lugosi gives an agreeable comic performance as he torments Brown's amiable lead at every corner.

It was then back to Fox again for Lugosi's most substantial film role to date. *The Black Camel* (1931) was the fourth in a series of second features based on the adventures of Earl Derr Biggers' inscrutable detective Charlie Chan and starring Swedish actor Warner Oland. Getting third billing, Lugosi plays murder suspect Tarneverro the psychic. The cast also includes Dwight Frye. One of the earliest surviving Chan movies, it makes great use of its Honolulu locations, while Oland is in typically good form and Lugosi hams it up for all he's worth. *The Black Camel* was released on 21 June 1931 – five days before Lugosi finally became an American citizen.

Lugosi had moved from stage star to film star, from supporting actor to leading man, on the strength of *Dracula*. But if he thought his success hung on his talent or star quality, he was mistaken. Dracula wasn't a part he played, but a persona he created, and ultimately it worked against him. Writer John Brosnan summed up the situation perfectly: 'At the time, his acting methods were heavily stylised – something he inherited from his Hungarian film days – and he spoke in a very slow and precise enunciation. But one must admit that his portrayal of the vampire was certainly a distinctive one; and for many, even since the arrival of Christopher Lee, he remains *the* Count Dracula.'

Brosnan added: 'Lugosi obviously believed that his overnight fame in Hollywood had come about because of his acting ability and personal charisma. He didn't realise it was due to the bizarre nature of his Count Dracula role. He certainly didn't think of himself as the successor to Lon Chaney.'

Universal however definitely did think that way when they put Lugosi under contract. Shortly after completing his stint on *The Black Camel*, the actor got lined up for another horror role, and one that he famously turned down. The circumstances of his decision became Hollywood folklore, but it was a professional misstep that may have cost him the major stardom he thought he had achieved with *Dracula*.

There are many stories about Lugosi's participation in *Frankenstein* (1931), and the reasons for him not playing the Monster. The film originated from a treatment by writer Garret Fort and director Robert Florey. Florey saw it as his pet project and, with support from Universal's story editor Richard Schayer, lobbied hard for the director's job. Although Carl Laemmle Jnr didn't formally hire Florey, he did commission him to write the script. Florey wrote the part of Baron Frankenstein for Lugosi, but Laemmle insisted that the actor be tested for the role of the Monster instead.

According to the famous rumour, Lugosi, an actor who felt he needed to be seen and heard, objected to playing the Monster because of the heavy make-up and lack of dialogue. He did however agree to star in two test films directed by Florey and featuring Edward Van Sloan and Dwight Frye; and it is also said that he did not photograph well under the make-up.

Unimpressed by the test films, Laemmle felt that Lugosi looked like something out of the fairytale operetta *Babes in Toyland*, and nine days into the production he fired both him and Florey. Laemmle then set his sights on British director James Whale, who had scored a hit with *Journey's End* (1930). Not only did he lose out to Whale as director, Florey also saw his script thrown out in favour of a new one written by Whale – although one scene set in an old windmill was retained from the original. Bitter about being replaced, Florey felt that Whale's film was a total travesty.

Generally, though, *Frankenstein* is regarded as one of the greatest films ever made. Unlike *Dracula*, it has all the hallmarks of a true horror classic. More importantly, it made a star out of Boris Karloff, a previously unknown British actor whose performance as the Monster is nothing short of brilliant. Lugosi's decision not to play the role backfired in his face. Critic Donald Glut summed it up best: 'He made perhaps the greatest mistake of his life when he turned down the role of the Monster in *Frankenstein*. The Englishman Boris Karloff accepted the part instead and, being a far better actor than Lugosi, nosed the Hungarian performer into second-place status.'

Glut added: 'In the minds of the motion picture executives, [Lugosi] was eternally Count Dracula of 1931, and he was condemned to continue enacting virtually the same performance in numerous films that were to follow.'

In an attempt to put things right with Florey, Laemmle assigned him to write and direct *Murders in the Rue Morgue* (1932), a loose adaptation of the classic Edgar Allan Poe detective story. Keen to retain Lugosi's services, Florey wrote the part of Darwin-inspired mad scientist Dr Mirakle with the actor in mind. 'I wrote the *Rue Morgue* adaptation in a week,' he said. 'I used the same device I employed in my *Frankenstein* adaptation. Bela Lugosi became Dr Mirakle – a mad scientist desirous of creating a human being – not with body parts stolen from a graveyard and a brain from a lab, but by mating of an ape with a woman.' Pretty daring at the time – but since the restrictive Hays Production Code, though introduced in 1930, would not start to be fully enforced until 1934, filmmakers like Florey could do pretty much as they wished, within budget and tight shooting schedules.

Murders in the Rue Morgue was reportedly shot in three days during November 1931, and the success of *Frankenstein* allowed for it to be given an increased budget of $25,000 to film additional scenes. The film was clearly inspired by *The Cabinet of Dr Caligari*, and Florey brought in cinematographer Karl Freund, whose expressionist camerawork lends an evocative atmosphere to art director Charles D Hall's interesting 19th Century Paris backdrop. The result is a good-looking and occasionally effective chiller that suffers from a weak supporting cast. Florey seems to have been preoccupied with recreating the style of *Caligari*, at the expense of his actors.

With second billing behind Sidney Fox (whose promising career would be cut short in 1942 by a drug overdose at the age of just 31) and sporting a weird-looking perm, Lugosi turns in a performance of ham-slicing relish. Given some juicy dialogue to make a meal out of, he excels as Mirakle, a once great scientist reduced to working in a carnival sideshow. The storyline involving Mirakle's gruesome experiments to prove man's link to the apes did not escape controversy at the time – especially from America's Anti-Evolution League – and it's never clear exactly what he is trying to prove, as the central theme of bestiality is a little obscure. This may be due to the fact that Universal edited the film and employed several other writers, including John Huston, to extensively rework the script, a state of affairs that prompted a furious Florey to walk off the set.

Despite Florey's attempts to ape (!) the style of *Caligari* and Lugosi's typically bravura performance, *Murders in the Rue Morgue* was too dark and violently graphic for the audiences of the day. It also suffered badly in comparison with *Frankenstein* when it was released in February 1932. Not surprisingly it failed at the box office.

Lugosi's next effort was *Chandu the Magician* (1932), a low-budget effort adapted by 20th Century Fox from a popular radio serial starring Edmund

Lowe as a westerner who becomes a superhero after learning the powers of eastern mysticism. Lugosi has a thankless part as super-villain Roxer, a deluded madman hell-bent on destroying the world with a powerful death ray.

Much more satisfactory, and certainly unusual, is the independently-made low-budget chiller *White Zombie* (1932). Produced by Edward Halperin and directed by his brother Victor Halperin, both first-time filmmakers, it has achieved a cult following thanks to its strange, dreamlike quality. Shot on the Universal backlot with a reputed $50,000 budget, it was completed in March 1932 after 11 days' filming. It was Hollywood's first venture into zombie territory - although much tamer than George Romero's later exploits with flesh-eating ghouls.

The Halperins scored a coup by bringing in Universal's make-up man Jack Pierce along with the distinguished cinematographer Arthur Martinelli, who made effective use of camera angles and lighting. 'We never went off the Universal lot,' recalled second assistant cameraman Enzo Martinelli. 'Even the night exteriors on the backwoods roads were shot there. All the night shots were night for night. My uncle [Arthur Martinelli] always made sure it was possible to recognise the source of the light in those scenes.' It sounds painfully arty, but the striking visuals remain as fresh today as they were in 1932. The zombies themselves are a chilling lot that must have inspired Romero in some way when he directed *Night of the Living Dead* (1968).

Playing necromantic zombie master Murder Legendre, Lugosi gives a pitch-perfect performance. Clearly the screen magnetism he displayed in *Dracula* wasn't just a one-off. The part of Legendre is a one-dimensional one, but was rewritten to fit the actor's persona and voice, and he makes for an effectively sinister villain, aided by some creepy set-pieces and the film's sparse dialogue. According to Victor Halperin, 'Only 15% of a talkie should be composed of dialogue.' *White Zombie* works on many levels, but it is Lugosi who makes it, with one of his best post-*Dracula* turns. According to his friend, filmmaker Edward D Wood Jnr, '*White Zombie* was his greatest film. He liked that even better than *Dracula*.'

Lugosi next reunited with David Manners and Edward Van Sloan for the independently-produced *Death Kiss* (1932), a routine murder mystery that has the actor playing movie mogul Joseph Steiner. This gimmicky effort has the novel premise of a murder taking place during the making of a film. That and the use of tinting for several scenes depicting flashlights, fires and guns gives it some curiosity value. Lugosi's screen time is limited to a few scenes, and the film's poverty row look is an uncomfortable indication of how his career would develop.

It became clear to Lugosi that it was his horror image and not his acting talent that was keeping him employed. The curse of Dracula had hit home in the form of typecasting. He lobbied hard for other roles – including that of Rasputin in *Rasputin and the Empress* (1932), on which he lost out to Lionel Barrymore – but without much success. Even the theatre world now saw him in the same light, as demonstrated when he went to Los Angeles to play a murderer in the horror play *Murdered Alive*. Although *White Zombie* was a massive success, he regretted taking part in it, especially as he had been paid a meagre $800 a week for his few days' work. But by this time he could not afford to be choosy.

It's fair to say, though, that Lugosi brought a lot of his career problems upon himself. Since becoming a Hollywood star he had developed expensive tastes, and to maintain his new lifestyle he had to work in cheap B-movies and serials rather than hold out for decent film roles. A popular party host within Los Angeles' Hungarian community, he often threw lavish gatherings for fellow ex-pats including director Michael Curtiz and actors Ilona Massey and Joe Pasternak. To show his off-beat sense of humour, Lugosi hired comic Vince Barnett to play a clumsy waiter whose job was spilling drinks and dropping plates to the delight of everyone.

'In the course of his lifetime Lugosi earned thousands of dollars,' said his manager Don Marlowe. 'He was, however, always in two extreme predicaments – either incalculably wealthy or completely broke. He never worried about money. He spent it faster than anyone I have ever known. He lived luxuriously in a stately mansion with lavish surroundings, wore elegant clothes and entertained in superlative taste. He owned a priceless stamp collection and his only other hobby, to which he devoted his leisure time, was reading books, mainly dealing with scientific subjects and world history.'

In stark contrast to Marlowe's comments, Lugosi claimed, 'My only ambition in life is to retire from the screen and settle down in peace and solitude on a little farm far away from Dracula and other of my monsters.' The actor's spendthrift ways and acceptance of roles in poverty-stricken movies weren't going to help him realise this ambition, and before long it all caught up with him. Lugosi's careless spending coupled with his lack of business sense resulted in him filing for bankruptcy in October 1932.

The financial problems may explain why he accepted the role of the Sayer of the Law in the infamous *Island of Lost Souls* (1932), adapted from H G Wells' novel *The Island of Dr Moreau* (1896), his $800 fee being far lower than that of any other actor on the production. Charles Laughton is excellent in the finished film as the white suited, bull whipping Moreau, creator of the man-beasts that reside on a remote island where the doctor rules from his 'House of Pain.' Among the unknown actors who played the beasts were allegedly Alan Ladd, Randolph Scott and Buster Crabbe, although this remains unconfirmed. Thanks to a competition organised by Paramount, a dentist's assistant named Kathleen Burke got chosen from 60,000 entrants to play Moreau's sexy Panther Girl!

Although his part is quite small, and his face hidden by a mountain of fur, Lugosi's distinctive tones are unmistakable. He is able to invest such lines as 'That is the law' and 'Are we not men?' with customary panache. This was also a rare chance for him to play a sympathetic role, especially in the scene where his character finds out the horrific extent of Moreau's vivisection work. 'You made us in the House of Pain!' he shouts impotently, 'You made us *things*!' It's a beautifully played performance; the pain and anguish in his voice are as poignant as they are disturbing.

In fact the film was a little too disturbing for both the censors and the paying public, who objected to its high level of sadism. Even Wells felt the film was a dreadful vulgarisation of his book. The Rt Hon Edward Short, Secretary of the British Board of Film Censors, took the objections a stage further by banning the film in the UK. It didn't turn up on British shores until the '50s.

Intensely directed by Earl Kenton, *Island of Lost Souls* is a savage chiller that hasn't dated with time. What she lacked in acting experience, Kathleen Burke made up for with a truly amazing performance that oozes sexuality. Despite his inadequate salaries on both *Island of Lost Souls* and *White Zombie*, these films remain Lugosi's best post-*Dracula* work.

In 1933 Lugosi famously said, 'I can blame it all on Dracula. Since then Hollywood has scribbled a little card of classification for me, and it looks as if I'll never prove my mettle in any other kind of role.' Did the Count finally take hold of Lugosi to such an extent that he was now unable to escape his clutches?

In addition to typecasting, financial woes and appearing in films beneath his dignity, there was another factor that limited Lugosi's options, and one that Boris Karloff nailed on the head: 'Poor old Bela. He really was a shy, sensitive and talented man. But he made one fatal mistake. He never took the trouble to learn our language … [He] had a real problem with his speech and difficulty interpreting his lines. I remember he once asked a director what a line of dialogue meant. He spent a great deal of time with the Hungarian colony in Los Angeles, and this isolated him.'

Lugosi may not have fully mastered the English language, but he was fluent enough to get by. In January 1933 he married again, this time to his former secretary and fellow Hungarian Lillian Arch, who was thirty years his junior. The start of the year was a period of upheaval within Hollywood. The Great Depression had gripped America, with businesses folding, banks closing and unemployment increasing to 16 million. Thanks to the introduction of sound, Hollywood was initially immune to the country's problems, with ticket sales averaging around 90 million per week. By 1933, though, it could no longer escape the realities of the Depression; and it was further constrained by the increasingly rigid enforcement of the puritanical Hays Production Code, under which elements such as sexual perversion, nudity and the suggested bestiality of *Murders in the Rue Morgue* and *Island of Lost Souls* were no longer considered acceptable material for cinema audiences.

The financial downturn quickly affected the studios. Universal in particular felt the pinch, scaling down their operations, firing long-term staff and suspending star contracts. Boris Karloff threatened to walk out when Carl Laemmle Jnr decided not to honour his salary increases, and he still had enough clout at the studio that Laemmle responded by actually offering him a more lucrative contract – although it cost the actor the title role of *The Invisible Man* (1933). Karloff was shrewd enough to beat the studios at their own game. Having achieving stardom after years of struggle, he wasn't about to be fobbed off by false promises. Becoming a founder member of the Screen Actors Guild also helped him considerably. Formed in 1933, the SAG had the goal of eliminating exploitation of actors by the studios. Lugosi was one of the first actors to join. He may not have had Karloff's influence, but this at least put him in a stronger position regarding pay and conditions.

Work-wise, Lugosi made another low-budget serial for Mascot Pictures called *The Whispering Shadow* (1932); his role was as Professor Anton Strang, another egocentric villain armed with a death ray that could destroy the world. The serial was made back to back with a chiller for Bryan Foy Productions called *Night of Terror* (1933). Lugosi is top-billed in this routine programmer as the turbaned, mystical Hindu servant Degar, and rises above the material with a performance of ripe menace, something that had by this point become his stock-in-trade.

More satisfactory was a supporting role in the Paramount musical comedy *International House* (1933) starring W C Fields as drunken Professor Quaill, one of several oddball characters (including two played by George Burns and Gracie Allen) who meet at a hotel to bid for a brand new invention – television! Being billed way down the cast as General Nicholas Petronovich can't have been great for Lugosi, but at least it wasn't a horror film. The weak plot just provides a link between various hit-and-miss musical and comedy numbers. Comedy may not have been his forte, but Lugosi's deadly serious turn adds a little unintentional humour.

Lugosi's next film performance was in an unbilled but quite large role as a military prosecutor in Fox's French Foreign Legion drama *The Devil's in Love* (1933). By July 1933, however, the film work had dried up, so the actor returned to Broadway for the last time in the short-lived musical comedy *Murder of the Vanities*. He then joined a vaudeville company touring the States with a new production of *Dracula*. With Broadway becoming a distant memory, Lugosi's theatre career would in future be restricted to summer stock and low-key provincial tours. The curse of Dracula had taken hold.

It was only a matter of time before Universal teamed Lugosi up with Boris Karloff. Allegedly based on the Edgar Allan Poe story of the same title (although it has nothing to do with it), *The Black Cat* (1934) was the first of eight films to co-star the two actors. With a $96,000 budget (the main set was built for $1,500), the film was shot in 19 days by Austrian director Edgar G Ulmer, with Lugosi and Karloff cast as Satanic rivals Dr Vitas Werdegast and Hjalmar Poelzig.

There were rumours circulating about Lugosi's apparent hatred of Karloff. A mistrustful person by nature, he probably resented Karloff for getting better acting roles. 'He was very suspicious,' recalled Karloff. 'Suspicious of tricks, fearful of what he regarded as scene stealing. Later, when he realised I didn't go for such nonsense, we became friends.' Once Lugosi relaxed in Karloff's company, both men enjoyed a happy working relationship, although they never socialised off screen. Karloff spoke very highly of his co-star and felt sorry for his later circumstances; he always referred to him as 'Poor Bela'.

Further down the cast list of *The Black Cat* was John Carradine, who enjoyed working with Lugosi. 'He was a charming man,' he recalled with great affection. 'He always had a bucket of red wine on the set, which he pulled out gracefully all day long. He never forgot his lines and never lost his affability. He was a very affable man.' But his drinking of red wine, especially Burgundy, on the set concealed a much darker side to Lugosi's affability; it helped camouflage his increasing drug addiction.

In Universal's eyes, Karloff was the star. He always had top billing, even when Lugosi had the more interesting role. Financially, the British actor was better off; for *The Black Cat*, Lugosi was paid just $3,583, a paltry sum compared with Karloff's $7,500 fee. Lugosi though gives the better performance. Originally conceived as a depraved villain, his character Werdegast was rewritten to become more ambiguously heroic. Lugosi makes the most of some excellent lines and plays the part to perfection. More importantly, the chemistry between him and Karloff is a natural, with both men at the peak of their satanic powers.

The Black Cat was Universal's biggest hit of 1934, grossing a profit of $140,000. However, the religious overtones and perverted nature of the film prompted the formation of the Production Code Administration, which was empowered to vet all scripts and edit any film that contained anything it considered of an offensive nature – right down to the title! So any movie containing elements of a sexual, religious or obscene nature would be hauled over the coals. This naturally had a highly negative effect on horror film production.

Lugosi's and Karloff's second shared film was, uncharacteristically, a screwball comedy called *Gift of Gab* (1934); they guest star as themselves but have no scenes together.

Lugosi's next solo starring effort was in the serial *The Return of Chandu* (1934), in which he replaced Edmund Lowe as the mystic crime fighter. It was a bad idea for him to star in another low-budget serial following his good work on *The Black Cat*, but at least he plays the hero and gets the girl. There was also an equally ill-advised return to B-movies with *The Mysterious Mr Wong* (1934), a poverty-stricken second feature that has the actor as a sinister Chinese villain who acquires the 12 coins of Confucius. Lugosi then returned to Chandu once more in the serial *Chandu on Magic Island* (1935), and made a ten-minute cameo as villain Doc Boehm in Columbia's *The Best Man Wins* (1935).

'Every producer in Hollywood had set me down as a type,' Lugosi recalled with an air of disenchantment. 'I was both amused and disappointed.' His reasoning was sound. 'Because of my language and gestures, I am catalogued as what you call a heavy. My accent stamped me, in the imagination of the producers, as an enemy. Therefore I must be a heavy.' But then he had to earn a living regardless. 'I'll be truthful. The weekly pay cheque is the most important thing to me.' These low budget flicks may have earned him much-needed cash, but really they caused far more harm to his career than Dracula ever could.

Even with typecasting, Lugosi was unable to secure plum horror roles. He was up for the part of Dr Pretorius in *The Bride of Frankenstein* (1935), but lost out to that great theatrical eccentric Ernest Thesiger. Thesiger is so brilliant as the overtly camp Pretorius that it's impossible to imagine anyone else in the role. The film grossed just under $1 million at the box office; but for Lugosi, it was a missed opportunity to break away from standard screen villainy.

Lugosi's horror career peaked in January 1935 with a memorable cameo as vampire Count Mora in MGM's *Mark of the Vampire* (1935). This production also reunited him with director Tod Browning, whose career had never recovered from the disastrous *Freaks* (1932). *Mark of the Vampire* was Browning's lavishly-mounted remake of his Lon Chaney-starring classic *London After Midnight* (1925), with Lugosi in the Chaney role. The actor is third-billed, but he doesn't do much and speaks only at the end of the film, when it's revealed that he's really an actor hired to play Mora in order to trap a killer. His presence however adds to a dated but atmospheric murder mystery.

Playing Mora's sinister daughter Luna is cult favourite Caroll Borland, whose stunning necrophile appearance and mesmerising presence form the prototype for all future vampire brides and undead femme fatales. She clearly inspired future television horror hostesses Vampira and Elvira, and probably influenced Charles Addams when he created Morticia for his comic strip *The Addams Family*. As well as achieving horror immortality on the strength of one film, Borland had the distinction of being Lugosi's greatest admirer. 'Let me admit with no apology that to me Lugosi is Dracula, and Dracula is Lugosi. There is no distinction between the two,' she said of her co-star. 'Many have donned his nocturnal cloak, and some, like Christopher Lee, have presented most credible representations of the great undead Count – but can never be Dracula.'

As a teenager Borland had first met Lugosi in 1931 when he appeared as Dracula on stage in Los Angeles. So mesmerised was she by his performance that she wrote the sequel *Countess Dracula* and submitted it to him. Of course it could not be made, because Florence Stoker owned the rights, but Lugosi took the impressionable girl under his wing and cast her as Lucy in his 1933 vaudeville production. It was Lugosi who told Tod Browning that Borland would be perfect as Luna. 'At the time I never knew why I was chosen to be his companion,' she said. 'I had great affection for him as a person and he knew it. He was my idol, yet I was not a "fan". I found him fascinating, intimidating, charming, exasperating, demanding and generous all at the same time. Years later I began to wonder what he had ever seen in me and why it was I had been so fortunate.'

Borland also said: 'When we were making *Mark of the Vampire*, there was never any intention that Lugosi was replaying his famous Dracula part.' Universal however had their suspicions to the contrary, and threatened legal action if there were two many similarities between Mora and Dracula. Lugosi counteracted this by devising his own costume for the part with screenwriter Guy Endore.

The relationship between Mora and Luna may have incestuous overtones, but Borland stressed that her own relationship with Lugosi was strictly platonic: 'He liked young women. He was much married and quite a domestic gentleman by then. I called him Mr Lugosi. We chatted together between takes, but I was just a junior member of the cast. We were just a pair of working actors.' She also noted that Lugosi liked to discuss biographer Emil Ludwig's book *Napoleon* in great detail with co-stars Lionel Barrymore, Lionel Atwill and Jean Hersholt.

Robert Bloch, who knew Borland, confirmed her description of her off-screen relationship with Lugosi: 'He was an easy-going, genial man who took a very paternal interest toward her and was very prim and proper.'

Unimpressed by Tod Browning's direction, Borland took advice from Lugosi as to how Luna should be played: '[Browning] was a big negative. "Caroll, I want you to walk in front of Lugosi. You're gonna be holding a candle, so look out for your hair." "What am I supposed to do?" "Walk over and down the steps and walk out." That was it. He expected Lugosi and me to go be vampires.'

One of Lugosi's better efforts, *Mark of the Vampire* netted a profit of $54,000. Unfortunately his next film, the thriller *Murder by Television* (1935), was another low-budget programmer. It cost $35,000 to be exact – less than half the $75,000 value of the television equipment the filmmakers borrowed for the production. Playing twins Arthur and Edward Perry, Lugosi remains the only saving grace of this worthless mess.

In May 1935, Lugosi returned to Universal to re-team with Boris Karloff in *The Raven* (1935). Lugosi is in fine form in this Edgar Allen Poe-inspired tale as surgeon Dr Richard Vollin, whose obsession with a recovering patient prompts him to hold a house party where he dispatches the guests in grizzly fashion. Along for the ride is Karloff's wanted criminal Edmund Bateman, whom Vollin disfigures as a way of blackmailing the fugitive into playing his reluctant accomplice.

Lugosi excels in a juicy role of ripe villainy and quotable lines. And once again he acts Karloff off the screen with unquestionable authority. Despite this, Karloff got the $10,000 pay cheque, whereas Lugosi received only $5,000.

The level of sadism in the film proved too much for the censor, who heavily cut it on its release, but nevertheless it was a huge box office hit.

Shortly after completing work on *The Raven*, Lugosi set sail for England on the *Berengaria* to make a film for a fledgling company called Hammer. *The Mystery of the Marie Celeste* (1935) was the studio's second film and the first to dabble in horror. The celebrated mystery surrounding the disappearance of the crew of the 19th Century sailing ship the *Mary Celeste* had been considered as a subject by several Hollywood studios before Hammer decided to make a film of it. Lugosi, wrongly thinking it was a big-budget British production produced by Alexander Korda, signed up without reading the script.

Arriving in England on 13 July 1935, Lugosi attended a reception two days later, then started location work on board the schooner *Mary B Mitchell*, with interior shooting at Nettlefold Studios. Hammer's continuity girl Tilly Day's impression of Lugosi was of a 'very tall, and somehow rather terrifying man.' She added: 'He was always nice to me though. He called me "the English rose" and once made a pass at me!'

Lugosi felt a tinge of disappointment that the film wasn't what he had expected. 'Bela was loath to talk about the film,' said producer Richard Gordon. 'Everybody thought it was going to make a big British picture out of [the story]. After all, it was a big subject. I think Bela thought the same thing.'

At least Lugosi was on extremely good money. 'They pay me all the money in the world in London,' he said. 'I don't get half as much in Hollywood.' Cast as sinister old sea dog Anton Lorenzen, he had a decent role on top of his $10,000 pay cheque, and he gives a solid, multi-layered performance. Menacing though he is, the film is far too slow, although critical reaction at the time was very favourable.

By the time Lugosi returned to Hollywood, Universal's worsening financial situation had prompted Carl Laemmle Jnr to obtain a loan from Standard Capital Corporation to save the studio from going under. But under the new arrangement, SCC would take hold of Universal if Laemmle could not raise the required $5.5 million to pay back the loan. This began a long period of uncertainty for Lugosi.

In September 1935, the actor was back at Universal for his third pairing with Karloff. *The Invisible Ray* (1936) is a science fiction film with Karloff dominating the proceedings as Dr Janos Rukh, a misguided scientist who discovers Radium X only for his discovery to be stolen by rivals. Like King Midas, his deadly touch kills everyone in his path. Stuck with a subdued but sympathetic role as rival scientist Dr Felix Benet, Lugosi is good value, but is no match for Karloff in excellent form.

Once again Karloff was better off financially, being paid $18,750 to Lugosi's $4,000. The shoot lasted several months, to allow John P Fulton time to complete his excellent special effects. Released in January 1936, the film garnered favourable reviews and respectable box office takings.

The box-office success of *The Bride of Frankenstein* prompted Universal to make a *Dracula* sequel. David O Selznick owned the film rights to Bram Stoker's short story *Dracula's Guest*. He sold them to the studio, along with John L Balderston's screenplay. Rewritten by R C Sheriff, it was scheduled to start production in February 1936. James Whale was initially pencilled in as director, but then Edward Sutherland was given the job, while Lugosi and Edward Van Sloan were lined up to return as Dracula and Van Helsing respectively.

However, Universal then threw out Sheriff's version of the script in favour of a new one by Garrett Ford, and Lambert Hillyer took over as director, at a reduced fee of $5,000 compared with Sutherland's $17,500. Renamed *Dracula's Daughter* (1936), the new script omitted Dracula altogether, except for a brief shot of him lying dead in his coffin – except it's not Lugosi in the coffin but a dummy that looks nothing like him. Lugosi, along with Sutherland, Balderston and Sheriff, was actually paid off, the actor receiving $4,000 for his non-participation, which was more than he had earned when he had actually played Dracula in the original film. Essentially a B-movie programmer, *Dracula's Daughter* was one of Universal's most expensive films of the year, but much of the $278,000 budget was used to pay off Lugosi and others involved.

In February 1936 SCC demanded immediate repayment of their loan. Carl Laemmle asked for an extension, but was turned down, and on 14 March 1936, only four days after the completion of work on *Dracula's Daughter*, SCC took control of Universal and unceremoniously kicked out the Laemmles. The British ban on horror films also had an effect on the Hollywood production line, and before long the genre was moribund.

Lugosi's future now looked dire. 'I am definitely doomed to be an exponent of evil,' he said, expressing his increasing frustration. 'But I want sympathetic roles. Then parents would tell their offspring "Eat your spinach and you'll grow up to be a nice man like Bela Lugosi." As it is, they threaten their children with me instead of the bogeyman.' He added that he would, 'like to quit the supernatural roles and play just an interesting down-to-earth person.'

Lugosi auditioned for the role of villain Surat Khan in the Errol Flynn film *The Charge of the Light Brigade* (1936) but lost out to C Henry Gordon. This was just one of many unsuccessful auditions that also included one for his stage role of Gorotchenko in the film version of *Tovarich* (1937); on that occasion he lost out to Basil Rathbone. Rathbone was among the increasing number of talented stage stars making their mark in Hollywood. With such fierce competition, an actor of Lugosi's limited range had trouble winning roles. Now settled in Hollywood, Rathbone became one of the film community's most popular actors. Only Lugosi, for reasons best known to himself, disliked him.

The fact that Boris Karloff had no problems getting work can't have helped Lugosi's self-confidence. Because Karloff had appeared in a variety of films outside the horror genre, he quite easily returned to other top supporting roles, avoiding any downturn in his career. Lugosi remained with Universal to play mob boss Greg Benez for the implausible low-budget crime thriller *Postal Inspector* (1936); but with his contract now up, the new management had little use for a washed-up horror star.

For Victory Pictures, Lugosi appeared as villain Victor Poten in the serial *Shadow of Chinatown* (1936). His association with no-budget serials then continued with Republic's *SOS Coastguard* (1937); filmed in August 1937, this was his only film work that year. As super-villain Borof, Lugosi is out to destroy the world with a deadly nerve gas. Although more action-packed than the previous outing, *Coastguard* sees the actor looking bored; he agreed to appeared in it only because poor health had prevented him from taking part in another serial he was contracted to.

But there was always Dracula, who guaranteed Lugosi stage work when the film offers dried up. 'It's a living but it's also a curse,' he bemoaned. 'It's Dracula's curse.' The actor made periodic returns to the role in summer stock theatre, including one production that reunited him with Edward Van Sloan and Dwight Frye. But there were still long spells of unemployment. Such was his financial situation that he had to borrow money from the charitable Actors Fund to pay the hospital bills when his son, Bela George Lugosi, was born in 1938.

Around August 1938, Lugosi was driving past the Regina Theatre in Beverly Hills when he saw something that lifted his heart: 'One day I drive past and see my name and big lines of people all around. I wonder what is giving away to people – maybe bacon or vegetables. But it is the comeback of horror, and I come back.'

Lugosi was absolutely correct. Horror films were popular once more, and

Universal quickly capitalised on it. Following the ousting of the Laemmles, Charles R Rogers was appointed as Vice President in Charge of Production, only to be replaced by Cliff Work after the studio quickly lost over $3 million. Work had a much sounder business ethic than his predecessors, so when it came to his attention that movie distributor E Mark Umann had successfully screened *Dracula* and *Frankenstein* at the Regina Theatre, he quickly produced 500 new prints of both films for a proposed cinema double bill. The official opening at New York's Rialto Theatre went under the title 'Revival of the Dead.'

In October 1938, Universal initiated the production of *Son of Frankenstein* (1939). Boris Karloff returned for his third and final time as the Monster, with Basil Rathbone in the title role. Brought in to direct was Rowland V Lee, a reliable journeyman who could finish a film on time and within budget. Lugosi, cast as Igor the sly hunchback, was clearly happy to be working again, and his performance ranks among his best. He is unrecognisable under thick grey hair and beard and with a crocked head (Igor has survived a hanging and wants revenge), but his voice is unmistakable. It is a great part, and the actor throws himself into it with the sort of enthusiasm lacking in many of his previous assignments.

What makes his performance all the more impressive is the fact his part was made up on the fly. Willis Cooper's original script did not feature Igor, but Lee wanted to retain Lugosi's services for as long as possible. He rewrote several scenes minutes before shooting started and allowed the actor to improvise his role on a daily basis. Aware of the fact that he got only half the salary of Karloff and Rathbone, Lee kept him on the payroll throughout the production to help make up the difference. Lugosi responded by doing some of his finest screen work.

Son of Frankenstein is a well staged and efficient chiller that cost more money to make than any previous horror film, its $420,000 final budget being twice the amount Universal had estimated. They need not have worried too much as the film went on to make a smart profit of over $1 million. Horror had well and truly returned.

Lugosi went to 20th Century Fox next for *The Gorilla* (1939), a good-natured comedy-thriller starring the Ritz Brothers, a vaudeville trio whose mugging can be either funny or annoying. The actor has a nicely played supporting role as Peters the butler, who spends most of the time in the background staying calm and collected while everyone else gets hysterical. He lends quiet presence and dignity, even if his role is little more than a red herring to the comic proceedings.

In March 1939, Lugosi made his second trip to England, at the request of producer John Argyle, to star in the Edgar Wallace crime thriller *The Dark Eyes of London* (1939), the first British film to receive the infamous H for horror certificate. Lugosi plays two parts: the first is as Dr Feodor Orloff, an insurance broker who signs people up on his policies and then kills then for the returns; the second is as blind Professor John Dearborn, for which he donned a white wig and moustache that made him unrecognisable. (His voice was re-dubbed by O B Clarence to complete the disguise.) Making the most of his dual role, the actor is in his element. His newfound confidence after his stint as Igor enabled him to give an excellent performance.

As on *The Mystery of the Marie Celeste*, Lugosi got paid a lot more for his services on *The Dark Side of London* than he did for his Hollywood roles. Considering how financially better off he was in England, and the availability of Anton Walbrook/Conrad Veidt-type roles in British films, he might well have had a more satisfactory career had he relocated permanently. It would certainly been a better-paid one.

Lugosi's time in England provided a unique opportunity for him to meet the man who had first brought Dracula to the stage. Hamilton Deane had revived his play in London, and it was currently being performed at the Lyceum Theatre (which had once been managed by Bram Stoker). Now playing Dracula, Deane was pleasantly surprised when Lugosi turned up during a performance, complete with evening suit and cape. The two men met on stage during the curtain call, to tremendous audience applause.

The good work continued on Lugosi's return to Hollywood, with a brief but high-profile role as Commissar Razinin in the classic Greta Garbo comedy *Ninotchka* (1939), a big-budget MGM production. Clearly happy to escape the clutches of mad scientists and monsters, Lugosi turns up late in the proceedings, but makes the most of his one, three-minute scene.

Both *Son of Frankenstein* and *Ninotchka* should have led to better things, but once again Lugosi's financial need to work dictated his next move, which was to appear in Universal's low-budget serial *The Phantom Creeps* (1939). It was back to mad science mayhem in his role as Dr Zorka; but this was still a cut above his next small, thankless part as a henchman in *The Saint's Double Trouble* (1940), a routine RKO B-movie starring George Sanders as Leslie Charteris's crime-busting sleuth.

Returning to Universal in December 1939, Lugosi appeared in a film that would have seen him again working alongside Boris Karloff, had it not been for a last-minute change of plan when it went into production. *Black Friday* (1940) tells the story of Dr Ernest Sovac, a scientist who saves the life of a friend, Professor George Kingsley, by using part of the brain of murdered gangster Red Cannon. Discovering the existence of a hidden fortune, Sovac tries to locate it by using hypnosis on Kingsley to bring out Cannon's personality. However, the gangster quickly asserts himself and sets about murdering those who double-crossed him. Originally Sovac was to have been played by Lugosi and Kingsley by Karloff. In the end, however, Karloff was given the role of Sovac and British stage actor Stanley Ridges was brought in as Kingsley, leaving Lugosi, miscast, as Cannon's former associate Eric Marney. As a result, the two horror stars share no scenes together – although Lugosi retained second billing.

Black Friday isn't a bad movie. It gave Stanley Ridges, an actor who specialised in doctors, lawyers and other assorted professionals, the role of his career, and one that he plays to the hilt, upstaging Karloff in one of his stiffer performances. Although he does his best, Lugosi doesn't add anything to the film other than an effective death scene in which he is suffocated in a kitchen cupboard (?). It was rumoured that technical adviser Manley P Hall had put Lugosi under hypnosis to make his death scene more effective, though this turned out to be a hoax for publicity purposes.

Black Friday premiered in Chicago on 29 February 1940 as part of a double bill with *The House of Seven Gables* (1940) starring Vincent Price. Lugosi and Price attended, before joining Boris Karloff for the San Francisco opening.

In August 1940, Lugosi, Karloff and Peter Lorre appeared in the RKO screwball musical comedy *You'll Find Out* (1940), a vehicle for radio star bandleader Kay Kyser. This was the only time Lugosi appeared alongside fellow Hungarian Lorre. The actors played second fiddle to Kyser, and a proposed musical number to be performed by them never materialised. A proposed sequel that would have reunited 'the Three Horror Men' with Kyser also came to nothing.

In October 1940, Lugosi starred in his only feature for low-budget specialists Public Releasing Corporation. PRC made good use of actors who were either hard up or had had their careers damaged by scandal. It is a sad fact that Lugosi must have been obliged to accept a role in one such film for financial reasons. As it was, *The Devil Bat* (1940) became a big box office hit!

The Devil Bat has one of the silliest movie premises ever. After being robbed of his invention of a cold cream by a cosmetics firm, Dr Paul Carruthers (Lugosi) trains an army of newly enlarged bats to kill in response to particular aftershaves. Yes, it's that daft. But Lugosi give an agreeably malevolent performance as Carruthers; a winning turn that gives the film undeserved respectability.

Writer Tom Weaver memorably summed up Lugosi's career at this point: 'By 1941 the only way Lugosi was getting into a straight picture was by buying a ticket.' The work was coming in, but it was uninspired, low quality stuff. *Invisible Ghost* (1941), which was shot in March 1941, was the first of nine low-budget chillers the actor made for Sam Katzman at Monogram Pictures. Cast as Dr Charles Kessler, he had a rare chance to play a sympathetic role, even if the character is driven to madness by the spectre of his wife. Lugosi makes the most of his role, but the thin plot and dreadful dialogue finally defeat him.

Marginally better was his return to Universal for *The Black Cat* (1941), a murder mystery that had nothing to do with Edgar Allan Poe, or to the actor's 1934 film of the same title. It's an efficient enough thriller, but Lugosi's turn as Vigos the gardener is a red herring role with only a few minutes' screen time. At least it is better than *Spooks Run Wild* (1941), a witless farce, and Lugosi's second for Monogram, in which he plays stooge to the unfunny juvenile gang the East Side Kids.

With Boris Karloff taking Broadway by storm with his performance as Jonathan Brewster in *Arsenic and Old Lace*, Lugosi had high hopes of regaining his title as Universal's king of horror. But there was now a new king on the lot, in the massive shape of Lon Chaney Jnr, an actor with even less dramatic acting range than him. The success of *Mad-Made Monster* (1941) established Chaney as a leading genre figure, much to Lugosi's chagrin. If the actor resented Karloff and disliked Rathbone, he absolutely hated Chaney, whose hard-drinking antics and boisterous practical jokes upset a lot of people at Universal.

The antipathy must have hit home with Lugosi's next film, *The Wolf Man* (1941), a handsomely-mounted horror that gave Chaney his best-known role as werewolf Larry Talbot. Lugosi has another brief cameo in this as Bela the gypsy, who also happens to be the werewolf who bites Talbot. It's a decent flick, even if it lacks the clout of Universal's best horror work. Playing Bela's sinister mother Maleva is that diminutive Russian actress of the Moscow Art Theatre, Maria Ouspenskaya – who happened to be only six years older than Lugosi!

The release of *The Wolf Man* coincided with the Japanese attack on Pearl Harbor, and the executives at Universal grew nervous that the market for horror movies might be adversely affected by the prospect of America going into the war. However, they could breath a sigh of relief, as *The Wolf Man* grossed over $1 million at the box office. Lugosi could too, although by 1942 he was forced by circumstances to accept every film role on offer.

Returning to Monogram for the wartime thriller *Black Dragons* (1942), Lugosi played Dr Melcher, yet another villain. Shot in January 1942, this film made history by being the first to respond to the Pearl Harbor attack. Unfortunately Lugosi, making what would be his only espionage thriller, began to suffer from crippling arthritis on top of his ongoing sciatica, so his morphine dependency also increased considerably. It never affected his performance, but by this stage of his career it was all about money. Artistic success was no longer an issue.

Ghost of Frankenstein (1942) marked Lugosi's return to his role as Igor the hunchback. Although less impressive than before, he keeps things in order with a less feral but still sly performance. This time Igor's brain is transferred to the Monster; he now speaks in that distinctive voice but goes blind as a result of the surgery. *Ghost of Frankenstein* is not up to the standard of the first three films in the series, but is reasonably enjoyable nonetheless. It also did well at the box office, which showed that the market for horror films, even in wartime, remained strong.

It was back to Monogram for *The Corpse Vanishes* (1942), featuring Lugosi as Dr Lorenz, a mad horticulturist who kidnaps girls for their glandular fluids in order to keep his elderly wife young – a forerunner to the infamous Peter Cushing slasher *Corruption* (1968). Zany, to say the least, but it turned out to be one of the better Sam Katzman productions, with Lugosi in surprisingly fine fettle, making the most of a better-than-average role and savouring some choice dialogue.

From Monogram the actor returned to Universal, and received top billing for the first time since *Dracula*, in what would be his last film for the studio. Unfortunately his role as Rolf the butler in *Night Monster* (1943) is a red herring cameo that doesn't advance the plot. Filmed by Ford L Beebe in July 1942, *Night Monster* is fun chiller that was intended as a quickie. 'I always was kind of proud of it,' recalled Beebe. 'Hitchcock, who was also making a picture on the lot, screened a rough cut, and couldn't believe the picture was shot in 11 days.'

The following month Lugosi was back at Monogram for the low-budget potboiler *Bowery at Midnight* (1942) as Professor Brenner, a criminologist who uses a soup kitchen as a front for his gang to carry out bank robberies and murder. Once again Lugosi makes the most of the poverty-stricken trappings of his role to create something memorable. As career-damaging as these B-movies were, he always gave a good performance, leaving aside his lacklustre cameo in *Night Monster*.

Lugosi rounded the year off with the worst of the Monogram films in which he appeared, *The Ape Man* (1943). Decked out in ridiculous ape-like make-up as mad scientist Dr Brewster, he looks embarrassed. At least the other Monogram efforts gave him something to work with, but this one isn't even in the so-bad-it's-good category. It was at this stage of his career that the Lugosi name became of little more than marquee value. And so desperate was his situation, he had to accept a role that he had declined all those years ago – the Frankenstein Monster.

It was writer Curt Siodmak who originally proposed making *Frankenstein Meets the Wolf Man* (1943). Seizing on this idea as a sure way to increase box office receipts, Universal assigned Siodmak to write a script, with George Waggner as producer and Roy William Neill as director.

There was one problem: Lon Chaney Jnr had played both title roles in the past and wanted to do so again. This, though, was ruled out by budget restrictions, the tight shooting schedule and the heavy make-up requirements, so in the end Chaney stuck to playing just the Wolf Man. Because the story involved the Monster being given Ygor's brain and speaking with his voice, logic dictated that Lugosi should play the role. On paper it sounded reasonable, even though the actor was in his sixties. The part also had dialogue, so Lugosi accepted without hesitation.

The film begins with the newly-revived Larry Talbot travelling to Frankenstein's homeland, where he meets Maleva the gypsy woman (Maria Ouspenskaya). Arriving at Dr Frankenstein's ruined castle, he finds the Monster frozen in a block of ice. The Monster is alive but blind and weak. The two sit together by a campfire where the monster starts speaking.

MONSTER: I can't see you. I'm blind, I'm sick. Once I had the strength of a hundred men. If Dr Frankenstein were alive he'd give it back to me … so I can live forever.

TALBOT: Do you know what happened?

MONSTER: I fell into a stream when the village people burned the house down. I lost consciousness. When I woke I was frozen in the ice.

TALBOT: Buried alive. I know, I know.

MONSTER: Dr Frankenstein created my body to be immortal. His son gave me a new brain, a clever brain. I will rule the world forever if we can find the formula that can give me back my strength. I will never die.

TALBOT: But I *want* to die. If you wanted to die, what would you do?

MONSTER: I would look for Dr Frankenstein's diary. He knew the secret of immortality. He knew the secret to death.

The dialogue is decent enough, and an actor like Lugosi could make it sing. The Monster is given several scenes where he speaks. So far so good, but Universal did not see it that way, especially with the idea of the Monster wanting to rule the world being a little too close to Adolf Hitler's ideals. As a result, all of the Monster's dialogue and references to his blindness were removed, leaving Lugosi with little do except lumber around with his arms stretched out as if he was sleepwalking.

Despite his advancing years and increasing frailty, Lugosi still had to undergo the ordeal of Jack Pierce's make-up. His wife Lillian recalled, 'He had to be in the chair at five in the morning. The head weighed five pounds; those boots weighed over twenty pounds; the whole schmeer took like four hours to get on. They had a special chair on the set for the Monster to sit in.'

However, Waggner took one look at Lugosi and realised they had made a mistake hiring him. So they brought in stuntman Gil Perkins, who at 6ft looked more convincing as the Monster. Perkins also performed all the demanding scenes, while Lugosi featured just in the close-ups.

Lugosi's total screen time amounts to only six minutes. The final confrontation between the Wolf Man and the Monster was not even performed by the two actors; Perkins donned the Monster's costume, while fellow stuntman Eddie Parker doubled for Chaney in full werewolf mode.

Chances are the actors were away from the set drinking each other under the table while the climax was being filmed.

If playing the Monster proved an unpleasant experience for Lugosi, he must have been mortified when Universal chose Chaney to star in *Son of Dracula* (1943). The studio's faith in Chaney was dubious to say the least. As good as he was as the Wolf Man, he owed his success to Jack Pierce's excellent make-up. He was far too big and overweight to pass himself off as the suave European gentleman Dracula, complete with evening attire and black cape. In his defence, Chaney battles hard against miscasting and gives a reasonable performance. The film as a whole is entertaining, but it could have been a lot better if Lugosi had played Dracula, even though he was now a tad too old for the role.

So next it was back to Monogram for another East Side Kids screwball comedy, *Ghosts on the Loose* (1943), as Nazi agent Emil. Directed by William 'One Take' Beaudine, this dismal effort is memorable mainly for having Ava Gardner in an early film role. It is also notable for Lugosi, standing still in one scene, saying 'shit' under his breath when he sneezes. Beaudine kept the scene in the film, making it the first time a four-letter word was used in a Hollywood movie – unless you count Clark Gable saying 'damn' in *Gone With the Wind* (1939)!

Shortly after completing *Ghosts on the Loose* in February 1943, Lugosi returned to the stage for a brief tour of *Dracula*. He then assumed Karloff's role of Jonathan Brewster in *Arsenic and Old Lace*, which played in San Francisco and Los Angeles. It was a far cry from Karloff's Broadway achievement, but its successful opening at the Music Box Theatre in Los Angeles on 20 August 1943 brought the actor favourable notices.

During his time on stage in *Arsenic and Old Lace*, Lugosi signed a three-picture deal with Columbia. The first film was meant to be a direct sequel to *Dracula*, but Universal, who had just completed *Son of Dracula*, threatened Columbia with a plagiarism lawsuit, forcing the studio to change the vampire character's name from Dracula to Armand Tesla.

Despite being paid only $3,500 for four weeks' work on *Return of the Vampire* (1944), Lugosi was happy to have another starring role in a major studio film. Playing Dracula in all but name, he made a welcome return to form. 'Bela was a real professional,' said director Sam White. 'The rest of the cast were top notch. They were all imbued with the parts, and Bela was the motivating factor. The film cost approximately $75,000 and grossed for Columbia close to a million dollars.' Actress Nina Foch, who had her first starring role in the film, recalled that Lugosi's breath reeked of sulphur water, a health tonic that gave off a bad odour.

Return of the Vampire provided Lugosi with his last starring role for a major studio. Columbia announced plans for a sequel called *Bride of the Vampire* and retained his services; but the film was eventually renamed *Cry of the Werewolf* (1944) and did not feature Lugosi, although Nina Foch again appeared. Nor did the Columbia deal lead to anything permanent.

February 1944 had Lugosi playing Merkil, another sinister red herring butler, in *One Body Too Many* (1944) for Pine Productions. He has little to do in the action other than offer cups of coffee (which may or may not be laced with rat poison) to the other characters. But the film itself isn't too bad, and a distinctly deadpan Lugosi wrings out a few laughs to his advantage.

Unfortunately the actor then made the mistake of returning to Monogram for *Return of the Ape Man* (1944). Co-starring in this inept chiller was John Carradine, who took on the assignment in order to finance his newly formed Shakespearean Players. Third-billed as the Ape Man was British actor George Zucco, who must have realised what he had let himself in for and feigned illness to get out of the film. Frank Moran took over his role, but for reasons of cost, the producers decided to keep Zucco's name on the credits, even though he appeared in only a couple of early scenes. Lugosi and Carradine should have followed Zucco's lead. Playing potty scientists Professor Dexter and Professor Gilmore respectively, Lugosi maintains his dignity but Carradine, doubtless having more important things on his mind, walks through his role with no conviction. Perhaps the greatest credit goes to Zucco – for bowing out of the film!

Lugosi, Carradine and Zucco then appeared together in another Monogram clinker. *Voodoo Man* (1944), a return to zombie territory, would be Lugosi's last film for the studio. Once again he rises above the silly premise as Dr Richard Marlowe, a loony doctor who kidnaps lone female motorists for his own necromantic pleasures, with the help of Zucco's garage manager Nicholas and Carradine's dim-witted handyman Toby. The presence of these three actors should have made the film bearable, but Carradine gives an awful performance. Filming *Voodoo Man* during the day, he spent his evenings performing with the Shakespearean Players at the Pasadena Playhouse. Zucco, looking silly in his feather voodoo costume, was just happy to make a few dollars to maintain his beloved ranch.

Carradine's dream of taking his Shakespearean Players to Broadway was never achieved. When the company folded following an abortive coast-to-coast tour, he returned to Hollywood to play Dracula in Universal's monster rallies *House of Frankenstein* (1944) and *House of Dracula* (1945). With his silver hair and moustache, Carradine comes perhaps closer than any other actor to the description of the Count in the novel. He gives a suave enough performance in both films, but this still leaves the baffling question as to why Lugosi wasn't even considered to reprise the role. Given that he had recently played the very similar Armand Tesla so effectively, Universal's decision not to use him seems rather odd. But then Carradine doesn't have much to do in either film, and his character is killed off halfway through both.

Signing a three-picture deal with RKO, Lugosi next appeared in *The Body Snatcher* (1945), which is notable for being his final film with Boris Karloff, who was on a similar deal with the studio. Unlike Universal's monster cycle, the RKO chillers were visually atmospheric pieces that emphasised suggestive rather than outright terror. These films, which include *Cat People* (1942) and *I Walked with a Zombie* (1943), are now regarded as horror classics. *The Body Snatcher* goes back to the old gothic style, but retains the same dreamlike quality that made *Cat People* so distinctive. Based on Robert Louis Stevenson's short story of the same title, it is an interesting reworking of the infamous Burke and Hare legend, with Karloff as grave robber John Gray. Although Karloff and Lugosi share top billing, the real star is Henry Daniell, giving the performance of his career, as the Dr Knox-inspired surgeon MacFarlane. Karloff is equally effective as Gray; the mind games played between the two men are brilliantly executed, and the eerie climax remains one of the most suspenseful in screen history.

Lugosi's role as MacFarlane's creepy manservant Joseph is little more than an extended cameo. The actor looks pale and gaunt; it seems the Burgundy could no longer hide the morphine addiction. But his performance is a welcome return to ghoulish form. There is an excellent scene where Joseph makes the fatal mistake of blackmailing Gray and gets dispatched for his troubles. Even in this one scene, the chemistry Lugosi and Karloff share is as effective as ever. It may have been a fitting end to their association, but once again Karloff was financially better off, with a $16,000 pay cheque compared with Lugosi's $3,000.

Karloff also fared well with the other two films made under his RKO deal, *Isle of the Dead* (1944) and *Bedlam* (1945), the latter being one of the best of his career. Lugosi, by contrast, had to make do with lesser assignments, both of them comedy vehicles for the duo Wally Brown and Alan Carney. The first, *Zombies on Broadway* (1944), has Brown and Carney as two press agents sent to San Sebastian to find a real zombie for the New York nightclub Zombie Hut. Lugosi has a brief cameo as zombie master Dr Paul Renault. The other, *Genius at Work* (1946), features Lionel Atwill, in one of his last films, as criminal mastermind the Cobra, with a pale-looking Lugosi as his sidekick Stone. The film wasn't released until October 1946; by that time, Lugosi had entered another period of uncertainty in his career, and one that would prove terminal.

With World War II coming to an end, horror films became redundant in the face of public indifference. The documentary evidence of the real life horrors performed at the Nazi death camps by Josef Mengele and his SS doctors made the movie exploits of Frankenstein and his fellow mad scientists disturbingly uncomfortable. Another factor was the declining standard of the genre. Universal had their monster rallies, but once they were done there was nowhere to take the series. Even Val Lewton's

207

atmospheric chillers became passé in the face of these changing times.

Filmed in February 1947 by Golden Gate Productions, *Scared to Death* (1947) is notable for being Lugosi's only colour horror film. Sadly it has little going for it other than his presence as hypnotist Professor Leonide, with George Zucco as Dr Van Ee. With an atrocious script and sloppy direction, Lugosi and Zucco do their best but are unable to rise above film's ineptitude. Even Lugosi's Monogram efforts had more charm than this.

Lugosi's drug use had become so well known in Hollywood by this point that most producers refused to hire him. With movie obscurity staring him in the face, he returned to the stage in another revival of *Dracula* and toured in a special adaptation of Edgar Allen Poe's *The Tell-Tale Heart*. He also went on tour with *The Bela Lugosi Revue*, a Dracula-style burlesque that did reasonably well thanks to the advance publicity organised by his manager and friend Don Marlowe. Personal appearances at various cinemas screening his older movies also brought in much-needed income.

Lugosi next returned to Dracula on film, for only the second time in his career, and once again he wasn't first choice for the role: such was his inactivity at this time in his career that Universal's new management thought he was dead and opted for Ian Keith instead. It was up to Don Marlowe to sort it out. Marlowe met with the new head of Universal and shamed him into changing his mind and giving the role to Lugosi. 'He *is* Dracula,' said Marlowe. 'You owe this role to Lugosi!'

The film was *Abbott and Costello Meet Frankenstein* (1948). By this time comedy duo Abbot and Costello were experiencing a career slump. As a way of bolstering their sagging fortunes and wringing a bit more mileage from the horror cycle, Universal decided that they should team up with Dracula (Lugosi), the Wolf Man (Lon Chaney Jnr) and the Frankenstein Monster (Glenn Strange). Even the Invisible Man (voiced by an uncredited Vincent Price) makes a guest appearance. Shot in February 1948 for $792,000, the film grossed over $3 million at the box office and briefly put everyone involved back on top.

Abbott and Costello Meet Frankenstein is one of those rare comedy horror films that works. Thanks to a sharp script that combines the scares and the laughs in equal measures, and first rate acting from all concerned, it's one of the best horror spoofs ever made. It also sees Lugosi give one his finest latter day performances. He is more convincing here as Dracula than he was 18 years earlier. With nearly twenty years of film experience behind him, he is thankfully more restrained, with none of the heavily stylised and over-the-top theatrics that hampered his original interpretation. He adds dignity to the proceedings and plays it totally straight.

Lugosi enjoyed working with Abbot and Costello. So much so that when the duo starred in a television series in the '50s that used all their classic routines, the actor made a guest appearance as Dracula.

Following the success of *Abbott and Costello Meet Frankenstein*, Lugosi planned a return to Broadway with *The Devil Also Dreams*. Sadly the initial tour did not do very well and the play was closed before it reached New York. This marked the end of his legitimate stage career.

Despite making a couple of early live guest spots, Lugosi had never been happy appearing on television. In September 1949 he featured in a Milton Berle sketch for CBS Television's *Texaco Star Theatre*. He had memorised the script, but during the performance Berle began to ad lib, completely confusing the actor. More satisfactory was his only dramatic television appearance, when he played General Fortunato in *A Cask of Amontillado*, an adaptation of the Edgar Allan Poe story for the CBS anthology series *Suspense*. The episode, which was aired in October 1949, is notable for being his last quality screen role.

The '50s turned out to be a washout for Lugosi. Advancing years, poor health and that morphine habit had all but killed his Hollywood career. With no film appearances throughout 1950, he went to England the following year to play Dracula on stage for a six month tour organised by film producer Richard Gordon. It would be the last time that he portrayed the Count.

Arriving in London in April 1951, accompanied by his wife and son, the actor was in fine fettle, especially when journalists questioned him about his association with Dracula. 'Now that I have played the role of Dracula on stage and screen for almost a quarter of a century, people often ask me if I still retain my interest in the character. The answer is I do – intensely.'

He also explained how his performance had changed over the years: 'It is now played perfectly straight and has been modernised since I first took it on the American stage. You see, horror is not what is used to be. Nowadays the customers – even the children – know it all. They have seen plenty of horror films. But we believe there is still a demand for an old-fashioned spine-tingling horror play – and always will be as long as it is properly presented.'

When asked by a reporter if he ever scared his wife or son, showing good humour he replied, 'How could I? They see me in my underwear, and how can a man have any dignity in his underwear?'

Lugosi must have been happy with the initial critical response to the tour from the British press. One British newspaper stated that it was, 'melodrama in the Henry Irving tradition, magnificent, macabre and gloriously blood-curdling; not staged but invoked, and declaimed rather than acted. Hollywood could never provide realism like that.'

Sadly, though, the tour turned out to be an unqualified financial disaster. The production was more threadbare than anything produced by Hamilton Deane, and the terrible performances from the supporting cast left poor Lugosi, who at least knew the play backwards, completely on his own.

Worse still, the play proved such a failure that it left the actor and his family with no money for the return fare back to Hollywood. It proved a sad and undignified end to his long and turbulent professional association with Dracula.

Salvation of sorts came from Richard Gordon, who got Lugosi a film role to finance his trip home. *Mother Riley Meets the Vampire* (1952) was a massive step down from *The Mystery of the Marie Celeste* and *The Dark Eyes of London*, although the $5,000 flat fee must have helped considerably. The film is notable for Arthur Lucan's last appearance as the popular Irish washerwoman. But like Lugosi, he too was at the end of his tether.

Lugosi fares better than Lucan. He doesn't however play a vampire. His role of Van Housen is actually a mad scientist who creates a radar-controlled robot with the intention of world domination. Getting thwarted by an Irish washerwoman can't have been particularly dignified for Lugosi, but at least he hams it up with good humour. What else could he do?

Returning to Hollywood, Lugosi was signed up for a film that was even worse. During a television interview, he expressed a desire to do more comedy. Low-budget film producer Jack Broder took him at his word and cast him as mad Dr Zabor in *Bela Lugosi Meets a Brooklyn Gorilla* (1952). Shot in nine days at a cost of $50,000, this dismal farce is notable as the only film to star comedy duo Duke Mitchell and Sammy Petrillo, who were a blatant imitation of Dean Martin and Jerry Lewis. The 17-year-old Petrillo looked like Lewis, and he copied the comedian's goofy act so closely that a furious Lewis successfully sued. While researching Lugosi life prior to appearing in the biopic *Ed Wood*, actor Martin Landau watched the film. 'It was so bad,' he said with absolute dismay, 'it made the Ed Wood films look like *Gone with the Wind*!'

Lugosi made sporadic stage and personal appearances that included taking *The Bela Lugosi Revue* to Silver City, Las Vegas in 1953. This proved very successful and one of the few high spots in his dwindling career. Unfortunately his poor health forced him to abandon the show.

Lugosi's personal life took a bad turn at this time. In an attempt to make ends meet, Lillian got a job as a personal assistant to Irish actor Brian Donlevy on his television show *Dangerous Assignment*. Lugosi was by all accounts jealous of her blossoming friendship with Donlevy. Lillian finally left Lugosi after twenty years of marriage. She divorced him on 17 July 1953, and would eventually marry Donlevy in 1966 – they would remain together until his death in 1972.

1953 was also the year Lugosi met the man who would become his closest friend during his sad final years. It was one of the strangest relationships in existence. This man was Edward D Wood Jnr.

A former war hero and devoted Lugosi fan, Wood was trying to make his name as a filmmaker when their paths first crossed. He was a notorious transvestite with a penchant for pink angora sweaters, but his blind optimism and misguided belief in his abilities must have appealed to the veteran actor. The two men became close friends; Lugosi even went on honeymoon with Wood and his second wife.

Wood also directed Lugosi's Las Vegas show and later became the actor's manager and dialogue consultant. Lugosi always felt Wood could write effective dialogue for him. 'There were certain words that had to be changed,' said Wood. 'He couldn't form them properly.' When Lugosi did a stint on *The Red Skelton Show*, he turned to Wood and said, 'Eddie, they don't know how to write for me. You write. You write.' Lugosi's faith in Wood's literary skills seems pretty strange in view of the fact that the dialogue in an average Ed Wood film was atrocious!

Lugosi had one good reason to be grateful to Wood – work! Anything to pay the bills. 'No-one was lining up to help Lugosi,' said writer Robert Cremer, author of *Lugosi: The Man Behind the Cape*. 'He was just closed out of the marketplace altogether. The fact is Ed always felt that he was the sole individual concerned about Lugosi in his later years, and the only one who came forward and tried to help him.' 'Bela appreciated Ed as an artist,' said actor Carl Anthony. 'There was deep mutual respect.'

Wood was equally grateful for the friendship. He knew that despite the actor's poor health and financial problems, his name still had enough marquee value when it came to financing movie projects. And boy, what movies they were!

The first Lugosi/Wood collaboration was the bizarre low budget transsexual flick *Glen or Glenda* (1953). Produced by exploitation filmmaker George Weiss, it was meant to be a serious account of transsexual Christine Jorgensen, whose sex change operation shocked the world. Wood took a different approach by making it both documentary and drama. The former is the story of how Glen (played by Wood) comes to terms with his *alter ego* Glenda. The latter is that of how a man decides to have a sex change to break away from the curse of transvestitism. It's preposterous stuff; but when one considers that Wood was a war hero who had fought against the Japanese in the Pacific wearing pink women's underwear under his combats, it can be seen as an unusual piece of forward thinking for 1953.

Surprisingly enough, Lugosi initially didn't want to do the film. 'Lugosi turned the thing down flat,' said Wood. 'He didn't want anything to do with it. He knew it was about the Jorgensen thing.' However a fast $1,000 flat-rate fee for one day's filming was enough to secure the actor's participation.

Any film that features Lugosi more or less playing God must have something going for it, even if his part doesn't make a blind bit of sense – a common trait in a Wood movie. Having already played Jesus in a possible 'lost' Hungarian film, Lugosi has the rare (if somewhat dubious) distinction of having played both Father and Son on film. His participation in *Glen or*

Glenda must rank as one of the strangest moments in cinema history.

But other than Lugosi's performance, *Glen or Glenda* is a badly made, poorly acted and incoherent mess – and that's what makes it fascinating. What Wood lacked in technical ability as a director, he made up for with his self-assured belief in himself. On that basis, watching *Glen or Glenda*, for all its ineptitude, is a unique experience.

With *Glen or Glenda* behind him, the over-enthusiastic Wood had a slew of Lugosi projects up his sleeve. These included *The Phantom Ghoul* and *Dr Acula*, the latter of which was a proposed television series. As the friendship developed, Lugosi became a member Wood's oddball entourage, which also included the phony psychic Charles Jared Criswell and statuesque actress Maila Nurmi, who was better known as television horror hostess Vampira.

'I first bumped into Bela Lugosi on Hollywood Boulevard,' recalled Nurmi, 'with a beret and roller skates. He came around the corner, Las Palmas and Hollywood Boulevard, and he bumped into me.' The two of them worked together on the *Red Skelton Show* in June 1954. 'We took a curtain call together,' she added. 'He got his arms out from under his cape, and took my arm in the good old Victorian or European manner, and made me feel such a lady. He was so genteel and so elegant and so regal. He made me feel like a noblewoman, that's what. And here I was this Hollywood tramp.'

Lugosi didn't look out of place among Wood's assorted weirdoes and dope addicts. 'Bela got way far out, man,' said actor John Andrews. 'Those parts really affected him. They became part of his psyche.' Actress Mona McKinnon shared this view: 'I've been to Bela Lugosi's apartment and it was really weird. He had more strange stuff. Skulls and different voodoo things, all kind of weird stuff.'

Another person who became close friends with Lugosi during his final years was Forrest J Ackerman, editor of the magazine *Famous Monsters of Filmland*. 'Lugosi was completely different from Karloff,' he said, 'Lugosi with his huge ego and Karloff with virtually none at all. When I was in Karloff's home I was disappointed, as a collector and admirer, that he didn't have all kinds of scrapbooks and everything on display. But no, if he had any such thing he kept them hidden. Whereas Lugosi had an infinity of scrapbooks on every movie he made. He got every shot that he was in. He must have subscribed to collectors who sent him clippings from all over the world.

'During the years that I knew Lugosi, he never said anything to me that suggested he resented Dracula. His classical acting career was long in the past. I imagine there was a time when he felt he was being wasted and felt he should have been a romantic or Shakespearean figure. But I have the feeling in the end he took a great deal of pride in having added his indelible impersonation to the lore of the world. He was Count Dracula right up to

212

the end.'

Ackerman also noted that Lugosi's final years were far from happy, both professionally and health wise: 'During the last three years of his life, he was desperately trying to get a little work and to hang on to his fame. And one whole year went out of his life when he had to have an operation. He had taken drugs for many years to kill the sciatic pain that he had, but finally his doctor felt it was no longer safe to give him such quantities of painkillers and that he would have to have an operation. But though the operation killed the pain, to his dismay he found his system still required the drugs.'

The next Wood production was *Bride of the Monster* (1955), a hilariously bad science fiction thriller with a bare bones budget, atrocious acting, dreadful dialogue and a motorised rubber octopus that didn't work! Hardly a dignified film for Lugosi to star in (he was paid $500 for five days' work), but it did provide him with the last decent role of his career. As mad scientist Dr Eric Vornoff, he is out to conquer the world with a deadly ray gun that looks like a photographic enlarger! The rubber octopus had previously been used in the John Wayne film *Wake of the Red Witch* (1948); Wood stole it from Republic Studios!

'The money for *Bride of the Monster* took me almost a year to raise,' said Wood. After three days' shooting the money ran out and Wood had to promote the film by any means possible. Several weeks down the line, he obtained finance from wealthy Arizona farmer Donald McCoy, who gave him $50,000 on condition that his son Tony played the hero and that the film ended with a nuclear explosion as a warning against the use of nuclear weapons.

Like a trouper, Lugosi worked all hours in the freezing cold. According to cinematographer Ted Allan, 'Bela Lugosi was in pain during the shooting of *Bride of the Monster*. And he would relax every once in a while, but we thought maybe he was taking aspirin or something a little stronger. He would get a sort of glow, and then he would be very relaxed. A painkiller; I guess a good strong painkiller of some sort.'

Allan added, 'Wood wasn't a martinet or anything, but he was trying to produce, direct and write the whole thing, so he was kind of short with [Lugosi] on occasions in his directing, when he couldn't remember his lines. But Bela just went on his way, and did his job, and went home.'

As a reward for the actor's commitment to the film, Wood wrote a speech especially for him, which he delivered with the grand eloquence unworthy of such a bad production:

'Home. I have no home. Hunted, despised, living like an animal. The jungle is my home. For twenty years I have lived in this jungle hell. I was classed as a madman, a charlatan, outlawed in the world of science, which had previously hailed me as a genius. Now, here in this jungle hell, I have proved that I was right.'

The speech had an impact. Did it sum up the sad loneliness of the actor's life, or did it reflect the way his career had gone? Either way, it is a sadly fitting epitaph for an actor who simply had nowhere to go in a world that had no further use for him. It was a piece of dialogue he loved to recite at inappropriate moments to bemused passers-by. 'Bela and I were walking on Hollywood Boulevard,' said Wood. 'He just stopped dead. All of a sudden, with his big booming voice, he went into his speech. And he did the whole thing on the corner. A crowd gathered and applauded him at the end.'

However, the actor's recitation of his speech on Hollywood Boulevard could also have been indicative of his declining mental state. By 1955 his morphine and methadone (and formaldehyde, according to Wood regular Paul Marco) addictions were affecting his mind. His addled brain started having visions of Boris Karloff trying to kill him. Worse was to come – he became increasingly suicidal.

Shortly after completing work on *Bride of the Monster*, Lugosi committed himself to the Metropolitan State General Hospital in Newark, California to try to kick his addiction. 'I would say,' said Forrest Ackerman, 'he dared public disapproval and revealed to the newspapers that he was a drug user.'

With Lugosi unable to pay the medical bills, Wood organised a special screening of *Bride of the Monster* to raise money for the frail old man's benefit. 'It was advertised,' said Maila Nurmi, 'and they sent invitations to everyone that said all the money goes to Bela, he's sick and he needs it. Nobody came. Nobody.' But then Wood had no control over the finished film, so any profits made (which were very little) went to its backers. Lugosi eventually got placed in a ward filled with drug addicts and alcoholics. 'They shit all over me,' he said to Wood of his terrible experience.

There was however a generous benefactor in the shape of Frank Sinatra. After reading about Lugosi's drug problems in the newspapers, and mindful of his own career slump a few years earlier, Sinatra wrote a letter wishing him well and sent it with a fruit basket to the hospital. He later paid all of Lugosi's medical expenses and regularly visited him. Up until then Lugosi had never met Sinatra, who asked for nothing in return. 'That's a side of him people ought to know more about,' said Lee J Cobb, whom Sinatra also helped out after the actor suffered a serious heart attack.

There was also a pretty young blonde woman who wrote regularly to Lugosi during his recovery. 'It took him a year to get his system cleaned up,' said Forrest Ackerman, 'and during that time he became involved with a woman who was to become his fifth and final wife. She was a strange person called Hope Linniger, and she had decided, many years before, that one day she would marry Bela Lugosi.' Hope had followed Lugosi's career for many years. Having moved to Hollywood to work as a studio clerk, she began writing to the actor when he was admitted to hospital, signing her letters 'A Dash of Hope.' 'She said in her letters that it was ironic that her name was Hope and that she, in effect, gave him hope,' Ackerman added, 'and she was someone who cared about him. So when he was released he naturally wanted to meet this woman.'

Bela Lugosi and Hope Linniger married on 25 August 1955 at Manly Palmer Hall Home. Ed Wood accompanied them on honeymoon!

Although cured of his drug use, Lugosi still had a serious drink problem, so he regularly attended Alcoholics Anonymous. 'He even wanted me to go,' said Ackerman, 'and I don't drink!'

'Bela was in hospital when *Bride of the Monster* was released,' said Wood, 'but I took him to see it after he was released, at the UA theatre in LA, and he liked it. He really liked that speech.'

Lugosi briefly returned to the stage to appear in a West Coast production of the anti-drug play *Devil's Paradise*. A compilation film of his Monogram chillers was also released as *Lock Up Your Daughters* (1951), with Lugosi doing a newly-filmed introduction. Then he was back to Ed Wood for the proposed horror film *The Ghoul Goes West*. When that project failed to materialise, he shot test footage for Wood's next mooted project, *The Vampire's Tomb*. When nothing came of that, he returned to horror in February 1956 with United Artists' *The Black Sleep* (1956), working alongside Basil Rathbone, Lon Chaney Jnr and John Carradine, with Russian actor Akim Tamiroff deputising for Peter Lorre.

Directed by Reginald Le Borg, *The Black Sleep* isn't a great film, but it was miles ahead of Lugosi's recent efforts. Unfortunately the part of Casimir the mute butler doesn't stretch his talents. Chaney too fares badly in the non-speaking role of Mongo; and Carradine turn up only toward the end, as a mental patient who's convinced he's Bohemund of Antioch. Only Rathbone comes out of it with any credit, with the plum part of scientist Sir Joel Cadman. 'There is Basil playing my part,' Lugosi said. 'I used to be the big cheese. Now I'm playing the dumb part.'

Unhappy about the lack of dialogue, Lugosi asked Le Borg to give him some lines. Le Borg did eventually shoot some scenes with Lugosi speaking, but they were never used. Despite this setback, Lugosi gives an excellent mime performance, even if he hasn't much to do except look sinister.

The filming of *The Black Sleep* was a happy experience for Lugosi. 'I play the role of a mute, but even with no lines to speak, it's tiring just getting to the set each day. But everyone is kind and it's good to be working with old friends.' Considering how much he had previously disliked Rathbone and hated Chaney, age must have mellowed him. He even wrote Rathbone a letter of good fellowship, which the British actor kept with his mementos.

Forrest Ackerman joined Lugosi at the premiere of *The Black Sleep*, when it opened as part of a double bill with Hammer's *The Quatermass Xperiment*

(1955). 'He was an inveterate cigar smoker,' he recalled, 'and in that particular theatre you couldn't smoke downstairs, so I went upstairs with him, along with this devoted young fan he had. For the last three years of his life he had this young man at his every beck and call.'

Lugosi and Ackerman were then spotted by a television crew and were asked to come over. 'He was too proud to wear glasses in public,' Ackerman said, 'so he whispered, "Boys, point me in the right direction." Here was this broken, decrepit old man admitting to 72 years of age but probably older, but the world wanted him, the eye of Hollywood was upon him and the limelight was shining – so right before my eyes he changed! It was like Mr Hyde changing back to Dr Jekyll. It just seemed like he filled out and rose three or four inches taller. He was proud and strong as he strode toward the camera, and once again the magic and charisma of the great Count Dracula was pouring out for the public.'

Lugosi also joined Lon Chaney, John Carradine and co-star Tor Johnson (the massive shaven-headed Swedish wrestler who had also appeared in *Bride of the Monster*) on several promotional tours and personal appearances for *The Black Sleep*. Although these engagements had a positive effect on him, Lugosi suffered a relapse while promoting the film in Washington. Sharing a hotel room with Tor Johnson, he threatened to commit suicide. 'I'm going to jump out the window! ' he said frantically. 'I'm jumping! You can't stop me!' This happened for two nights running, and a fed up Johnson finally said, 'Go ahead and jump, just *jump*!' Get it over with!' Lugosi finally replied, 'Well, I go back to bed now.'

Made for $400,000, *The Black Sleep* took a healthy domestic gross of $1,600,000 following its opening at the Loew's Metropolitan in Brooklyn on 13 June 1956. With Hammer spearheading a gothic horror revival, its success was assured, even if it wasn't without controversy; a family threatened to sue the theatre and the film distributor for $25,000 when their son suffered a ruptured artery during the screening.

But Lugosi was now a frail old man at the end of his life. 'It was pitiful to see pictures of Lugosi in the last year of his life,' said Forest Ackerman. 'He really looked like someone who had been in a concentration camp – just skin and bones.' Maila Nurmi last saw the actor three weeks before his death, when they were promoting *Bride of the Monster* at the Pic Theatre in LA. 'He looked very ominous,' she recalled, 'like a mad scientist. I was lying in the coffin in the back [of our rented hearse] as Vampira. Anyway, we went into the theatre, and I had to guide Tor Johnson down the aisle because he couldn't see with those white contact lenses. Bela was staggering, and Tor couldn't see. People were throwing popcorn, they were so disrespectful and angry, and one woman yelled, "The blind leading the blind!" They hated Bela. He had so much bad publicity about being a drug addict, and they were vicious. Bela got out of his deathbed to make that appearance that night. He was staggering because he was dying. And this woman was saying, "The blind leading the blind!" He was such a sweet man, one of the sweetest people I've ever met.'

The Black Sleep was technically Lugosi's final completed film, a half-decent flick to bow out with. His very last film, though, is one for which he will always be remembered, and that is *Plan 9 from Outer Space* (1956), considered by many fans and critics to be the worst movie ever made.

Lugosi's few scenes in *Plan 9 from Outer Space* consist of test footage from *The Vampire's Tomb* and that heart-wrenching home movie of the elderly actor leaving his home and smelling a rose. He actually died before the film started production.

On 18 August 1956, Hope Lugosi went out shopping. When she returned to their modest Los Angeles home, she found her husband dead on the couch from a heart attack. 'I think his heart just simply stopped from old age,' said Forrest Ackerman.

There were rumours that Lugosi had died while reading a script for a new Ed Wood project called *The Final Curtain*. According to Wood's wife Kathy, 'Eddie gave him *The Final Curtain* script, which he had written for Bela, and Bela loved it. Bela was sitting in his apartment in Harold Way and was reading the script when he died. It sounds like a stage play, but that's what happened. When Hope came home, she saw the script lying on his lap.' Others, however, have said this story is untrue.

With his star dead, Wood pressed on with *Plan 9 from Outer Space*. He obtained finance from Minister J Edward Reynolds of the Baptist Church of Beverly Hills, whose members cashed in their life insurance policies and savings to raise the budget. With a cast comprised of Wood's entourage of Charles Jared Criswell, Maila Nurmi, Tor Johnson and the ultra camp John 'Bunny' Breckenridge as the Supreme ruler, the odds of the film being remotely good were minimal. Aside from those inserted scenes, Lugosi's role was doubled by Kathy Wood's chiropractor Dr Tom Mason, who was twenty years younger and a foot taller than the actor – even the cape that he wrapped around his face to disguise his features was phony!

The original Dracula cape was buried with Lugosi at the request of his son Bela Jnr and his mother Lillian Arch. (Contrary to popular belief, Lugosi never made that decision.) He was laid to rest at the Holy Cross Cemetery in South Los Angeles; Frank Sinatra quietly paid for his funeral. 'There were 101 people at the funeral,' said Forrest Ackerman. 'For some reason I just happened to count them as they passed by his coffin.' Among those people also in attendance were Caroll Borland, Peter Lorre, Vincent Price, John Carradine and filmmaker Zoltan Korda. Boris Karloff wasn't present. He was living in England at the time of Lugosi's death and only found out about it afterwards.

John Carradine read the eulogy, calling Lugosi 'a great craftsman and a considerate and kind gentleman. As for the parts we both played, he was the better vampire. He had a fine pair of eyes. Nobody will ever be able to fill his shoes. He will be missed by us all.'

'Earlier in the day,' said Ackerman, 'I looked at [Lugosi] in his coffin, and it passed my mind that if there was such a thing as survival of the personality after death, and Lugosi was there in spirit looking at himself, he would have been very pleased with his final appearance. You almost expected him to open his eyes and rise once again from the grave. And his young acolyte, knowing his attachment to cigars, told me that when no-one was around he had sneaked a last one into Lugosi's coat pocket. So he took a cigar to the grave.'

Vincent Price and Peter Lorre also viewed the coffin. Seeing Lugosi dressed in his formal evening attire, Price turned to Lorre and asked, 'Do you think we should drive a stake through his heart just in case?'

Edward D Wood, who was executor of Lugosi's will, acted as front pallbearer. 'I touched his hand,' he recalled, 'and the large ring of Count Dracula as he lay in the coffin. He was buried in full Dracula costume, full dress suit, cape and crest. I said "Goodbye, dear friend Bela."'

Hope Linniger quickly grew tired of being Mrs Lugosi. She thought she had married a movie god, but in reality he was just a flawed, elderly and now dead mortal. 'I'm afraid the world used her rather badly,' said Ackerman. 'People constantly came and took up her time asking about Bela, and she told her stories, but she never got anything out of it. Finally she got tired of it all. And here was a woman who, for maybe twenty years before she ever laid eyes on him in the flesh, had decided she was going to marry him.'

When Ackerman paid Hope a visit at her home, he was in for a shock. 'She kept scrapbooks on him and had seen his pictures many times. But a year after his death I was in her apartment and was looking at a scrapbook that she had there. It was her wedding photos, all the congratulations that famous people had sent them at the time, Lugosi's work permit, his birth and death certificates and other collectors' items. All of a sudden my eyeballs popped out of my head when she said, "Forry, would you want this? I was going to throw it away but you can have it if you want." She really seemed to be quite sincere about no longer caring. She was sick and tired of the fact that nobody regarded her as a human being but only as the wife of the late Bela Lugosi.'

After Lugosi's death, Edward D Wood Jnr's life spiralled downhill in a mess of alcoholism and financial destitution. On 10 December 1978, he died from a heart attack aged 54. He had just been evicted from his apartment with only a suitcase and a handful of belongings. Among the stuff thrown out with the garbage was a manuscript and screenplay on the life of Bela Lugosi.

In the early '60s, Bela Jnr, who became a lawyer, entered into a lengthy court wrangle regarding personality rights. He claimed that Universal Studios had exceeded the terms of his father's contract on *Dracula* by licensing his image for reproduction for toys and other merchandise that had nothing to do with the film. The Los Angeles County Superior Court initially ruled in favour of the Lugosi estate, but in 1979 the opinion was overruled on appeal to the California Supreme Court, which held that Bela Lugosi's personality rights could not be passed to his heirs as a copyright would be. The court ruled that under Californian law any rights of publicity, including the right to his image, terminated with Lugosi's death.

Tim Burton paid homage to Lugosi in his film *Ed Wood*, with Martin Landau winning an American Golden Globe and an Oscar for his portrayal. It seems rather sad considering that Lugosi himself never came close to receiving such accolades. Furthermore, Bela Jnr and Forrest J Ackerman stated that the actor never swore as much as Landau did in his portrayal. Clearly the film took some liberties regarding Lugosi's life and career.

But the legacy still remains; a statue of the actor can be seen outside Vajdahunyad Castle in Budapest. But Dracula is never far away, and the actor summed it up best when he said, 'Never has a role influenced and dominated an actor as the role of Dracula. He has, at times, infused me with prosperity and, at other times, he has drained me of everything.'

So ends the Curse of Dracula.

Bela Lugosi Filmography

A Leopard (1917), *Alarscobal* (1917), *Az Elet Kiralya* (1917), *A Nasdal* (1917), *Tavaszi Vihar* (1917), *Az Ezredes* (1917), *Casanova* (1918), *Lulu '99'* (1918), *Kuzdelem a Letert* (1918), *Sklaven Fremden Willens* (1919), *Der Fluch der Menschen* (1920), *Der Januskopf* (1920), *Der Frau im Delphin* (1920), *Caravan of Death* (1920), *Nat Pinkerton in Kampf* (1920), *Lederstrumpf* (1920), *The Devil Worshippers* (1920), *Johann Hopkins II* (1921), *Der Tanz auf dem Vulkan* (1921), *The Last of the Mohicans* (1922), *The Silent Command* (1923), *The Rejected Woman* (1924), *The Midnight Girl* (1925), *Daughters Who Pay* (1925), *How to Handle Women* (1928), *The Veiled Woman* (1928), *Prisoners* (1929), *The Thirteenth Chair* (1929), *The Last Performance* (1929), *Such Men Are Dangerous* (1929), *Wild Company* (1930), *Renegades* (1930), *Viennese Nights* (1930), *Oh, For a Man* (1930), *Dracula* (1930), *Fifty Million Frenchmen* (1931), *Women of All Nations* (1931), *The Black Camel* (1931), *Broadminded* (1931), *The Murders in the Rue Morgue* (1932), *White Zombie* (1932), *Chandu the Magician* (1932), *The Death Kiss* (1932), *The Island of Lost Souls* (1932), *The Whispering Shadow* (serial - 1933), *International House* (1933), *Night of Terror* (1933), *The Devil's in Love* (1933), *The Black Cat* (1934), *Gift of Gab* (1934), *Return of Chandu* (1934), *The Best Man Wins* (1934), *Chandu on the Magic Isle* (1934), *The Mysterious Mr Wong* (1935), *Murder by Television* (1935), *Mark of the Vampire* (1935), *The Raven* (1935), *The Mystery of the Marie Celeste* (1935), *The Invisible Ray* (1936), *The Yellow Phantom* (serial - 1936), *Postal Inspector* (1936), *SOS Coastguard* (serial - 1937), *The Dark Eyes of London* (1939), *The Phantom Creeps* (serial - 1939), *Son of Frankenstein* (1939), *Ninotchka* (1939), *The Gorilla* (1939), *The Saint's Double Trouble* (1940), *Black Friday* (1940), *You'll Find Out* (1940), *The Devil Bat* (1940), *The Invisible Ghost* (1941), *The Black Cat* (1941), *Spooks Run Wild* (1941), *The Wolf Man* (1941), *The Ghost of Frankenstein* (1942), *Black Dragons* (1942), *The Case of the Missing Bride* (1942), *Night Monster* (1942), *Bowery at Midnight* (1942), *Frankenstein Meets the Wolf Man* (1943), *The Ape Man* (1943), *Ghosts on the Loose* (1943), *Return of the Vampire* (1943), *Voodoo Man* (1944), *Return of the Ape Man* (1944), *One Body Too Many* (1944), *The Body Snatchers* (1945), *Zombies on Broadway* (1945), *Genius at Work* (1946), *Scared to Death* (1946), *Abbott and Costello Meet Frankenstein* (1948), *Mother Riley Meets the Vampire* (1952), *Bela Lugosi Meets a Brooklyn Gorilla* (1952), *Glen or Glenda* (1953), *Bride of the Monster* (1954), *The Black Sleep* (1956), *Plan 9 from Outer Space* (1956).

The Curse Of Yorga:
Robert Quarry

'They let me go down the drain.' Robert Quarry

In April 2008, Kryten Syxx wrote for the webmag *Dread Central* a disturbing article entitled *Robert 'Count Yorga' Quarry Needs a Helping Hand*. According to Syxx, 'a disgusting and manipulative fan' had befriended the veteran horror star and proceeded to take over his life through, in Syxx's words, 'manipulation and bullying.' By passing himself off as a business manager, this con artist had accessed the elderly actor's bank account and personal information, leaving the poor soul vulnerable to fear and abuse. 'We're not talking about gold digging,' said Syxx, 'but nickel and dime digging, stealing dollars and postage stamps that fans send to have their items autographed and returned.' This 'fan' had also apparently stolen memorabilia and sold it on various websites, claiming it was on Quarry's behalf. Keeping all the profits for himself, he had even committed the sickening act of charging the actor for his time. Syxx's article ended with a message to fans, asking them to write to Quarry offering good wishes and support.

The following month, *Cinefantastique* magazine launched The Robert Quarry Appreciation Week on their webpage. Steve Biodrowski's article for this, entitled *Sense of Wonder: Robert Quarry Appreciation Week*, contained a piece previously published by Mark Redfield on The Classic Horror Board, requesting financial support from fans to help with medical costs and other expenses following the actor's move to the Motion Picture Country Home retirement facility.

The response was overwhelming. With his company New Rebellion handling the finances, filmmaker and journalist Tim Sullivan happily reported in an article on the website Icons of Fright that within two weeks Quarry's 'new crypt' had been completely furnished with gifts sent by fans and friends. This outpouring of affection, respect and admiration from all over the world enabled Quarry to live in comfort and protection.

But despite the brilliant work of all concerned, the circumstances of Quarry's final months were hard for true fans to stomach. When he had left his Los Angeles home of forty years to move into the retirement home, their rules had forbidden him to bring his personal belongings with him – even though it was okay for him to buy new stuff. At least, thanks to the support of his fans, Quarry had new furniture, possessions and clothes to help him adjust to the final phase of his life.

Once tipped to eclipse Vincent Price as horror king, this versatile actor suffered an unkind fate. Although the horror magazines and webmags covered his death in great detail, it passed unnoticed by the major tabloids. And the incident with the con artist rounded off a series of events that had blighted Quarry's life, derailed his career and taken its toll on his already fragile health.

Was Robert Quarry a cursed horror star? He wasn't a drug addict, an alcoholic or financially destitute. Nor was he the perpetrator or victim of an infamous scandal. As for typecasting, that's a handicap that follows all actors; especially those associated with the horror genre. No, Quarry wasn't really cursed. He was just an extremely unlucky man.

With his formidable stage presence, well modulated speaking voice and sophisticated manner, Quarry was perfect for the genre. But just when he seemed about to achieve horror stardom, following his enigmatic performance in the title role of *Count Yorga, Vampire* (1970), his film career surprisingly faded. Having come to the horror circuit too late to make a major impression, he was in the right place at the wrong time.

Quarry's distinctive mid-Atlantic voice enabled him to adopt an English accent with ease. But he was as American as they come. He was born Robert Walter Quarry on 3 November 1925. 'I was born in Fresno (a city situated in the San Joaquin Valley of Central California),' he said, 'but pretty much raised in Santa Rosa, up in Northern California.' The first known European settlement in America, Santa Rosa had a ferry link across the San Francisco Bay to the city. 'I used to get to San Francisco a lot on the ferry boat,' he recalled, 'before the Golden Gate Bridge was built. (It opened in 1937). When I say that, people will think, "Christ, how old are you?"'

The son of Dr Paul Quarry and Mable Shoemaker (affectionately known as Mimi), Quarry had a secure upper-middle class childhood. As a child he developed a lifelong passion for cooking. 'When I was a kid, we always had help, and every maid we got – Chinese, Mexican, Italian – was a marvellous cook, and I learned cooking from all those wonderful girls.'

With an IQ of 168, he was an academically gifted student and, like many fit, good-looking California boys, excelled in most high school sports, especially swimming. At 6' 1", with striking blue eyes and jet black hair, the handsome Quarry looked set to follow his father's footsteps in the medical profession. However, fate took a different turn.

Quarry got introduced to acting via his grandmother, a frustrated actress who performed in amateur theatre. Graduating from high school in 1940, the 15-year-old won a drama scholarship to the Pasadena Playhouse, California's historic performing arts venue that was first started in 1912 as the Little Theatre Movement by actor-director Gilbert Brown. The Playhouse Theatre was built in 1924, and a theatre of performing arts was set up in 1928. It became an official college in 1937. Among those luminaries who studied there were Ernest Borgnine, Charles Bronson, Gene Hackman, Dustin Hoffman, Victor Mature and Tyrone Power.

'As a kid from California,' Quarry said of his early acting days, 'I had worked very hard with a good voice coach to learn that transatlantic accent so I could play something besides Kansas City and Brooklyn.' It was a wise move, especially after his voice had lost him a stage role. 'I auditioned for an actor named Alfred White and said "I'm Robert Qwayry." He said, "Mr Quarry, your name is spelt Q-U-A-R-R-Y. How can I hire an actor who cannot pronounce his own name?"' Years later, Quarry would get his revenge on Alfred White!

Few details are known for certain about Quarry's film debut in Alfred Hitchcock's *Shadow of a Doubt* (1943). Some sources say that the director secured the teenager's services after he had enrolled at the Pasadena Playhouse, others that it was actually prior to that. According to an excellent article by Anthony Petkovich in *Psychotronic* magazine, Quarry got into the film mainly by chance – and 'no small degree of schmoozing!'

'It was springtime in Santa Rosa, 1942,' recalled the actor himself, 'when I heard that Alfred Hitchcock and a Hollywood crew were coming to shoot a film on location there. So I got a job as a bellhop at the hotel where the cast were staying, and then proceeded to kiss ass and run around with all those movie stars.' The ploy worked, and Quarry ended up with a part in the film. Allegedly he was originally to have taken the juvenile role of Roger Newton, which was eventually played by Charlie Bates, but he ended up in an uncredited and undetermined bit part.

Shadow of a Doubt was a box office failure disowned by Hitchcock. For Quarry, however, it proved an invaluable experience. 'They were wonderful, darling people,' he said of the cast and crew. He especially liked the film's star Joseph Cotton, who took the teenager under his wing. 'Joseph Cotton and his wife Lenore were particularly wonderful to me; they asked me to stay in their home in Pacific Palisades.'

It was the summer of 1942, the film had been completed and Quarry had just graduated from the Pasadena Playhouse. Taking up the Cottons' offer to stay with them, the teenager arrived in Los Angeles, only to be in for a big surprise when he turned up at their home. 'When I walked in, I couldn't believe it – Katherine Hepburn, Ginger Rogers, Bill Tilden, David Selznick – they were all there. Nothing but famous people! So I was in the "A" group of movie stars before I knew what hit me.' Quarry's meeting with Katherine Hepburn at the Cottons' home led to a lifelong and 'most beneficial' friendship.

Quarry spent his weekends with the Cottons and their 14-year-old daughter Judy, whom he started dating. 'But in those days,' he said with typical candour, 'dating wasn't what it is now – you know, fucking and "Make sure you wear a condom." Judy was a really nice kid. They just adopted me and took me everywhere. I met every top star, producer and director ' Among the influential figures he met was Cotton's friend Orson Welles. 'He was about 28 years old at the time, a good-looking man. I had no idea who he was.'

There was another big name that Quarry met at a party hosted by the Cottons. A long time before gaining his horror title, Vincent Price was big star under contract with 20th Century Fox. Their first meeting was simply between an established Hollywood actor and a starstruck teenager; their next would be in less pleasant circumstances.

In 1943 Universal put Quarry under contract at their juvenile actors' training school on $97 a week, but he hated the experience. 'I did a lot of movies, the Donald O'Connor movies, but I was just a glorified extra.' As Quarry was an accomplished dancer, these unbilled appearances would probably have been in the chorus line; fans would need to look *very* hard through every Donald O'Connor movie to find him!

Quarry's first chance of involvement in the macabre never came to pass. He won a tiny role opposite Basil Rathbone in *Sherlock Holmes and the Spider Woman* (1944) but got replaced when he objected to having tarantulas crawling over him. The Universal contract didn't amount to much, although he spent six months of it working as an apprentice editor.

With many actors fighting in World War II, and his ability to mimic a variety of accents, Quarry landed full time radio work with the Mercury Theatre Company and Lux Radio Theatre. 'Everybody who was 18 to 26 years of age had been drafted, yet I was too young to enlist. But I was very good at doing different voices. I could do German, Japanese, Chinese, French and English.'

Quarry's radio output included recurring roles in the popular dramas *Dr Christian* and *A Date With Judy*. 'I was making a damn good living. The consistently best living I ever made, actually averaging about $750 a week. I was a valuable commodity because I was the only one with a voice range who could play different age groups and yet still wasn't quite 18.'

In 1943, Quarry got drafted into the US Army, but he never saw combat. 'I hate to say it, but I had a good time.' Following basic training he got posted to the Army Combat Engineers. 'I went to Washington, where they found out I didn't know anything about demolition, and I was transferred to Camp Lee in Virginia to start basic training all over again. But I just goldbricked my way out if that one.' With typical candour he noted, 'The people around me were dumb as shit. I know that's a terrible thing to say, but they were!' Fortunately Quarry had taken typing and shorthand in high school, and this led to a job as an office clerk.

The love of acting did not diminish. Quarry started a theatre group at Camp Lee, where he acted in and produced *The Hasty Heart*. The production received a special viewing from President Franklin D Roosevelt and his wife Eleanor.

Transferring to Special Forces, Quarry went through basic training again, but still avoided combat. 'They needed a disc jockey to play the records, so, among the many records I spun, I had to religiously play Reveille in the morning.'

Getting his discharge in 1945, Quarry moved to New York to establish himself on the Broadway stage. With the Big Apple also at the forefront of a new entertainment medium known as television, the opportunities to act in the theatre and on the small screen held great possibilities for the ambitious actor.

Whereas he had earned good money on radio, life in New York proved a bit of a struggle – he lived on cream cheese, nut sandwiches and milk shakes! To expand his talents further, he joined the Actors Studio. Founded in 1947, the Actors Studio is famous for introducing to the American theatre a radical acting new style known as 'the Method.' The basis of 'the Method' is for an actor to find reality, individuality and truth in his performance. When Lee Strasberg joined the Studio as artistic director in 1948, his name became synonymous with Method acting. Among those influenced by Strasberg were Marlon Brando, James Dean and Paul Newman.

Considering his future career in classical theatre, it is hard to imagine Quarry having been linked to this new style, since it defined the bad boy screen images of Brando and Dean. But this was a beneficial period in his life. 'I studied with Lee Strasberg and Stella Adler. Those were the days when you had real acting training. Now it's more about working out in a gym and being willing to take your clothes off!'

It was Strasberg who was responsible for teaching Quarry a valuable, if controversial, acting lesson that influenced his future career in the horror genre. 'Lee Strasberg taught me that there are no villains; which means the so-called villainous character doesn't think he's wrong at all. He truly believes he is right in all his actions. And that's how I played Yorga. My whole approach to playing horror characters and bad guys is that there's no such thing as somebody who thinks he's bad or rotten. He thinks he's right; that's why he does what he does, immorally or violently. And there's nothing wrong with him, because he's right. I don't shoot you because I'm wrong and you're right. Just like the guy who blew up everybody in Waco, Texas. He thought he was right. Jim Jones thought he was right when he killed all those people. There's nothing villainous about what he thought he was doing. I always played the villains like the heroes. The best villains are the ones who are both protagonist and antagonist.'

While in New York, Quarry took a vocational course at the famous Le Cordon Bleu Cooking School in Manhattan. The school was set up in 1942 by celebrated chef Dione Lucas, a British-born graduate from Le Cordon Bleu in Paris who became the first woman to present a cookery show on American television. Now an accomplished cook, Quarry always put his culinary skills to good use at parties. According to his old friend, journalist David Del Valle, 'Bob was a gourmet cook who loved to give dinner parties at home; or he would pack up his pots and pans and do it at your place if that was what the party called for.'

Returning to Hollywood, Quarry signed with RKO. The contract did not lead to anything, but he re-established his friendship with Katherine Hepburn, whom he taught to play tennis. Then came a lucrative offer from Louis B Mayer at MGM. He signed on the dotted line, his contract providing for stage and television work, plus acting classes and dating female starlets.

In 1948, Quarry appeared with John Carradine in the screen short *Hollywood Canteen*. He later moved in with Carradine and his wife Sonia Sorel. 'John and Sonja had a house in Greenwich Village that was very nice. He couldn't quite pay the rent. Veronica Lake rented the house from him, and Norma Connelly and I also lived there and chipped in to pay the rent.'

The following year, Quarry returned to New York to appear in the television anthology series *Starring Boris Karloff*. He enjoyed working with Karloff but became aware of the downside of typecasting, especially in the horror genre. 'He really was the kindest man you'd ever met. Boris and I were talking about careers, and Boris said, "Playing the Frankenstein Monster turned out to be a very profitable mistake, but a mistake, nonetheless." Karloff wanted to do other things, but once he played [the Monster] he was always typecast. And the same thing happened to me when I played Count Yorga.'

Quarry hung around MGM just waiting to be discovered. 'I was going to be the next Robert Montgomery, but Louis Mayer got fired and was replaced by Dore Schary, who didn't want me.' By 1948, Mayer's old-fashioned values were out of step with the changing times, so Schary was brought in to streamline the studio and produce harder-edged films. When he became studio head in 1951, many of their top contract players were dropped, along with Quarry.

But there was still his 'most beneficial friendship' with Katherine Hepburn, who had left Hollywood to establish herself on the New York stage. Forming the Katherine Hepburn Company, she personally chose Quarry for a part in her 1950 Broadway production of Shakespeare's comedy *As You Like It*. It marked the actor's official Broadway debut.

As You Like It was a big success, and Quarry continued his Shakespearean phase when director Margaret Webster chose him for the part of Lucentio in the well-received 1951 Broadway production of *The Taming of the Shrew*, and then when he had another important part in *Richard III*, opposite Maurice Evans in the title role. 1951 also marked his first known television appearance, for *The Philco-Goodyear Television Playhouse*.

Quarry maintained his Broadway profile by starring opposite Veronica Lake in *The Gramercy Ghost*. This comedy by John Cecil Holme had Lake playing Nancy Willard, a young woman who inherits from her landlady the ghost of Nathaniel Coombes, a handsome soldier killed in 1776 but doomed to an Earthbound existence for something he failed to do during the War of Independence. Cast as Coombes, Quarry made his first venture into horror-fantasy, as the spirit succeeds in turning Nancy's life upside down.

Opening on Broadway in 1951, *The Gramercy Ghost* was a huge hit that led to a successful American tour the following year. The natural chemistry between the two stars was an important factor that made the play so popular. It's little wonder that the towering 6' 1" Quarry and the tiny 4' 11" Lake briefly became an item.

Unlike Katherine Hepburn's, Veronica Lake's post-Hollywood career turned into a tragedy. Never a great performer ('You could put all the talent I had in your left eye and still not suffer from impaired vision,' she admitted), her success had been built around her looks and famous 'peekaboo' hairstyle, where her long blonde hair partly covered her right eye ('I just use my hair'). But she had provided adequate glamour throughout the '40s. Describing herself as a sex zombie rather than a sex symbol, she turned to the stage when her film career faded, but her deteriorating mental health meant she also turned to alcohol.

The couple continued their professional association in 1953 with a successful American tour of *Peter Pan*, featuring Lake as A A Milne's eponymous boy hero. Quarry, in his first stab at villainy, was well cast as Captain Hook. When their relationship ended, Lake remained in New York but was unable to build on her stage success. She did star in a television version of *The Gramercy Ghost*, but without Quarry. Disappearing into alcoholic obscurity, she was rediscovered a few years later working in a cocktail bar.

Around this time Quarry got revenge – of sorts – on the actor who had turned him down years earlier. 'I was in a play, and I was sitting next to Ethel Barrymore when Alfred White showed up. This was the time of Brando and Dean when you couldn't understand the language. Mr White came up to me and said, "Mr Quarry, I want to say it is a joy to see a young American actor who can speak good theatrical speech." So I told the story, and Ethel said, "Alfred, you were always a pompous prick! That's P-R-I-G!"'

Quarry remained in New York to play Bushy in *Hallmark Hall of Fame*'s television production of Shakespeare's *Richard II* (1954), working once more with Maurice Evans, who adapted the play for television as well as took the role of the king. Then it was a return to television anthologies with an appearance in *The Net Draws Tight*, an episode of *Schlitz Playhouse*.

That same year, Quarry appeared in the series *The Lone Ranger*, starring Clayton Moore in the title role and Jay Silverheels as loyal sidekick Tonto. 'I was signed to do three episodes at $150 a day,' he recalled. 'Anyhow, when we were shooting my very first show, Clayton Moore was busy walking around, wearing his mask, and handing out silver bullets to children who came on the set. So I figured this would be a good time to go over and pet his horse. But just as I was about to pet his horse, Moore came over to me and said, "Don't touch my horse!" And Jay Silverheels, who was maybe the funniest man I've ever met, he just got hysterical. So did I. And I got fired! For laughing at the Lone Ranger! Jay Silverheels didn't like him very much either, but unfortunately he had to travel the US with Moore, promoting the show.'

In 1955 Quarry appeared in two episodes of the CBS crime series *The Millionaire*, a show he would be involved in again twenty years later. Returning to Hollywood, he attended the Actors Lab to gain more experience. Quarry always maintained strong links to the Lab and attended classes whenever possible.

After being put under contract by Darryl F Zanuck at 20th Century Fox, Quarry appeared in the crime thriller *House of Bamboo* (1955). Starring Robert Ryan, Robert Stack, Cameron Mitchell and Brad Dexter, the film was directed by the formidable Samuel Fuller, who pretty much scared Quarry. 'Fuller was tough. He believed in using real bullets in guns. And here we are in our big heist scene, and they hired Japanese marksmen to shoot at us. A great believer in authenticity, Sam wanted real bullets. We could have been killed. And I had to run first, because I was the youngest I guess. So I'm running, getting shot at with real bullets by Japanese marksmen. But the bullets just penetrated the oil drums as I ran past. They didn't ricochet, luckily.

'I spent most of my time absolutely terrified working with Sam. And he never said "Action". Instead he shot off a revolver! Very talented man, but all his films were violent. He was a war veteran, and I think the problem with "Colonel Fuller" was that he got a little shell-shocked somewhere along the line.'

Quarry enjoyed working with Cameron Mitchell, whom he knew from his New York days. He also described Robert Stack as a 'very nice guy, [though he] couldn't act worth shit. Still can't. In one scene I realised he was terribly insecure as an actor, because he just couldn't look at anyone. He'd just drop his eyes when he did a scene with you.'

Although *House of Bamboo* was a well-received film – it became a personal favourite of famous director Jean-Luc Godard – Quarry's uncredited role of henchman Phil passed unnoticed. ('If you cough you'll miss me!'). Much the same could be said of his whole time with Fox. He was set to play dashing ladies' man Wilfred Pendleton opposite Jennifer Jones in *Good Morning Miss Dove* (1955), only to get fired. 'Jennifer Jones' character stays an old maid throughout. But she does have one segment in the film where she's young. And in that particular scene I played the young beau. The director [Henry Koster] and producer [Samuel G Engel] thought I was terrific, but Bobby Adler [associate producer] said our love scene questioned her virginity. So they hired Marshall Thompson to [replace me in a] re-shoot [of] all those scenes that I did. I mean, Marshall Thompson! He wouldn't challenge the Witch of Endor's virginity!' Despite being cut out of the movie, Quarry still appeared on some of the promotional posters, holding Jennifer Jones in his arms, because it looked romantic!

Quarry fell foul of Clark Gable on his next film, *Soldier of Fortune* (1955). This espionage drama was Gable's first film after being dropped by MGM. He plays a mercenary who joins forces with Susan Hayward to find her captive husband, played by Gene Barry. Shooting took place on location in Hong Kong, and Quarry was originally cast in Barry's role. 'I was all set to go to Hong Kong, but when we went in for wardrobe, Gable took one look at me and said "No." You see, when Gable and Susan were together on screen, it looked okay. But when I came into the scene, I looked like their kid. So it was an age thing. Gable was not a young leading man anymore.'

It took a while to sink in with Quarry what had happened. '[Gable] came over to apologise to me. At the moment, I thought, "Oh, what a nice man." But when I got halfway home, I hit the roof of my convertible so hard, I tore the canvas. That son of a bitch fired me!'

Quarry did still fly to Hong Kong to play a small, uncredited part in the film. 'It was a one-day shoot for me. At least Susan and I became good friends out of that whole fiasco.'

Quarry rounded off 1955 with an episode of the television anthology series *Studio 57*. 'Young Couples Only' is an adaptation of a Richard Matheson story, with Quarry appearing opposite Peter Lorre as the sinister Mr Grover, a custodian who lures young couples to his exclusive modern apartment, which turns out to be a spaceship!

'Zanuck put me under contract. But a year after I was there, he was fired. And that was it for me at Fox.' It was just as well, because Quarry had grown fed up with the studio system. 'I had been under contract to several film studios. They would contract you for a year, and give you fencing and horseback lessons. I felt like I was being trained for the Olympics rather than an acting gig. So I soon tired of that.'

In his book *Vincent Price: The Art of Fear*, Denis Meikle describes Quarry as, 'a low-level figure on the Hollywood circuit,' famous for, 'playing opposite the derriere of Jeanette MacDonald when the popular 1940s songstress had been required to sit alongside him while he lay in a hospital bed.' This description is unfair. Quarry may not have been sufficiently successful in Meikle's eyes, but he was a dedicated working actor who pursued his career like a holy cause.

Quarry's view of his profession was an honest one: 'If you want to last in this business you have to give a lot. You can't just take it. My motive is simple: I want to continue to earn a decent living and earn the respect of the people I work with. I'm a positive thinker. I don't panic. I don't scare myself. I've seen lots of brilliant actors go under because they panicked, got scared and ran. I'm hard to scare.'

With his good looks, muscular frame and versatility, why Quarry never became a big star is a mystery. He may not have been attracted to the trappings of stardom, but it's true to say he was unlucky in his timing. Approaching 30, he was now too old to challenge the new wave of testosterone-fuelled juveniles and too young to challenge older established hands – the situation with Clark Gable being a prime example of this problem.

Quarry's classical background also made him unfashionable with the actors influenced by Strasberg. Bad boys Marlon Brando and James Dean brought a raw and dangerous edge that represented America's rebellious teenage culture. Even within Hollywood's mainstream cinema, Quarry looked out of place among the new generation of studio-groomed pretty boys that included Tony Curtis, Rock Hudson, Jeffrey Hunter and Robert Wagner.

There do however appear to have been two occasions when Quarry made cross-over appearances with these other, opposing types of actors. *Robert Montgomery Presents* was a popular anthology series that ran between 1950 and 1957, and – although this is unconfirmed – it is believed that one episode featured Quarry and James Dean as feuding brothers. Although the Internet Movie Database makes no mention of Quarry having ever appeared in the series, it does credit Dean for an episode entitled 'Harvest'. Sadly this, like many television shows from the '50s, has been long regarded as lost, so fans may never know if Quarry and Dean did indeed act together.

Quarry did definitely, however, cross over into pretty-boy territory with his most memorable film performance to date. Based on Ira Levin's novel of the same title, *A Kiss Before Dying* (1956) was a thriller directed by Gerd Oswald and starring Robert Wagner and Jeffrey Hunter in uncharacteristic roles of serial killer and academic respectively. The plot has Wagner's ambitious student Bud Corliss getting involved with the daughter (Joanne Woodward) of a wealthy industrialist (George Macready), only to murder her when she falls pregnant (fearing the worst if she is disinherited) and making it look like suicide. He then sets his sights on the dead girl's sister (Virginia Leith), who suspects foul play and enlists the help of her brilliant criminologist boyfriend Professor Gordon Grant (Hunter) to do some amateur detective work.

Robert Quarry's contribution is an excellent cameo as Dwight Powell, a college student who stumbles on Corliss's nefarious activities, only to be found out and murdered by Corliss. Quarry comes into his own when the sweaty Powell breaks down in tears and nervously pleads for his life. Despite the limited screen time, he gives a brilliantly timed performance. 'Yeah, that was a good scene,' he later acknowledged.

Quarry became good friends with Gerd Oswald, 'because he thought I was funny,' and rated him one his favourite directors. 'He use to hire me to find ways to kill me. In those days, a lot of actors had to do their own stunts or they didn't get hired. I don't mean life-threatening stunts, but they were difficult. And every time I was going to die in one of Gerd's movies, he'd take pages out the script to see if I really did die!'

Despite a few stylish moments, *A Kiss Before Dying* is a routine potboiler that suffers from the fatal miscasting of the leads. Wagner comes off best, but while he tries hard, he doesn't convince as a serial killer. Hunter on the other hand overdoes the pipe smoking and spectacle wearing in an attempt to play a dull, intellectual type. Even Quarry is miscast. At 31 he's too old to be a college student, and would have been better suited to playing Hunter's role.

David Del Valle remembers watching *A Kiss Before Dying* on television with Quarry. 'Bob set this one up by saying, "I was younger than springtime and stupider than shit if memory serves! Joanne Woodward was and is a close personal friend from that picture, and R J [Robert Wagner's nickname] was such a pretty boy that it was hard to take him seriously in those days."' Del Valle added that, on seeing Virginia Leith's appearance in the film, 'Bob looked over at me and said, "Would you believe that girl is now remembered by the fans as *The Brain That Would Not Die* (1960)? While I am now and ever shall be *Count Yorga, Vampire*! What kind of fucking business is this?"'

After rounding off 1956 with a television appearance in the anthology series *Navy Log*, Quarry reunited with Gerd Oswald for *Crime of Passion* (1957), a film noir crime thriller with social overtones, starring Sterling Hayden, Barbara Stanwyck, Raymond Burr, Fay Wray and Stuart Whitman. His brief, but credited, appearance as Sam the reporter passed largely unnoticed.

For the remainder of the year, Quarry concentrated on television. He appeared in an episode of the medical drama series *Dr Hudson's Secret* and had three roles in the anthology series *Lux Video Theatre*. Much more interesting was the short-lived anthology series *Panic*, a well-staged effort about ordinary people in life-threatening situations. 'The Airline Hostess' feature Quarry as Father Malone, a passenger on a plane that has a bomb on board – hence the panic!

After roles in episodes of *Official Detective* and *The George Sanders Mystery Theatre*, Quarry rounded off 1957 with the first of three appearances in the crime series *Richard Diamond, Private Detective*. Another crime show followed in 1958, this time *Mike Hammer*. He followed it up with a role in *The Shirley Temple Storybook*. The latter series had the former child star introducing adaptations of classic fairytales. Quarry's appearance as Perriscale in 'The Sleeping Beauty' was his first venture into television fantasy. 1958 ended with another television spot in the Western series *Frontier Doctor*.

Between 1957 and 1958, there ran a popular series called *Mr Adams and Eve*, starring Howard Duff and Ida Lupino. According to some sources, Quarry had a recurring role in this, yet there is no mention of him in the cast on the Internet Movie Database, and the series itself seems not have been screened for a very long time. As with his appearances in Donald O'Connor films and opposite James Dean on television, it seems that fans may never know the exact extent of the actor's film and television work.

But the television work continued in 1959 with a role in the entertaining Lloyd Bridges-led show *Sea Hunt*. And after making his third and final appearance in *Richard Diamond, Private Detective*, Quarry guest-starred in another crime series, this time *The Thin Man*. Although television kept

Quarry steadily employed, his roles were hardly brilliant, and consisted of brief, one-off appearances.

The start of the new decade brought a well-received return to the theatre when Quarry starred alongside Cloris Leachman in *Design for Living* for the Los Angeles Stage Society. In between the play's eight-month run, he managed to squeeze in a television appearance in the Western series *Wichita Town*.

In 1960, the Ford Foundation funded a new drama programme that aimed to bring Shakespeare to America's schools and colleges. When *Design for Living* ended its run, the Foundation hired Quarry, and with the allotted money he spent the next two years visiting regional theatre groups, campuses and high schools across America. This tour was an artistically rewarding experience, enabling Quarry to give young actors the benefit of his stage experience. His one-man Shakespeare performances were equally well received at the Arena Theatre in Washington DC and the Alley Theatre in Houston. He was now an expert on the Bard, and his popular campus lectures were singled out in favourable reviews by the *New York Times*, the *Herald Tribune* and *Time* magazine.

In between his extensive speaking engagements around the college circuit, Quarry gave the practical benefit of his experience by acting in a variety of Shakespeare productions for several regional theatres. He also squeezed in a couple of television appearances, in *The Best of the Post* and *77 Sunset Strip*.

In 1962, with the triumphant tour over, Quarry returned to television for a series of commercials for a variety of products – including one for Joy Soap, which he recorded in Japanese! The remuneration for his work made him financially secure enough to pick and choose his roles. After purchasing an apartment in North Hollywood, he devoted his spare time to a small drama group at the Guthrie Theatre in Los Angeles. As an influential figure at the Guthrie, he was extremely proud of his work developing the talents of many young stage actors.

Quarry's one television acting appearance of 1963 was in an episode of *The Fugitive*. Unfortunately this was also the year when he suffered his first serious health problem.

Quarry was only 38 years old when he got diagnosed with cancer. This period of his life, and even the type of cancer he had, remains a mystery, since he refused to discuss his illness with anyone. By this time, his mother had permanently moved into his apartment to look after him. Because his apartment was more like a duplex, 'Mimi' had her own living quarters, allowing her son to retain some privacy while she kept an eye on him.

During his two-year period of convalescence, the actor concentrated his mind by playing the complex card game bridge. Not only did this help in his recovery by keeping him completely focused, his efforts also won him coveted Life Master status with the game's federation. A fiercely independent and positive man throughout his life, he successfully fought off the disease with typically strong determination.

Quarry returned to work in 1965 with appearances in two episodes in the popular legal series *Perry Mason*, starring Raymond Burr as the crusading lawyer. The first of these, 'The Case of the Deadly Debt', sees him playing Danny Talbert, a Los Angeles Police Detective Sergeant who is wrongly arrested for the murder of a gangster. Although it is not one of the better episodes, he turns in a good performance as the framed policeman. The second episode is 'The Case of the 12th Wildcat', which features Quarry as Coach Casey Banks, one of several suspects who may have killed the unpopular owner of a local football team.

Quarry returned to films in *Agent for H.A.R.M.* (1966), a dismal science fiction thriller directed by Gerd Oswald. Originally intended for television, the film stars Mark Richman as Adam Chance, a wimpy agent assigned to protect a scientist who has created a deadly gun used by an evil Pee-Wee Herman lookalike to shoot boogers at people! Quarry appears as villainous henchman Borg, and the eclectic cast includes alcoholic actor Wendell Corey, '60s glamour girl Barbara Bouchet and second-string villain player Martin Kosleck.

Quarry doesn't do much in the film, but at least Oswald gave him the ultimate death scene: 'I had to jump out of a plane that was taxiing down the field to take off. I limped for about seven months after we shot that scene, because I really jumped out of the plane. Gerd knew I'd do anything, because he always challenged me to do things. But in those days, Spanish boots with the high heels were the "in" thing, and I didn't realise when I jumped that my heel was gonna catch. So as I started to jump out the plane, I suddenly realised, "Jesus, here comes the tail assembly, I'm gonna be decapitated!" And I really had to throw myself out the plane.' Consequently the actor injured his leg. 'By the time I hit the pavement, however, my feet had gone numb, because of these tight-fitting boots.' Not one to allow his actor any leeway, Oswald lined Quarry up to do another dangerous take. 'Gerd wanted to shoot the scene from inside the plane, so I had to do it all over again.'

Once fully recovered from his injury, Quarry returned to the stage later in the year, playing the title role in the San Fernando Theatre production of *Butley*. He followed this up with a well-received performance as Henry II in James Goldman's *The Lion in Winter*. Of all his stage roles, it was this one that he was always most proud of.

Who's Afraid of Virginia Woolf (1966) was an enormously successful, Oscar-winning film starring Richard Burton and Elizabeth Taylor, so a stage version looked a guaranteed winner. Cast in Burton's role as weak-willed history lecturer George, Quarry scored the best reviews of his stage career, and the subsequent year-long American tour met with great success. It would remain his finest theatre triumph.

David Del Valle recalls an amusing story related to him by Quarry about Richard Burton that reflected the actor's down-to-earth personality. 'Oh my god, Richard Burton – let me tell you about Burton,' Quarry would say. 'He had the worst body odour on the planet, because he never bathed. I ought to know – I sat in his dressing room when he was on stage on Broadway in *Camelot!'*

Quarry's next film was the motor racing story *Winning* (1969). Initially a low-budget television movie, it turned into an expensive, high-profile cinema feature once Paul Newman, who had taken up racing, got involved. With Newman and his wife Joanne Woodward also on board, Quarry landed a nice supporting role as Sam Jagin, a racing driver romantically involved with Woodward's character. 'I'd been out touring in *Who's Afraid of Virginia Wolf*, playing the role of George, when I got an offer from Paul to do *Winning*. I still get residuals from it, but I was never in the movie.'

Quarry's character was removed from the film prior to release, leaving his remaining appearances in a few racing track scenes uncredited. 'My character was this English racing car driver who was really just another guy in the story whom Joanne was sleeping with. And I got cut out as a result of our big seduction scene, where I was swimming in the pool. In those days I worked out and had a good build. And Joanne had to be in a bathing suit, sitting at the pool's edge, sunning herself. Somehow or another, the way they photographed her, when she saw the footage she said, "Oh! Those thighs!" And she did have heavy thighs at the time. This was before she started taking ballet lessons to trim down. But the producers figured, "Hey, if two guys other than Paul's character are sleeping with her" – Robert Wagner's character and mine – "it makes her seem too trashy."' Wagner was the better known actor, so Quarry had to go!

Although *Winning* is effectively shot, its appeal is really limited to motor racing fans. Away from the racing, it's standard Hollywood soap opera stuff wrapped around a weak story. But despite Quarry's removal from the film, he remained close friends with Newman and Woodward. His professional association with the couple continued with *WUSA* (1970), a downbeat political drama co-starring Laurence Harvey, Anthony Perkins and Cloris Leachman. Newman plays Rhinehardt, a cynical drifter who gets a job on a right-wing radio station in New Orleans, only to find himself at odds with the neo-fascist station executives. Quarry was well cast as the slimy radio manager Noonen – and this time his part didn't end up on the cutting room floor.

Quarry's excellent performance is the best thing in the film. 'I played a right-wing DJ, the ass-kissing production head of the radio station in the film. As far as *WUSA* goes, I heard throughout 1969 that I was going to win the Academy Award for Best Supporting Sctor.' However, any chance of him receiving such an award got ruined by studio interference. 'Producer Bob Evans cut one hour of the film. Cloris Leachman got cut to three lines, and I got cut to about, on again, off again, thirty lines.'

During the making of *WUSA*, however, Quarry received an interesting offer that would change the course of his career and bring him the kind of movie fame previously denied him.

So began the curse of Yorga.

One evening, Quarry visited the home of his old friend, actor George Macready. Later, Macready's son Michael, who was a member of Quarry's theatre group, turned up with a script written by his friend Bob Kelljan. According to Quarry, 'Michael Macready came to me and told me he had $64,000 to make a movie, and that he was going to make a "nudie" – a soft-core porno film – and he wanted to make it about vampires. The film was going to be called *The Many Loves of Count Iorga*.'

Michael Macready did not have Quarry in mind for the role of principal vampire, since this was to be a porno flick and beneath the dignity of a middle-aged Shakespearean actor. However, Quarry liked the script, because he felt it would make, 'a neat little horror film.'

'I read the script, which I thought was actually quite good, and asked him why he just didn't do it as a straight horror film.' From a financial point of view, Michael had his doubts. 'He was concerned about getting his money back, as it was his own personal cash, and he knew nudies were a sure sell. Well, I also knew that horror pictures were a sure sell.'

George Macready agreed with Quarry's reasoning and, according to the actor, said, 'Okay. We'll do that if you play the lead role.' To this Quarry replied, 'Sure. Just cut out the porno shit.' If the film didn't do well as a horror, Michael could shoot additional soft-core scenes that could be inserted later. 'That's why there are so many random female characters such as the nurse and the secretary,' Quarry added. 'If the film didn't sell, they could cut to a shot of [the secretary] bopping her buns off in the outer office with a lesbian or a male client.'

Changing the film's name to the less erotic *Count Iorga, Vampire*, Michael Macready assembled his team. With Quarry on board, the producer went up-market by bringing in two other legitimate actors: television star Roger Perry, who played the nominal hero, and Michael Murphy, a veteran of several Robert Altman films. Even George Macready contributed, providing off-screen narration. In addition to producing the film, Michael Macready, a reasonably successful television actor, played a supporting role. With the possibility that the film might have to revert to being a porno if it wasn't a hit, Macready hired several porn actresses to play Iorga's vampire brides, among them the pretty and extremely buxom Marsha Jordan, America's porn queen of the '60s.

As well as writing the script, Bob Kelljan took on the directorial duties. New Jersey-born Kelljan had acted since the early '60s, making appearances in the television shows *Alfred Hitchcock Presents*, *The Twilight Zone* and *The Outer Limits*, and in the films *The Glass Cage* (1964), *Hells Angels on Wheels* (1967) and *Psych-Out* (1968). He had teamed up with Macready to co-direct for the soft-core flick *Flesh of My Flesh* (1969). Little is known about the latter film, although it probably made the money used to pay for *Count Yorga, Vampire*, as the new project would eventually be retitled.

Because of Quarry's commitments to *WUSA*, the shooting schedule was limited to evenings and weekends. 'Well, Paul [Newman] always quit at six o'clock,' explained the actor, 'and since we were shooting *Yorga* on location, and as vampires only "work" at night, we could only shoot when the sun went down, right up until it came up again. So I was shooting *Yorga* from 8.00 pm until 4.00 am.' Unfortunately, problems between Quarry and the filmmakers began early on.

'I quit the first night,' he recalled. 'They called me at 12.30 in the afternoon. We were on location in Agora (an isolated part of north Los Angeles), where it was about 100 degrees. So I got there and put on all that vampire drag. I sat there, and waited, and waited. They said, "We can't shoot you until the sun goes down." I thought, "Well, why did you call me at 12.30?" So I sat there patiently and ate some cold pizza.' Eventually Quarry got his call to the set – at 4.00 am! 'The first shot I did was one where the kids are in the station wagon and my feet walk across the grass. The director said, "Cut, that's a print. That's it for the day."' To say Quarry got angry would be an understatement. 'I stormed off! I got out into the night, and I got lost. They came by in a car and said "Do you want a ride?" I said, "No, I'm quitting this movie! I'm going home and never coming back." They said it was a mistake, so I said, "Okay, you get your act together, and I'll come back."'

The crew did exactly that, and Quarry reported for work. However, the amateurish nature of the production had further drawbacks for the actor, who found the experience, on top of getting little sleep between the two films, harder than he thought. 'We just had four crew members. That's it! They were all happy on plum wine and grass. There was one make-up man and a few guys with little arc lights. You say the film was "dark and mysterious". The film was dark and mysterious because we didn't have enough lights!' Small wonder Quarry was embarrassed by the rough cuts of the film.

However, the actor pulled enough weight to play Yorga a certain way. 'Once Bob Kelljan, who wrote and directed the picture, realised we were constrained to modern Los Angeles, he embraced the concept as did I.' Kelljan adapted the role of Yorga to suit the place and period, and allowed Quarry to develop it his own way. 'Bob certainly wrote a place for with me to go with Yorga, and I always want to credit him with that, but so many of the choices were mine. I feel that, as an actor, you have to go for it.'

Taking Lee Strasberg's advice, Quarry gave Yorga a heroic side. 'Running down the halls wildly chasing after my vampire brides, that showed the animal side of Yorga. But I also wanted him to have a human side. I wanted to show the human side of a non-human character. So I constantly insisted and got more scenes, more dialogue. Once the producer and director saw how I was playing Yorga, they let me run with it.'

Quarry also added class, style and a hint of sardonic humour that didn't teeter into camp. 'With Yorga, I had the opportunity to show his charm and his elegance. I figure if you've lived 250 years, buddy, you better have a sense of humour, or else you're not gonna make it through lunch!'

Wisely, Quarry didn't give Yorga a European accent. Michael Macready wanted him to play the character like Bela Lugosi's Dracula, with the same distinctive delivery and mannerisms, but Quarry knew better. 'I didn't want to do that, but I could get some kind of European thing going. So I learned the whole part with an accent, with a dialect, and then just took it out. I started with a voice in a register up (high), and I had to get it lower to work on the thing. Christopher Lee is still working on it!'

It was the dialogue and Quarry's delivery of it that set him apart from Lee's Dracula, because he made Yorga a three-dimensional person and a vampire in his own right, not a Dracula clone. 'I had more dialogue in the first Yorga picture than Christopher Lee had in all his *Dracula* movies combined! Poor Christopher! They would just have him up there with red contacts and whitened face, lightning and fog behind him. He had very little to do other than play the fangs and play the costume. And that is what I think is wrong with so many of the "monsters" in movies of late. They're just men with masks and knives going "boo"! There's very little for them to do as an actor.'

Quarry did have some difficulty with the film's coffin scenes. 'The hardest thing was being out in that coffin and having the lid closed down on my face. That was really tough, because I'm a little claustrophobic. Boom, down came the lid, sitting on my nose, and I thought, "God, get me out of here!"

'I was the first vampire to have upper and lower fangs. That was a big innovation in those days. My dentist gave them to me – I had a wonderful dentist who made them.' However, the impressive new fangs made it impossible for Quarry to deliver his dialogue. 'I couldn't talk with them. In that first movie there was a line, "Soon I will suck from your veins the sweet nectar of your soul. Then we shall be one. A lifetime of eternal bliss." That's a lot to get your mouth around, but with the teeth it came out like, "Thoon I will thuck from your veinth the thweet nectar of your thoul!" That got cut out! The line found its way into the second *Yorga* script, but got cut out again, for the same reason!'

To avoid costly re-dubbing, it was decided that Yorga should show the fangs only when he attacked someone. When Yorga acted human, the fangs wouldn't be present. It's a nice touch, although it doesn't explain how his ordinary teeth turn into fangs at a moment's notice. The best way to explain it was suggested in the British horror spoof *The Monster Club* (1980) when John Carradine's character asks Vincent Price's vampire about his missing fangs. The vampire replies, 'Retractable when not in use!'

With the editing completed and the film ready for distribution, Quarry attended the first test screening at the Fox Wilshire Theatre in Los Angeles. 'I was hiding in the balcony. But when the movie was over, the theatregoers were saying to each other how good this guy Quarry was, and there I was, right in the middle of the crowd! But not a soul recognised me.' Quarry did however recognise the film's amazing impact. 'It's very funny when you do something like that, it becomes your identity. And because it's a make-believe character, people don't think anybody human could possibly do it. I was never Robert Quarry, I was always Count Yorga.' It may not have been apparent at the time, but the curse of Yorga had taken root.

Thanks to a massive publicity campaign, the film grossed around $8 million the first weekend of its release. It also attracted the attention of Samuel Z Arkoff, head of American International Pictures. Michael Macready and Bob Kelljan owned the film rights but they arranged a distribution deal with Arkoff, who released it through AIP.

AIP made further cuts to the film and, on Arkoff's request, altered the character's name from Iorga to Yorga because it would be easier for paying audiences to pronounce. According to Quarry, 'Sam said, "If it's I-O-R-G-A, no-one will know what it is," and he was probably right. But for the next five years of my life, he always called me "Count Yorba." I thought. "This thing made a little money for you, at least get the name right!" They changed the name for him, but he still couldn't get it right!'

Count Yorga, Vampire grossed several million dollars worldwide – way beyond the $64,000 budget. Despite the cheap looking production and amateurish acting, the film is effective. Kelljan directs with a strong visual style and Quarry rises above the obvious sloppy workmanship with a performance of rare distinction. He gives Yorga a real heart and soul (albeit evil). With his impeccable diction and formidable stage presence, he plays Yorga with a sophisticated style and a sardonic wit.

More importantly, he effortlessly transports a 19th Century vampire to a modern day California. Yorga was a vampire for a new generation of young film fans. When Hammer tried the modern approach with *Dracula AD 1972* (1972), it botched up an interesting premise. While Yorga mingles with humans and looks completely at ease with his modern surroundings, Dracula in the Hammer film spends his limited screen time within the confines of an abandoned church, with no contact with the outside world. The fact that Christopher Lee looks well and truly bored as Dracula further emphasises the superiority of Quarry's amazing performance.

Count Yorga, Vampire may have been a commercial success but only Bob Kelljan, Michael Macready and AIP benefited financially. According to Quarry, 'Bob and Michael got their $2 million cut from the film, and they were so grateful to me that they sent me a bonus cheque. I had made only $1,249 for the whole thing. We had shot it over three or four weeks and I had charged them $5 more than minimum. Well, they sent me a cheque for $350 out of their $2 million – a cheque I was going to tear up, I was so angry about the whole thing. But then I thought, "Well, $350, I can take four people out to the best restaurant in town." So I gave a dinner party on my $350 bonus. I was going to frame it and write under it, "Their gratitude knew a lot of bounds!"'

Shortly after completing *Count Yorga, Vampire* Quarry went back to ordinary acting work with the now long forgotten television movie *A Clear and Present Danger* (1970). But the chiller worked its magic enough for the actor to instigate his next venture into vampire cinema. 'I had an idea,' he recalled. 'This was at the time of the Manson murders, so I thought, just make Charles Manson a vampire. That's logical!' Quarry then hooked up with actor friend Fred Sadoff to work on the idea. Sadoff became producer and Quarry associate producer, and with a budget of $120,000 as their disposal, Sadoff hired R L Grove to write a script.

Deathmaster (1972) has an interesting premise about a vampire named Khorda taking over a local LA hippie commune. Quarry had a definite idea on how to play Khorda. 'Charles Manson was definitely in the consciousness, so much so that I truly decided to expand upon the theme in the film ... There was no beating about the bush there. I played a vampiric Charles Manson who lived in a commune with a bunch of hippies, whom he used to bring him victims.'

Quarry's feeling about *Deathmaster* was, 'Great idea, terrible picture.' And the main fault was the script. 'I wanted to turn the Manson family into vampires. But when I got back from some location shooting for another film, I saw the script, and it was unbelievable. Apparently [Fred Sadoff] gave [R L Grove] just enough drinking money to keep him blotto the entire time he wrote the script. So when I got back I was stuck with this terrible script.'

Chosen by Quarry to direct *Deathmaster* was actor Ray Danton. After achieving brief Hollywood success in the late '50s, Danton had moved to Europe, where he got involved in film production. On his return to America in 1970, *Deathmaster* was his directorial debut. Quarry decided to use him even though he knew that he had a reputation for being difficult. 'Even though nobody could stand Ray, I liked him, thought he was a talented guy, so I hired him. Besides, I knew how to push Ray.' Quarry also appreciated

Danton's filmmaking background in Europe. 'He'd already made a couple of cheapies in Italy with Mario Bava, who was kind of king of horror films in Italy for a long time. A very strange, imaginative director! Too much symbolism for me, but it was unique stuff. Anyhow, Ray did a film or two with Bava and learned many things about directing from him. I was the only one who could handle Ray's ego, which of course meant he had absolutely no ego. Everybody thought he was the most egotistical son of a bitch that ever lived.'

Decked out in bright, elaborate Masonic robes, hippie jewellery, long black wig and a thick beard, Quarry's Khorda is different from Yorga, although he uses the same fangs. He gets to spout a great deal of guru-inspired rhetoric to his followers, which he puts over with some style. 'We really had to wing those scenes!' Quarry exclaimed. Despite his effective improvisation of his dialogue and Ray Danton's imaginative directorial touches, *Deathmaster* falls way short of the mark. Already dated on its general release in 1972, it suffers from a weak script and a dreadful supporting cast. If it wasn't for Quarry's charismatic performance, it would have nothing going for it.

Deathmaster wrapped a couple of days ahead of schedule, but prior to it going on general release, AIP threatened to sue, claiming it was ripping off *Count Yorga, Vampire*. 'Gimme a break!' exclaimed Quarry. 'I told them, "If I stole *Count Yorga* from you, then you stole *Count Yorga* from Bram Stoker's *Dracula*." But what happened was that AIP wound up scaring off the money people for *Deathmaster*, who made about $30,000 beyond what they invested in the picture. So it really cost them nothing.'

Ironically AIP bought the distribution rights and released *Deathmaster* purely as a tax loss. Quarry also lost out financially. 'Ray, Fred and I were supposed to get a share of the television sales, but we never did.' To confuse things further, the movie posters for *Count Yorga, Vampire* referred to Yorga as 'The Death Master,' implying that the two films were connected, which was never the case.

Deathmaster had been long forgotten in the cinema vaults when Fred Olen Ray's Retromedia Company acquired the rights for DVD distribution in 2002. Thanks to him, *Deathmaster* now has a belated but well deserved cult following, even if it hardly ranks as a horror classic.

By the time *Deathmaster* went on release, Quarry had signed a lucrative contract with AIP. The seven-year deal put him on good money, with the promise of starring in several horror pictures as well as regular salary increases. It was a pay-or-play contract, meaning he was guaranteed a salary whether he appeared in an AIP film or not in any given year, because the exclusivity clause prevented him from accepting other work. 'Sam Arkoff would rather have you do anything than pay you and not play you,' Quarry commented.

AIP was a two-prong organisation run by Samuel Arkoff and James H Nicholson, with Louis M 'Deke' Heyward in charge of British film production. Arkoff and Nicholson both had their own specific roles within the company. According to Quarry, 'Jim was the artistic supervisor. Sam was money and promotions – though God knows he was clever.' It was Nicholson who put Quarry under contract.

In addition to being on good money, Quarry was set to take over as their main horror star from Vincent Price, who was winding down his career. In an interview with Steve Biodrowski for *Cinefantastique*, Quarry elaborated on the arrangement: 'Vincent didn't care to work anymore at AIP. His contract was up; they were not going to re-option it. They wanted rid of him, because his salary was going up and up and up, and his last two pictures had not done that well. They didn't know where the horror thing was going, and I was being brought in.

'Vincent had an exclusive contract with AIP to do horror films; he had the same contract I had, except mine started down here in salary and his was already up there, with a much higher *per diem*. In me, they thought they had somebody new that they could build into the horror thing.'

Considering Price's popularity, Quarry admitted that achieving this would not be easy. 'I was told that I was going to be set up to take Vincent's place at AIP, but that was between [me and the studio]. And it was not that I was ever gonna be as big a star as Vincent – it would have taken seven more years of good horror films to have gotten me up to a position where I might have an established name as a horror star.' Though daunting, it might not have been an impossible task to achieve, had fate not taken a different turn.

Quarry was quickly put to work by AIP on the sequel *The Return of Count Yorga* (1971), the script of which omits to explain how Yorga, his servant Brudda – played as before by Edward Walsh – and his vampire brides get revived after their demise at the end of the first film. Quarry had his own idea about how to rationalise Yorga's glorious return from the grave: 'He simply shows up and is asked, "How did you get there?" to which he replies, "I flew!"' On viewing, the film looks less like a sequel and more like a remake, because several elements and situations are repeated from the first film. In retrospect, *The Return of Count Yorga* can be seen as an effective re-imagining of the original.

With a larger budget at his disposal this time, Michael Macready assembled a better cast. Roger Perry returned as a different hero, while George Macready was brought out of retirement for a hilarious cameo as a doddery old vampire expert. Lower down the cast list were Craig T Nelson (making his film debut) and Michael Pataki, a genre favourite who would go on to play the Yorga-inspired Caleb Croft in *Grave of the Vampire* (1974) and to make an unconvincing Dracula in *Zoltan, Hound of Dracula* (1977).

The film also boasts a strong female character, played effectively by the underrated Mariette Hartley. An accomplished stage actress, Hartley had made an excellent cinema debut in Sam Peckinpah's *Ride the High Country* (1962). She had never quite fulfilled her early promise, however, and alcoholism and mental health issues had brought about a career slump in the '60s.

Bob Kelljan returned as director as well as co-writer of the script, and his actress wife Yvonne Wilder also appears in the film.

Thanks to a polished production and the superior cast, *The Return of Count Yorga* is a vast improvement on the first film. Tightly constructed, it looks far more professional – no plum wine consumed or joints smoked by the crew this time! Quarry relishes every moment of screen time, with plenty of sardonic lines for him to savour in a script overflowing with them. The best scene comes early on, when Yorga attends a fancy dress party at an orphanage in a remote rural town not far from San Francisco. (No explanation as to how he has got there, but he has conveniently bought a large mansion nearby.) The cheap Dracula costume worn by one of the partygoers, played by Michael Pataki, is tacky compared with the attire of the nattily dressed Yorga! Listening to an orphan playing Beethoven on an off-key piano, a guest asks Yorga if he likes this kind of music. Without missing a beat, the vampire disdainfully replies, 'When played well, yes!'

Another great moment comes when Yorga sits quietly in his mansion watching *The Vampire Lovers* (1970), dubbed into Spanish, on television. It's hard to imagine Christopher Lee's Dracula doing something like this; but then it's the nature of Yorga's existence that makes the film special; Dracula doing the same thing would just look weird!

Yorga is a more complex individual this time around, and his love for Hartley's Cynthia Nelson is human – perhaps too human for someone who kills without mercy. This plot element slows things down, despite excellent acting from Quarry and especially Hartley, who convincingly plays a Christian woman torn between her faith and her attraction to Yorga. Admittedly Cynthia spends a lot of time wandering around the mansion looking confused. Why Yorga doesn't just put the bite on her and be done with it is never explained. The camp, tongue-in-cheek humour is also at odds with the romantic overtones between Yorga and Cynthia, as the vampire's dialogue, when he declares his undying (!) love for her, is a bit pompous.

The Return of Count Yorga is far more savage than the first film. A scene of the decaying female vampires rising from their graves is reminiscent of the classic dream sequence from *Plague of the Zombies* (1966), and evocatively shot by Kelljan, as are the dark, sinister settings inside Yorga's mansion. 'We shot an awful lot of that in a huge mansion house in Santa Barbara,' recalled Quarry. 'Here we are in this house all done up, and there's this incredible looking thing over there.' He was referring the Edward Walsh's shabbily-dressed servant Brudda. 'I kept telling the director, "Can't I take him to Sears for a new suit? We'll all chip in and dress him up a bit!"'

The film's scenes set at the dockside are very effective, and the brilliantly staged massacre of Cynthia's family by Yorga's female minions uncomfortably echoes George Romero's *Night of the Living Dead* (1968) and the Charles Manson murders. Quarry was quick to make comparisons with Romero's work: 'That whole situation was very much on our minds when we made Yorga.' The film's twist ending is genuinely jolting.

The animalistic side of Yorga is retained, and Quarry remains as frightening as ever. The supporting cast are good value, with comedian Rudy DeLuca in fine form as an out-of-his depth police detective. He too gets a few good lines, which he probably improvised. ('Nobody plays hero; the first one to find the vampire screams his ass off!') The best performance comes from Yvonne Wilder as Jennifer, a deaf-mute maid who witnesses the massacre but is unable to convince the police of what has happened, since Yorga has ensnared Cynthia's younger brother as his servant so that the evidence can be cleared away. The character's eventual suicide is a tragic moment in horror film history.

Once again the fangs proved a problem when Quarry tried to speak, especially when Yorga came to declare his love for Cynthia. 'One of the problems of the Yorga pictures,' said the actor, 'was that any time I had to speak my lines with the fangs in my mouth, it was impossible! They gave me a lisp that made me sound like Daffy Duck. Every line had to be dubbed in later, but getting it in the can was a living hell, especially with Mariette Hartley, who simply could not stop laughing at me! I don't blame her!'

Quarry enjoyed working with his co-star. 'Mariette Hartley and I had a lot of fun. We're both great gigglers.' However, Hartley wasn't happy doing the film. 'Mariette talks about *The Return of Count Yorga* like it's the great "shame" of her life. At the time, however, she couldn't get a job. She was an alcoholic and her career had taken a really bad fall. When she did *The Return of Count Yorga*, of course she was sober, but still, she had to rebuild her career. I think she was only about 26 at the time, and it was the first movie she'd done in quite a while. But she went from *Return* to doing commercials with James Garner for Kodak. Made a ton out of that.'

But despite thumbing her nose at the film, Hartley was apparently fond of Quarry. 'In her [autobiography, *Breaking the Silence*], she never mentioned me or *The Return of Count Yorga*, although she did call me her "dear friend" when we worked together.'

Unfortunately Quarry found working with Michael Macready a less pleasant experience. 'Michael Macready got all "bent out of shape" over *Deathmaster*. He said I was ripping off *Yorga*, and actually sued me, for God's sake! He said I ripped off the Brudda character by having this brutish character as the Deathmaster's sidekick. Since [Bela] Lugosi's Dracula set the pattern, certain themes are always repeated over and over again. Every vampire needs a guy to lock him in the coffin! Anyway, Macready was so out of shape, he never forgave me. AIP did the second Yorga picture, but Michael was so horrible to me I vowed never to work with him again.'

Because Quarry was under contract with AIP, he was more actively involved in the promotion of *The Return of Count Yorga*. This meant radio and television interviews across America and personal appearances wherever the film was being screened. But it was hard work. 'I'd get up at 5.00 am to promote that sequel at the strangest stations in the Midwest, and in between the hog reports they'd interview me!'

Meeting fans turned out to be a creepy experience, despite the PR men assuring Quarry that horror films weren't supposed to have a bad influenced on people. 'Some really sick fans would show up at my guest appearances,' he recalled. 'But in some ways, it's really like porno, and you're really just jerking off at both. But the strange thing, which I never understood, was that Count Yorga was sexual, for some reason or another. I never saw him that way. He was sensual I suppose. There's that oral thing about vampires.'

Sexual or sensual, Yorga certainly had an effect on female fans, as Quarry soon found out. 'When I went on tour, girls and women would crowd in on me to get my autograph, get right up against me, and just pee right down the front of my clothes! They'd be so beside themselves that they'd actually wet themselves. I never understood it.

'I'll never forget this one theatre in St Louis. The place was packed, and I was supposed to sign at the concession stand. So they had this little roped off area where I was supposed to sign. I came down the side aisle to walk out there, and suddenly this flock of fans just runs out of the theatre and jams me up against the wall. I shout "Security!" because they were coming close to breaking my ribs.

'I sort of halfway turned my back, and I felt a kind of pressure. And then the whole back of me was wet. As it turned out, some guy masturbated behind me and shamelessly came on my clothes. A fairly nice looking guy, I'd say about 19 or 20 years old, but he just came all over the back of me. Of course he ran as fast as he could. But at least he could say he got his rocks off on Count Yorga! And I'm standing there saying, "Will somebody please get a towel and clean this guck off my back? ", because everyone was pushing. They were really out of control.'

Worse still was a situation that arose while Quarry was promoting the film in Chicago, doing three shows a day around the various cinemas. After finishing the morning show, he returned to his dressing room to rest. On his way to the afternoon show, he encountered a fan. 'Here was this kid whose skin was pale white, whose hair was jet black, and he was in a black sort of silky, satin shirt. And this kid says, "Can I have your autograph, Mr

Quarry?" "Oh, sure kid," I tell him, and sign his autograph book. So I come out after the afternoon show and the kid is there again, asking me to autograph some more pictures. So I did.

'Third show, I come out, he's there again. "Can my girlfriend take a picture of you and me together?" So I said, "Oh, sure kid." Believe me, I was better looking than his girlfriend! She was one of those unfortunate fat girls with a lot of hair on her face, and pimples. And here was this little skinny guy. So I put my arm on his shoulder and she said, "Smile.' So I turned to him with a smile and he turned to me and smiled, and do you know that he had filed every one of his teeth down in fangs? All of them! My jaw just dropped! And I thought, "Two years from now, this kid's going to be the vampire killer of Chicago and they're going to find the picture of me with my arm around him." So in total disgust I just told him, "Get outta here!", and he didn't come back after that.'

Even back home, he attracted unwanted attention: 'I've been getting very funny mail, and I've had my number taken out of the phone book as I've been getting obscene phone calls. I mean, strange things really happen. I always figured that if people made obscene phones calls, it would be at a decent time, say 2.30 in the afternoon, but they always call at 8.00 am or midnight, or just as you're sitting down to dinner. And who wants to listen to "Oh, Count Yorga" and then the sound of heavy breathing over the phone. I'll say, "Listen, call me at 1.00 pm tomorrow when I haven't got anything to do and when there's nothing on TV. I'll get a drink and we'll lap it up a little."'

The Return of Count Yorga did not repeat the first film's success. But it made enough money for AIP to consider a third film, and it was Quarry who instigated it. 'My idea for the third film was for him to return a complete mess. Someone inherits the house, does a Masonesque blood ritual, which spills on Yorga's ashes, and he returns. He's completely broke and broken. Everything he had is gone, he's completely scarred. So he turns to the streets. Lives in the sewers, where he becomes king of the homeless, the addicts. Turns them all into vampires, and has one final bloody laugh on LA.'

Unfortunately Michael Macready was still mad as hell at Quarry about *Deathmaster* and refused to give the go-ahead for the new film, insisting on directing any further sequels himself instead of Bob Kelljan. 'He wouldn't let anyone else direct a Yorga picture, ' said Quarry, 'so there you go.' With both men refusing to work together, Count Yorga remained permanently in his coffin.

But despite the series ending on a bitter note, Quarry would always be Count Yorga to his fans. It was a role he was most proud of. 'I enjoyed playing Yorga,' he reflected. 'The fun of making movies is the fun of getting outside yourself.'

246

With a new star to promote, AIP next lined Quarry up to play wealthy industrialist Jason Crockett in *Frogs* (1972), an effective ecological horror in which local swamp animals, telepathically guided by intelligent frogs, wipe out a family attending a birthday party at an isolated plantation. But at 46 the actor was a bit young to play a tyrannical, wheelchair-bound millionaire grandfather, so he got replaced by the older Ray Milland, whose stalwart presence had enlivened several routine chillers in the '60s.

Count Yorga resurfaced in another proposed sequel that was actually a sequel to another AIP chiller. But with Macready on the warpath, the script was hastily rewritten and the character's name changed. This new production took Quarry to England, where he was to team up with the man he was being groomed to take over from. It also led to an acrimonious relationship that became Hollywood horror folklore.

The Abominable Dr Phibes (1971) had been a return to form for Vincent Price following a trio of indifferent British chillers that had heightened his disillusionment with the genre. And he had almost passed on the role, after a falling out with Sam Arkoff over the lack of good scripts. Once the pair had patched things up, Price had been given a witty script written by James Whiton and William Goldstein originally called *The Curse of Dr Phibes*. Playing a long dead doctor of music and theology who uses the ten biblical plagues to eliminate the physicians who failed to save his beloved wife, Price is in his element with an excellent performance. The fact that he acts in mime makes this all the more remarkable: for once he does not use his famous voice; when the character does speak, it is through a microphone.

The film is directed by Robert Fuest, a talented painter and set designer, who effectively combines humour with horror. The lavish art deco-style sets give the film an expensive look that belies the modest £300,000 budget, making *The Abominable Dr Phibes* one of most visually striking horror films to come out of Britain for some time.

When the film took more than $3 million at the box office, a sequel was inevitable. The original James Whitton and William Goldstein script for this proved unworkable, so Robert Blees wrote a new one, which then underwent extensive rewrites by Fuest. Price returned as Phibes, but this time the story has the doctor travelling to Egypt to seek out the River of Life, in order to revive his wife. On the same journey is Darius Biederbeck – Quarry's character – a 150-year-old archaeologist, whose elixir of youth has run dry and who needs to find the River first, before he starts aging. So begins *Dr Phibes Rises Again* (1972).

'Well, that was really the only expensive film I ever did,' said Quarry. 'It was also the best film I ever did. Simple as that.'

The casting was down to Louis M Heyward, who was instrumental in bringing back his favourite actors Hugh Griffith and Terry-Thomas (replacing first choice Frankie Howerd) from the first film (albeit in different roles). However he was none too happy about using Quarry. 'In my opinion,' he said, 'Robert was the weakest thing in the film. He didn't integrate, and he didn't have the fun that such a picture demands.'

The working relationship between Quarry and Price started happily enough. However, as David Del Valle explained, 'Bob and Vincent Price had so many things in common, and yet they never connected.' This is rather surprising, as both men were intelligent and cultured individuals, veterans of classical theatre, and brilliant gourmet chiefs. 'They never traded recipes!' exclaimed Del Valle.

Quarry's early memories of Price were extremely positive. 'I can't describe what it is like to work with Vincent. I mean, Phibes is a silly role. How do you know how good an actor you worked with? God knows you couldn't tell anything from the silent facial expressions. The hardest acting I ever did in my life were those scenes – keeping a straight face and playing it with anger while Vincent was mugging.

'Working with Vincent was hysterical, because as Dr Phibes he couldn't talk. So when we had our dialogue together, I would talk to him and someone would then read his lines from off stage and Vincent would tilt his head and start talking with his mouth shut, and it sounded like he had a mouth full of fudge. Trying to keep a straight face and work with him was hard, because my lines were very serious.'

Price's mischievous behaviour caused Quarry to blow his takes. 'He had to learn the scenes so that his expression matched the dialogue. That isn't easy to do, either; it looks easy, but trust me, it is not. He said, "Just wait until you do this scene. Joe Cotton [who starred in the first film] couldn't stand it." [I blow the first take, and] Vincent is enjoying every minute of it, because he knows what he's doing to me.' To overcome the problem, Quarry adopted a new approach. 'I thought I'd just relate it to somebody I really hate, in real life, and just look at his ear.' The plan worked, and Price told him later, 'You did a better job than Joe Cotton did.'

Quarry was in awe of Price as an actor and a person. 'He's a funny man; he's also a hard worker. People think it isn't tough to act in horror films. It's the toughest acting in the world. That's why I have nothing but admiration for all those years Vincent played those horror films. They're all peak emotion; they're all phony. And you have to create a characterisation out of something that doesn't exist. There's a great difference between that and being able to play scenes with real situations where emotion come honestly.'

Quarry did feel that Price 'over egged the pudding' when it came to playing villains. 'Vincent was always playing the boogeyman thing, overdoing stuff, and I was like, "Vincent, for once just play it straight." I mean, I played Count Yorga straight, I played Biederbeck straight, I played Deathmaster straight. But Vincent's mannerisms took him over. As an actor you should never allow that to happen.'

Unfortunately, as filming progressed, Quarry found that, 'the atmosphere was decidedly Macbethian,' due to an unfortunate incident that happened one evening. 'We were put at odds by the bastard Sam Arkoff and his slimy errand boy "'Deke" Heyward.'

A week into production, Heyward threw a big cocktail reception. According to Quarry, 'An English publicist came up to Vincent and asked, "How do you feel about Mr Quarry coming in as your replacement at AIP?" He wasn't happy at all about it. He was hurt. It was as if I was a "threat" to Vincent's career – to this man with this long, distinguished career that nobody could replace. It was the wrong thing for that man to say. That man should have been fired.'

Quarry naturally wanted to smooth things over. 'I went to [Heyward] and told him what had happened. Well, it was too late. The damage was done. The publicist made it sound as if I was out to dethrone the king. That made a rift between us. I never saw Vincent socially after that. Not ever.'

Quarry was further incensed when Heyward went behind his back by telling his London friends about the situation. Not only did this break the confidentiality agreement Quarry had with AIP, it destroyed any good will he had with Heyward.

But the damage had been done and relations between the actors permanently soured. 'Vincent was never the same. That made a rift between us. As far as our working together, it was extremely pleasant. Our sense of humour was the one bond that made working with him a pleasure. We had an awful lot of laughs on the movie.' Away from work, though, things were different. 'Vincent tried to pretend we were friendly, but he wasn't really that nice ever again. And he was very funny, you know, like when the press came over to interview me in London; he'd try to take over. And when the press came over to see Vincent, I wasn't allowed to even come near him.'

Robert Fuest recalled an infamous incident that summed up the resentment between the two actors: 'In make-up, Robert Quarry used to sing Gershwin, and Vincent Price looked around the corner, and Quarry said, "Didn't know I was singer, did you Vincent?", and Vincent said, "Well I knew you weren't a fucking actor!"'

Given that Price was a man known for his warm, generous nature and fun loving-affability, his resentment toward Quarry was surprisingly out of character. He was a serious and sensitive individual behind his casual exterior, and Peter Cushing once described him as a man 'who cares more about his work than he allows his public to know.' In the early '70s, though, with his $90,000-a-year endorsement contract with Sears Roebuck coming to an acrimonious end and his marriage to costume designer Mary Grant going through a rough patch, Price was a deeply unhappy, insecure and vulnerable individual. Already tiring of horror films, he was now re-evaluating his position with AIP, having had an unhappy experience making *Cry of the Banshee* (1970) and been obliged to turn down a role in *The House That Dripped Blood* (1970) because his contract prevented him from doing horror films elsewhere. Not surprisingly, his relationship with Sam Arkoff had deteriorated. 'There was some kind of bad blood between him and Sam,' observed director Gordon Hessler, who worked with Price on three films. 'I think Vincent resented the fact that he was taking Sam's money for doing things he disliked. Sam tried to make believe that he was a friend of Vincent's, but Vincent didn't reciprocate. I think sending Vincent to England was probably the line of least resistance for Sam.'

Price could pull a certain amount of weight at the studio, but the arrival of Quarry undermined his position further. Having a younger man assuming his role as king of horror, even if it was a title he resented, had a negative effect on his mindset.

Ironically, Quarry cultivated happier friendships with Price's British horror contemporaries Christopher Lee and Peter Cushing. 'While I was at AIP, Christopher was much nicer to me than God knows Vincent was. Chris and I were supposed to do a film together, but nothing ever came of it. And yet, he and his lovely wife Gitte would take me out to see all the gardens in England, and they had me over to dinner a couple of times, always very nice to me. Chris might come across as pompous, but he's really a very decent man.'

Quarry may not have had the chance to appear on screen with Lee, but he did work with Cushing, a man he once described as 'a saint.' They first met on the set of *Dr Phibes Rises Again*, where Cushing had a guest appearance as a ship's captain. 'Loved working with Peter Cushing!' he exclaimed fondly. 'He was the greatest. When I first met Peter he was just getting over the death of his wife. Actually, he never did get over her passing; he was just waiting to die and go to heaven.'

Quarry also enjoyed working with Robert Fuest, but felt he over-emphasised the film's comic elements. 'He never went berserk. He had a lot of that hyper energy that Quentin Tarantino has. A lot of great kinky grey hair that was all over the place, just mad as a hatter! But he knew how to put a movie together. Bob didn't know how to control Vincent, though, so he let the farce thing in the *Phibes* sequel go a bit too far. I think the first one was better, actually. There was just too much of the "big joke" in *Rises Again*.'

Filming had its drawbacks, as Quarry told interviewer Anthony Petkovich for *Psychotronic Magazine*: 'The soundstages were freezing cold, and the boots [I had to wear], since they were old-fashioned and up to the ankles, proved very difficult for me to get out of in between takes.' The discomfort was particularly acute when he was filming the scenes where his character had to rescue supporting actress Fiona Lewis's from drowning. 'I was always wet too, because I kept going down to help Fiona, [whose character] Phibes had tied up and was trying to drown in a sort of *The Perils of Pauline* fashion. So when it was time for my character to jump into the canal at the end of the movie and swim helplessly after Phibes, I'm sitting there sopping wet and freezing to death.

'Anyhow, Fuest said, "Well, we don't want you to hurt yourself, so all you have to do, instead of jumping over the edge of the canal and swimming after Phibes, is kind of go over the edge, and we'll put a platform down there, and then you can go into the water later. We'll just cut it that way." And I said, "Oh fer christsakes, I can swim, I'm not gonna drown! Get that junk outta there!" So I went jumpin' off the edge. It was no big deal. So I start to swim, and Fuest says, "Fer christsakes, it's Johnny Weissmuller." And I say, "Hey, you're talking to a California boy. I grew up in the water."'

Toward the end of the film, Phibes beats Biederbeck to the River of Life, leaving the archaeologist to age rapidly. According to Quarry, 'The make-up process was broken down into various stages of ageing. So, for each of the various stages, I'd swim back and they'd put this make-up on me, and then I'd have to get back to the same position deep in the water for the camera. But in between the make-up changes, it was like half an hour, and I'm still soaking wet, because there was simply no time to change. It was hard fucking work. Any work where you have to deal with fire, water, floods, things blowing up, is hard fucking work. But being wet is the worst, because you don't get dry. For one week I was sopping wet from the moment we started to do that scene. I could take the shirt off but not the pants or boots.'

Responsible for Quarry's make-up in the scenes where Biederbeck ages was Trevor Crole-Rees, who would leave the film business shortly after this to run a pub. Crole-Rees wrote to Price soon after the actor's return to Los Angeles after completing his work on the film, stating: 'Quarry took the old age make-up very well and it stopped him from talking for a while – however he was very pleased with the rough cut he saw, and I think he learnt a lot from the film.'

Although it lacks the charm of the first film, *Dr Phibes Rises Again* is enjoyable. Fuest directs with the same visual style as before, and many of the set-pieces are well done. It's more comical than the original, but this does not detract from its effectiveness. Price is in fine form as Phibes, giving his customary high camp performance despite the discomfort caused by his make-up and the preoccupation with his personal and professional problems.

As Biederbeck, Quarry gives his best film performance. The character is essentially an evil one, but the actor plays him with more sympathy than the script suggests, making him more of a centrepiece than Phibes. His serious performance does go against the film's tongue-in-cheek nature, but then his approach to Biederbeck, as with Yorga, was to play it straight. In doing so he nearly acts Price off the screen.

Dr Phibes Rises Again was not as successful as the original but it made enough money to warrant a third film. Several ideas were in the pipeline. *The Bride of Dr Phibes* had originally been mooted as the first sequel (with Quarry as Count Yorga), but Louis Heyward had dropped the idea (although he kept the Egyptian scenario). Another idea proposed for the third film would have had Phibes up against Adolf Hitler and the Nazis, with Quarry returning, possibly as Biederbeck. Fuest had been approached to direct, so it looked certain a new film would go into production.

'There was talk,' observed actress Caroline Munro, who had played dead as Phibes' wife Victoria in the first two films, 'and the talk that I'd heard, that seemed quite fascinating to me, was that [Victoria] would actually come back, and she'd be far worse than [Phibes] was.' The idea sounded promising, but all was not well at AIP, with Quarry finding out the downside of being tied to a long-term contract.

The Arkoff/Nicholson partnership was never perfect, but as the years went on, things got worse between them. 'It was not a happy marriage,' said Robert Fuest, observing the tension between the two men during the making of *Dr Phibes Rises Again*. In 1964, Nicholson, then president of AIP, had been having an affair with a young actress named Susan Hart (whom he would subsequently marry). When his wife filed for divorce, she ended up with a 50% share in AIP, leaving Arkoff in sole charge of the company. With his position at the company constantly undermined by Arkoff's belligerent attitude, Nicholson wanted out.

Fuest also felt, 'AIP was a very fragile empire.' With British film production in sharp decline at the time, Arkoff decided to cut considerable overheads by moving AIP's London base from its elegant office suite in Upper Grosvenor Street to the more economical Berkeley Square. And with film budgets facing further cuts, he focused on getting *Dr Phibes Rises Again* ready for distribution.

Once the production wrapped, tempers frayed between Arkoff and Nicholson over the final cut. Scenes with Terry-Thomas and Beryl Reid were chopped for being too light-hearted. It proved to be the last straw for Nicholson, who resigned his position in January 1972 to become an independent producer. Sadly his only subsequent film was *The Legend of Hell House* (1973); he died from brain cancer before it was released.

Robert Quarry's own career looked unsteady. 'Once Nicholson and his business manager Paul Zimmerman left,' he said, 'I was just a piece of meat on a rack to be used. I was under contract, but it was the beginning of the end of AIP, though it lingered on, doing one ghastly film after another. Sam Arkoff had little enthusiasm for me. Sam always dismissed me and Yorga.'

With Nicholson gone, Arkoff didn't know what to do with Quarry. As the businessman of the company, he wasn't interested in producing traditional gothic horrors. 'They didn't develop me as a property at AIP,' recalled Quarry. 'They just let me go down the drain. Well, Sam didn't know what to do. He knew how to buy movies, but that's about it. [Nicholson] was my back up. If he had stayed at AIP, I would have been all right, but I had no protection against Arkoff, who was a gross pig. A gross pig! Unfortunately there really isn't anything good I can say about that man. He was even terrible to Vincent. But Vincent knew how to screw him up one side and down the other. Vincent used to lie about his *per diem* in London just to steal money from Sam. Trust me, Sam was not the nicest man in the world. Rude, vulgar, crude, and he did absolutely nothing.'

Surprisingly, Louis M Heyward, who had his own problems with Arkoff, was sympathetic to the actor's position. 'He was a delight to work with,' he said. 'I felt he was misunderstood. He was given short shrift at AIP. He had a decent role in *Phibes*, but his career was being mangled.'

Quarry concurred with Heyward. 'They never developed any properties for me to do. I just went from one piece of junk to another. And I couldn't do horror things for anybody else, which was unfortunate.'

Quarry could have taken some comfort by appearing in the proposed second sequel, which had the working titles *Dr Phibes and the Holy Land* and *Phibes Resurrectus*. 'It's a marvellous script,' said Price. 'A very funny script. I wanted Bob Fuest to direct it. He's the only person in the world who is man enough to direct the *Dr Phibes* films. He's a genuine, registered nut! He even looks like a madman. He's all over the place, like an unmade bed. What an imagination he has! They were all his ideas.'

However, Fuest turned the assignment down, and the film was dropped. He also turned down *Theatre of Blood* (1973) and *Madhouse* (1974) because he didn't want to be too closely associated with Price, who starred in both, and he turned down *The Legend of Hell House* to avoid being pigeonholed as a horror director. 'They're all frightened that they're going to get stuck in the horror genre,' said Price regarding Fuest's decision.

Instead Fuest directed his pet project, *The Final Program* (1974), but it wasn't very successful and his cinema career quickly faded after that. 'Bob has never done anything as good as *Dr Phibes*,' said Price. Quarry concurred, with some regret: 'I never understood Bob Fuest's career just going downhill like that. He's a brilliant, wonderfully eccentric man. Bob was under contract with AIP and did a couple of things after *Phibes*. A very good director, very imaginative, very crazy. Likeable crazy though.'

Eight months after Nicholson's resignation, Louis Heyward also quit after one too many disagreements with Arkoff. 'Things fell apart after Jim left,' he said. 'I told Sam, "I don't want to do any more horror films; I don't want to do any more sex movies."' In the end, with his options severely limited, he had no choice but to resign.

It was Quarry who had the last word, when he accurately summed up the turmoil within AIP: 'It was like everybody pulled the plug and the ark sank – or the Arkoff sank!'

The actor added: 'Its too bad they didn't make another *Dr Phibes* film. Go ahead and blame it on Sam, because he hooked up with a producer who wanted to make blacksploitation horror films.' Heyward's departure effectively ended the *Dr Phibes* series. 'When I left AIP, Jim was already gone,' said Heyward. 'You couldn't do those pictures in the States. Plus, they lost the production team they had. Bob Fuest knew design, and I'd say [production designer] Brian Eastwell was very important. You need people like Bob and Brian, who have lovely pictures in their head and understand the beauty of what they construct. And you need someone like myself, who controls the dollars with compassion, with not a bread knife but a scalpel, to say, "Hey, it's great, but for the dollars we have to do this; without emasculating, let's take it here, and save."'

Talk about resurrecting *Dr Phibes* went on in one form or another for the next twenty years. This included the idea of bringing the character back in a television series. However, Price would never consider returning unless Fuest was involved. And as far as AIP was concerned, the franchise, and gothic horror in general, had become passé. 'That was the end of the horror cycle,' said Quarry. 'After that came blacksploitation pictures.'

Blacksploitation may have been the order of the day in Hollywood, but Heyward's departure left the UK production arm of AIP in a mess. Between 1972 and 1973 there were no films in the pipeline for Quarry and Price to get their teeth into. Arkoff agreed to loan Price out to United Artists, to play demented Shakespearean actor Edward Lionheart in *Theatre of Blood*. If the actor was reluctant to do yet another horror film, he soon changed his mind. As it turned out, *Theatre of Blood* was a life-enhancing experience that gave Price the performance of his career.

In the meantime, Quarry had to make do with television guest appearances in *Kojak*, *Cannon* and *Ironside*, the latter providing some good memories: 'What I really remember most about that programme was working with Myrna Loy. Darling, darling lady! Boy, was she a smart cookie. On the one episode I did with her, I played her scumbag nephew, but we had a lot of sophisticated dialogue between us, which she loved because it let her play an acid-tongued yet adorable character, which she's perfect at.'

Unfortunately Quarry's AIP contract also prevented him from doing horror stuff for television. 'I was given some scripts from a wonderful television series back in 1974 called *Kolchak, The Night Stalker*. I was going to have a running role as a vampire in the series, and Darren McGavin as Kolchak, the misunderstood reporter in Chicago, would be chasing me, this vampire, all over town. But AIP wouldn't let me do that, and I couldn't do horror films for anyone else.'

It was back to England in the late spring of 1973 for *The Revenge of Dr Death*. Based on Angus Hall's novel *Devilday*, this had been on AIP's production schedules since 1969. With a script provided by Murray Smith, production had been due to start in 1971. But with Nicholson quitting, things got delayed 18 months before the project finally got the green light. There was minimal AIP involvement after that. Unable to mount a UK production without extensive costs, Arkoff entered into a co-production deal with American-born British horror specialists Milton Subotsky and Max J Rosenberg of Amicus Productions. The film's original title got changed to *Madhouse*, with former editor Jim Clark replacing Robert Fuest as director.

By the time *Madhouse* went into production, Quarry wanted out of his contract. He wasn't enthusiastic about the film either. 'They had a very good script, which Sam Arkoff, with his usual back-handed "brilliance", fucked over.' Quarry was even deprived of the role he was originally slated to play.

Madhouse stars Vincent Price as Paul Toombes, a washed up horror star who, after spending several years in an asylum following his wife's murder, reluctantly makes a television comeback with his famous Dr Death character. Quarry was set to plays Toombes' best friend Herbert Flay, only to be replaced by Peter Cushing, leaving Quarry with the thankless role of producer Oliver Quayle. 'Originally I was to play the Peter Cushing role,' he bemoaned, 'but age-wise that didn't work out, so they manufactured a part for me.'

The year between *Dr Phibes Rises Again* and *Madhouse* had been a tumultuous one for Price. In addition to the positive professional experience on *Theatre of Blood*, his personal life had changed when he began an affair with one of that film's other actors, Coral Browne. *Theatre of Blood* had strengthened his desire to quit horror films and return to the theatre, so it is somewhat surprising that he agreed to appear in *Madhouse*. In all probability, the reason he accepted the role had lot to do with getting away from the pressures of his impending divorce and spending some quality time in London with his new lady.

'My contract had finished and I hoped it would be my last,' said Price, expressing his dissatisfaction with AIP. Not surprisingly, he had scant regard for the film. '*Madhouse* was ill-fated from the start,' said the equally disillusioned Quarry, 'thanks to Vincent's shaky status at AIP after years of contract disputes.' Price was further incensed by an article in the *Sunday Mirror* newspaper claiming that he was broke, living from film to film and using quiz show fees to support his family. In retaliation, Price barred AIP's PR man Dennison Thornton from assisting the press in further articles.

'None of us could really prepare for *Madhouse*,' Quarry added, 'because we got the script on the actual day before we were supposed to start shooting. And I read the thing and just said, "You've got to be kidding." What could we do? It was Vincent's last movie with AIP. His contract was up. We never got the script until Sunday morning, and we were to start shooting the next day. This gave us no time to bitch and scream. They knew if they'd sent it to us two weeks before, we'd have called them up and said, "Hey, work this over, as it's terrible." So they were very smart there.'

Denis Meikle described *Madhouse* as a 'tense' production where, 'the two Americans consequently spent most of the time bitching at each other or avoiding each other as much as possible. Quarry whiled away his off-duty hours schmoozing with David Hemmings and his then wife Gayle Hunnicutt, while Price concentrated on his transatlantic love affair with Coral Browne.' Meikle's comments are a little inaccurate. Although they were never friends, Price and Quarry did become confidants. 'The script we ended up with,' recalled Quarry, 'was so bad that I started rewriting my dialogue, and then Vincent asked me if I wouldn't mind rewriting some of his dialogue too.'

After the tense atmosphere of *Dr Phibes Rises Again*, the actors joining forces to make *Madhouse* work was rather surprising. In addition to the script, Quarry had an issue with the director's inexperience. 'Jim Clark may have been a good editor, but he was ill-prepared to direct a movie; he was just gonna shoot what was there. So I would change the dialogue around so it was speakable and then leave the last line, the cue-line, in. They never knew what hit them: when I finished talking and gave the cue-line, the other actor spoke.

'About the second day, I told Vincent I had made some changes, so I wouldn't have to speak this shit. He said, "God, help me with my stuff – could you rewrite some of this?" I was flattered that Vincent trusted me enough to let me rewrite some of the scenes. I couldn't change the scenes, but at least we put a little edge on some of them ... We didn't really improve the movie though.' Summing up his work with Price, Quarry said that *Madhouse* was 'the only serious work we did together, trying to find ways to do this dreadful movie.'

Price also confided in Quarry about an expenses fiddle he was working. Although his marriage had ended, he was still claiming for ex-wife Mary and daughter Victoria so that he could buy artwork on the quiet. 'Vincent told me that if anybody asked if Victoria and Mary were there, I was to say yes, because he wrote it in his expenses. All that expenses money for two weeks: first class air fare, food ... I said, "Oh, I love it, I love it. Can't you get anybody else on there?" After all, he made a great deal of money for AIP. He was their only superstar. And they should have been damn grateful to him, and they should have paid him more money. Frankly, anything he could steal out of that studio, I said, "Steal baby, steal."'

It is to Quarry's credit that he managed to add substance to his virtually non-existent role in the film. As an act of revenge, he rewrote his role of boorish television producer Oliver Quayle to resemble Sam Arkoff as closely as possible, having him be belligerent and rude to his actors. If there was any ill-feeling shown on screen by Quarry and Price, it was clearly aimed at

Arkoff rather than each other. 'At least it gave me something to work with,' Quarry added.

If Quarry had reservations about Jim Clark's inexperience, the director had his own beef with the producers. Arkoff's involvement in *Madhouse* was minimal, leaving Milton Subotsky in charge, and he had the annoying habit of interfering in post-production when not needed, souring any good will he had with a director. In a letter to Price, Clark claimed, '[Subotsky has] bulldozed his way into the cutting room and is at this moment cutting a swathe through the film. They are retaining all the action, of course, but every time anybody opens their mouth, Milton tries to cut the line for no other reason than, "It bores me." It is pure butchery.'

Subotsky, on the other hand, said that Clark, 'did a terrible job,' and added, 'When AIP got it, they re-edited the picture entirely, and I nearly died when I saw it. What they did made no sense at all.'

To sum up the controversy surrounding *Madhouse*, it seems that everyone involved was blaming each other for the shortcomings of the end result.

Even though he lost his role to Peter Cushing, Quarry was more than grateful that the British actor was involved. 'Thank goodness Peter was on the thing!' he exclaimed. 'We became very good friends. The nicest gentleman, and a darn good actor. It's too bad Peter got stuck in the horror category, because he is really a much better actor than that. But, then again, years before that, Karloff told me that once you got started in the horror field you couldn't get out of it, as Vincent also found out. You just got labelled as a horror film actor, like there was something wrong with you. And I remember when it started happening to me, it really pretty much ended everything.'

Quarry quickly bonded with Cushing, and often cooked dinner for the actor at his Chelsea apartment. 'Peter Cushing is the nicest man – ever. I still get tears in my eyes just thinking about him.' Quarry was also one of the few people to visit Cushing at his seaside home in Whitstable, Kent, but saw the sad and introspective person he had become after his wife's death. 'I visited his home in Whitstable. We sat for dinner and I noticed that Peter had laid out cutlery for a third person, which was actually for his late wife. He was a very strange guy.'

British actress Natasha Pyne, who played doomed PR girl Julia Wilson in *Madhouse*, had nothing but fond memories of Quarry. 'Robert was great fun to work with. In fact we became good mates, as his sense of humour coincided with mine. We had lots of good laughs talking about the business. Toward the end of shooting he took me and my husband Paul Copley out for a long, hilarious supper at Da Angela, his favourite Chelsea restaurant at the time.'

Madhouse isn't a bad film, but it's fair to say it could have been better. London Weekend Television Studios were used for some of the location shooting, and this gives the production a cheap look. The well-staged death scenes also lack the originality of those in the *Dr Phibes* movies. After his career-defining turn in *Theatre of Blood*, Price spends much of the time in *Madhouse* looking uninterested. He reverts to his customary warmth only when he is acting opposite Cushing; the final confrontation between their two characters (famously described by Cushing as a 'titanic ding-dong!') remains the highlight of a jaded film that has little to offer aside from their long overdue teaming.

Despite the thankless nature of his role, Quarry emerges from the film with some credit, and more than holds his own with the two horror legends by giving an excellent performance, achieved on the strength of his unofficial work as a script editor.

The hugely successful *The Exorcist* (1973) gave cinemagoers a taste for a new type of horror film, and the release of *Madhouse* the following year met with indifference. Taking only £1,901 in its first week in London, it did slightly better at regional cinemas, but it was not enough to halt the overall decline of British-made horror films as the studios found themselves unable to compete with Hollywood's big-budget special effects-laden chillers. Even low-budget American fare such as *Night of the Living Dead* (1968) and *The Texas Chainsaw Massacre* (1975) had the benefit of a vicious streak that made the average Hammer horror look conservative by comparison.

Although AIP considered a proposed follow-up to *Madhouse* called *The Naked Eye*, Vincent Price was finished with both the company and the genre. 'I didn't see anything that I wanted or needed,' he said. With his contract now coming to an end, he had no wish to renew, although the decision was effectively made for him when Arkoff closed AIP's London base and moved the company into other, more lucrative fields of exploitation. Price was loaned out for one final project, the woefully unfunny sex comedy *Percy's Progress* (1974), then his long, successful but tumultuous association with AIP came to a quiet end.

Never having been close friends in the first place, Quarry and Price unsurprisingly did not stay in touch. David Del Valle recalled a conversation he had with Price while working as a publicist on his film *The Offspring* (1987): 'Price brought [Quarry] up in conversation, asking if I knew what had happened to him. After I explained that Bob was still around, Price shook his head and reflected, "This town can be a paradise or a hell, and I have seen it both ways in my career. He should have had a bigger career than he did. Robert was a good character man; he just couldn't carry a tune.'

Hammer horror icon Ingrid Pitt met Quarry many years later and heard her own version of his relationship with Price: 'There were a lot of stories about Bob and Vincent Price not getting on. Bob denied this. He said it was all to do with Price's sense of humour, which, he said, was rather British!'

With no pure horror projects available, Sam Arkoff next decided to place Quarry in a horror-tinged blaxploitation film. This was *Sugar Hill* (1974), starring Marki Bey as Diana 'Sugar' Hill, a woman who takes revenge on Mafioso gang boss Morgan, played by Quarry, by using voodoo to resurrect a zombie army. Production began in February 1974, and Quarry had more than a few doubts about how the film was going. If the script for *Madhouse* had been bad, that for *Sugar Hill* was even worse. 'If Sam went out and had his cleaning lady write a movie, it couldn't have been any worse than this piece of junk they dumped on me. And everything was judged by Mrs Arkoff, who sat home and ate chocolates and read paperbacks all her life.

'[The film] was such camp. The producer Elliot Schick and director Paul Malansky were both white, and of course it was an all-black movie. They [originally] had a black actor set for the part [I played]. So I walked in as "Mr Whitey" to play the head of the Mafia in Houston, which was where they shot it.' By this time, though, Quarry was past caring. 'I didn't give a shit. They paid me.'

Filming posed a few problems for Quarry, especially when he encountered some racist attitudes. 'During the shoot, my rich white friends in Houston wouldn't call me, because they thought I'd bring somebody black to lunch with me. The racism was that subtle. And of course they hired so many blacks for the movie, and here I was saying [in my dialogue] things like "nigger" and "jungle bunny". The extras who weren't actors were going to kill me, because they thought I was a big racist. But I won them over eventually. And we all laughed so hard. I'd tell them all on the set, "Okay, easy fellas, get ready, because I'm going to say the 'n' word again."'

Sugar Hill is actually one of the better blacksploitation films. Marki Bey is no Pam Grier or Tamara Dobson, but she's incredibly sexy and turns in a great performance. Equally good is Don Pedro Colley, who gives a fine ham-slicing turn as voodoo priest Baron Samedi. The zombie make-up is effective and the film generates a creepy atmosphere that compensates for a dreadful script. Despite the thankless nature of his role, and his visible discomfort with the racist insults he is required to deliver, Quarry is in fine menacing form. He gets a chance to speak some juicy dialogue and hold his own with the lead actors.

By 1974, though, blacksploitation had become as passé as the type of horror films Quarry had been making before. With no further projects in the pipeline, Arkoff let the actor go by mutual consent, making *Sugar Hill* his last AIP film. Looking back, Quarry's horror career had been fraught with unrealised projects, unsatisfactory films, personal friction and internal squabbling. *Count Yorga, Vampire* may have started it all with a bang, but *Sugar Hill* ended it all with a damp squib.

Quarry's post-AIP career got off to a decent start. *The Midnight Man* (1974) sounds like the perfect title for a vampire movie, but the film is in fact a downbeat crime thriller starring Burt Lancaster, who also co-wrote, co-produced and co-directed it with Roland Kibbee. Based on David Anthony's novel *The Midnight Man and the Morning Lady*, it sees Lancaster play a former police detective who takes a job as a security guard at a college, where he investigates the murder of a wealthy female student. As part of a solid cast that includes Susan Clark, Cameron Mitchell, Catherine Bach and Ed Lauter, Quarry has the good supporting role of Dr Prichette, a lecherous campus psychiatrist more interested in chasing the young girls in his charge than sorting out their emotional problems.

'It was Burt's movie all the way,' said Quarry. 'Roland Kibbee, who had written a number of hit movies for Burt, was in dire trouble with work. And Kibbee came to him with a script he called *The Midnight Man*, and asked Burt to do it. So, as a favour to Kibbee, Burt took on the movie.'

Quarry's involvement in the movie was initially confined to pre-production work with Lancaster. 'Well, for about three weeks before the entire production crew arrived [for filming] in South Carolina, Burt was checking all the locations, rehearsing and blocking the part using me [as a double for him], so that he could stand away and see how it all fit in. I was with him for about three weeks before the whole production really began. And while we were doing all this, there was a part available, and I asked for it; hell, I was going to be on location anyway.

'When we finally began filming the movie, Burt would watch the scene through the lens with me playing his part, then I would step out, and he would step in and shoot the thing. Well, Kibbee was supposed to direct when Burt was in front of the camera. But when Burt was done with each of his scenes, he'd look at me and sort of expect me to either nod if it was a good take, or shake my head if it was a bad one. So, in essence, I was directing Burt in that one. And people said, "How did you direct Burt Lancaster?" I told them the truth – I nodded or shook my head!'

Although it's a serviceable enough thriller, *The Midnight Man* lacks that film noir touch to make it a classic, despite solid performances from all concerned. Lancaster's direction does tend to be heavy-handed but otherwise he does a decent job, and he is in typically good form in the lead role. After a well-established and nicely-played early scene, Quarry appears only fleetingly. But then his real contribution to the film was as Lancaster's stand-in director.

The Midnight Man should have led to supporting roles in other films. However, while Quarry continued his involvement with local theatre in Los Angeles, his next two television appearances the following year were the nadir of his career, and both were courtesy of the strange, comedy science fiction world of producers Sid and Marty Crofts.

Far Out Space Nuts stars Bob Denver and Chuck McCann as incompetent maintenance men working at a space station, who accidentally shoot themselves into space in a rocket. Flying from planet to planet trying to get home, they encounter various oddballs. Brought in to replace a cartoon series that got scrapped at the last minute, it has the look of a zero-budget porno. There's even a muppet-like alien character called Honk, who just makes honking noises! Quarry appears in the episode 'Tower of Tagot' as a villain called Zarlam, and gets to camp it up, which at least makes the episode passable – but only just.

Worse still was *The Lost Saucer*, starring Jim Nabors and Ruth Buzzi as aliens Fi and Fum, who after landing on Earth take a boy and his babysitter on board their flying saucer, only to get lost in a time warp. The series has the ship landing on Earth at different stages of the future while trying to get home. The episode 'Beautiful Downtown Atlantis' has Quarry as Emperor Nepto, ruler of the underwater city. He converts the saucer into a television studio and persuades the aliens to perform in front of the cameras. Once again the actor camps it up for all he's worth.

More satisfactory was a film role in *Rollercoaster* (1977), an efficient thriller starring George Segal as a safety inspector trying to thwart a pathological explosives expert played by Timothy Bottoms, who blackmails various amusement park companies by threatening to blow up their rollercoaster rides. The film also stars Richard Widmark, Susan Strasberg and Henry Fonda, with Steve Guttenburg, Craig Wasson and 13-year-old Helen Hunt making their film debuts. There is even an appearance by bizarre pop duo Sparks. Quarry turns up briefly as the Los Angeles mayor.

'It was the most money I ever made in a movie,' recalled Quarry. 'I'd done a television movie that Jim Goldstone directed called *A Clear and Present Danger* with Hal Holbrook, and suddenly the phone rings and it's Jim asking me if I'm available. And when the director calls you for a part, you know it's nothing. Very common! It's like doing them a favour. So I asked, "Is the money any good?" and he said, '"Yeah, you'll be working for two or three days." So I said, "Get me my top price." And he called me back and told me $3,000 a day. I couldn't believe how cheap they were being. So I told Jim, "One line a day for three days." So it was three days, one line a day, and I made $9,000! And they cut one of the lines too!'

Quarry's character doesn't have much to do in the film other than turn up at the press opening of a new rollercoaster, declare it open and look smug in a very mayor-like fashion. The film is lively, but is essentially an intriguing battle of wits between the lead characters played by Segal and Bottoms, so anyone expecting *The Towering Inferno* (1974) will be disappointed.

Quarry's next television appearance is his most memorable. *The Rockford Files* was a popular series starring James Garner as good-humoured private eye Jim Rockford. The episode 'Requiem for a Funny Box' features Quarry and Chuck McCann as feuding former comedy duo Lee Russo and Kenny Bell. When Russo steals Bell's funny box (containing his gags), Jim is hired to pay the ransom. Russo then turns up dead, and Jim and Bell stumble on a guilty secret that Russo was the homosexual lover of a Mafia hitman played by Herb Evers.

Quarry's involvement in this episode turned out to be financially beneficial. 'They initially hired Shecky Greene, and at the time the top [fee] for the show was [usually] $3,000. But to get Shecky, they paid him $7,000. It turned out in the story that Shecky's character was gay and his lover killer him. Well, Shecky got afraid of playing the part for some reason or another. I mean, who cared whether Shecky Greene was gay or straight or whatever? So Jimmy [Garner] said, "Well, let Quarry play the part." According to [Screen Actors Guild rules], if you replace an actor, they have to pay you that actor's salary. So I ended up with $7,000 instead of $3,000.'

In the autumn of 1978, Quarry landed the starring role in a made-for-television movie. *The Millionaire* (1978) was a pilot for a proposed revival of a popular '50s series. Quarry plays Michael Anthony, a millionaire who gives complete strangers £1 million each. The plot focuses on how the money affects the lives of those people. It was a novel concept, and the pilot did well in the ratings, so it is no surprise that it did lead to a series. However, that series failed to find an audience, despite a solid cast of guest stars that included Martin Balsam, Eddie Albert, Ralph Bellamy and John Ireland.

Quarry returned to *The Rockford Files* in January 1979 in the episode 'Guilt', where he played a character named Joe Zakarian. It was a less showy role than the previous one, but he always enjoyed his time on the series. 'I did several of those *The Rockford Files*,' he said. 'Pretty good salary, too. I loved working with Jimmy Garner.'

Later in the year, Quarry put in another memorable television performance in an episode of the science fiction series *Buck Rogers in the 25th Century*. 'Return of the Fighting 69th' has the actor in fine form as disfigured villain Commander Corliss. A group of elderly pilots, including two played by Peter Graves and Woody Strode, are brought back into service to attack Corliss's fortified base and prevent the vengeful Corliss and his disfigured cohort Roxanne Trent, played by Elizabeth Allen, from unleashing a deadly nerve gas on Earth. Quarry gives a nicely slimy performance and plays well off the equally brilliant Allen. The episode is also an interesting piece of social commentary, as it focuses on attitudes toward the elderly and the handicapped.

David Del Valle recalls an amusing incident told to him by Quarry about his guest appearance in this episode: 'I remember Bob telling me that after he had done the show, he was walking through the Universal lot in full half-man/half-robot regalia, and as he went by James Garner, the *Rockford* star looked up and said, "Hi Bob," as if noticing nothing unusual – which just cracked Bob up. He also hit if off with co-star Elizabeth Allen, whose sense of camp matched his. He told me it was such fun to get up and work with talent like that.'

At the beginning of 1980 Quarry made his final television appearance, as John P Ellison in 'Diplomatic Immunity', an episode of the crime series *Quincy M.E.*, starring Jack Klugman as the New York coroner. The episode also reunited him with Ray Danton. 'Ray had a tough last few years of his life,' said Quarry. 'But he was still directing. Jack just loved working with Ray. If you just cut out the bullshit and let Ray do his stuff, he was talented. A rather good actor too.'

With film and television work winding down, Quarry turned his attention to writing. 'In the early '80s,' he explained, 'a merchandising company paid me a flat fee for a cookbook I'd written, took out forty pages of it, and printed it. A little paperback that sold a lot! Something like 60,000 copies. *Wonderfully Simple Recipes for Simply Wonderful Food* was the title, and it included recipes people would typically have, like for a meatloaf or a stew, but with my particular alterations to them. For instance, a lot of people use Canadian bacon on pizza, but I make it with plain bacon. I lost money on the project because I didn't take a percentage. I mean, I didn't know it would sell that well. But it did.'

Quarry's cookbook sold well enough for a proposed follow-up. 'They wanted me to do another one. They were going to put it on nicer paper and I took a $3,000 advance and a big percentage out of the book. But while they were in the process of preparing the book for publication, they went bankrupt.'

Why Quarry never built on his cookbook success is a mystery, but then the '80s weren't exactly kind to him. In 1980 he was walking across a road when was knocked over by a lorry. He was dragged along the road for several minutes before being left for dead as the lorry sped off. When the police apprehended the vehicle, they found that the driver was both drunk and uninsured. Quarry was left with severe facial injuries and unable to work for a while. Worse still, the extensive plastic surgery he needed and other extensive medical bills used up a large portion of his life savings.

Quarry recovered sufficiently enough to be considered for two proposed horror films. *The Boarding House* was instigated in 1982 by David Del Valle, who designed a poster for it and put together an interesting cast that included Quarry, Deborah Blair (sister of *The Exorcist* star Linda), Katherine Wallach (daughter of Eli Wallach), British actress Elizabeth Shepherd (who had almost played Emma Peel in the famous spy series *The Avengers*) and genre favourites Reggie Nalder and Angus Scrimm. Sadly this came to nothing. 'I did try to put a film together for Bob,' said Del Valle, 'but the money could not be raised for something that did not have more explosions and sex.'

That same year Count Yorga resurfaced again, and with the same idea Quarry had earlier envisioned regarding the Count's homeless, drug fuelled existence. 'I had a very good idea for the third Count Yorga, but there were some problems about the rights. By that time Bob Kelljan had just died, and the rights had lapsed to Michael Macready. I found a director who wanted to make the movie, but Michael wouldn't give up the rights unless he directed. I don't want to speak ill of anyone, but I didn't want to work with Michael. Bob Kelljan wrote the first one, and he and his wife wrote the second script; they just had a touch for it. I think the studio might have done it, but Michael wouldn't give up the rights.'

Unfortunately, any thoughts of a horror comeback were put on hold when Quarry suffered a serious heart attack that kept him out of action for quite a while. Then, in 1985, there was another setback that nearly cost him his life.

'After the heart attack, I didn't work for a while. Then I was almost killed when these two guys mugged me right outside my North Hollywood apartment; it was before they put in a security gate. They broke my knees, my ribs, smashed my cheekbone, knocked all my teeth out; just kicked the shit out of me. But they didn't have to. I mean, after the first punch I was on the ground. The first guy that hit me, I swear he could take on Mike Tyson. I never saw a fist that big. I just turned around after getting out of my parked car and – bam! – right into this fist. Shot me right to the ground. And then the other guy started to kick me. So then I could not work.'

Not only was Quarry left for dead, he suffered another heart attack, and all this for a mere $27 stolen by the muggers. 'But it cost me cost me $177,000 in doctors' bills, because I hadn't worked enough the year before to get my Screen Actors Guild insurance. Like a fool, I had let my SAG insurance lapse – lesson to all you SAG members out there – and within a year my nest egg was completely gone. I was broke, and not in the best physical shape.'

The mugging and heart attack had left Quarry a wheelchair-bound recluse with only his devoted mother for company. Fortunately, he still had a loyal friend in Katherine Hepburn, who helped him out financially with his ongoing medical bills.

He was thrown a professional lifeline from another source. 'Thank God for Fred Olen Ray!' he later said. While going through his very lengthy recuperation, Quarry received a phone call from Ray, a prolific producer of low-budget features, with the offer a role in his thriller *Cyclone* (1987), starring Heather Thomas as the owner of a futuristic motorbike wanted by various shady governments. As part a solid cast that included Jeffrey Combs, Martin Landau and Martine Beswick, Quarry plays double agent Knowles, and has several good scenes with Beswick as his partner Waters. The British actress had fond feelings about her co-star. 'Oh my God!' she exclaimed. 'He was an absolute nut, but so great to work with.'

Quarry described *Cyclone* as, 'a piece of shit film,' but he was grateful because, 'Fred kept me working.' Quarry became part of Ray's stock company of actors. 'I hire a lot of old veterans, ' said Ray, 'because you're not worried about whether they can act or not. You hire Leo Gordon or Bob Quarry or Martin Landau or guys like that, they *are* good.'

Quarry was equally glad of the employment. 'Fred hired me to do bits and pieces in films for him. They were nice little bits. He was doing budget movies so, of course, there wasn't an awful lot of money. But by that time I was three years out of work, what with my heart attack and the beating. I couldn't get up and down out of my wheelchair, and I had three operations on my knee.

'Fred said to me, "I don't put myself in the movies like Hitchcock, but I'll put you in all of them." Well of course it was like a joke: I'd do three lines in many of his films and then just disappear.'

The professional association between Quarry and Ray turned into a friendship that lasted to the very end. 'We became fast friends. Fred and his wife and I were as close as can be. I'd nickname myself "Uncle Bob" on the set of Fred's films, so suddenly all the people on the set would call me "Uncle Bob"; they all thought I was really Fred's uncle.'

Quarry added, 'Fred pretty much kept me alive.' Fellow actor and writer Mark Redfield agreed: 'Fred Olen Ray was able to cast Robert in a string of films that, on its important practical level, allowed Robert to stay in the actors' union to navigate the gross expense of countless surgeries and rehabilitation. But more importantly, a friendship between Fred and Robert grew and lasted to this day.'

The late '80s marked Quarry's welcome return to the cinema as a featured player, mainly in films for director Ray. These included the action film *Commando Squad* (1987), the Gary Graver-directed horror flick *Moon in Scorpio* (1987), in which the actor played Dr Khorda, and the fantasy adventures *The Phantom Empire* (1988) and *Warlords* (1988).

Quarry also wanted to return to the stage. He had an idea to do a production of *I Never Sang for My Father*, which was his own personal favourite play, and even approached Mark Redfield with the idea of casting him in one of the central roles. Sadly a further heart attack in 1988, just before the opening of a Las Vegas show, brought a permanent end to his stage career.

Quarry continued working, however, and made a welcome return to vampire cinema courtesy of Ray's *Beverly Hills Vamp* (1989), a comedy flick about three nerds going to a brothel populated by vampire hookers whose leader was played by Britt Ekland. Quarry doesn't play a vampire. Instead he represents the side of good as Father Ferraro, a kooky, wheelchair-using priest who wants to be a screenwriter. It's a long way from Count Yorga, but it's a fun film and Quarry is in fine form.

Quarry continued the ham-slicing in the Jeff Broadstreet-directed *Sexbomb* (1989) as a slimy, low-budget movie producer, King Faraday, who pulls out all the stops to make a cheap horror film, only to find his statuesque wife is out to kill him. Unlike Quayle in *Madhouse*, Faraday is the ultimate producer from hell, treating everyone with total contempt – no doubt inspired once more by Sam Arkoff!

After appearing briefly in the Worth Keeter-directed crime film *LA Bounty* (1989), the actor was back to Fred Olen Ray and the horror genre as Doc Burnside in *Alienator* (1990). Then came a fun cameo as Hawaiian-shirt-wearing mob boss Visconti in the effective Ray chiller *Haunting Fear* (1990), and a tiny appearance in the same director's *Mob Boss* (1990), in the credits of which he was jokingly billed under the pseudonym Darius Biederbeck.

'I think I had a pretty good part in *Spirits* (1990),' noted the actor. In fact it was his best film performance in years. As psychic expert Dr Richard Wicks in Ray's solid haunted house chiller, he gives a nice sardonic turn that shows he hadn't lost his flair for the genre. His scenes with popular scream queen Brinke Stevens, giving her best dramatic performance, display a warm chemistry between the actors that makes one regret a sequel wasn't forthcoming. Quarry rounded off the year with a brief appearance as a doctor in the Gary Graver-directed *Evil Spirits* (1990).

Quarry worked again with Brinke Stevens on the Ray-written but Grant Austin Waldman-directed *Teenage Exorcist* (1991), a comedy horror based on the actress's own story idea. As Father McFerrin, a priest completely out of his depth as an exorcist because he's totally unprepared for the events that befall him, the actor has a fun time. 'I played this kooky Irish priest,' he recalled. 'It was a good part, and at least it let me be funny for a change, let me do comedy, which I really love.' Quarry steals the film, whether crooning dreadful Irish ditties or wailing out biblical verses for no apparent reason.

It is surprising that despite his good work for Fred Olen Ray and others in these low-budged films – some of which went straight to video – Quarry never had the chance to appear in anything more substantial at this point in his career. His poor health had ended his stage career, and television work had dried up. Writer and Quarry fan Steve Biodrowski vented his own frustration at the dearth of good film roles for the actor: 'In his later years, it seemed as if only low-budget filmmakers like Fred Olen Ray would employ him. I could understand that Quarry did not have the stature that would land him in mega-million-dollar productions, but you have to wonder why film-buffs-turned-filmmakers like Joe Dante and Quentin Tarantino never gave him the comeback role he deserved.'

Quarry himself was quick to agree, but with plenty of good humour that showed no bitterness whatsoever regarding his circumstances. 'I keep hearing Quentin Tarantino is a big fan. Quentin, if you're listening, I may not be able to be on the edge of a bushido blade, but I can still shoot a gun from a wheelchair! Call me!'

Teenage Exorcist gave Quarry's his last leading part of any note. His poor health restricted the size of his roles thereafter, but his presence was still always welcome. His wonderful voice got put to good use in *Evil Toons* (1992), and he popped up in a tiny cameo in *Angel Eyes* (1993) – wearing the same Hawaiian shirt from *Haunting Fear*!

Then there was another bit part in *Mind Twister* (1994), directed by Ray and notable for being Telly Savalas's last film. Quarry appeared alongside actress Paula Raymond, an old friend of his, who also had a bit part. 'Well, it was a joke,' recalled Quarry, 'for both Paula Raymond and me; a real Hitchcock appearance. See, Paula and I hadn't worked together since 1951. Of course Fred likes to get people like us in these bit parts. Back then Paula was crazy about me and I was crazy about her. And then, all these years later, here we are, these old people, she in her curlers and I unshaven for five days, my hair messed up and in a baggy old robe. We just came out and did that one little bit on the movie. Telly was a love. I'd worked with him on *Kojak*, so we just sat there and reminisced the whole time.'

Quarry carried on, with another tiny appearance in *Inner Sanctum II* (1994) and a larger role, working once more with Brinke Stevens, in the futuristic *Cyberzone* (1995). Other brief appearances followed in *Caged Fear* (1996), *The Shooter* (1997), *Rapid Assault* (1997), *Hybrid* (1997) and *Dear Santa* (1998). His voice was used once more for the comedy *Jungle Boy* (1998).

As the '90s drew to a close, Quarry continued working with appearances in *Mom's Outta Sight* (1998) and *The Prophet* (1999), the latter being notable for the presence of British horror actress Barbara Steele. He rounded off the end of the 20th Century with *Invisible Mom II* (1999) and *Fugitive Mind* (1999), the latter of which reunited him with *Buck Rogers in the 25th Century* colleague Gil Gerard.

At the start of the new millennium Quarry finally retired from acting, but he remained a firm favourite among fans, appearing at many conventions and giving interviews about his career. 'Make no mistake,' said Mark Redfield, 'Robert is a brilliant raconteur. A man whose career in film spans the end of Hollywood's golden era, through the anything goes period of the '60s and '70s, with solid work in live theatre and television, and radio, Robert has an endless supply of wonderful stories of the famous and infamous.'

Steve Biodrowski agreed with this assessment when he met Quarry at one of the many conventions he attended. 'He was still dapper and healthy-looking when making appearances at fan conventions. He remained an engaging and amusing speaker, a rare actor not ashamed of his association with the horror genre, and one not afraid to poke fun at himself or take a stab at his former colleagues when the occasion demanded. He had a sharp – one might say acid – tongue, but he put it in the service of being a great raconteur, regaling listeners with outrageous behind-the-scenes tales, and to be fair, he was not averse to taking himself down a peg or two.'

Biodrowski added that, when he approached him for an interview, the actor 'expressed some reservations about rehashing old news, but he agreed to meet with me, and gave me a hilarious interview in which no punches were pulled and no insult went unuttered. Although understandably disappointed that his career did not turn out as it should have done, he did not strike me as particularly bitter while dishing the dirt. He refused to sugar-coat the truth, and he didn't stand in reverent awe of people [generally] regarded as hallowed icons not to be impugned under any circumstances.'

But behind his good humour and way with a story, there was great sadness in Quarry's life, with the declining health of his devoted mother. 'Bob was a good son in every way,' recalled David Del Valle. 'I remember how my heart went out to him when she was getting weaker. He called me one afternoon from the hospital, and I could tell he was worried.'

Del Valle arrived at Quarry's apartment fearing the worst. 'The doctor asked me if I would mind if they called a priest to give Mimi the last rites, and I simply had to get out of that room. I couldn't take any more. Bob said to me, "David, you will go through this someday, so try and remain strong when it comes your way." Now I think of that just about every day of my life.'

Tragedy did befall Del Valle when he lost his partner Chris Dietrich to HIV and liver cancer in 2004. 'It was later in the following year that I saw Bob. He had put on quite a bit of weight but he was still Uncle Bob. I went over during a break and knelt down by Bob's chair and told him we lost Chris. The look on his face said more than I could bear, and we quickly hugged.'

Another loyal friend to Quarry at this time was John Seastone, who has fond memories of the actor. 'I managed the building Mr Quarry lived in from 2004 to 2007. He was a very nice man. He used to tell me all kinds of great stories about his career and people he worked with; I lost touch with him when I moved. I won't forget him. Nice man.'

In fact Seastone's admiration for Quarry went beyond just managing the actor's home, especially when his health got worse. 'He had been living in that apartment for over twenty years, and the former manager never updated or fixed it. It was pretty bad. He went into the hospital for some minor surgery at one point and, with the help of a close friend of his, we gave him all new flooring, repainted the walls and remodelled the whole place. He was so happy when he returned, he cried.'

In 2007 Quarry was set to make a movie comeback in *The Tell-Tale Heart* as creepy recluse Mr Ambrose. Cast to play his equally creepy wife was Ingrid Pitt. Arriving in Los Angeles during pre-production, Pitt met Quarry via Fred Olen Ray. She then spent a wonderful couple of days with the actor. 'I think Bob must be one of the most underrated actors of all time. If not, he was terribly unlucky,' she said with great affection and sadness. 'In spite of the fact that he was friendly with some of the biggest guns of studio-led Hollywood, he never seemed able to get the right chance at something substantial.'

Pitt added, 'I never met anybody who had anything bad to say about him. In spite of being in loads of films, it wasn't until he took up the cape and fangs that he came into his own. Bob had a wonderful voice, like jelly-covered titanium in a mink glove.'

She was equally impressed with Quarry as an actor. 'Tall, dark and handsome, with an easy manner, he could have given his successor [Christopher Lee] a run for his money in the fanging stakes. But once again ill luck blocked his path.'

All concerned had high hopes for the film project, but there were setbacks, as Pitt explained: 'We were to play husband and wife in a screenplay adapted from Edgar Allen Poe's *The Tell-Tale Heart* with embellishments from an American Civil War story by Ambrose Bierce. Originally it was supposed to be shot in spring, but shooting was postponed because the money man kicked the bucket!'

Production was rescheduled for September 2007, but by this time Quarry's age and poor health had become a problem. 'He was still fairly upbeat,' said Pitt, 'but he admitted that he wasn't so confident about the film. He felt that if the film didn't shoot before the end of the year, he wouldn't be around to do it.'

The film never got off the ground.

Quarry's health went into further decline. 'Robert's body continues to fight against everything his heart and mind desires,' said Mark Redfield. 'A series of small heart attacks, his health continually giving him trouble, an endless list of drugs that he hates having to take to keep all his moving parts working. Robert remains a fighter.'

But Quarry could not go any further, and the incident described at the start of this chapter with the vindictive fan meant that he needed to take drastic steps, as Redfield explained:

'Two years ago, Robert began to realise that maybe he had better do something that most dread and fear, and that is to move himself into a retirement home. As he had gotten older, and found it more and more difficult physically to do the simple things, he made his decision, and was lucky to get an opening at the Motion Picture Country Home in Woodland Hills. For a man so fiercely independent, to uproot himself from a home he'd lived in for nearly forty years was an emotionally and physically devastating experience. But he handled the transition with his usual aplomb and humour. A most wrenching factor in this new ordeal was the fact that, because of the very specific rules of the Country Home, Robert had to leave virtually all his possessions behind him. His clothes, furniture, and many personal belongings.'

Thanks to Tim Sullivan's extensive campaign, and the financial and moral support of his fans, Quarry got everything he could have needed or wanted. 'Robert has been overwhelmed, in a good way, ' said Redfield, 'and indeed overjoyed by all the attention. Slowly, he is coming to like the new place. It's clear the quality of his life has improved, his circle of friends has widened, and the old rascal may just be with us for a long time to come. I hope so.'

Robert Quarry was to live in relative comfort for only a few months before being moved to a nearby hospice. On 20th February 2009, close friend Fred Olen Ray made the following announcement:

'A short while ago, earlier this evening, my good friend Bob Quarry passed away at the Motion Picture Hospital in Woodland Hills. He'd been in poor health for some time and this wasn't sudden or unexpected, but it hurts nonetheless. He was 83 years old. I sat at his bedside yesterday for hours looking for some sign of hope, but it just wasn't there. It truly is, for me, the end of an era that began in 1987 when Bob and I first met and I tried to coerce him into my stable of "regular" stock players. He became a *bona fide* member of my family and we're going to miss him dearly. I don't think any of us can tell you how much.'

Robert Quarry was an unfortunate man. A fine actor who, through no fault of his own, suffered at the hands of heartless people who took both his career and his life for granted. Was it bad luck? Well, he had bad breaks and suffered a dreadful series of events that were undeserved. He may have been cursed, but at least there was one positive constant that came late in his life, and that was the support of Fred Olen Ray and the stream of loyal fans who went beyond the call of duty to help him when everything looked bleak. It's a testament to their own love and admiration for a great man; their support in his final years can best be described as a big thank you for his fine work for the horror cinema.

Robert Quarry Filmography

Shadow of a Doubt (1943), *Soldier of Fortune* (1955), *The House of Bamboo* (1955), *A Kiss Before Dying* (1956), *Crime of Passion* (1957), *Agent for H.A.R.M.* (1966), *Winning* (1969), *WUSA* (1970), *Count Yorga, Vampire* (1970), *A Clear and Present Danger* (TV – 1970), *The Return of Count Yorga* (1971), *Deathmaster* (1972), *Dr Phibes Rises Again* (1972), *Madhouse* (1974), *Sugar Hill* (1974), *The Midnight Man* (1974), *Rollercoaster* (1977), *The Millionaire* (television movie - 1978), *Cyclone* (1987), *Commando Squad* (1987), *Moon in Scorpio* (1988), *The Phantom Empire* (1988), *Warlords* (1988), *Beverly Hills Vamp* (1989), *Sexbomb* (1989), *LA Bounty* (1989), *Alienator* (1990), *Haunting Fear* (1990), *Mob Boss* (1990), *Spirits* (1990), *Evil Spirits* (1990), *Teenage Exorcist* (1991), *Evil Toons* (voice only – 1992), *Angel Eyes* (1993), *Mind Twister* (1994), *Inner Sanctum II* (1994), *Cyberzone* (1995), *Caged Fear* (1996), *The Shooter* (1997), *Rapid Assault* (1997), *Hybrid* (1997), *Jungle Boy* (voice only – 1998), *Dear Santa* (1998), *Mom's Outta Sight* (1998), *The Prophet* (1999), *Invisible Mom II* (1999), *Fugitive Mind* (1999).

Bibliography

Anger, Kenneth: *Hollywood Babylon*
Barnes, Alan: *Sherlock Holmes on Screen*
Bradley, Doug: *Sacred Monsters*
Brosnan, John: *The Horror People*
Bryce, Alan: *Amicus: The Studio That Dripped Blood*
Cushing, Peter: *Peter Cushing: An Autobiography*
Cushing, Peter: *Part Forgettings*
Davies, David Stuart: *Starring Sherlock Holmes*
De Cocteau, David and Ray, Fred Olen: *Attack of the B-Movie Makers*
Del Vecchio, Deborah and Johnson, Tom: *Hammer Films: An Exhaustive Filmography*
Del Vecchio, Deborah and Johnson, Tom: *Peter Cushing: The Gentleman of Horror and his 91 Films*
Earnshaw, Tony: *An Actor and a Rare One: Peter Cushing as Sherlock Holmes*
Gifford, Denis: *Horror Movies*
Grey, Rudolph: *Nightmare of Ecstasy: The Life and Art of Edward D Wood Jnr*
Haining, Peter: *The Dracula Scrapbook*
Halliwell, Leslie: *The Dead That Walked*
Hamilton, John: *Beast in the Cellar: The Exploitation Film Career of Tony Tenser*
Lindsey, Cynthia: *Dear Boris*
Miller, Mark A: *Christopher Lee and Peter Cushing and The Horror Cinema: A Filmography*
Jones, Stephen: *The Illustrated Frankenstein Movie Guide*
Jones, Stephen: *The Illustrated Werewolf Movie Guide*
June, Andrea and Vale, V: *RE: SEARCH: Incredibly Strange Films*
McCarty, John: *The Sleazemerchants*
Meikle, Denis: *Vincent Price: The Art of Fear*
Pitts, Michael R: *Horror Film Stars*
Price, Victoria: *Vincent Price: A Daughter's Biography*
Quirk, Lawrence and Schoel, William: *The Rat Pack*
Rathbone, Basil: *In and Out of Character*
Rigby, Jonathan: *American Gothic*
Rigby, Jonathan: *English Gothic*
Ross, Jonathan: *The Incredibly Strange Film Book*
Skal, David J: *V for Vampire*

BIBLIOGRAPHY

Svelha, Gary J and Svelha, Susan: *Vincent Price*
Williams, Lucy Chase: *The Complete Films of Vincent Price*
Wright, Bruce Lanier: *Nightwalkers*
Youngkin, Stephen D: *The Lost One: A Life of Peter Lorre*

Index

About the Author

Mark Iveson was born in Gateshead. He spent his early childhood in London before returning permanently to the North-East as a teenager. He currently works as a civil servant for the Department for Work and Pensions.

A horror movie buff from a young age, Mark has a near photographic knowledge of the genre. He also loves science fiction, British film comedy and the James Bond series.

Mark began writing film, theatre and gig reviews for several work-related magazines and periodicals. He went on to write for the Glasgow-based vampire magazine *Bite Me*, provided theatre reviews for the North East arts magazine *Up Front* and non-film-related articles for the Swiss-based English-language magazine *The Geneva Times*.

Mark currently writes for the movie webmag *Shadowlocked*, where he has over thirty articles and reviews to his name. The articles are available at www.shadowlocked.com.

In addition to writing and cinema, Mark has a passion for music; he plays guitar, bass, mandolin and banjo. He sings and performs at several buskers' nights around Newcastle as well as organising his own. He also plays the odd pub gig.

To help develop his writing skills further, Mark attends the Swanwick Writers' Retreat at the Hayes Conference Centre in Swanwick, Derbyshire.